D1547943

FLORIDA STATE
UNIVERSITY LIBRARIES

JAN 15 2001

TALLAHASSEE, FLORIDA

Documentation Improvement Methods
The New Accounting Manual

Subscriber Update Service

BECOME A SUBSCRIBER!

Did you purchase this product from a bookstore?

If you did, it's important for you to become a subscriber. John Wiley & Sons, Inc., may publish, on a periodic basis, supplements and new editions to reflect the latest changes in the subject matter that you **need to know** in order to stay competitive in this ever-changing industry. By contacting the Wiley office nearest you, you'll receive any current update at no additional charge. In addition, you'll receive future updates and revised or related volumes on a 30-day examination review.

If you purchased this product directly from John Wiley & Sons, Inc., we have already recorded your subscription for this update service.

To become a subscriber, please call **1-800-225-5945** or send your name, company name (if applicable), address, and the title of the product to:

mailing address:

Supplement Department
John Wiley & Sons, Inc.
One Wiley Drive
Somerset, NJ 08875

e-mail: **subscriber@wiley.com**
fax: **1-732-302-2300**
online: **www.wiley.com**

For customers outside the United States, please contact the Wiley office nearest you:

Professional & Reference Division
John Wiley & Sons Canada, Ltd.
22 Worcester Road
Rexdale, Ontario M9W 1L1
CANADA
(416) 675-3580
Phone: 1-800-567-4797
Fax: 1-800-565-6802
canada@jwiley.com

Jacaranda Wiley Ltd.
PRT Division
P.O. Box 174
North Ryde, NSW 2113
AUSTRALIA
Phone: (02) 805-1100
Fax: (02) 805-1597
headoffice@jwiley.com.au

John Wiley & Sons, Ltd.
Baffins Lane
Chichester
West Sussex, PO19 1UD
ENGLAND
Phone: (44) 1243 779777
Fax: (44) 1243 770638
cs-books@wiley.co.uk

John Wiley & Sons (SEA) Pte. Ltd.
2 Clementi Loop #02-01
SINGAPORE 129809
Phone: (65) 463-2400
Fax: (65) 463-4605, (65) 463-4604
wiley@signet.com.sg

Documentation Improvement Methods
The New Accounting Manual
Second Edition

Athar Murtuza

JOHN WILEY & SONS, INC.
New York • Chichester • Weinheim • Brisbane • Singapore • Toronto

This book is printed on acid-free paper. ∞

Copyright © 2000 by John Wiley & Sons, Inc. All rights reserved.

Published simultaneously in Canada.

No part of this publication may be reproduced, stored in a retrieval system or transmitted in any form or by any means, electronic, mechanical, photocopying, recording, scanning or otherwise, except as permitted under Sections 107 or 108 of the 1976 United States Copyright Act, without either the prior written permission of the Publisher, or authorization through payment of the appropriate per-copy fee to the Copyright Clearance Center, 222 Rosewood Drive, Danvers, MA 01923, (978) 750-8400, fax (978) 750-4744. Requests to the Publisher for permission should be addressed to the Permissions Department, John Wiley & Sons, Inc., 605 Third Avenue, New York, NY 10158-0012, (212) 850-6011, fax (212) 850-6008, E-Mail: PERMREQ@WILEY.COM.

This publication is designed to provide accurate and authoritative information in regard to the subject matter covered. It is sold with the understanding that the publisher is not engaged in rendering legal, accounting, or other professional services. If legal advice or other expert assistance is required, the services of a competent professional person should be sought.

Designations used by companies to distinguish their products are often claimed as trademarks. In all instances where John Wiley & Sons, Inc. is aware of a claim, the product names appear in initial capital or all capital letters. Readers, however, should contact the appropriate companies for more complete information regarding trademarks and registration.

Library of Congress Cataloging in Publication Data:

Murtuza, Athar.
    Documentation improvement methods: the new accounting manual / Athar Murtuza.—2nd ed.
        p.cm.
    Earlier ed. published: The new accounting manual. New York : Wiley, 1995.
    Includes bibliographical references and index.
    ISBN 0-471-37938-7 (cloth : alk. paper)
        1. Accounting—Handbooks, manuals, etc.—Authorship.   I. Murtuza, Athar. New accounting manual.   II. Title.
    HF5657.M88 2000
    808'.066657—dc21   00-022255

Printed in the United States of America

10 9 8 7 6 5 4 3 2 1

To my parents
and
their parents
for having taught me
about the importance
of documentation

O you, who believe! When you deal with each other in transactions involving obligations, reduce them to writing. Let a scribe write down faithfully the nature of the obligation. Scribes must not refuse to do what has been taught to them.

(Qur'an, 2:282)

ABOUT THE AUTHOR

Athar Murtuza, PhD, CMA, is currently associate professor of accounting at the W. Paul Stillman School of Business at Seton Hall University. In addition to accounting documentation, his research and consulting interests include effective communication of accounting information, linguistic approaches to accounting, and the use of accounting as a decision-making tool. An expert in cost and management accounting, Dr. Murtuza has written chapters for several professional books, including John Wiley & Sons' *Handbook of Budgeting, Third Edition* by Robert Rachlin and H. W. Allen Sweeny, and has been published widely in both professional and academic journals, including *Management Communication Quarterly*. He also has been an invited speaker at some of the accounting industry's largest associations, such as the American Accounting Association, Institute of Management Accounting, and Academy of Accounting Historians.

PREFACE

Documentation Improvement Methods: The New Accounting Manual, Second Edition, seeks to change the popular perception of the documentation process as well as to the end product, the procedures manual. Within the documentation process is the potential for illuminating the functions, processes, and procedures of the organization. This potential turns the documentation process into an opportunity for organizational learning, since it is well recognized that questioning the status quo facilitates innovation.

In the past, those assigned the chore of documenting procedures have merely recorded the status quo without asking any questions about it. This led to the process being accorded scant respect. One could ignore the state of affairs in the area of procedure documentation were it not for the outpouring of reports describing organizations busily redesigning their work. Given such changes in the way various processes are being performed throughout organizations, why not improve the process used for procedure documentation as well? It seems well suited to spark questions concerning the status quo within the accounting departments. Through such questions, one could turn the documentation process into an occasion for learning.

The basic idea expressed here was put forth in my paper "Procedures Documentation Ought to be Illuminative Not Just Archival" published in a Sage Publications, Inc. journal *Management Communication Quarterly,* Vol. 8, Issue 2, November 1994, pp. 225–243.

Organizational change is becoming globally endemic. Corporations are busily reshaping the processes and procedures they rely on to get things done. Even though organizations have begun to reinvent what they do and how they do it, these emerging management concepts and organizational practices have yet to reach procedures documentation, an organizational communication genre. The winds of change have yet to reach the procedures documentation process.

Academics do not even teach procedures documentation, let alone teach it as an activity whose uses and value reside in the entire process and transcend the end product, the documentation itself. Like academics, managers continue to see documentation as an afterthought rather than the learning organization paradigm and extension of process redesign that it is. Professors and practitioners both mistakenly see procedures documentation as merely archival.

Seeing procedures documentation as merely archival has isolated this organizational communication genre from the developments taking place within contemporary organizations. Such isolation has prevented procedures documentation from becoming a useful tool, an occasion to review and prune outdated, inefficient, or redundant procedures, and to think of newer ways to do things in view of changing environments and technologies.

By not limiting procedures documentation to merely the final act of writing the procedures manual, but seeing it broadly as an illuminative tool, an organization can learn how to streamline its own processes. The value of procedures documentation resides in the process of creation as well as in the document created.

Current practice only mirrors the existing process, thereby perpetuating the status quo with all its flaws. Rather than simply reflecting the status quo like a mirror, procedures documentation should also illuminate like a lamp the adequacy of current practices and processes. The axiom that an unexamined life is not worth living can apply not only to individuals but to organizations as well.

Attempts aimed at continuous improvements or even periodic review and updating of procedures can go a long way in preventing the accumulation of deadwood by replacing them with productive and efficient procedures and policies. Such ongoing reviews and incremental steps have had a major role in the emergence of Japan as a manufacturing giant. Despite the demonstrated efficacy of periodic procedures review not only in Japan but also here in the United States, documentation experts have not added such reviewing to the process governing procedures documentation. They continue to limit the documentation process to the actual writing of the manuals rather than as an occasion for periodic organizational self-examination. Such failure wastes potential opportunities to examine, reflect, consult, improve, learn, and prosper.

WHAT IS THIS BOOK ABOUT?

This book explains the process involved in documenting the accounting manual without limiting the documentation process to merely describing the various procedures and policies in place within the accounting departments. The current perception of documentation as essentially archival permits irrelevant, redundant, non–value-adding procedures to continue within an organization. All too often, archival documentation becomes obsolete even as it is written because it makes no provision for the changes that are constantly taking shape within the accounting department, throughout the organization, and in the environment in which the organization operates. The world is constantly changing, and what does not change with it soon comes to regret its immobility.

The documentation process can be an occasion to examine the very nature of accounting functions within the organization, to review how they are being carried out, and to reengineer them if necessary. Such a perception of what the documentation process ought to be is quite practical. The practicality of activity management, process redesign, and learning paradigm has been well-documented in recent years. This book shows how these emerging ways of doing business can be incorporated as part of the process dealing with the documentation of the accounting procedures manual.

Incorporating the knowledge of the new ways of doing work as an integral part of the procedures documentation process can change the documentation from being an afterthought, a necessary nuisance, into a chance for improvement not only for the accounting department but for the entire organization.

So even though we will focus on the process that governs the documentation of accounting policies and procedures, in effect we will be seeking to affect the role accountants perform for the organization. If the accounting department itself is not operating efficiently and does not seek ongoing improvements, then the efforts aimed at organization-wide improvement through such means as activity-based costing and process reengineering cannot have optimum impact. To increase the potential of success for organization-wide improvements, do not ignore the work of the accounting department. The process concerned with procedures documentation provides an ideal occasion to institutionalize continuous improvement and learning within the controller's department as well as the rest of the organization. Procedures documentation can become a safeguard against obsolescence.

Given the great organizational diversity that exists in the workplace, no attempt is made to provide sample documentation for various accounting functions. One size cannot fit everyone! Instead of outlining the specific way various functions ought to be documented, the book describes the nature of various accounting functions, such as those dealing with sales and the collection of accounts receivable. While all organizations are concerned with collecting accounts receivable, payroll, and accounts payable, they do not perform them in an identical manner. Each organization needs to have its own unique set of procedures to help fulfill its particular needs. All organizations must pay their bills, accordingly, the existence of the accounts payable function is fairly universal. Each organization, however, is likely to structure the functions in keeping with its unique constraints. If the goals to be attained with the help of various accounting functions are clear, then procedures can be developed to help attain these goals in keeping with organizational constraints. Accordingly, an overview of an accounting system, rather than an accounting manual containing a set of sample procedures, is provided. When armed with the knowledge that an overview of accounting functions can provide, managers in charge of reviewing procedures or developing new ones can do a more effective job of ascertaining whether the current procedures are adequate and in line with the needs of their particular organization before they document the procedures.

A book's germination comes about with the support and encouragement of others. Among those who helped nourish this project are Virginia and Miriam—their contribution cannot be sufficiently acknowledged with mere words, whose efficacy is limited.

Professor Joseph Wilkinson's books on accounting systems have helped me greatly in understanding the nature and working of accounting information systems. His books helped give form to this book. I have also learned a great deal from another John Wiley book, *Core Concepts of Accounting Information Systems*, written by Stephen Moscove, Mark Simkin, and Nancy Bagranoff.

I am also grateful for Tim Burgard and Sheck Cho at John Wiley for their patience and advice.

South Orange, New Jersey   Athar Murtuza

CONTENTS

Introduction   Procedures Manuals: Past, Present, and Future   1

Chapter 1   Changing Role of the Accounting Profession   7

1.1   Introduction   7
1.2   AICPA's Vision of the Future   8
1.3   Nature of Evolutionary Competence   8
1.4   Expanding the Services Accountants Provide   9
1.5   Core Competencies for New Services   11
1.6   Expanding Role of the Management Accountant   13
1.7   Highlights of the Institute of Management Accountants Study   15
1.8   Highlights of the Association of Chartered Certified Accountants Study   16

Chapter 2   User-Friendly Accounting Manuals   19

2.1   Introduction   19
2.2   The Message and the Medium   19
2.3   Program for Starting an Accounting Manual   20
2.4   Organization of the Accounting Manual   22
2.5   System Maintenance   22
2.6   Review and Maintenance of the Manual   23
2.7   Policing the Manual   24
2.8   Physical Attributes   24
2.9   Core of the Accounting Manual   24
2.10   Directives   25
2.11   Policy Statements   25
2.12   Procedures   25
2.13   Policy and Procedure Statements   26
2.14   Illustrating Accounting Manuals Preparation   27
2.15   Budget Manual   30
2.16   Contents of a Budget Manual   31
2.17   Conclusion   31

Chapter 3   Illustrating the Illuminative Approach to Documentation   33

3.1   Introduction   33
3.2   Deconstructing a Procedure   33
3.3   Raising Some Questions About the Procedure   34
3.4   Tracking the Components of the Procedure   35
3.5   Explaining the Illuminative Approach   37
3.6   Elements of the Illuminative Approach   37
3.7   First Understand, Then Deconstruct   37
3.8   Conclusion   38
        Appendix   38

Chapter 4   Organizational Controls   55

4.1   Introduction   55
4.2   Nature of Control   56
4.3   Historical Development of Control   57
4.4   Control Process   58
4.5   Systems within the Control Structure   62
4.6   Other Control Classifications   63
4.7   Organizational Structure   64
4.8   Manual Systems Control Organization   65
4.9   Computer-Based Systems Organization and Control   66
4.10   Documentation Controls   70
4.11   Management Practice Controls   70
4.12   Asset Accountability Controls   71
4.13   Planning Practices   73
4.14   Personnel Practices   73
4.15   Audit Practices   74
4.16   Communication Audit in Accounting Context   75
4.17   When to Conduct a Communication Audit   77
4.18   How Is a Communication Audit Accomplished?   79

Chapter 5   Threats to the Control Process   83

5.1   Introduction   83
5.2   Impediments to Effective Control   83
5.3   Types of Risk Exposure   84
5.4   Degree of Risk Exposure   85
5.5   Conditions Affecting Exposures to Risk   86
5.6   Fraud and Control Problems Related to Computers   86
5.7   Types of Computer Crimes   87
5.8   Reasons Underlying Computer Control Problems   87
5.9   Other Control Considerations for Computer Systems   89
5.10   Forces for the Improvement of Controls   91
5.11   Auditors' Responsibilities Regarding Fraudulent Financial Reporting   91
5.12   Forensic Accounting and Fraud Auditing   93
5.13   Forensic and Investigative Accounting   94

Chapter 6   Documenting Accounting Information Systems   97

6.1   Introduction   97
6.2   What Is Information?   97
6.3   Information Systems   98
6.4   Roles Performed by Information Systems   98
6.5   Limitations of Information Systems   99
6.6   Components of an Information System   100
6.7   Types of Information Systems   102
6.8   Accounting Information Systems   102
6.9   Subsystems of Accounting Information Systems   104
6.10   Documentation Tools and Techniques   104

6.11   Varieties of Visual Representations   105
6.12   Flow-Charting Symbols   105
6.13   Flow-Charting a Process   108
6.14   Guidelines for Preparing Flow Charts   112
6.15   Data Flow Diagrams   115
6.16   Illustrating Data Flow Diagrams   116
6.17   Guidelines for Preparing Data Flow Diagrams   119
6.18   Additional Techniques   120
6.19   Narrative Documentation of Information Systems   121
6.20   Manual Systems   124
6.21   Computer-Based Systems   124
6.22   Additional Documentation Needed   127
6.23   Conclusion   127

Chapter 7   The Working of Accounting Information Systems   129

7.1   Introduction   129
7.2   Bricks and Mortar of Accounting Information Systems   129
7.3   Impact of Complexity on Accounting Information Systems   131
7.4   Transaction Processing Cycles   132
7.5   Computer Transaction Processing Approaches   133
7.6   Batch Processing Approach   134
7.7   Contrasts with Manual Batch Processing   136
7.8   Advantages and Disadvantages of Batch Processing   137
7.9   Computer-Based On-Line Transaction Processing   138
7.10   Contrasts with Computer-Based Batch Processing   140
7.11   Advantages and Disadvantages of On-Line Processing   140
7.12   File Processing and Management   141
7.13   Nature of File Storage   141
7.14   Classification and Coding of Data   142
7.15   Coding Systems   143
7.16   Coding and Computers   144
7.17   Attributes of Codes   145
7.18   Conclusion   145

Chapter 8   General Ledger and Financial Reporting Cycle   147

8.1   Introduction   147
8.2   Objectives and Functions   147
8.3   Data Sources and Inputs   150
8.4   Database Used for General Ledger System   153
8.5   Data Flows and Processing   155
8.6   Accounting Controls   158
8.7   Financial and Managerial Reports   162
8.8   Coding of Accounts   163
8.9   Charts of Accounts   164
8.10   Conclusion   165
         Appendix   166

Chapter 9   The Revenue Cycle   171

9.1   Introduction   171
9.2   Organizational Context   171
9.3   Documentation of the Revenue Cycle   172
9.4   Documentation for Computer-Based Systems   175
9.5   Journal Entries Used for the Revenue Cycle   175
9.6   Transaction Coding   176
9.7   Database Files   177
9.8   Working of the Revenue Cycle   179
9.9   Credit Sales Procedures in Manual Processing Systems   179
9.10   Cash Receipts Procedure   182
9.11   Accounts Receivable Maintenance Procedure   185
9.12   Computer-Based Processing Systems   188
9.13   Credit Sales Procedure in Computerized Systems   188
9.14   Cash Receipts Procedure in Computerized Systems   192
9.15   Advantages of Computer-Based Processing Systems   194
9.16   Controls Needed for the Revenue Cycle   194
9.17   General Controls   196
9.18   Transaction Controls   197
9.19   Managerial Reports   198
9.20   Conclusion   199

Chapter 10   The Expenditure Cycle   201

10.1   Introduction   201
10.2   Organizational Context of the Expenditure Cycle   202
10.3   Managerial Decision Making   205
10.4   Documentation Needed for the Cycle   206
10.5   Documentation for Manual Systems   206
10.6   Documentation Needed by Computer-Based Systems   208
10.7   Accounting Entries   208
10.8   Transaction Coding   209
10.9   Database for the Expenditure Cycle   210
10.10   Data Flows and Processing for Manual Systems   212
10.11   Computer-Based Processing Systems   218
10.12   Controls Needed for the Expenditure Cycle   223
10.13   Control Objectives   225
10.14   Reports and Other Outputs   229
10.15   Conclusion   230

Chapter 11   The Resources Management Cycle: Employee Services   233

11.1   Introduction   233
11.2   Resources Management: An Overview   233
11.3   Objectives of Employee Services Management System   233
11.4   Organizational Context of Employee Services   234
11.5   Documentation Needed for Employee Services   237
11.6   Accounting Entries   238
11.7   Transaction Coding   239

11.8   Database Needed for Employee Services   239
11.9   Data Flows and Processing for Manual Systems   240
11.10   Computer-Based Processing System   244
11.11   Controls Needed for Employee Services   244
11.12   Reports and Other Outputs   248
11.13   Conclusion   248

Chapter 12   The Resources Management Cycle: Inventory Management   251

12.1   Introduction   251
12.2   Merchandise Inventory Management System   251
12.3   Inventory Valuation Methods   255
12.4   Organizational Context of Inventory Management   258
12.5   Components of Merchandise Inventory Management System   259
12.6   Raw Materials Management (Product Conversion) System   260
12.7   Production Logistics   261
12.8   Emerging Organizational Context of Production   261
12.9   Material Requirements Planning   261
12.10   Inventory in the JIT Environment   264
12.11   Production-Related Managerial Decision Making   264
12.12   Documentation for Product Conversion   265
12.13   Accounting in a Manufacturing Context   265
12.14   Database for Product Conversion   266
12.15   Data Flows and Processing   267
12.16   Reports and Other Outputs   275
12.17   Conclusion   275

Chapter 13   The Resources Management Cycle: Facilities and Funds   277

13.1   Introduction   277
13.2   Facilities Management Cycle   277
13.3   Capital Budgeting Concept   277
13.4   Capital Budgeting Process   279
13.5   Maintenance and Disposal of Capital Assets   279
13.6   Organizational Context of the Cycle   280
13.7   Documentation Needed for the Cycle   280
13.8   Accounting for the Facilities Management Cycle   281
13.9   Database for the Facilities Management Cycle   281
13.10   Data Flows and Processing   282
13.11   Controls Needed for Facilities Management   283
13.12   Reports and Other Outputs   286
13.13   Funds Management System   286
13.14   Objectives of the System   286
13.15   Conclusion   288

Chapter 14   Evolutionary Competence   289

14.1   Introduction   289
14.2   What Is Evolutionary Competence?   289

14.3   A Short List of Evolutionary Competencies   290
14.4   Building Blocks of Institutional Evolutionary Competence   292
14.5   Primary Forms of Evolutionary Behavior   294
14.6   Implementing Evolutionary Strategies   296
14.7   Elements of Tools and Techniques   300
14.8   Brainstorming   300
14.9   Benchmarking   304
14.10 The Process of Benchmarking   306
14.11 Benchmarking Accounting Functions   307
14.12 Potential Benchmarking Pitfall   307
14.13 Benchmarking Networks   308
14.14 Future of Benchmarking   308

Chapter 15   Organizational Flexibility   309

15.1   Introduction   309
15.2   What Is a Flexible Organization?   309
15.3   How Is Organizational Flexibility Achieved?   310
15.4   Product Modularization and Flexibility   311
15.5   Administrative Flexibility   312
15.6   Flexibility through Optimum Capacity Utilization   313
15.7   Making Agile Manufacturing American   314
15.8   Strategic Alliances   315
15.9   What Allows Alliances to Work   315
15.10 Future Prospects   316
15.11 Realizing the Maximum Customer Potential   317
15.12 Impediments to Attaining Adaptability   317
15.13 Implementing a Strategy for Change   318
15.14 Why the Imperative to Evolve?   319
15.15 Time-Based Competence   320
15.16 Various Time-Based Competencies   320
15.17 What Does It Take to Reduce Cycle Time?   321
15.18 Using Cycle Time to Gain Competitive Advantage   322
15.19 Concurrent Engineering   323
15.20 Theory of Constraints   324

Chapter 16   Repertoire of the Deming Approach   327

16.1   Introduction   327
16.2   What Is Total Quality Environment?   327
16.3   Not Being Content with the Status Quo   328
16.4   Change Is Inexorable   328
16.5   System as a Process   329
16.6   Cross-Functional Cooperation, Not Departmental Competition   330
16.7   Who Does What in Total Quality Environments   331
16.8   Implementation Levels for Total Quality Environment   332
16.9   Setting the Stage for Total Quality Environment   332
16.10 Implementing Total Quality Environment   334
16.11 Policy Implementation   336

16.12 Control Points and Checkpoints   337
16.13 Tools Used for Total Quality Environment   337
16.14 Business Process Redesign   340
16.15 The Information Technology Connection   342
16.16 Business Process Redesign Versus Total Quality Environment   344
16.17 Predecessors of Business Process Redesign   344
16.18 Benefits of Business Process Redesign   345
16.19 What Does Business Process Redesign Involve?   346
16.20 Process Management   346
16.21 How to Redesign?   347
16.22 Organizational Learning   349
16.23 Rethinking the Documentation Process   349
16.24 What Prevents Organizational Learning?   350
16.25 Rethinking the Perception of Work   350
16.26 Learning Paradigm   351
16.27 Frame Breaking   352

Chapter 17   Activity-Based Costing and Activity-Based Management   353

17.1   Introduction   353
17.2   Cost Tracking to Help Managerial Decisions   353
17.3   Focus on Activities   354
17.4   Accurate Reflection of Resource Usage   354
17.5   Definition of Activity-Based Costing and Activity-Based Management   354
17.6   Direct Versus Indirect Costs   355
17.7   Cost Behavior   356
17.8   Cost Behavior Under Activity-Based Costing   356
17.9   Activity Levels for Activity-Based Costing   357
17.10 Search for More Accurate Allocation   358
17.11 Acceptance of Irrational Allocations by Generally Accepted
       Accounting Principles   358
17.12 Trying to Do without Allocations   359
17.13 Tracking Activity-Based Costing   360
17.14 Activity-Based Costing Minus the Hype   361

Chapter 18   Information Technology as an Agent of Change   363

18.1   Introduction   363
18.2   Promise and Performance   363
18.3   Technology Is Not at Fault   363
18.4   Demonstrating the Usefulness of Information Technology   364
18.5   Assessing the Promise of Information Technology   369
18.6   Emerging Information Technology   371
18.7   Data Warehouses and Datamarts   371
18.8   Wide Area Networks   371
18.9   Extranets and Intranets   372
18.10 Electronic Data Interchange   372
18.11 Value-Added Networks Versus the Internet as a Basis for Electronic
       Data Interchange   373

18.12 Illustrating the Uses of Electronic Data Interchange   374
18.13 Client/Server Computing   375
18.14 Auditing Client/Server Systems   376
18.15 Handling Expense Accounts   377
18.16 Handling Information Technology with Care   378
18.17 Changing Systems   379
18.18 Outsourcing   380
18.19 Enterprise-Wide Accounting   380
18.20 Conclusion   380

Chapter 19   Electronic Commerce and Computer Security   383

19.1   Introduction   383
19.2   Overview of E-Commerce   383
19.3   Security on the Internet   385
19.4   Overview of Computer Crime   388
19.5   Understanding Computer Crime   388
19.6   Inadequate Computer-Crime Statistics   389
19.7   Understanding the Nature of Computer Abuse   390
19.8   Identifying Computer Criminals   391
19.9   Recognizing the Symptoms of Employee Fraud   391
19,10 Preventing Computer Abuse   393
19.11 Computer Virus Problems   395
19.12 Computers and Ethical Behavior   395
19.13 Protection from Computer Abuse   398
19.14 Federal Legislation Affecting the Use of Computers   399
19.15 Fraud on the Internet   400
19.16 Providing Assurances for E-Commerce   401
19.17 Example of a WebTrust Application   402
19.18 Securities Fraud on the Internet   403
19.19 Internet Mutation of Investment Frauds   404
19.20 Illustrating Cyberhighway Robberies   405
19.21 Dealing with Securities Fraud on the Internet   406
19.22 Disaster Readiness   407
19.23 Organizational Complacency   408
19.24 How to Get a Disaster Plan in Place   409
19.25 Content of a Disaster Recovery Plan   409

Index   411

Documentation Improvement Methods
The New Accounting Manual

INTRODUCTION

PROCEDURES MANUALS:
PAST, PRESENT, AND FUTURE

I.1 HISTORICAL ORIGIN

JoAnne Yates, a management communication expert who has written extensively on procedures documentation and other forms of organizational communication, has shown how developments in office technology, such as the invention of the telegraph, the typewriter, the mimeograph, and the vertical filing system, combined with the growth of various communication genres, the executive summary, the interoffice memo, and the procedures manual, helped bring about the advent of modern control systems between 1870 and 1920.

The growth of office technology made documentation more accessible. The growing accessibility of documentation allowed managers to record procedures and to communicate their expectations to employees. This downward flow of internal communication, in turn, permitted performance measurement and evaluation, thus leading to better organizational control and coordination. The upward flow of information in quantitative terms enable upper management to monitor and evaluate processes and individuals at lower levels. It made possible improved managerial control of organizational processes and assets. In addition to upward and downward communication flows, due to the new office technology, it also became possible to communicate laterally, thus promoting the staff functions within organizations.

Yates has shown convincingly that the developments in office technology and the newer organizational communication genres such as the procedures manual permitted the emergence of a formal communication system, which became an important control mechanism. Indeed, it allowed formal internal communication to become the dominant tool for managerial control. The documentation of procedures, policies, and rules and the reporting of financial and operational information on a regular basis led to the emergence of an organizational "memory," which facilitated organizational learning. She notes, however, that the advent of technology alone was not enough; the vision to use the new tools in creative ways was also necessary. Nor would gains have been realized by simply extending the communication patterns current during the period from 1870 to 1920. According to Yates's research, attention to potential human problems can facilitate organizational and technological changes. Moreover, documentation of the past for its own sake is not very useful for making decisions in the present; systematic recording and analysis of data allows informed decisions to be made.

Notwithstanding the negative aspects of bureaucracy, the antidote is not to dispense with the bureaucracy itself but to create conditions that will allow an organization to adjust to changes in the environment and to take advantage of the evolution of technology.

1

In the last twenty years, American management has relied on a number of techniques, such as quality circles, participative management, activity management, continuous learning, and process reengineering, to ensure that organizations can adapt to meet the demands of external changes. But because these management changes have not yet found their way to the process involved in the documentation of procedures manuals, the end product of the process has been an ignored resource for organizational learning.

1.2 PROCEDURES MANUALS GET NO RESPECT!

Today, accounting manuals that set forth organizational policies and procedures are not perceived as a learning tool; instead, they are often the neglected afterthoughts of management.

Most firms have procedures and policy manuals; however, they are rarely used in an optimum manner. The procedural and policy manuals on hand are all too often inadequate because of poor writing, cumbersome organization, and out-of-date information. The presence of such unusable manuals represents a twofold waste: On one hand, the preparation of the inadequate manuals was a waste of resources; on the other hand, by not using them, the firm is denying itself optimum use of potentially useful learning tools.

1.3 REASONS FOR THE INADEQUATE DOCUMENTATION

Among the reasons for the inadequacy and the resulting suboptimum use of manuals is that documentation is given low priority in the world of controllers and managers. Because of the lack, and at times absence, of respect given to the preparation of the documentation, manuals remain inadequate and underutilized. Within the universe of controllers and managers, other tasks, other crises seem to get a faster track. As a result, the writing and maintenance of manuals remains an afterthought.

Another reason for the poor quality of documentation is its absence in the educational training of future accountants, engineers, programmers, and other professionals. Their professional education does not prepare them for the writing of manuals. College accounting courses focus on the preparation of financial reports for disclosure but ignore the effective communication of those reports. Many of the labels hurled at accountants (e.g., bean counters and number crunchers) can be attributed to accounting professionals' inattention to the disparities between the information they provide and the actual needs of the users. It is no surprise, therefore, that accountants are unprepared and untrained for writing manuals. Too often, they are not motivated even to undertake documentation, let alone to do it well. It naturally follows that the documentation that results is not good and does not get used.

Accounting documentation does not have to be inadequate. But if it is to change into a productive tool, then both the perception of procedures manuals and the documentation process itself must change.

1.4 THE STAGNANT PERCEPTION OF MANUALS

In addition to the poor writing in manuals, their cumbersome organization and the failure to keep them current results in them being accorded low respect. An examination of the literature written in the last twenty-five years to instruct readers on how to write operating and systems manuals shows that there has been very little change in the way experts view them. The literature calls for manuals to be understandable, accurate, and professional looking. The experts think of manuals as archival instruments that merely describe current procedures. The same perception permeates advertisements for workshops on the preparation of organizational manuals.

Given the stagnant perception of procedures documentation and the low priority accorded it, it is no surprise that accounting manuals remain an ignored, wasted resource. As a result, their potential remains unrecognized and unused. The manuals have many traditional uses but their poor quality keeps them from being utilized optimally.

1.5 THE MANY USES OF MANUALS

There is no doubt that accounting manuals have many potential uses. Some are:

- Organizational Memory. Manuals can serve as the archive of a firm by providing knowledge about the development of a firm's policies and procedures. Such knowledge can prevent the firm from repeating its procedural mistakes.
- Reference Source. The manuals also can serve as a reference source, keeping employees from wasting time devising policies that already exist every time an infrequently used procedure has to be applied.
- Training Instrument. Manuals can help in the training of new employees. Instead of wasting the scarce, expensive time of experienced workers, newly hired employees can get their initial orientation by reading the operations and procedures manuals.
- Prevention of Work Interruption. Proper, well-written, current documentation also can allow work to continue if a key employee is absent or resigns. The key employee's departure does not lead to a crisis since others may refer to the manual for information and guidance.
- Regulatory Compliance. By documenting various regulatory requirements, manuals also can permit firms to comply with them. Workers are less likely to comply with requirements if they do not know what they are.

Accounting periodicals have documented many instances where manuals have been used successfully in various ways. In one instance, the productivity of a firm improved through the use of a procedures manual that provided those involved in the budgetary process with needed instruction about various steps in the process. Clearly, organizations, regardless of their size, should have a budget manual as part of their financial planning systems and procedures, so that employees do not have to start from scratch every year. The manual provides for an organized, centralized approach to the budget process by letting the workers know what needs to be done when, in what order, and by whom. It can be argued that manuals are needed not just for budgetary processes but for almost all the tasks undertaken by administrative units, in general, and the controller's department, in particular.

There are many other ways that procedures manuals can be useful. The Coca-Cola Company, for instance, found a comprehensive, easy-to-use manual to be an extremely important tool in maintaining financial controls in a multinational environment. The recently reported experience at Dow Chemical confirms the usefulness of accounting documentation to ensure consistent financial reporting. The giant chemical firm found a policy and procedures manual especially useful in policy formulation as well as in the implementation and administration of corporate strategy.

Even though manuals are potentially useful, instances of their successful use are the exceptions rather than the rule. They are, for the most part, an underutilized resource, but the organizational documentation does not have to be neglected. However, if the manuals are to change into a productive tool and regain their original use as a form of organizational memory and a learning tool in the twenty-first century, then the perception of documentation must not be limited to an archival role, nor should the process be limited to merely recording the procedures.

I.6 MAKING DOCUMENTATION AN ILLUMINATIVE ACT

It is common to find procedures and policies lingering on long after exhausting their usefulness. A periodic review and updating of manuals can go a long way in preventing the accumulation of deadwood by replacing it with productive and efficient procedures and policies in keeping with state-of-the-art technology. Such periodic reviews will allow the documentation process to become an occasion to learn.

The preparation and maintenance of procedures and operating manuals ought to be seen as the occasion for analyzing how the accounting department is carrying out its designated tasks. The writing should be an occasion for organizational self-examination and for learning. In a changing world, assigned departmental roles are subject to change. And even if the basic roles remain unchanged, certainly the implementation of them can evolve over time.

Before the procedures are documented they must be reviewed. Such a review can proceed by asking questions such as:

What is the given procedure seeking to accomplish?

Whose needs is the particular procedure seeking to meet? Can those needs be met in other ways?

Does the procedure enable the organization to better serve the customers? Does it add any value?

Are all the steps involved necessary?

Can the same goals be accomplished in another way?

How can technology be used cost-effectively to expedite the process? Can new technology provide an alternative approach that accomplishes the same goals?

The periodic review and analysis of the procedures used to carry out the functions assigned to accounting departments must be conducted with a view toward eliminating procedural gridlock, incorporating new technologies, and enhancing organizational productivity. Such analysis can ensure that the non–value-adding procedures are dropped or improved. A periodic review of what accounting procedures are meant to do, how they do it, and the extent to which they are meeting users' current and evolving needs can keep the procedures from becoming obsolete. By seeing to it that obsolescence does not infect procedures, accounting departments can prevent the spread of obsolescence to the information system of an organization and to the organization itself.

The obsolescence that plagued American accounting systems in the 1980s, and continues to do so, could have been avoided by periodic review of users' needs, the information provided, and the procedures used to generate the reports of the accounting information systems.

While writing procedures manuals, don't simply describe the way things are but think also about how they could be. The procedures analysis should become an occasion for cultivating employees' experience and knowledge in order to innovate. The centerpieces of the Japanese response to a constantly changing world are "knowledge-creating" companies that innovate continuously. They do so not by "processing" facts and figures of objective knowledge or by delegating to various departments such as research and development, marketing, or strategic planning, the task of innovation. Japanese firms like Honda and Canon create knowledge by taking a holistic approach that taps into the knowledge, experience, insights, and intuitions of all their employees and that emphasizes organizational self-knowledge and a collective sense of identity and purpose.

The task of organizational reexamination can benefit from the emerging tools such as activity management, process redesign, and the paradigm of learning organizations.

To summarize, accounting procedure documentation should not be an afterthought but a deliberate, illuminative act, an occasion for periodic self-examination on the part of the organization.

The preparation of manuals ought to be the result of teamwork, which uses collective knowledge and experience of the involved employees to periodically reexamine what the firm does and to explore ways of improving and evolving.

The documentation must not perpetuate the status quo. In a constantly changing world, maintaining the status quo can be the kiss of death. The fate of the dinosaurs testifies to that effect. Likewise, there is a lesson to be learned from Sears as it painfully paid in the 1990s for having played Rip Van Winkle in the American retailing scene in the 1970s and the 1980s.

I.7 THE TIME IS RIGHT FOR THE NEW PERSPECTIVE

This book brings a new perspective to the writing of accounting manuals by arguing that the documentation process can and should be an occasion to upgrade or even to redesign procedures in keeping with the changing environment and developing technology. That such a perspective is needed is borne out by the prevailing environment of the business organizations, professional groups, and emerging technology.

Seeing manuals as merely archival also has isolated the documentation process from the developments taking place in the world at large. Among the progressive organizations these days, the vogue is for activity management, process redesign, continuous improvement, and organizational learning. But so far no one has connected the new competencies developing in the organizational world with the process involved in the documentation of procedures. By studying the developments taking place in various managerial disciplines, those charged with writing accounting manuals can use the new techniques to broaden the perception of the documentation, making it a valuable contributor to the company's health rather than merely a record of company history.

Organizations, both public and private, must realize that the process that deals with the documentation of operating manuals itself can be useful for organizational learning and evolution. At present the focus of documentation is merely on the end product rather than the process that leads up to it. A broadening of the perception of the documentation process and an investment of resources to develop better manuals should more than pay for itself by making operations smoother and more efficient and by preventing organizational obsolescence. To live up to their potential usefulness, manuals must be current, available, readable, and easy to understand. Even if the actual writing is done by one individual, the preparation of manuals should be the result of teamwork, using the collective knowledge and experience of the involved employees to periodically reexamine what the firm does and to explore ways of improving and evolving. The documentation must not perpetuate the status quo, and it does not have to!

CHAPTER 1

CHANGING ROLE OF THE ACCOUNTING PROFESSION

1.1 INTRODUCTION

Four recent developments provide a significant insight on how the changes in technology as well as sociopolitical factors are altering the traditional roles performed by the accounting profession. The first of these four incidents involves the journal published by the Institute of Management Accountants (IMA). The journal was called *Management Accounting* for several decades; and in 1999 its name was changed to *Strategic Finance*. Clearly, when the flagship changes its banner, one has added incentive to notice. A 1999 study sponsored by IMA, and published under the name "Counting More, Counting Less: Transformations in the Management Accounting Profession," notes that the very name of the profession is in the process of becoming obsolete. The old label "management accountant" is still the norm in the academic accounting literature, but it is rarely used in practice by accountants themselves. Those who would have been considered management accountants refer to themselves as working in finance, as analysts, business partners, business managers, or controllers, but not in accounting. The third of these telling details was described in a conference paper. At the 1999 meeting of the American Accounting Association, which represents accounting academics, one of the papers described how the national advertising by Big Five accounting firms almost entirely omits words such as "accounting" and "auditing." According to the authors of the paper, other adjectives abound but not the phrases "certified public accounting" or "financial auditing." Last, there seems to be a decrease in management accounting courses being required of students in the graduate MBA programs. Other courses seem to be teaching business majors about the uses of information by decision makers and managers in planning and strategic contexts. Even the courses taught by information technologists seem to be recognizing that their profession combines the word "information" and "technology."

To better frame the changing nature of the accounting profession, this chapter starts by discussing three reports, by American Institute of Certified Public Accountants (AICPA), Institute of Management Accountants (IMA), and Association of Chartered Certified Accountants (ACCA), the British equivalent of the American certified public accountants (CPAs). The three reports show that changes taking place in the business environment are impacting the work of accountants. The first edition of this book argued that accountants must emphasize equally all three of their roles as score-keepers, attention-directors, and problem-solvers. What the three studies are saying is in fact the same: What is important is not only keeping score, but directing the attention of the management as information users to emerging issues and helping them solve problems as well as develop strategic goals.

1.2 AICPA'S VISION OF THE FUTURE

The CPA Vision Process was launched by American Institute of Certified Public Accountants to document the challenges and opportunities the accounting profession is likely to encounter by the year 2011. The AICPA's Vision, according to those who helped draft it, represents "an unprecedented, profession-wide initiative" seeking to make accountants the change facilitator for their clients and employers, in public practice, education, government, service, merchandising, or manufacturing. The statement seeks to make accountants, the proverbial bean-counters of yesterday, into the premier provider of information—and knowledge—in the new century.

The demand to formulate the CPA Vision was dictated by the pressures confronting the accounting profession, which in turn have been generated by the manifold changes that are taking place globally in every sphere involving the world of accounting and finance. "Evolutionary competence," using the term coined by this book's first edition and discussed at length in Chapter 14 of this edition, is what the AICPA Vision is seeking to help the accounting profession develop. The drafting of the statement seeking to promote evolutionary competence on the part of a profession historically seen as dronelike defenders of the status quo rather than vanguard of the organizational avant garde, was dictated by the realization that those who do not evolve end up going the way of dinosaurs, carrier pigeons, and horse buggies.

Allegedly, this exhortation to seize the opportunities inherent in a changing environment took nearly 3,500 accountants the equivalent of 21,456 hours to accomplish. The commitment of such resources was brought on not by any altruistic impulse, intellectual curiosity, or the desire to undertake introspection of the kind suggested in the philosophical maxim that an unexamined life is not worth living. Rather the task of developing a vision was undertaken by AICPA because of an economic imperative rooted in the realization that the monetary survival of the profession was dependent on developing new competencies that can respond to the demands of the information technology–driven twenty first century. Information technology is providing at the speed of light the kind of information accountants used to extract at snail's pace from their ledgers and journals. Furthermore, such instantly produced information can be tailored to the specific needs of the specific managers and their particular organizational function. Whatever the motivation, the redirection of the accounting profession sought by the AICPA is worth studying.

1.3 NATURE OF EVOLUTIONARY COMPETENCE

Accounting professionals are being asked to help their clients develop the competencies they would need to survive the future. Instead of merely keeping the books through financial statements that archive the performance score, accounting professionals are being urged to combine "insight with integrity," to help communicate "the total picture with clarity and objectivity" in order to provide value to their clients. To help earn their proverbial keep, CPAs are exhorted to render complex information into relevant knowledge meaningfully understandable to its users. Instead of playing the archival scorekeepers, accountants are urged to anticipate and to help create opportunities. Instead of just counting, accountants are being told to account for the organizational reality.

Accountants are being asked to start moving up the economic value chain. By thus migrating up the economic ladder, the accounting profession is to shift its attention away from the preparation of financial statements to providing knowledge-based products and services. Besides commanding higher fees, the so-called knowledge-based products are likely to remain in demand, in contrast to the technology now available that lets clients obtain on their own the sort of information that accountants used to provide, such as financial statements, and instantaneous ones at that. The technology represented by the current hardware and software is making information available on demand, instead of through laborious monthly closings that used to be the preoccupation and the focus of the accounting professional ritual.

Among the activities that are unlikely to bring a greater prosperity to the accounting profession is tax preparation. Such services have reached the stage where they can largely be prepared electronically, often by the clients themselves. Tax form preparation is itself no longer a moneymaker. However, the higher economic value of this information lies in helping clients reach a better understanding of their financial position and providing them with investment and tax options. Tax professionals must shift to provide clients with such strategically useful and financially more lucrative advice.

Through additional and revitalized education and training, which could be available through the 150 hours of education that CPAs are required to take to practice, accountants can use tax services as a foundation to provide such expanded value-added services as investment services. CPAs' understanding of investment and financing strategies will add value to the services they provide to their clients. Not the preparation of the tax form itself, but services such as estate and financial planning are where higher economic benefits exist for future tax accountants. Such work is now, and in the future will be, increasingly in demand and will provide higher fees and salaries. The key to a more lucrative income is in providing services where one must use professional judgment in combination with solid values. Such services require accountants to apply strategic thinking and professional acumen. The basic services provided by yesterday's accountants, such as basic tax filing and financial statement preparation, will no longer be lucrative enough.

In the business sector, the basic services such as maintaining financial records and preparing financial statements kept accountants busy, overwhelming them to the extent that they could not step back from putting out fires to take a strategic look at the employer's current situation and future strategy. Using technology to take care of the routine but time-consuming work, accounting professionals can move up the economic value chain by providing insight and strategies designed to deliver clients higher values and to help accomplish desired outcomes. Among the activities that can serve a strategic, illuminative role rather than routine, archival roles are:

- Involvement in broader business issues
- Providing assurance services and information integrity
- Helping clients through technology competence
- Serving as management consultants
- Advising clients in financial planning
- Providing international services

1.4 EXPANDING THE SERVICES ACCOUNTANTS PROVIDE

Next, the services accountants are to provide are discussed at some length. It should be obvious that these services are very different from what accountants provided in the past. To a very large extent, they involve broader business issues. Organizations that employ and/or consult with accountants do not exist in a vacuum. Environmental, social, political, and cultural factors have a considerable impact on organizational performance. Given this imperative, accountants, if they are to be relevant as employees or as consultants, will need to develop an understanding of the global, national, and marketplace environment. They will need to find ways in which various tangible and intangible factors can impact various types of organizational decision making and strategy formulations. Accountants must be able to make sense of the overall realities of the business environment. For this they must have technological acumen and be able to cultivate a "big picture" perspective in place of a bottom-line–focused financial reporting orientation. The development of such perspective demands an increased understanding of the economics as well the social, political, and cultural factors that impact society. No longer can accountants limit themselves to ledgers and journals, debits and credits.

(a) Assurance Services and Information Integrity

The portfolio of services provided by accountants have expanded into assurance services, and the change is not without controversy. Assurance means providing a variety of services that presumably improve and assure users about the quality of information being provided to organizational decision makers—such as the credibility of a web-based business. Such services have generated a greater income through a lucrative expansion of services CPAs provide. However, they also mean more regulatory standards and potential oversight, governmental as well as professional. It is likely that legal liabilities will increase for the profession. Beside the conflict of interest it could create for those accountants involved in public auditing, such an expansion of assurance services requires the acquisition and continuing cultivation of new skills that have been considered nontraditional accounting competencies by the profession. CPAs will not simply audit the extent to which the financial reports are in accordance with generally accepted accounting practices (GAAP); they also must provide assurance and interpretations as to the quality, accuracy, and meaning of diverse information in all settings. They are to provide quality advice to their client that can enhance their respective abilities to make decisions in relevant and all-too-often unfamiliar contexts.

(b) Technological Competence

Changing technology also provides another potentially lucrative opportunity to the accounting profession. Accountants can provide services that will enable their clients to use technology for improved decision making. Such consulting can pertain to business application processes, system integrity, knowledge management, system security, and integration of new business processes and practices. To do so, accountants will need to understand technology systems and how they can enhance the ability to process and integrate information on the part of organizations. Besides system technology, accountants must understand the nature of an organization's mission, objectives, and business environment. By acquiring such knowledge of technology and awareness of various areas of business practice, they can help provide solutions to complex questions through integrating specialized technology with their extensive experience. They can help clients create new strategic business processes. Accountants ought to be able to advise regarding security, relevance, and reliability of information being generated and consult regarding business applications and newer business practices and processes that help generate information. But to do so, they need to become more than archival scorekeepers of an organization that employs them or uses them as consultants.

(c) Management Consultants

Accountants provide advice regarding a host of financial and nonfinancial matters as well as the operational and strategic processes that impact the performance of organizations. While such consulting involves broad business knowledge and judgment, it also increases the potential for growth and new income opportunities. Consulting requires enhanced communication skills and additional education and training leading to new competencies. To be effective in their role as consultants, accountants must have a comprehensive set of problem-solving skills that apply to a wide range of business management and performance issues. They also will need to develop understanding about the environment within which businesses operate and be able to link internal operations and marketplace issues.

(d) Financial Planning

By using a wide range of financial information, accountants provide a variety of services to organizations and individuals that interpret and add value. These services include everything from tax planning and financial statement analysis to structuring investment portfolios and complex financial transactions. These areas will continue to be major avenues for professional involvement by accountants.

(e) International Services

Last, accountants provide services to support and facilitate trade commerce in the international marketplace. Being able to do so requires not only technical knowledge but multinational and multicultural communication skills. These services can lead to strategic alliances that provide leverage for taking advantage of opportunities available in global capital markets. Accountants also assist clients and employers moving into new foreign markets and in coping with the complexities of import and export regulations and cultures.

1.5 CORE COMPETENCIES FOR NEW SERVICES

Given the new roles accountants are expected to assume, they must be educated and trained with a focus very different from the one used to educate accountants in the past. Accountants of the twenty first century will need to develop a wide variety of skills that are markedly different from those currently emphasized in the college curriculum and continuing professional education. In some cases, the skills may be similar to the current ones, albeit with a different kind of emphasis. In recognition of the fact that accountants must actively compete with others by effectively marketing their professional talents and abilities, the AICPA's Vision Statement has specified a number of skills accountants of the future must be taught. To beat out the competition, accountants must understand how to help their employers and clients maneuver in the competitive environment by identifying strategic choices and by mobilizing resources to capitalize on opportunities in a timely manner. Accountants must understand the needs of clients, customers, or employers better than they do themselves.

The skills AICPA wants accountants to develop include:

- Communications and leadership skills
- Strategic and critical thinking skills
- Focus on the customer, client, and market
- Interpretation of converging information
- Technological competence

(a) Communications and Leadership Skills

This category requires an ability to exchange and extract information that can then be used to make decisions. Accountants not only provide information; first they must extract and receive it. The processing of data into information requires a set of skills and technologies different from those needed for effective organizational communication. Communicating information is different from organizational communication; the latter requires appropriate delivery and interpersonal skills and for the development of the ability to actively listen, but the former calls for additional technical skills. Both kinds of communication require accountants to gain an understanding of the explicit and implied needs of their customers, clients, and employers. They must learn to ask targeted questions that probe for valuable information. They have to be able to influence, inspire, and motivate others to achieve results. Increasingly, for timeliness of communication, accountants must learn to use technology. They also need to realize that different communication skills are needed for internal and external communication. Both the informational and organizational communication mandates require accountants to use a broad range of techniques, including process consultation, teamwork, and people skills far beyond traditional written and oral skills. Given how problematic traditional written and oral skills have been for accountants, developing the broader expertise is likely to require an even greater commitment, especially when considering that information communication is different from the general form of communication circumscribed by culturally aware reading, writing, and speaking.

(b) Strategic and Critical Thinking Skills

Information providers must have the ability to make sense of data and knowledge. Doing so calls for experience and insights so that accountants can provide relevant advice for decision making in operational and strategic contexts. Instead of simply checking the bottom line while preparing financial statements for their employers, accountants will be required to focus on how the firm can add value by broadening services, which will in turn enhance income. The newer technologies will expand accountants' abilities to gather data from a wide variety of sources and increasingly provide valuable, strategic interpretations for decision making. But increased data will not mean much unless accountants are able to find the real meaning behind financial and nonfinancial information while still protecting the broader public interest. They must invent new criteria to evaluate performance in a variety of business areas. They must use strategic and critical thinking skills to pinpoint untapped areas of financial growth, opportunity, and success. They will be well off if they understand new techniques such as visioning, scenario planning, and environmental scanning to keep the focus on the desired results. These skills require both a proactive stance and future rather than archival thinking.

(c) Focus on the Customer, Client, and Market

Accountants will need to develop skills that allow them to become the eyes and ears of their employers and clients. They must be able to anticipate and meet the changing needs of clients, employers, customers, and markets better than their customers and their competitors. They must have the ability to recognize market needs and anticipate new markets as well as help in the cultivation and development of such markets. To do so, accountants must proactively and continuously investigate current and emerging market trends.

(d) Interpretation of Converging Information

As the availability of data increases, so does the pressure to interpret such data. Such interpretation must be located within a broad-based context comprising both financial and nonfinancial information. If information provided is to facilitate interpretations that are timely and of value, accountants must increasingly utilize a systems approach, including formal and informal networks, to gain information and provide interpretations and insights for effective managerial decision making. Accountants will have to develop methodologies to measure and value intangible assets, such as the knowledge, experience, and intellectual capital of the organizational employees, that currently are excluded from the financial statements.

(e) Technological Competence

Since information technology consists of two words, information and technology, accountants as information providers must be capable enough to utilize and leverage technology in ways that add value to clients, customers, and employers. All too often the hype that accompanies adaptation of technology remains just hype—since many times the promised benefits do not materialize. Technology increases overhead costs for firms and organizations. To realize positive returns on costly capital investments, accountants must have the ability to combine critical thinking and professional judgment with the use of technology. They must not only be able to assess the cost benefits of technological projects; they should also be sensitive to myriad ways in which technology reinvents lifestyles, working environments, education, and communication skills. They must also be able to redesign the practices and processes that they and managers rely on in the public and private sectors. Accountants must cultivate expertise involving current and emerging technologies; be able to use technology to efficiently enhance the interaction of people, processes, procedures, structures, and systems; and help facilitate change by identifying, selecting, and maximizing the use of technological resources. They must use the technology not just to do what they have always done but to find new ways of working. Computers are not faster calculators or better typewriters; they help change how and why things are done.

1.6 EXPANDING ROLE OF THE MANAGEMENT ACCOUNTANT

A survey sponsored by the Institute of Management Accountants (IMA) first called "Counting More, Counting Less: The 1999 Practice Analysis of Management Accounting" but later changed to "Counting More, Counting Less: Transformation of the Management Accounting Profession," reveals how the role of the accounting profession is changing within corporate America. According to this study, the 1990s led to a changed perception of management accountants in leading-edge companies in the United States. In such firms, accountants are no longer bean-counters on the outer edges of organizational decision making; instead they are seen as valued team members very much involved at the very center of the organization's strategic activity. The study, a follow-up to the IMA's first practice analysis conducted in 1995, found accelerating changes taking place in the management accounting profession.

The 1995 Practice Analysis yielded an invaluable database that ultimately was used by at least some colleges and universities to revise curricula. Beyond fulfilling its specific charge, the 1995 Practice Analysis revealed the emerging contours of a new management accounting in which practitioners were breaking out of staff positions, working on cross-functional teams, and becoming more involved in decision making. While they still performed the traditional role of scorekeepers, company historians, and controllers, they were devoting increasing amounts of time to their new roles as analysts, consultants, and business partners. The 1999 Practice Analysis sought to locate and understand the changes in the work done by management accountants and their role in their companies over the past five years. The study also wanted to learn about the changes that are likely to occur in the work done by accountants working for organizations over the next three years. The IMA Practice Analysis documents that the changes in the management accounting profession are reflecting a much broader pattern of change in the way business is done in American companies. By focusing a lens on the accounting function, the 1999 Practice Analysis, in effect, permits a glimpse of even greater change under way in corporate America in the Information Age.

The 1995 Practice Analysis described a transition occurring in the profession. In the early 1980s, management accountants held corporate staff positions. As staff accountants, they were outsiders to the central work of their companies. They were physically separated from the operating departments and had relatively little face-to-face communication with people in line positions. If a factory manager needed product cost information, he or she would send a memorandum to the management accountant on staff, who would fill the request as received, even though a good business decision might require other, more relevant information.

Management accountants were not participants in the decision-making process. Instead, they provided support for the decision makers, even though such support did not seem to be all that appreciated. Management experts have argued that accountants were called in to defend decisions already made and were often informed of key decisions after the fact. Accountants spent the bulk of their time performing the mechanical aspects of accounting—scorekeeping after the game was over. They manually entered, added, and balanced pages upon pages of numbers on multicolumn papers. Accountants also documented budgets agreed to by managers and checked expense reports, often by spending more time and resources than those being reported by employees while traveling on organizational business. They also produced inventory cost reports by trying to track all the many copies of purchase orders, and generated a variety of standardized financial statements, which often were considered less than accurate valuation of organizational assets because of the adherence to the historical cost in valuating the assets owned by the firm. They were the scorekeepers (the bean-counters) and, sometimes, the corporate cops. Fulfilling the traditional accounting role, they were the keepers of financial records, the historians of the organizational archives.

(a) Management Accounting in the Twenty-First Century

The role of management accountants is very different today. Growing numbers of management accountants spend the bulk of their time as internal consultants or business analysts within their companies. Technological advances have freed them from the mechanical aspects of accounting. They can spend less time preparing standardized reports and more time analyzing and interpreting the information they are supplying to the managers. Many have moved from the isolation of accounting departments to be physically positioned in the operating departments where they work. They work in cross-functional teams, have extensive face-to-face communications with people throughout their organizations, and are actively involved in decision making.

In the late 1980s many corporations adopted a customer focus as part of quality improvement programs. This led to management accountants being seen as service providers to their organizational customers. The underlying philosophy of this approach is that the customer is always right. Thus, if a product designer requested particular financial information from an accountant, it would be provided even if not really appropriate to the business decision being made. Since then, the role of management accountants has evolved from serving internal customers to being a business partner. A business partner is an equal member of the decision-making team. As a business partner, a management accountant has the authority and responsibility to tell an operating executive why particular types of information may or may not be relevant to the business decision at hand and is expected to suggest alternative forms of information better suited to improving the quality and usefulness of the decision.

1.7 HIGHLIGHTS OF THE INSTITUTE OF MANAGEMENT ACCOUNTANTS STUDY

The 1999 Practice Analysis results provide both a snapshot of the current state of the management accounting profession in the United States and an indicator of where the profession is heading. When compared to the baseline measures established in the 1995 Practice Analysis, the current results show ongoing and escalating changes taking place not only in the work done by management accountants but in their very role in the organization and in the value they add to organizational decision making.

(a) Providing More Value to Organizations

If bolstered by the skills required to function in the technological revolution that fostered the new information economy, management accountants' expertise is in greater demand within their organizations. Management accountants say that a growing number of people outside the finance function perceive them as providing greater value to the company than they did in the past.

(b) Not Being Perceived Negatively

In many companies, management accountants believe they are shedding the number-cruncher and bean-counter stereotypes and are instead perceived as business partners.

(c) Increased Communication with Other Departments

Management accountants spend more time communicating with people in their company today than they did five years ago. Indeed, respondents universally agree that good interpersonal skills are essential for success. This dispels the outdated stereotype that accountants are devoid of people skills.

(d) Improved Business Decisions

In corporations where management accountants function as business partners, anecdotal evidence suggests that better business decisions are being made.

(e) Changed Work Location

Accountants traditionally worked in accounting departments that were physically isolated from the operating departments of their companies. In 1999, however, 20 percent of all respondents report that at least half the management accountants in their company have moved out of the central accounting area and are located with the operating departments they service. In larger finance organizations, 45 percent of respondents say that at least half the management accountants are located with the operating departments they service.

(f) Team Members

More than 50 percent of management accountants now work on cross-functional teams and are increasingly likely to take on leadership roles. More than 70 percent work in companies in which at least some management accountants are cross-functional team members.

1.8 HIGHLIGHTS OF THE ASSOCIATION OF CHARTERED CERTIFIED ACCOUNTANTS STUDY

The July/August 1999 issue of *Accounting and Business,* a publication of ACCA, included the results of a research study that reveals expectations about finance professionals' ability to add value to the organization that employs them. The study reveals that industry chiefs globally "are increasingly worried that their companies' key financial managers lack the skills necessary to adapt to a changing global environment." This survey commissioned by ACCA reveals that a perceived inability of finance professionals to take a broad strategic perspective and see the bigger picture is a corporate chief's greatest fear.

The key finding of the survey is the realization that the globalization of business is leading to both strategic opportunities and new anxieties. Directors are increasingly dependent on their financial experts to help them navigate through the maze of new economic, legislative, and commercial risks. The research shows that, while there is perceptible need for finance professionals to be involved in developing strategic plans, the corporate accountant's traditional role in financial reporting, taxation, and compliance has not diminished in importance. However, finance professionals are expected to do more than merely contribute number-crunching to strategic decision making and the development of corporate financial strategy. Corporate managers wish to see their finance people take on a strategic involvement well beyond scorekeeping through numbers. But the survey also reveals the critical nature of traditional financial skills; 90 percent of respondents believe that these skills will remain the foundation of strategic financial management now and in the future.

The survey consisted of in-depth telephone interviews with eighty senior executives in

Europe, China, Japan, Singapore, South Africa, and North America. Of those interviewed, 20 percent were chief executive officers, managing directors, presidents, or chairmen; 59 percent were finance directors or chief financial officers; 20 percent were human resources directors, or the equivalent.

Like its counterparts AICPA and IMA in the United States, ACCA has committed to a strongly enhanced and broadened customer focus, based on a flexible package of support for members throughout their careers, delivered through interactive training and information technology (IT). The study makes clear that once they have joined the profession, accountants are largely expected to be responsible for their own further professional development.

CHAPTER 2

USER-FRIENDLY ACCOUNTING MANUALS

2.1 INTRODUCTION

Historically, accounting manuals fall into the category of imposing professional references that sit on shelves, rarely used, their bulky binders never opened. This "HANDS-OFF" policy is in large measure responsible for the lack of attention accorded the accounting manuals. If accounting documentation is to be illuminative, it must be usable and useful. The big binders are among the impediments that make the manuals less usable.

Fortunately, the advent of desktop publishing has helped remedy the formidable look of accounting documentation by giving manuals user-friendly appeal. Even now it is entirely possible to think about the accounting manual as a part of the information bank on client server systems, linked to far-flung users on the information highway. Today's information technology links data, jobs, and employees in ways that was not possible until recently. Now there is software that interprets and extracts information from many sources; there is also software for relational databases, structured query language, hypertext, and graphical user interface (GUI). Given such technological tools, the black-and-white, yellowing, small prints of accounting manuals are a thing of the past.

This chapter is about the accounting manual itself. It describes the content, the organization, the logistics, and the mechanics involved in documenting an accounting manual.

2.2 THE MESSAGE AND THE MEDIUM

A well-developed policy and procedures system facilitates the performance of accounting functions. The accountant's role as a member of the management team can be accomplished more effectively in an environment where policy and procedures are well defined, documented, and accessible. The accounting documentation, an integral part of an effective accounting department, is extremely useful in the preparation of reports in which relevance, uniformity, and continuity are important. Management should use the manual to establish uniform standards for evaluating the results of different divisions, plants, and products. If the same system of accounting is used in all locations, it is much easier to identify and analyze variances. In fact, if a company operates on the management-by-exception principle, common bases are absolutely essential. Without a common frame of reference, it would be impossible to classify results as standard or nonstandard.

The value of effective documentation is not limited to the accounting department. It benefits the entire organization. Effectively communicated policies and procedures enable all segments of operations to start from a commonly understood base. This ensures that comparisons are accurate between plants, departments, people, and products, enhancing performance evaluations. Time requirements and errors are reduced when proper procedures can be confirmed by consulting the manual.

However, the policies and procedures outlined in the manual must be followed in order to realize the benefits of a streamlined, efficient process. This requires that the process be reviewed constantly. Revisions and improvements should be made periodically so that the policies and procedures do not become obsolete.

2.3 PROGRAM FOR STARTING AN ACCOUNTING MANUAL

The scope of a policy and procedures manual is determined by the complexity of the organization. The greater the number of departments or plants, the diversity of products or procedures, and the echelons of management, the more thorough the manual must be. The planning process is outlined in Exhibit 2–1, and the critical factors that must be taken into account are given in Exhibit 2–2. The decision to prepare or to revise an accounting manual must have a commitment from management, or the manual preparation process will lack the resources it needs to become fully established and operative. A person or committee should be designated to develop and manage the process.

The next step is to obtain the necessary personnel and resources to develop the manual. This requires selection of an editor; designation of the people who will review the final drafts to see that errors have not slipped through; designation of people who are to receive

---

Outline of the Manual Planning Process

Planning the actual writing of the manual
- Defining the subject matter
- Deciding who will collect the data
- Deciding who will write the manual
- Establishing a timetable for data collection and writing

Planning the mechanics of production
- Developing an efficient clearance and review process
- Deciding on layout format and binders
- Determining distribution
- Determining method of reproduction
- Establishing a control point
- Developing and distributing a work schedule
- Anticipating and preventing problems

Collecting and organizing the data
- Collecting the data
- Who should collect the data
- Methods of data collection
- Anticipating and preventing potential data collection problems

Organizing the data in a working outline
- The importance of outlining
- Guidelines for outlining

Explore the use of information technology

Exhibit 2–1. Planning an accounting manual.

IDENTIFYING YOUR MANUAL NEEDS

Benefits that manuals provide to the organization
Different types of manuals in use
Determining your manual's specific objectives

DESIGNING AN ATTRACTIVE, READABLE MANUAL

Choosing the appropriate format
Using layout to increase readability
Selecting the appropriate binder, index tabs, and paper

PREPARING THE MANUAL'S INTRODUCTORY SECTION

Preparing a table of contents
Developing an index
Writing effective introductory material

WRITING FOR MANUALS

Reviewing the principles of effective writing
Using step-by-step listing to simplify your writing
Using formats that clarify procedures

USING VISUAL SUPPORT TECHNIQUES IN MANUALS

Using flowcharts in manuals
Using forms effectively
Determining when to use special exhibits

THE REVIEW PROCESS

The reviewer's role and responsibilities
Scheduling reviews
Techniques for ensuring that reviewers meet deadlines

THE PRODUCTION, STORAGE, AND DISTRIBUTION OF MANUALS

The role of word processing in manual production
The printing of manuals
Determining the appropriate distribution
Handling the storage of extra copies

Exhibit 2–2.   The critical factors impacting documentation of an accounting manual.

and maintain the manual; and selection of people responsible for the filing and maintenance of copies in all locations. The program also should specify those who may issue, revise, or rescind bulletins.

After the project has been properly staffed, the next step is to select and organize the topics to be covered in the manual. A company-wide manual may have the following general sections:

- General matters
- Operations
- Sales
- Accounting
- Credit and collections

Accounting manuals in theory do not devote much space to topics that do not concern them directly. However, there is very little that occurs within an organization that does not eventually flow into the accounting system. Consequently, it is wise to include peripheral procedures that may affect the accounting department.

2.4 ORGANIZATION OF THE ACCOUNTING MANUAL

There are a number of ways in which an accounting procedures manual can be organized. It may be split into two volumes: One volume describes the accounting system in terms of the chart of accounts, the coding scheme, account descriptions, and the general accounting principles and policies being followed; the second volume deals with the specific procedures that are in place.

Other manuals may follow a scheme where the material is divided into several volumes. One way to divide the material is as follows:

- Overview of Accounting System. Gives information about the organization of the system and the chart and description of accounts; discusses the organizational structure and its relationship with accounting information system; provides a directory of the employees.
- Policy and Procedure Statements. Gives the actual policies and procedures that are in place in the system; describes how the various accounting subsystems work and the procedures they employ to accomplish their objectives.
- Budget Manual. Gives information about the budget process as well as identifying the components of the budget.
- Year-end Procedures. Gives the procedures to be used for the year-end work that must be done in order to generate the financial statements.
- Data Processing Manual. Gives information about the data processing needs of the accounting system; facilitates the interactions between accounting and systems.
- Forms Manual. Collects the forms and worksheets that are used by the accounting system to process its transactions and facilitate the data collection.
- Information Release. Collects directives about topics of interest to employees.

The topics that may be included in an accounting manual are listed in Exhibit 2–3.

2.5 SYSTEM MAINTENANCE

It is not enough merely to know how to initiate a manual system for policies and procedures; it is equally important to establish a system that will maintain the manual. To accomplish this there must be a person in charge of the documentation who will have the master copy and will see to it that it is being kept up-to-date. This responsibility is best delegated to a person who has the knowledge and ability to write new bulletins or revise existing ones. In a large company this is a full-time job; in smaller companies the job is often handled by the controller or the treasurer.

The person in charge of documentation may write the proposed material and submit it to management for review and approval. Following approval, the material is issued under the name of the individual who has authority over the particular policy or procedure. This practice is important, since it establishes the source of authority over documentation. In

---

ACCOUNTING MANUAL
  Overview of accounting system
  Need for and source of accounting policies
    Scope of an organization's accounting policies
  Writing and updating accounting policies
    Drafting, gaining approval, and updating policies
  Internal control policies
  Code of business and personal conduct, incidental gifts, managerial authorizations,
      entertainment, and cost transfers
  Accounting and financial management policies
  Signature authorities, cash management, investments, revenue recognition, inventory
      valuation, inventory adjustments, incurred costs, multi-year budgets, audits, and
      record retention
  Cost accounting policies
    Labor, material, direct/indirect costs, other direct costs, compensated absences,
    leases, capitalization, depreciation, insurance, pensions, and credits
  Employee compensation and disbursement policies
    Timecard preparation, overtime, bonuses, 401 (K) plans, relocation, exempt/non-
    exempt employees, employees vs. consultants, travel reimbursement, and frequent
    flyer awards
  Property management policies
    Policies regarding organization-owned, leased, and small-dollar items, computer
    hardware, software, and physical counts
  Purchasing policies
    Ethical conduct, full and open competition, adequate number of bidders, source
    selection, cost and price analysis, and purchase order processing

---

Exhibit 2–3. Contents of an accounting manual.

some instances, management prepares its own material, and after approval it is given to the controller for proper indexing, classification, and inclusion in the manual.

All of the documentation maintained in respective departments of an individual plant or location need not be complete, since each individual needs only the section of the manual that pertains to his or her job. However, one complete and intact copy should be in each location. One person at each location should be responsible for the maintenance of manuals in all departments. This method is more effective than permitting each department to maintain its own manual, which results in the task of filing changes and adding new material being performed unevenly throughout the organization.

2.6 REVIEW AND MAINTENANCE OF THE MANUAL

As a matter of general policy, manuals should be periodically checked for revision. The person in charge of the manual should schedule and record such reviews. The date of any revision should be shown in the body of the particular bulletin, and the date of review should also be noted in order to facilitate later reviews. The department that suggests the revision should review the bulletin at the same time it is reviewed by the manual manager.

There are always changes being made to procedures, and the organizational structure also keeps changing. All such changes require adaptations in the manual. Such maintenance will ensure greater respect for the manual as well as greater adherence to the procedures it documents.

2.7 POLICING THE MANUAL

There may be times when employees seek to do things their own way. Such customization of work may not be the optimum way to achieve the organization's objectives. Given this tendency, it is important to police the compliance with standard operating procedures.

Independent auditors can use company manuals to check the performances of various units against prescribed policies and procedures. A company's internal audit staff also checks on compliance with standard procedures as a part of their audit program. A third method of policing is to set up a task force whose sole function is to check on compliance throughout the company. If a program is well maintained, cooperation and communication already exists between the plants and the general office. There will be little danger of noncompliance because all will be aware of the benefits to be derived from the system. If the system is not well maintained at its source, then trouble may be expected from the field.

2.8 PHYSICAL ATTRIBUTES

Even though on-line documentation is becoming more common, one still must have available a "hard-copy" version for legal and other reasons. Careful attention to the physical characteristics of the accounting manual can go a long way in making the manual user-friendly. Following are some factors to be considered when planning the "hard copy" version of the manual:

- Type of binder—should be loose-leaf post or ring-type to allow for insertions
- Type of page presentation—stationery should be identifiable as pertaining to the manual
- A system of indexing
- Page format
- Numbering of bulletins, pages, and paragraphs
- Method of reproduction

The manual must allow for expansion, as revisions will certainly come as the system progresses.

2.9 CORE OF THE ACCOUNTING MANUAL

The heart of the accounting documentation is the portion dealing with policies and procedures. It is quite important to understand the distinction between policies and procedures. The topics covered in a manual can be either a matter of policy or a matter of procedure, or they may be both. All policy matters are approved by the appropriate level of management, but procedures may be approved by lower management as long as they do not contradict the policy they are intended to serve. The distinction between them is important because the person who sets policy generally does not perform the related procedures. This separation is used to argue that policy and its related procedures should exist as separate documents. Even if policies and procedures are to be combined in a manual, a clear distinction should always exist between a statement of policy and a statement describing the procedural details.

2.10 DIRECTIVES

Directives are an important tool for the accounting department in communicating with both internal and external customers. They are meant to inform about pending policy changes, staff changes, organization changes, and holiday schedule, and to announce minor procedural changes. Directives also may be issued as reinforcement to recent policy changes. They should be communicated on official stationery that will identify them as directives. They may be numbered so that a record can be maintained.

2.11 POLICY STATEMENTS

Policy statements, or bulletins, are those documents that concern matters of policy, both external and internal. They have official standing, and they are formal documents. They have direct impact on the organizational culture of an institution and at the same time are the outgrowth of the organizational culture. The environment also may be influenced with policy statements. In an environment dominated by litigation, there may be more of them.

Common subject matter for these bulletins may include:

Absence from work due to: accident, sickness, approved leaves, personal business, jury duty, military service, death of a relative, National Guard duty, tardiness, pregnancy
Office or plant hours

Advancement and promotion	Overtime
Car pooling	Parking
Coffee or rest breaks	Pensions and retirements
Company stationery and logo	Personal telephone calls
Disabled employees	Personal work
Discipline and discharge	Picnics and parties
Educational assistance to employees	Rehiring
Employee purchases	Relatives (nepotism)
Ethical codes	Repairs and maintenance
Expense allowances	Safety
Garnishments	Seniority
Holidays	Service recognition
Insurance	Smoking
Intoxicants	Tools and tool boxes
Inventions and patents	Travel time
Keys	Unclaimed wages
Mail	Use of personal car on business
Moving expenses	Vacations
New equipment acquisitions	Visiting and visitors
Outside business or employment	

2.12 PROCEDURES

Procedure bulletins cover the procedures required to implement policy but, as stated previously, they should be distinguished from policy. Procedures change more often than policies, and procedures spell out exact details, whereas in policies, broad outlines are drawn.

The documentation of procedures can take a number of forms. It could be designed to follow the document flow that occurs in the performance of a given procedure. Or it may describe individual transactions in a narrative style, set off by the person responsible for the task. Following is an example of the narrative layout—the step being described is from the procedure for cash collection during registration at a university:

1. Assistant Controller   Will prepare a cash change fund to give back change to students registering. This will be handed over to Head Cashier for use during registration.

2. Head Cashier   Will sign receipt for cash received. Prepares change drawer for each station as the shift begins.

The range of procedure bulletins is unlimited but, to ensure company-wide comparability of results and uniformity in the execution of policies, they should at least include the following:

Absence from work	Job evaluation and rating
Accidents and disability benefits and claims	Key control
Address changes	Memberships and fees
Admittance to plant and office	Moving expenses
Advances on pay	New products
Applications and employment	Overtime
Badges and numbers	Part-time employees
Bathing and clothes change	Payroll deductions
Company tools	Payroll rates, ranges, classifications, changes
Contributions and fund drives	Personnel records
Discharges and dismissals	Repair and maintenance
Employee purchases	Requisitions and returns to stock
Employment benefit plans	Safety and safety equipment
Empty bottles	Scrap
Endorsing, cashing, and handling paychecks	Stationery and supplies
Error reports	Storeroom
Errors in pay	Suggestions or idea awards
Expense reimbursement	Supper or meal allowance
Filing	Toolroom
First aid and dispensary	Unclaimed wages
Insurance coverage for personnel	Worker's compensation

2.13 POLICY AND PROCEDURE STATEMENTS

Policy/procedure statements (P/PSs) combine the description of the policy and a summary of the procedures being used. The description of the procedure is aimed at the users and generally leaves out the actual processing details. Even the simplest form of procedures, with just one form, may require fifteen to twenty identifiable steps to be performed by several different clerical employees. Omitted from the P/PS are details concerning tasks performed, such as initiating, checking, approving, distributing, calculating, balancing, cross-checking, reviewing, and filing. Such omissions make the document easy to read; however, these omissions make it difficult to analyze those tasks from a value-adding or cost-benefit perspective.

An example provided in the appendix for Chapter 4 serves to illustrate the form and content of a policy/procedure statement. The range that can be covered by policy/procedure statements is illustrated in Exhibit 2–3.

2.14 ILLUSTRATING ACCOUNTING MANUALS PREPARATION

To help illustrate the process involved in the preparation of an accounting manual, two articles that have described the experiences of two major corporations with regard to their respective accounting manuals are summarized here. Between the two, almost all the issues concerning the logistics of accounting manuals are illustrated.

(a) The Coca-Cola Company*

The use of a comprehensive, easy-to-use accounting manual became an important tool at the Coca-Cola Company for maintaining strong financial controls in a globally active organization, whose overseas operation is staffed with individuals whose native language is not English and who have no knowledge of the U.S. accounting principles. Management's demands for timely, reliable financial information required that the worldwide accounting reports be uniform.

Such reporting required a universal chart of accounts to facilitate consolidation, auditing, and communication of accounting reports. It also mandated standard practices and procedures throughout the organization and a uniform data collection system.

In response to such needs, the company developed an all-purpose accounting manual for use in foreign offices. The manual is divided into two parts; the first part contains a chart of accounts along with account definitions, and the second part contains standard practices and procedures.

The initial step in the preparation of the manual was the appointment of a project team charged with its writing. The project team initially sought to rehash the old manual, but they found that simply editing the old manual was not helpful. The company's needs had changed since the previous manual was issued, and functions that were deemed important only a few years ago were no longer relevant in an automated environment with high-speed bottling equipment, preselling, automated warehousing, and satellite communications.

The project team sought to determine what to include in the manual. One essential was a universal chart of accounts. Creation of such a chart became a project in itself because of the new emphasis on automation. After deciding on a logical numbering scheme, the chart of accounts was created. It was detailed enough to identify activities important to the company, so that data collection would not require extensive account analysis. Information that was not reported on a regular basis was maintained at the subaccount level, whereas main accounts were set up to meet management and tax reporting needs. The accounts were described, as was the expense account distribution. The chart of accounts and the explanation became a volume called *Accounting Manual Part I*.

The writing of the policies and procedures became the next concern. These procedures became *Accounting Manual Part II*. The procedures' arrangement followed the structure of financial statements. Therefore, cash was the first section, followed by accounts receivable, inventories and cost accounting, properties, and sections on internal control and the translation of foreign currency statements into U.S. dollars. A "general" section contained procedures on record retention, insurance, travel expenses, a glossary of terms, and a few other areas of concern to international businesses.

The company used tabs to separate the sections and wrote the procedures in outline format so that inquiries from field operations or auditors were easily referenced as to section and paragraph.

The next step was to determine the content of each section.

- The section on cash included procedures dealing with the opening and closing of bank accounts and the handling of cash receipts along with remittances to headquarters.
- The accounts receivable section dealt with the company's procedures for aging, collection, extension of credit, order entry, and invoicing.
- Inventory procedures dealt in general terms, leaving specifics of inventory management to the discretion of the operating unit. Areas that were detailed were physical security of the inventories, physical counts, and reconciliation. A uniform costing procedure also was included here. In an extensive manufacturing environment, cost accounting procedures would be in a separate manual.
- The properties section included property control, asset depreciation rates, and property disposal procedures.
- The procedure for translating local currency statements into U.S. dollars took up another section.
- A separate section dealing with considerations such as the Foreign Corrupt Practices Act and security over automated systems, financial records, data files, and user documentation was included.

The writing was assigned equally among the team members, as was editing for content and form. Once drafts were completed, they were reviewed by the audit, legal, and tax managers. Then the drafts were distributed to a select number of field accounting managers for comments, since they were the actual users of the document. The writing style was determined to a great extent by the company's personality, but the goal was to keep the prose simple, especially since, for the majority of users in a multinational company, English is a second language.

The distribution of the volume also was important. Because the manual contained certain sensitive information, it had to be restricted to a select number of recipients. The list needed to be periodically reviewed and updated.

It took twelve work-months from the initial planning stage to design, write, edit, and distribute the finished product.

(b) Dow Chemical Company*

The philosophy that guides Dow Chemical's documentation is driven by the following perceptions:

- It provides improved, consistent decision making.
- It helps delegate accounting functions.
- It enhances communication.
- It provides coordination across and within subunits.

Another factor that affects Dow's documentation is its belief that the procedures documentation should be detailed enough to meet both local and corporate reporting requirements.

Dow's first accounting manual consisted of a chart of accounts and an accumulation of policy and procedure letters written over a period of time. It provided no formal mechanism for updating the documentation, nor was it possible to determine if all concerned parties, functions, and locations were operating in accordance with the most recent version of a policy or procedure. During the late 1960s, Dow was becoming a global company and needed a uniform system of accounting policies and procedures with worldwide application. To address these needs, Dow's *Accounting Policy and Procedures Manual* was formalized and became effective as of January 1, 1971. It consisted of two volumes: *Policies and Procedures* (AP Volume) and *Chart of Accounts* (AC Volume). It was anticipated that the revised coding arrangement of the accounts would aid in the accumulation of information and facilitate the preparation of Dow's financial reports. In 1990, after a twenty-year trial, it was reported to have been effective in meeting these objectives.

Dow's *Accounting Policy and Procedures Manual* (AP Volume) contains eighteen sections. The sections are family groupings within which related subjects appear and each family or major category has been assigned a section number. The first section, numbered 000 to 099, provides an overview of Dow as an organization by discussing locations, divisions, subsidiaries, and related companies. This discussion of the firm is followed by a corporate policy section, numbered 100 to 199, highlighting such areas as internal control, code of conduct, transfer pricing, and product policies. The third section discusses personnel practices, such as employee transfers and Dow's stock purchase plan. The remaining sections present Dow's policies and procedures relating to various financial statement items in addition to their cost accounting policies.

The *Chart of Accounts* (AC Volume) outlines the intended use of each account. The general ledger accounts are assigned by the corporate controller's office to provide for all eventualities for which a valid need is disclosed. The account number also serves as a document control number and is the principal reference number as indicated on each page. Since the manual undergoes continual changes, the pages are not numbered consecutively. Rather, each subject has its own document number with the pages numbered sequentially. With few exceptions, the assignment of subaccounts to the *Chart of Accounts Manual* is at the discretion of the local units of Dow.

All pages of the manual include a format section for the date of the current revision and a second formatted section for the date of the superseded section. Thus, the manual is always current, as superseded sections are removed and the current revisions inserted. In addition, the manual's index lists the most recent issue of a policy, procedure, or account revision against which any page may be compared. The dating feature facilitates worldwide communication by quickly enabling corresponding parties to determine if they are discussing a subject from the point of view of the most recent revision.

In some cases there is need for interim communication to help with rapid dissemination of procedural information, including clarification of new policies or the opening of new accounts. Such interim communication is followed with formal documents at the next official manual update. This interim method of communication was used recently to disseminate the new procedures required to implement SFAS No. 95, Statement Cash Flows. Several new general ledger accounts were opened to collect dollar amounts on investment and financial activities (new items from receipts or repayments) and also to segregate opening balances from current year activities. Dow has issued forty-four transmittal letters since

January 1971, which translates into slightly more than two revisions per year. Using interim communications allowed for data exchange between corporate and area representatives, which resulted in the modification of certain procedures before they were included in the manual as policy.

As an aid to the reader, revision symbols are used to identify and assist the manual user in locating the changes in the updated material. They include:

>>>>   Denotes a new or revised paragraph or that something has been added to the index.

<<<<   Points to the approximate location where something was removed.

<<>>   Points to a location where one thing has been added or revised and another has been removed.

In addition to these indicators, a brief explanation for the change is provided with the revision. Such explanations are dispatched to various locations via a numbered letter of transmittal.

The documentation is stored on floppy disks. About eight hundred pages are stored on twenty-six disks in five hundred files. As of 1990, Dow was searching for a package to help move the documentation on-line with worldwide access. Editing the documentation to ensure current usage of terms or proper names is done with the help of a software package that can examine all the files and report on the number of times a term is used. When the firm went to quarterly closing from monthly closings, it used a file search to help change to "quarterly" the word "monthly" when used in reference to closings. When the employee relations department changed its name to human resources department, a computer search helped with the revision. The search revealed that the words "employee relations" were used twelve times; those references were changed to "human resources."

Dow has distributed 507 copies of its manuals worldwide. They are issued to the locations rather than individuals, so that when managers transfer, the manuals remain at the location. A periodic audit is done to verify the existence of the documentation.

2.15 BUDGET MANUAL

The preparation of the budget is a major task in the lives of controllers and their staff. While it is important, it is only an annual event for most of those involved in the preparation of the budget. Not everyone remembers all the bits and pieces that are a part of the "how to" of budgeting. Because of its infrequency, and given its importance, budget preparation requires that a major portion of the accounting manual be devoted to it. It is recommended that there be a distinct volume entirely devoted to the budget process.

Such a manual will inform and instruct those involved in the process about the organizational policies pertaining to its budget preparation. The manual also will describe the procedures and the tasks that are necessary in putting together the budget. Such documentation will ensure that data flowing in will be processed uniformly. Since preparing a budget involves organizing, analyzing, and reporting large amounts of information, it is easy to overlook important details and tasks. If those tasks are prerequisite for subsequent processes, then the entire process may face roadblocks. Preventing such lapses due to the frailty of human memory is a function of the budget manual. It should list the various phases of the process as well as the tasks specific to each phase. It should also indicate who was assigned various tasks in previous years.

2.16 CONTENTS OF A BUDGET MANUAL

Organizations approach budget manuals in different ways. The approaches range from having no manual at all to having a very detailed, task-by-task set of instructions. Moreover, the contents of budgets themselves will vary from one organization to another, and the budget process will vary from industry to industry. It will also be affected by the size of the firm and its organizational culture. Notwithstanding such diversity, a budget manual should contain:

- A statement of the budget policy for the chief executive officer.
- A guide describing how to communicate the organizational goals for the budget period. The section also could contain the organizational goals used for previous budget periods. The presence of such historic awareness will aid managers in dealing with the present and the future.
- Definition of the responsibilities involved in the process.
- The procedures devoted to budget preparation and its review.
- The tasks involved in data collection and its consolidation.
- Principal forms and the worksheets used as well as a description of the software packages used. Preparing a budget manually for even a midsize firm can be a challenging experience.
- Calendar and time lines used for the budget.
- Procedures for changing budgets
- Distribution of the budget document.
- Explanation of how the budget is to be used by managers and supervisors.

2.17 CONCLUSION

Business firms must realize that operating manuals can be useful, productive tools. It will take an investment of resources to develop better manuals, but this investment will more than pay for itself by making operations smoother and more efficient. To live up to their potential usefulness, accounting manuals must be current, available, readable, and easy to understand.

In the spirit of continuous improvement and of keeping up with technolcgical changes, it may be advisable to rely on emerging information technology to make documentation less archival and more interactive. In keeping with the new emphasis on the process, on-line documentation is a wise investment, which will make changing or revising easier.

CHAPTER 3

ILLUSTRATING THE ILLUMINATIVE APPROACH TO DOCUMENTATION

3.1 INTRODUCTION

The documentation process can be changed from being merely an exercise in perpetuating the status quo into an instrument for improving organizational efficiency. There is nothing magical about such a transformation. One simply has to analyze a given procedure. One could do so by asking questions, such as: What does the procedure seek to accomplish? Is it doing so in an efficient manner? By exploring what the procedure is seeking, one is in effect trying to ascertain the value of a given procedure to the organizational purpose, in other words, its role in creating the so-called value chain. To do so, a given procedure first must be deconstructed to see its objectives and its value, and whether it can be modified and improved in any way. Once such questions are answered, the procedure may then be reconstructed with modifications and improvement. If the existing procedure is not worth redesigning, an alternative approach is called for and should be implemented.

Through the application of such a basic technique, the documentation process can become more than an exercise in maintaining the status quo in a world where the only constant is change. By trying to understand why a procedure is being done and how it is being done, one can make documentation into not just an archival act, an unevolving reflection of the status quo, but an occasion to ascertain the value of the existing procedures as well as to evaluate their efficiency and cost effectiveness.

Later in the book we will explore the various competencies, the veritable alphabet soup of TQE, BPR, ABC, and ABM, the organizational learning paradigm, and process consulting, because they can help an organization become more efficient. But at the core, the way to organizational evolution is simply asking why things are done the way they are.

3.2 DECONSTRUCTING A PROCEDURE

We will analyze an accounting procedure to help demonstrate the illuminative approach to procedures documentation, the approach proposed in the book. Our analysis is quite basic and does not make extensive use of the many tools that are being used in various approaches to organizational improvement that are discussed in chapters to follow. The procedure will be analyzed by deconstructing the documentation provided by a well-regarded book about accounting policies and procedures manuals. The procedure to be examined is one used to reimburse travel expenses incurred by the faculty at a state university. The complete documentation for the procedure chosen is provided in the appendix for this chapter, and we will refer to it throughout as we review it.

The documentation of an actual accounting procedure from the second edition of *Design and Maintenance of Accounting Manuals* by Harry L. Brown (New York: John Wiley & Sons, 1993), is used for two reasons. Perhaps the more important of the two is the fact that the procedure illustrated is quite representative of the practice at a large number of academic institutions. While the amounts available for faculty travel at different universities may vary, as would the actual processing and the extent to which the system in place is computerized, the procedure as described is typical. In contrast to some procedures, it is relatively uncomplicated. It also will serve to illustrate the differences between what may be called the archival versus the illuminative approach to procedures documentation.

Archival documentation reflects the procedures and satisfies the accepted standards for accounting documentation. But even though the documentation is dated September 2, 1986, it could just as easily have been written in 1976, or even 1966. The major difference over the three decades would have been in the amount allowed for daily meals. However, the procedures that will be written for 2000 are bound to be different, given the changes taking place in the environment within which accounting functions are performed.

3.3 RAISING SOME QUESTIONS ABOUT THE PROCEDURE

As we evaluate the procedures documentation included in the appendix to this chapter, a number of questions come to mind. Merely raising questions is a fact-finding exercise; it does not imply a negative judgment about the merits of whatever is being questioned. The judgment concerning the value provided by the procedure can be exercised only after the facts are available. There may be valid reasons for undertaking a certain task within a procedure in a given manner. If so, they can be allowed to remain in effect. If this is not the case, then different, more effective procedures could be put in place.

Below are questions and observations that ought to be considered in a review of the procedures such as the one being analyzed:

- The nature of the approval process
  1. Is it highly centralized?
  2. Is it cost-effective to have financial affairs be a part of the approval process?
  3. Does financial affairs have the resources to devote to such approvals for the entire university?
  4. Do the resources devoted to the approval of such travel take time and attention away from other tasks?
  5. What does it take in terms of costs and resources for financial affairs to undertake such approvals?
  6. Can the approval be delegated to a lower operational level and still be cost-effective?
- The nature of the paperwork required
  1. The procedure seems task-intensive; a faculty member wanting to travel may have to fill out rather lengthy forms with multiple copies as many as four times: to get the initial approval, to get the advance, to get reimbursed, and, if using a university vehicle, to get authorization.
  2. There seems to be considerable duplication between the different forms. A considerable amount of data is required afresh with each form.

3. What is the justification for requiring such detailed itemization for the expenses incurred for meals and lodging?

- The cost benefits of the procedure
  1. What are the clerical and administrative costs associated with such a procedure?
  2. Who pays how much for the cost of administering the procedure? Those to be considered are the faculty member applying for permission and reimbursement, the department, the college, the controller's department, the university, and the taxpayer.
  3. What is the ratio between the total amount allowed for such travel and the costs associated with this accounting procedure? Has it changed over the years?

- Positive attributes of the procedure
  1. The procedure has attempted to minimize the paperwork by not requiring documentation for all meals. Meals for less than $25 do not need validation with receipts.
  2. The procedure specifically points out the time it will take to get the reimbursement processed.
  3. The instructions for filling out the forms, as well the documentation for the procedure itself, are very understandable and well written.
  4. The procedure is quite specific, but is that extent of detail really needed? Why not trust the faculty's judgment for using the most economical and convenient means of traveling?

- Given the quantity of paperwork being generated, how can emergent information technology be of use in improving the process?

3.4 TRACKING THE COMPONENTS OF THE PROCEDURE

In addition to raising the questions listed in the previous section and having them answered, those seeking to review the procedure prior to documenting it will also need to track the steps required for its completion. In addition to listing the individual elements of the process, we indicate the following for each element: We will use the letter "V" to indicate whether the step adds value to the institution; the letter "P" will be used to show that it helps to move the process forward; the letter "N" will be used to suggest that it hinders the completion of the process–in other words, is non–value-adding. If the analysis were actually to be performed at the university, then we would also indicate the estimated time and costs incurred for each of the various elements. This is an essential part of the actual review process. Those estimates provide tangible measures about the value of the procedure being used. Of necessity, such estimates will be left out of the analysis being done here. It is also possible that some of the elements listed are not part of the process at a given school. If so, that institution has already embarked on a quest to improve the procedure.

#	Category	Element
1.	V	Professor's paper is selected for presentation at a conference.
2.	P	Professor fills out a travel request form and gives it to department chair.
3.	N	The travel request waits for the approval of the department chair.
4.	P	The department chair approves the request.

5.	N	The form goes to the dean of the college and waits for approval.
6.	P	The dean approves the request and sends it over to financial affairs (FA).
7.	N	The request waits for action at FA.
8.	P	FA checks the availability of funds.
9.	P	FA approves and informs the professor.
10.	P	The four copies of the form are distributed. Two go back to the professor, one goes to the controller's office for the records, and the last one goes back to the college where the professor belongs.
11.	V	The professor attends the conference and makes the presentation.
12.	P	The professor has to ensure that documentation for expenses is collected, and records expenses as they occur or soon afterward.
13.	P	The professor fills out the form called employee travel voucher and includes the necessary documentation in the package. It then is sent to the department chair.
14.	N	The voucher waits for the department chair's approval.
15.	P	The chair signs it and sends it to the controller's office.
16.	N	It waits for processing in the controller's office.
17.	P	One or more staff members there will take care of the tasks required to approve the reimbursement.
18.	P	The approval will be verified.
19.	P	The check will be written and sent to the professor.
20.	P	The professor will deposit the check in the bank.

As the result of analysis and as a part of the review, the steps involved in the process should be examined to see if they must remain. Certainly those labeled as N ought to go. Items categorized as P may remain, be altered, be dropped, or be replaced, depending on the costs incurred in processing them.

A number of the steps categorized as P really duplicate one another. For instance, the professor's department chair approves the travel voucher. This is to ensure that the correct and approved amount is being requested as reimbursement by the faculty member. The amount allowed is already on file in a number of places, including accounting. If the professor is submitting an excess amount, it will be noticed. Within the accounting departments, processing is followed by the verification. Such care—given that the amount to be reimbursed is already approved—may not be cost-effective; indeed, some will say that such redundancy amounts to costly overkill.

It should also be obvious that emerging information technology could help alter the procedure. There is technology available to help improve the process. Having the approval of the request on file in the system could save the professor from submitting a good deal of data twice: first in connection with the request itself, and second with the submission of the employee travel voucher. A good deal of paper, not to mention labor, could be dispensed with if the procedure were handled through a system that relies on client servers rather than old-fashioned forms with four different-color copies.

The review just suggested will not produce identical answers for all universities. Each academic institution is likely to have its unique arrangements for the implementation of the procedure, even though on paper the procedure is fairly uniform. Most colleges have faculty members fill out the request for permission to travel; these are reviewed by their chair and the dean of the college where the department is located. The dean may either provide the final approval, or, in some institutions, the level above the dean may also be involved. The rest of the steps involved in the procedure are quite typical.

3.5 EXPLAINING THE ILLUMINATIVE APPROACH

Using the illuminative approach to accounting procedures documentation implies more than simply writing down the status quo. The documentation process should begin with a review of the procedure currently in place to see the extent to which it is efficient, effective, and value adding. The impetus for such an approach comes from the organization's commitment to the continuous quality improvement as well as the learning organization paradigm. The actual procedures review and redesign should use all or some of the following nine steps.

1. Identify the process to be redesigned.
2. Analyze the effectiveness and the efficiency of the process.
3. Analyze the relationship between the procedure and the organization's strategic plans.
4. Identify how the procedure supports the mission and strategic goals of the organization
5. Explore information technology that may be useful.
6. Design a prototype.
7. Measure prototype for its effectiveness and efficiency.
8. Carry out full implementation.
9. Measure how well the redesigned process performs.

In this case, by being selected for analysis, the procedure has been already identified. However, were it a situation in a real university, the selection itself could have been the result of a process devoted to selecting procedures for review. Alternatively, the procedure could have been chosen for review after learning about how industry is handling its travel and expense reimbursement procedures.

3.6 ELEMENTS OF THE ILLUMINATIVE APPROACH

The illuminative approach to documention would include an analysis of the effectiveness and efficiency, as well as the cost-effectiveness of the procedure under review. It could be done by an individual charged with the assignment or by a group of employees who are already involved with the various elements of the procedures. Such a group would need less time in order to acquaint themselves with the process; however, they would still need to orient themselves because their knowledge of the process may well be limited to their particular slice of the action, and not the entire process.

3.7 FIRST UNDERSTAND, THEN DECONSTRUCT

Before trying to change things for the better, the reviewer(s) must understand the existing procedure well and develop an appreciation for the procedure's current performance and its resource usage. Such an understanding could be obtained by:

- Talking with those involved in administering the procedure
- Surveying the boundaries of the procedures

- Reading up on the currently available documentation pertaining to the procedure
- Talking with those performing the tasks involved
- "Walking through" the procedure
- Detailing the process on a flow chart, describing not just activities, but also the time involved in getting from one task to another and the time spent waiting for a given task to be performed
- Calculating or at least estimating the cost of the procedure
- Comparing the expense of the procedure with the actual budget for faculty travel, in order to put the costs into perspective

To help focus the review of the procedure, look for the following during the procedure review:

- Non–value-adding tasks
- Duplication; unnecessary administrative paperwork
- Potential for simplification/improved form design
- Opportunity for standardization
- Chances to improve relationships with customers
- Alternatives to the procedure
- Use of information technology to streamline, upgrade, or even reduce costs
- Proper implementation of the procedure

In looking for the above points, it is helpful to remember some of the tools used by TQE such as "Three-Mu checklists" as well as the "who, what, where, when, why, and how" approach.

In order to ensure that the review is effective, it should not be carried out in isolation of the organizational mission and strategic objectives.

3.8 CONCLUSION

This chapter illustrates the illuminative approach to procedures documentation. The use of the illuminative approach to documentation can help to bring learning to the accounting department. Procedures documentation can become the occasion to question the status quo in the accounting department. The ripple effect can even spread the learning to the rest of the organization.

APPENDIX: AN EXAMPLE OF PROCEDURES DOCUMENTATION

The sample documentation of a policy/procedure dealing with the reimbursement of faculty travel at a public university, which follows, is adapted from Brown's *Design and Maintenance of Accounting Manuals, Second Edition*.

Administrative Procedure

THE UNIVERSITY OF SOUTHERN MISSISSIPPI

ACCOUNTING SERVICES

- RETRIEVAL NO.   10,015
- PAGE   1 of 2
- ISSUE DATE   January 10, 1983
- ORIGINATOR   Accounts Payable
- SUPERSEDES

SUBJECT: NEW REMITTANCE VOUCHER (ACC 14)

Many expenditures for services do not require a purchase order and authority
to pay has been processed through the use of a memo, a purchase requisition
sent directly to Accounting Services, or by a remittance voucher. The new
Remittance Voucher form is to be used by anyone authorized to approve disbursements
for an account. The use of the purchase requisition for payment authorization
is no longer acceptable.

Use of the Remittance Voucher

Items which do not normally require purchase orders and for which this Remittance
Voucher is to be used are:

    Seminar and conference registration fees for employees
    Honorariums to nonemployees
    Speaker's fee
    Travel expense reimbursement for nonemployees(recruiting, speakers,
      professional fees and so forth)
    Stipends
    Agency accounts
    Items on contract (leases, land purchases, entertainment groups, Cablevision, etc)
    Legal, audit and other professional fees
    Payroll taxes and amounts withheld for payment to others
    Insurance
    Postage (Post Office only)
    Advertising
    Utilities
    Telephone
    Freight when shipper is USM
    Band and music awards (not trophies or plaques)
    Registration workers
    Officials — Athletic and Intramural Departments
    Sales Tax
    Refunds — housing deposits and Continuing Education fees

The form is used as a cover document for form ACC 14A — Multiple Vendor-Payee
Attachment.

Supporting documents are to be attached to the accounting copy of the form.
The preparing department retains the pink copy for comparison to the monthly
budget activity report.

Appendix 3–1. Example of procedures documentation.

Source: Harry L. Brown, *Design and Maintenance of Accounting Manuals, Second Edition* (New York:
John Wiley & Sons, 1993). Logo reprinted with permission from the University of Southern Mississippi
(both forms and logo are no longer in use by the university).

Completing the Form

Department enters:

A. Department name.
B. Account number.
C. Telephone number of preparer.
D. Name and address of vendor. If used as a cover form for the Multiple Vendor-Payee Attachment, enter "See Attached Forms." Social Security number must be supplied for payment to individuals.
E. Description of charge to be paid, including name of registrant(s) at a seminar or conference, purpose of payment and so forth. If registration form, document or letter is to be sent with check, indicate that enclosure is attached.
F. Amount to be paid. Attach supporting document, if any.
G. Total to be paid on this voucher.
H. Signature of person requesting payment and date signed.
I. Approval signature and date. Payments to individuals require two approval signatures if an invoice is not available.
J. General Ledger Code, Object Code and Department to be charged. If department is not entered, the charge will be made to the account shown at top of the form.
K. Amount to be charged to this account. Form provides distribution for up to eight accounts.

Accounting Services enters:

L. Vendor code number.
M. Voucher number.
N. Voucher date.
O. Purchase Order Number, if any.
P. Name of person processing the voucher and date processed.
Q. Name of person reviewing or verifying information.
R. Preprinted number of special check used to pay voucher.
S. Special handling required or enclosure to be mailed.
T. Amount of encumbrance to be liquidated, if any.

This form is available from Accounting Services, 201 Forrest County Hall. The use of unauthorized forms should be discontinued.

Any questions concerning this procedure should be directed to Accounting Services, Box 5143, Telephone 4084.

Attachment: Copy of Remittance Voucher

Appendix 3–1. Continued.

REMITTANCE VOUCHER
UNIVERSITY OF SOUTHERN MISSISSIPPI
HATTIESBURG, MISSISSIPPI   39406-5143

THE UNIVERSITY
OF SOUTHERN MISSISSIPPI

DEPT NAME	(A)
ACCT NO	(B)
TEL NO	(C)

VENDOR ___(D)___

VENDOR CODE
(L)

DESCRIPTION	AMOUNT
(E)	(F)

REQUESTED BY	DATE	APPROVED BY	DATE	TOTAL	
(H)		(I)			(G)

ACCOUNTING USE		GL	OBJECT	DEPARTMENT	LIQUIDATION	EXPENDITURE
VOUCHER NUMBER	(M)	(J)	(J)	(J)	(T)	(K)
VOUCHER DATE	(N)					
PURCHASE ORDER NUMBER	(O)					
PROCESSED BY DATE	(P)					
VERIFIED BY	(Q)	SPECIAL CHECK NO. (R)	ACCOUNTING USE (S)			

ACC 14 (REV 1-83)   WHITE — ACCOUNTING   CANARY — VENDOR   PINK — DEPARTMENT

Appendix 3–1.   Continued.

Administrative Procedure

THE UNIVERSITY OF SOUTHERN MISSISSIPPI

ACCOUNTING SERVICES

- RETRIEVAL NO.   30041
-
- PAGE   1 of 11
-
- ISSUE DATE   September 2, 1986
-
- ORIGINATOR   Controller
-
- SUPERSEDES   30023

SUBJECT: TRAVEL PROCEDURES

Employees of the University are reimbursed for reasonable and necessary expenses incurred while in the performance of approved travel. The following forms are used in the procedure.

Form	Source
Permission to Travel Form (ACC 1)	Printing Center
Travel Voucher (ACC 2)	Printing Center
Remittance Voucher	Financial Affairs

INDEX

Advance Payment, Registration Fees
Approval for Travel
Authorization for Travel
Cancellation, Travel Request
Change, Travel Request
Common Carrier
Domestic Travel
Employee Business Expense
Foreign Travel
High Cost Cities
Lodging, shared, spouse, family
Meals, day trips, overnight trips
Motor Pool
Other Expenses
Parking
Permission to Travel Form and Instructions
Personal Travel Log
Private Vehicle
Pro Travel
Receipts
Registration Fees
Reimbursement Procedure
Rental Car
Spouse Accompanying
Tips
Tolls
Travel Advance
Travel Voucher and Instructions
University Vehicle, Credit Card

Appendix 3–1.   Continued.

Retrieval No. 30,041
Page 2 of 11

AUTHORIZATION FOR OFFICIAL UNIVERSITY TRAVEL

Each employee required to travel in performance of official duties and entitled to reimbursement for expenses incurred shall have prior authorization from the department chairman and/or other designated officials. The Permission to Travel Form must be submitted at least two weeks in advance of expected departure date to conferences, conventions, and meetings. In the case of out-of-country travel, the request must be submitted at least 90 days in advance of the requested departure date.

The originating department should be certain that the travel request form is properly completed. The four-part Permission to Travel Form is prepared by the applicant and routed as follows:

A. Domestic Travel:
    (1) Department Chairman
    (2) Dean of College of School or Division Chairman
    (3) Financial Affairs (funds available)

B. Foreign Travel, including Hawaii and Alaska, add:
    (4) Vice President
    (5) President (after obtaining State approval)
    (6) Financial Affairs (for distribution)

When Financial Affairs receives the request for Permission to Travel, it will determine if funds are available. If there is a problem and the request cannot be further processed, it will be returned to the Dean's or Director's Office. If funds are available, Financial Affairs will retain the white and canary copies and return the other copies to the applicant.

Distribution

White — Financial Affairs (for encumbrance)
Canary — Employee (used to obtain travel advance, if needed)
Pink — Employee (to file with travel voucher)
Goldenrod — Departmental file

If a travel advance is requested, the employee will obtain the canary copy from Financial Affairs and take it to the Business Office to obtain cash advance. Money will not be advanced earlier than two weeks prior to the meeting or conference. No cash advance for trips within the State.

The pink copy of the travel request must be attached to travel voucher when it is submitted for payment. The goldenrod copy of the travel request should be maintained in the department's file.

Appendix 3–1. Continued.

Required Approvals

The approval requirements for travel are as follows:

A.   In-State and Out-of-State Business Trips require approval of
     immediate supervisor. No permission to travel form required.
     Categories 1 and 2 on Travel Vouchers.

B.   In-State and Out-of-State trips for conferences, conventions,
     associations and meetings require approvals of the Chairman,
     Dean, or Division Chairman and Financial Affairs. Permission
     to Travel Form required. Categories 3 and 4 on Travel Voucher.

C.   Travel outside the Continental United States requires the
     approvals in B above, the Vice President, President, Trustees,
     the Executive Director of the Commission of Budget and Accounting
     and the Governor of Mississippi. Category 5 on Travel Voucher.

Changes and Cancellation of Travel Request

An amended Permission to Travel request form must be submitted to change
place or dates of meeting or to change department account number.

When a Permission to Travel request has been canceled, a copy of the
request with the word "Canceled" written across the face should be sent to
Financial Affairs to release the encumbrance of funds. Funds will remain
encumbered until the travel voucher is paid or until notice is received of
cancellation.

Advance Payment — Conference Registration Fees

To pay registration fees in advance of the conference, these procedures
must be followed:

>   The request should be made at least 20 days in advance of the
>   start of the conference.
>
>   The request should be made on a Remittance Voucher form with
>   both the literature concerning the conference and photocopy
>   of the Permission to Travel Form attached.

University Vehicles

To obtain a vehicle from the Motor Pool, the request is made to the
Physical Plant Division as outlined in the University Motor Pool operating
procedures and regulations.

The University of Southern Mississippi uses the State Credit Card for
vehicles assigned to the Motor Pool and USM Gulf Park.

The Motor Pool will charge the account through a Motor Pool Invoice.
The amount charged is based on mileage with a $15.00 per day minimum.
Motor Pool charges should never be reported on a Travel Voucher.

Appendix 3–1. Continued.

REIMBURSEMENT OF TRAVEL EXPENSE

GENERAL

Travel Vouchers received in the Financial Affairs Office by 5 P.M. Thursday
will be paid the following Thursday, provided there are no problems with
the voucher.

Expense Reimbursement

Immediately upon returning from a trip, the traveler should submit a
voucher for reimbursement of travel expenses. If not filed within 30 days
of the return, any advance received will be deducted from the traveler's
pay check for the next full pay period. The first two copies of the Travel
Voucher, with required receipts attached, should be completed as outlined
in the attachment hereto and submitted to Financial Affairs. For other
than business travel, the pink copy of the Permission to Travel must be
attached to the Travel Voucher when it is submitted to Financial Affairs
for payment. The departmental account number shown on the Permission to
Travel will be charged regardless of the department shown on the Travel
Voucher. Vouchers submitted with errors other than mathematical errors
will be returned. Travel expenses will be reimbursed only for the
employee's own expense. One employee cannot submit expense for
reimbursement on the same voucher with another person.

If members of the family accompany the University representative, request
hotel clerk to note the single room rate on the bill; otherwise,
reimbursement will be made for one-half cost of the room. Expenses as a
result of unofficial stopovers, side trips, telephone charges, or any other
items of a personal nature should not be submitted for reimbursement. Long
distance telephone charges must be documented to show place, party called,
and purpose of call.

Reimbursement for Meals

Reimbursement for meals will be for actual expenditure (plus tips) at a
reasonable amount with the following maximum daily limits for three meals:

        In Mississippi   - $18 per day
        Out of Mississippi   - $24 per day
        High-cost cities (specific)   - $30 per day (receipts required)

Day Trips

No reimbursement is authorized for meals when travel is confined to the
vicinity of your home campus. For other travel, reimbursement for meals
shall be:

        Breakfast — When travel begins before 6 A.M. and extends beyond 8 A.M.
        Lunch — When travel begins before 12 P.M. and extends beyond 2 P.M.
        Dinner — When travel extends beyond 8 P.M.

No reimbursement is authorized for a dinner meal when the meeting is
completed in sufficient time for the traveler to return by 6 P.M.

Appendix 3–1. Continued.

Lodging Expenses

Reimbursement will be made for lodging expense incurred in a hotel or motel on the presentation of a paid original bill. When a room is shared with other employees on travel status, reimbursement will be calculated on a pro rata share of the total cost. The other traveler must submit a copy of the lodging receipt indicating that the room was shared. An employee on travel status, if accompanied by spouse who is not an employee on travel status, is entitled to reimbursement at the single room rate. Request the hotel clerk to note the single room rate of the bill.

Normally if the order of business for which the travel is authorized begins after 3 P.M., reimbursement will not be made for lodging prior to the first day of business. If the order of business begins prior to 3 P.M., reimbursement is made for lodging and meals for the preceding day if the lodging is necessary for the traveler to be present prior to the first order of business. Reimbursement is made for lodging the final evening of the trip if the traveler is not able to return home by 9 P.M.

Modes of Transportation

Transportation authorized for official travel include University vehicles (Motor Pool), private vehicles, common carriers, and rental cars.

If travel is by other than the most direct route between points where official University business is conducted, the additional cost must be borne by the traveler. No traveler can claim transportation expense when he is gratuitously transported by another person, or when he is transported by another traveler who is entitled to reimbursement for transportation expense. Private vehicle mileage reimbursement cannot exceed cost of round-trip air coach fare.

Private Vehicles

The employee shall receive the legal rate established by the State of Mississippi for each mile actually and necessarily traveled in the performance of official duties.

The following situations justify the use of private vehicles for travel:

1. When travel is required at such time or to such places that common carrier transportation may not be reasonably available.

2. When one or more persons travel to the same destination in the same car and total mileage claimed does not exceed the total airline tourist fares for transporting the same number of people.

Appendix 3–1.   Continued.

Common Carriers

Employees are reimbursed for actual airline and train fares. All airline tickets must be purchased from Pro Travel, the official travel agent of the University.

The employee will purchase his own common carrier transportation and claim reimbursement. Employees are not allowed to charge the transportation to the University. Ticket cost reimbursement must be handled through the travel voucher.

Travel by airline shall be at the tourist rate. Certification that tourist accommodations are not available will be necessary when travel is first class.

Rental Cars

Limit the use of rental cars as much as possible. There are times when common carriers, private cars, and University vehicles are not available and rental cars are the only means of transportation. Below are examples:

1. When a destination has been reached by common carrier and several locations in the same vicinity must be visited.

2. When transportation between airport terminal and destination is needed and taxi or limousine service is not fesible or available.

3. When a schedule cannot be met through the use of common carrier.

Before you accept the rental car, examine the vehicle for any prior damage. If prior damage is discovered, it should be reported immediately to the rental agency to prevent improper claims against the University.

At the time you return the rental car, report any accident involving the rental vehicle and file an accident report with the rental agency.

Other Expenses

Registration fees paid by the employee at the conference will be reimbursed on a travel voucher when supported by a paid receipt. The portion of the fees applicable to meals shall be reported as meal expense.

Tips for meals and taxi should be included as part of those charges. Tips reported here include baggage handling tips when arriving and departing a hotel or at airports.

Actual parking fees while away from home, and road and bridge tolls are reported here.

Appendix 3–1. Continued.

Receipts

Major expense incurred by an employee while on official travel for the
University require receipts. The receipts must be originals and not
copies.

Expenses that require original receipts:

1. Lodging
2. Rail, plane, or bus
3. Registration fees
4. Car rental (including gasoline tickets)
5. Telephone expense (only as listed on motel receipt)
6. Gas for University vehicle (see reimbursement procedure)

Expenses that do not require receipts:

1. Meals, including tips (receipt required for any meal if over $25)
2. Mileage of personal vehicle
3. Tips
4. Taxi/Limousine, including tips
5. Parking/Tolls

Reimbursement Procedure

Payment checks for travel expenses are sent to Business Services and
applied to the employee travel advance receivables. If reimbursement
exceeds advance, Business Services will send a check for the excess to the
traveler. If advance exceeds expenses, Business Services will notify the
traveler of the amount applied and amount due. Monthly statements are sent
also.

Appendix 3–1.   Continued.

COMPLETING THE PERMISSION TO TRAVEL FORM

a. Date submitted.

b. Employee name, title and social security number.

c. Name of convention, association or meeting. If for normal business travel out-of-state, enter "Business Travel."

d. Enter city and state where meeting is being held.

e. Enter dates of meeting.

f. Enter department name and account number to be charged for the travel.

g. Enter purpose of the meeting.

h. Estimated total cost of attending.

i. Signature and Southern Station Box Number.

j. Required approvals of domestic travel.

k. Additional approvals for travel outside continental United States.

l. Amount of advance when requested.

m. Signature of employee.

n. Date advance received.

o. Completed by Business Services when advance is issued.

p. Completed by Financial Affairs when Permission is approved.

All costs of conventions, associations and meetings are reported annually to the State Peer Committee. This report shows the convention name, place, dates, employee attending and total cost.

Appendix 3–1. Continued.

PERMISSION TO TRAVEL

Submit at least two weeks prior to date of proposed trip (90 days prior to foreign travel).

THE UNIVERSITY OF SOUTHERN MISSISSIPPI

a _____ , 19____

Name: **b** _____ Title **b** _____ S.S. No. **b**

In compliance with Section 25-3-45 Mississippi Code 1972, request is made for authorization to attend the following convention, association, or meeting:

c _____   **d** _____

Complete Name of Convention, Association or Meeting (Do Not Abbreviate)   Place of Meeting

e _____   **f** _____   **f** _____

Dates of Meeting   Department Name   Department Code

Purpose of convention, association, or meeting (If an advance is needed, but cost of trip will be reimbursed by an outside organization, please explain).

g

Estimated Cost $ **h** _____

I acknowledge that I have read and that I understand the summary of travel policies on the back of this form.

_____ **i** _____

Signature of Applicant

Southern Station Box No. **i** _____

Domestic Travel

1. Chairman **j** _____

2. Dean or Division Chairman **j** _____

3. Funds Available—Accounting (5143) **j** _____

Foreign, Hawaii, Alaska Travel

4. Vice President **k** _____

5. President **k** _____

FOR ACCOUNTING AND BUSINESS OFFICE USE ONLY

ADVANCE (Cannot exceed estimated cost above)

Amount of advance $ **l** _____ Signature **m** _____ Date **n** _____

I hereby certify that the above trip has been properly approved. The amount advanced will be repaid from reimbursement check for travel expenses, and it is expressly understood and agreed that unless this amount is repaid by me before the next full pay period after the date of my return, it may be deducted from my next salary check.

ACCOUNT RECEIVABLE . o

Date MMDDYY	F/GL	OBJ.	SOCIAL SEC. NO.	AMOUNT		DR
	1014	1169				4

ENCUMBRANCE   **p**

P.O. CONTROL	F/GL	OBJ.	DEPARTMENT	SOCIAL SEC. NO.	AMOUNT		DATE MMDDY

White Copy—Accounting • Canary Copy—Employee (For Advance) • Pink Copy—File with Voucher • Goldenrod Copy—Dept. File Copy

ACC 1 (Revised 7/84)

Appendix 3–1. Continued.

COMPLETING THE EMPLOYEE TRAVEL VOUCHER

a. Employee name, social security number and address.

b. Purpose of trip and city and state.

c. Department name and account number to be charged. Must be same as
    Permission to Travel.

d. Names of others on trip, whether traveling together or not.

e. Date of travel, departure and arrival times.

f. Meals -- Daily meal maximums are: In Mississippi $18
                                       Outside Mississippi $24
                                       Listed high-cost cities $30

g. Lodging -- Original hotel or motel bill required. If bill shows two
    persons, indicate single room rate for this room. Do not report
    charges other than room charges as lodging (telephone, room service, etc.)

h. Travel by personal vehicle -- Indicate if University Motor Pool vehicle
    was used. If so, do not enter any miles here. If personal vehicle is
    used, enter departure and arrival location and miles. Enter current
    approved rate (20¢ mile).

i. Travel by Public Carrier -- Date, city leaving from, destination city,
    mode and ticket amount. Airline ticket coupon must be attached.

j. Registration fees -- If paid by employee, receipt or copy of program
    stating fee must be attached.

k. Tips -- Only for baggage handling or valet parking.

l. Taxi/limousine -- Actual taxi fare plus tip or airport limousine
    charge.

m. Parking/Tolls -- Actual parking charges or road or bridge tolls paid.

n. Car rental -- Receipt required.

o. Check travel category. If category 3, 4 or 5 are checked, approved
    copy of Permission to Travel form must be attached.

p. If travel advance was received, enter amount and date received.

q. Enter total of all expenses on Travel Voucher.

r. Maximum Reimbursement Allowed -- If chairman approving enters a smaller
    amount here than the total amount, then the smaller amount will be
    paid. Some departments have a travel limit on each trip.

s. Signature of employee and account director and dates.

t. For Accounting use only.

Appendix 3–1. Continued.

COMPLETING THE EMPLOYEE TRAVEL VOUCHER

a. Employee name, social security number and address.

b. Purpose of trip and city and state.

c. Department name and account number to be charged. Must be same as Permission to Travel.

d. Names of others on trip, whether traveling together or not.

e. Date of travel, departure and arrival times.

f. Meals -- Daily meal maximums are:

In Mississippi	$18
Outside Mississippi	$24
Listed high-cost cities	$30

g. Lodging -- Original hotel or motel bill required. If bill shows two persons, indicate single room rate for this room. Do not report charges other than room charges as lodging (telephone, room service, etc.)

h. Travel by personal vehicle -- Indicate if University Motor Pool vehicle was used. If so, do not enter any miles here. If personal vehicle is used, enter departure and arrival location and miles. Enter current approved rate (20¢ mile).

i. Travel by Public Carrier -- Date, city leaving from, destination city, mode and ticket amount. Airline ticket coupon must be attached.

j. Registration fees -- If paid by employee, receipt or copy of program stating fee must be attached.

k. Tips -- Only for baggage handling or valet parking.

l. Taxi/limousine -- Actual taxi fare plus tip or airport limousine charge.

m. Parking/Tolls -- Actual parking charges or road or bridge tolls paid.

n. Car rental -- Receipt required.

o. Check travel category. If category 3, 4 or 5 are checked, approved copy of Permission to Travel form must be attached.

p. If travel advance was received, enter amount and date received.

q. Enter total of all expenses on Travel Voucher.

r. Maximum Reimbursement Allowed -- If chairman approving enters a smaller amount here than the total amount, then the smaller amount will be paid. Some departments have a travel limit on each trip.

s. Signature of employee and account director and dates.

t. For Accounting use only.

Appendix 3–1. Continued.

EMPLOYEE TRAVEL VOUCHER

THE UNIVERSITY OF SOUTHERN MISSISSIPPI

IMPORTANT—SEE INSTRUCTIONS ON BACK

Employee	**a**		S.S. No.	**a**

Address To Which Check Should Be Sent	**a** **a**

Purpose and Place of Visit	Dept.	**c**	Dept. No.	**c**
b	Others On Trip	**d**		

MEALS AND LODGING

	Date								Total
e	Departure Time	AM-PM	AM-PM	AM-PM	AM-PM	AM-PM	AM-PM	AM-PM	
	Arrival Time	AM-PM	AM-PM	AM-PM	AM-PM	AM-PM	AM-PM	AM-PM	
f	Breakfast								
	Lunch								
	Dinner								
g	Lodging								
	Total Meals and Lodging								

h TRAVEL BY PERSONAL VEHICLE (Did you use University vehicle? ☐ Yes ☐ No)

Date	From	To	Miles	
		Total Miles		X Rate	

TRAVEL BY PUBLIC CARRIER

i

Date	From	To	Mode	Ticket Amount
			Total Travel By Public Carrier	

OTHER EXPENSES

Item	Date	Place Where Expense Incurred	Amount
j Registration Fees			
k Tips (baggage handling)			
l Taxi/Limousine			
m Parking/Tolls			
n Car Rental			

o Check Category of Travel (3 Through 5 Require Permission to Travel Form)

1 ☐ Business Trip In-State/No Advance

2 ☐ Business Trip Out-of-State/No Advance

3 ☐ Business Trip Out-of-State/With Advance

4 ☐ Conventions, Conferences, Associations/In-or Out-of-State

5 ☐ Out-of-Country

Travel Advance For This Trip

$ **p** Date **p**

Employee Signature **s** Date **s**

Approved By **s** Date **s**

Total Other Expenses	**q**
Total Expenses	
MAXIMUM REIMBURSEMENT ALLOWED ▶	**r**

Accounting Distribution	F/GL	Object	Department	Liquidation	Expense
Voucher No. **t**					
Voucher Date **t**					
P.O. No. **t**					
Verified By Date **t**					

ACC 2 (4/85)   White Copy—Accounting • Canary Copy—Accounting • Pink Copy—Department • Goldenrod Copy—Emplo

Appendix 3–1.   Continued.

CHAPTER 4

ORGANIZATIONAL CONTROLS

4.1 INTRODUCTION

This chapter studies the concept of control from an organizational perspective. The word "control" has many meanings, literally speaking. Here we are concerned with two of them. The first pertains to the notion of domination, where an individual or a group imposes its will on others—it may do so through incentives, brute force, and/or manipulation. The second meaning sees control as a form of feedback that allows management to monitor and, if need be, regulate the workings of the organization. In this sense, control is similar to a thermostat that regulates the temperature in a building or a vehicle. Both meanings are relevant when we talk about organizational control. Managers want to dominate—control—not only how employees carry out their jobs but how organizational resources are deployed and used in order to help realize planned objectives and strategies. All organizations use a wide variety of controls to ensure that organizational resources, including employees, are employed toward the realization of planned organizational objectives, such as those contained in budgets and strategic plans. Organizational controls consist of formal rules and procedures that help govern working conditions, such as information access rules, holidays, job specifications, and physical control of assets, such as inventories and supplies. At the same time, controls can be less formal, unstated but understood by stakeholders. Dress codes subscribed to by employees are examples of such informal and cultural controls.

Internal control can be seen as an organization function performed by accountants which is concerned with the physical control and appropriate uses of assets, particularly cash and inventories. The internal control is carried out with the help of various procedures that are called controls. For accountants, internal control is of special interest. It is through internal control that they seek not only to physically safeguard organizational assets but also to ensure the integrity of information provided through the financial statements prepared by accountants for the benefit of decision makers and organizational stakeholders. However, internal control put in place by accountants is only a subset of organizational controls. Management control of an organization requires not only internal control but a variety of other controls. Throughout this book "control" is used to mean not only internal control of interest to accountants but more inclusive controls.

This chapter emphasizes the importance of documentation to organizational control. One could argue that the relationship between effective documentation and organizational control is similar to the relationship between organizational effectiveness and control. Without control, managerial plans may never be realized. Likewise, without documentation, control measures will not be effective. The chapter starts by discussing control from an organizational perspective. After the overview, the text moves to discuss internal controls, which remain of prime importance to accountants. The emphasis is on internal controls as recently redefined in Statement on Auditing Standard (SAS) No. 78, published by the American Institute of Certified Public Accountants (AICPA).

One item of special concern in the new SAS No. 78 is the focus on effective communication. It is not enough to have controls in place; it is also important to ensure that those controls and what they seek to accomplish are communicated to those involved within the organization. Since accountants have not been known to be effective communicators, the communication audit is of great use to accounting departments. The chapter includes an appendix that discusses the nature of communication audits. Since communication audits are not usually associated with accounting and information systems, the chapter also discusses how such audits may be carried out by information providers to ensure that information consumers are getting what they want, when they want, and in a manner that is useful to them.

4.2 NATURE OF CONTROL

The process of control is one of management's basic functions. Management must establish and maintain control over its operational system, organization, and information system. The decisions made by management in doing so are crucial to the organization's success. Effective control decisions enable a firm to employ its resources efficiently, to fulfill its legal responsibilities, and to generate reliable and useful information. It is important to distinguish between "control" and "controls." The term "controls" refers to various measures and procedures put in place to counteract exposure to certain risks. An integral part of a firm's control is a "framework of controls." The framework of policies and control procedures is also called a firm's internal control structure. Composed of underlying management policies and a wide variety of control procedures, this framework spans all of the firm's transactions. The overall purpose of this framework is to provide reasonable assurance that a firm's objectives will be achieved. Thus it also encompasses the firm's operations and system of management.

This structure is the means through which the process of internal control functions. If the internal control structure is strong and sound, all of the operations, physical resources, and data will be monitored and kept under control. Information outputs will be trustworthy. However, a weak and unsound internal control structure can lead to serious repercussions. The information generated and made available for managerial decision making by accounting departments and others in the organization is likely to be unreliable, untimely, and perhaps unrelated to the firm's objectives. Without control, the implementation of policies may be dysfunctional. Furthermore, the firm's resources may be vulnerable to loss through theft, carelessness, sabotage, and natural disaster.

Internal control, as both a process and a structure, is of great concern to accountants. As key users of the accounting information system (AIS), they need to know which control procedures are in effect. Therefore, accountants often take active roles in developing and reviewing control frameworks. They work closely with system designers during the development of information systems to ensure that the planned control procedures are adequate and auditable. For instance, accountants/auditors make sure that totals will be balanced and reconciled properly and that audit trails are clearly established. During audits they determine the adequacy of measures and procedures that facilitate the internal control process, so that they can assess the reliance to be placed on the internal control structure when performing subsequent auditing program steps. Developing and evaluating control frameworks are skills at which accountants can and are expected to excel.

4.3 HISTORICAL DEVELOPMENT OF CONTROL

In *Accounting Terminology,* published in 1931, the American Institute of Accountants (now known as the American Institute of Certified Public Accountants) defined internal control as an accounting device whereby a proof of the accuracy of figures can be obtained through the expedient of having different people arrive independently at the same result. In 1936 the same group in another book, *Examination of Financial Statement,* defined "internal check and control" as those measures and methods adopted within the organization itself to safeguard the cash and other assets of the company as well as to check the clerical accuracy of the bookkeeping.

In 1958 and again in 1972 the AICPA defined the difference between what it called administrative controls and accounting controls. Administrative controls focused on authorization by management, while accounting controls pertained to policies governing the safeguarding of assets and the reliability of financial statements.

Investigations by governmental agencies such as the Security and Exchange Commission (SEC) have revealed illegal activities within American firms that were not detected by their internal control structures. As a result, Congress passed the Foreign Corrupt Practices Act (FCPA) in 1977. In addition to prohibiting certain types of bribes and hidden ownership, this act requires subject corporations to devise and to maintain adequate internal control structures. Managers of these corporations are legally as well as ethically responsible for establishing and maintaining adequate internal control structures. They are expected to establish a level of "control consciousness," so that employees are not inclined to subvert the control structures. Those managements that do not comply with the Act's requirements are subject to large fines and imprisonment. It is not surprising that many managements have taken significant action. For instance, many corporations now maintain sizable internal audit departments.

The FCPA in 1977 changed the focus on internal controls by establishing legal requirements for firms that sold their securities to the public. The act was designed primarily to prevent bribery of foreign officials in order to obtain business, but its effect has required companies to have good systems of internal accounting control. American firms were using slush funds to bribe foreign officials as well as to make political contributions domestically. The act sought to make this more difficult. Specifically, the FCPA requires companies to make and keep books, records, and accounts that, in reasonable detail, accurately and fairly reflect the transactions and dispositions of the assets of the issuer of securities for sale to the public. Such firms must devise and maintain a system of internal accounting controls sufficient to provide reasonable assurances that:

- Transactions are executed in accordance with management's general or specific authorization.
- Transactions are recorded as necessary to allow preparation of financial statements in accordance with generally acceptable accounting principles and to permit accountability for asset.

- Access to assets is permitted only in accordance with management's general or specific authorization.
- Periodic inventorying of the firm's assets occurs, and action is taken when there are differences between the recorded and the actual quantities of assets.

In a related context, in 1986 Congress passed the Computer Fraud and Abuse Act. Under this law it is a crime to knowingly, and with intent to defraud, gain unauthorized access to data stored in the computers of financial institutions, the federal government, or those used for interstate or foreign commerce. This law applies to corporations as well as to individuals.

Another milestone was reached in 1992, when, after several years of study, a Committee of Sponsoring Organization (COSO) report was issued. It sought to define internal control as well as practical guidance to companies to help them assess and improve their internal control. COSO was set up by the American Accounting Association, the AICPA, the Institute of Internal Auditors, the Financial Executives Institute, and the Institute of Management Accountants. COSO asked the firm of Coopers & Lybrand to conduct the study on its behalf.

The COSO report looks at internal control in much more than purely financial terms; it attempts to unify the views on internal control held by the various groups that sponsored the committee. It defines internal control as a process put into effect by people (management, the board of directors, personnel) to provide reasonable assurance but not absolute guarantee of the attainment of objectives concerning: effectiveness and efficiency of operations, reliability of financial reporting, and compliance with applicable laws and regulations. In addition, the COSO report describes internal control as consisting of five interrelated components:

1. Control environment—the setting in which people operate
2. Risk assessment—necessary to design controls
3. Control activities—policies and procedures to manage risks
4. Information and communication—necessary to identify and manage risks
5. Monitoring—to evaluate performance

As one might expect, there are those who feel the COSO report did not go far enough in making management more responsible to its shareholders.

4.4 CONTROL PROCESS

In brief, the control process consists of measuring actual results against planned accomplishments and taking corrective actions when necessary. These corrective actions are the decisions that keep the firm moving toward its established objectives.

The best way to understand the nature of the control process is to see it in terms of a household heating system. The overall purpose of a heating system is to control the temperature, which is the characteristic or performance measure. A homeowner begins the process by setting the thermostat reading for the desired temperature (the benchmark). He or she chooses a setting that is determined by personal objectives such as comfort and economy. Then an automatic process takes over. As the furnace (the operating process) generates heat, the thermostat's thermometer (the sensor element) detects the actual temperature. Next, the thermostatic mechanism (the regulator element) compares the actual temperature (fed to it by the sensor element) with the benchmark temperature. When the actual temperature rises above the preset temperature, the control element notifies the activating mechanism in the thermostat to shut down the furnace. Later, when the actual temperature drops below the preset temperature, the information feedback leads to the furnace being turned on again.

What allows a thermostat to function is feedback. As the foregoing heating system example shows, feedback is an information output that returns ("feeds back") to a regulator element and then to the operating process as an input. Feedback therefore provides the means for deciding when corrective action, such as turning off the furnace, is necessary. Like the temperature control system, a control process also both monitors and regulates. What makes this possible is feedback obtained through various information systems.

(a) Elements of a Control Process

A typical organizational control process consists of six elements:

1. A factor being controlled, called the characteristic or performance measure
2. An operating process that gives rise to the characteristic
3. A sensor element that detects the actual state of the operating process
4. A planned accomplishment, or benchmark, against which the actual state of the characteristic is to be compared
5. A planner who sets the benchmark
6. A regulator element that compares the actual state of the characteristic against the benchmark and feeds back corrections to the operating process

An entity such as a business firm may employ a variety of control processes. They may be preventive, designed to keep problems from occurring in the first place. Wearing seatbelts or locking one's car are examples of preventive control. Controls also could be detective, aimed at discovering problems as soon as possible. A smoke detector is an example of a detective control. Alternatively, they could be corrective, meant to solve problems after they are discovered. Corrective controls work in association with detective controls. Hotels have automatic sprinkler systems meant to go on after the smoke detectors set off alarms.

As a firm grows in size and complexity, the number of needed control processes (and controls) is likely to increase. Moreover, these processes may vary in sophistication and could take the form of feedback or feedforward. The heating system is an example of a first-order feedback control process or system, if the benchmark is assumed to remain unchanged after being set. In a business firm a budgetary control system is an example of a first-order feedback control process. By contrast, a second-order feedback control system employs a benchmark that adjusts to meet changing environmental conditions. An example is a flexible budgeting system, in which the budget values are adjusted with changing levels of activity. A third-order feedback control system attempts to predict future conditions and results. Based on such predictions, the system anticipates future problems and suggests corrective actions before the problems occur. Several third-order feedback control systems, also known as feedforward control systems, typically are used by business firms. One example is a cash planning system. Based on periodic cash forecasts, the treasurer of a firm may anticipate seasonal cash shortages by arranging for bank loans before the shortages actually occur.

(b) Illustrating the Control Process

The accounting information system is central to a firm's control processes, since it can serve as both a monitor and a regulator. We can see how it functions through the example of inventory control systems. The inventory control process begins when an inventory manager decides how much to carry of each inventory item.

Let us assume that the only item carried by a firm is a wheelbarrow, and that the manager decides to carry at least one hundred wheelbarrows for sale. When the quantity on hand drops to one hundred (the reorder point), the manager acquires fifty more wheelbarrows from a wholesale store across town the same day. The AIS keeps track of the inventory level by deducting the quantity of each sale from the on-hand quantity shown on an inventory record. Thus the AIS serves as a monitor and provides feedback information to the manager via a first-order feedback control system.

Now assume that the firm recognizes that the sales of wheelbarrows face seasonal fluctuations. More wheelbarrows are sold each month in the spring when gardeners and contractors intensify their labors. Thus the manager adjusts the level of minimum inventory by referring to sales for the same month last year and adjusts the reorder quantity by reference to the current on-hand quantity. Now the AIS provides added feedback information that is affected by changing conditions; thus it acts as a second-order feedback control system.

Finally, assume that wheelbarrows can be obtained more cheaply from a wholesale firm in the next state, but the lead time is two weeks. Also, the firm's sales have grown substantially but fluctuate more significantly from week to week. The manager now employs a reorder point that is affected by the expected demand in the weeks ahead as well as by the lead time. The AIS automatically informs the manager when the reorder point has been reached. Then the AIS computes the economic reorder quantity, which also depends in part on the expected sales demand for the coming weeks. Because it provides inventory information that anticipates future needs, the AIS now acts as a feedforward control system.

Another illustration of the working of internal control may be seen in the recommendations for effective payroll procedures:

- A system of advice forms should be installed so that new hires, terminations, rate changes, and the like are reported to the payroll department in writing. Such forms should be approved by the employee's superior.
- Before applicants are hired, their background should be investigated by contacting references to determine that they are not dishonest and have no other undesirable personal characteristics. There are some legal limits on what may be asked of applicant's references.
- The supply of blank time cards should be controlled. At the beginning of each week the payroll department should provide each worker with a time card stamped with his name.
- Install a time clock and have the workers "punch" in and out. A responsible employee should be stationed at the time clock to determine that workers are not "punching" the time cards of other workers who may be late or absent, or who may have left work early.

- The foreperson should collect the time cards at the end of the week, approve them, and turn them over to the payroll clerk. All time cards should be accounted for and any missing cards investigated.

- If the company has a cost system that requires workers to prepare production reports or to account for their time by work tickets, the time cards and the production reports or work tickets should be compared.

- Payroll clerks' work should be arranged so that they check each other. As an alternative, one clerk may make the original computations for the full payroll and the other clerk do all the rechecking.

- Payroll checks should be prenumbered to control their issuance.

- Payroll checks should be distributed to workers by a responsible person other than the foreperson. Unclaimed checks should be held in safekeeping by the payroll department until claimed by the worker. Direct deposits in employees' bank accounts should be encouraged.

- A responsible person other than the chief accountant and the payroll clerks should reconcile the payroll bank account.

- From time to time, an officer of the company should witness a payroll distribution on a surprise basis.

An illustration of internal control is also seen in the following recommendations to help improve control over cash receipts.

- All sales tickets should be prenumbered, and all sales ticket numbers should be accounted for daily. All sales tickets stamped "paid" should be reconciled to the duplicate deposit slip receipted by the bank. This should be done by a responsible employee other than the cashier or a member of the credit department.

- An employee other than the cashier or a member of the credit department should open the incoming mail and prepare daily a list in triplicate of remittances received that day. The original of the list should accompany the checks (and cash, if any) turned over directly to the cashier; one copy of the list of remittances should be routed to the responsible employee mentioned above; and one copy should be routed to the person responsible for posting to the accounts receivable ledger.

- The responsible employee who received the copy of the list of remittances should compare the remittances shown thereon with the duplicate deposit ticket at the same time he or she reconciles the cash sales tickets to the deposit ticket. Any checks or cash not deposited the day received should be investigated.

- Different forms (or colors) of sales tickets for cash, cash on delivery (COD), and credit sales would facilitate the daily accounting for sales tickets used.

- The cashier, who should have no duties connected with accounts receivable, should prepare bank deposits and forward the deposit to the bank. Someone other than the cashier or a member of the credit department should establish agreement of the list of remittances and daily collections with the daily deposit ticket prepared by the cashier. It is better if this person who compares the list of remittances with the deposit slips is a different individual. In other words, three different individuals are involved.

- Remittances should not be held; those for each day or for each batch of mail, whichever is the more practical, should be deposited intact. The credit department may make whatever record it needs for further follow-up on the remittances that are not in the correct amount.

According to the American Institute of Certified Public Accountants, the internal control structure of a firm has the following objectives:

- To encourage adherence to management's prescribed policies and procedures
- To safeguard the assets of the firm
- To assure the accuracy and reliability of the accounting data and information

These control objectives, specified in the AICPA Committee on Auditing Procedure's "Internal Control—Elements of a Coordinated System and Its Importance to Management and the Independent Public Accountant" (Statement on Auditing Standards no. 1, section 320. New York: AICPA, 1973) pertain to the operational system of a firm. In essence, their purposes are to assure that operations are performed effectively in a manner that best achieves the firm's broad goals; that operations are performed efficiently in a manner that does not waste resources; and that resources are provided with adequate security. (Security consists of safeguarding and protecting a firm's tangible and intangible assets via physical measures and control procedures.)

4.5 SYSTEMS WITHIN THE CONTROL STRUCTURE

The control structure also may be viewed as a collection of three component control systems or processes. Although known by various names, we will label these systems as:

1. The management control system seeks to encourage compliance with management's policies and procedures with the help of administrative controls.
2. The operational control system seeks to promote efficiency in operations with the help of administrative and technological controls.
3. The accounting control system seeks to safeguard assets and ensure the accuracy and reliability of data and information with the help of accounting controls.

(a) Management Control System

The management control process focuses on managerial performance rather than on technical operations. Its purpose is to encourage compliance with the firm's policies and procedures. Policies are the strategies or guidelines by which the overall goals and objectives are to be achieved; procedures are the prescribed steps by which specified tasks are accomplished. If the policies and procedures are soundly developed, resources will be acquired and used effectively and efficiently. As the term implies, management control is exercised through the actions of managers. It follows the organizational structure of a firm, since the managers function through responsibility centers.

An example of the management control process can be drawn from the production function of a manufacturing firm. To fulfill her responsibility of controlling production-related resources, the production manager (planner) develops policies and production volume and cost targets (benchmarks). These policies and targets are embodied in a production budget for the coming year as well as in procedures concerning quality inspections and other matters. The budget is broken down by production departments (responsibility centers). Each department head is then evaluated by comparing the actual volumes and controllable costs against the budgeted amounts. When the variances in volumes and costs are significant, corrective action may be necessary. For instance, if the volume is below budget, the department head may be assigned more workers or he or she may be transferred.

All of the controls implemented by management control systems are known as administrative controls. These controls roughly parallel those encompassed by what are called the control environment. Specific administrative controls include:

- Preparing budgets
- Preparing documentation such as procedures manuals
- Establishing an organizational structure that provides adequate direction through supervision
- Providing adequate oversight of accounting policies and practices via audit committees, internal auditors, and external auditors
- Carefully selecting, training, and supervising employees

(b) Operational Control System

The process or system that promotes efficiency in performing tasks, the second listed objective of internal control, is called operational control. Examples of operational control systems within typical firms are the inventory control system, the credit control system, the production control system, and the cash control system.

Like the management control system, an operational control system incorporates administrative controls. In the context of operational control, however, the controls are related to specific transactions. For instance, a credit check is a central control within the credit control system; it is also a key control in a sales transactions processing system. Similarly, a bank reconciliation is an important part of the cash control system; it is also a key control in the cash receipts and cash disbursements transaction processing systems. Another example of an operational control system is the close electronic surveillance of the gambling area in Las Vegas casinos. The high degree of security in a casino ensures that the dealers do not take home any of the chips.

4.6 OTHER CONTROL CLASSIFICATIONS

Controls also may be classified by objectives, by risk aversion, by settings, and by system architectures. Such alternative perspectives on control enhance the perception of what control seeks to achieve within an organization.

(a) Classification by Objectives

Two major control categories under the objectives classification plan are the administrative and accounting controls previously discussed. Administrative controls relate to the broad objectives of encouraging adherence to management's policies and procedures and promoting operational efficiency. Accounting controls have the broad objectives of safeguarding a firm's assets and ensuring accuracy of the accounting data and information.

Controls based on objectives also can be categorized as operations controls, financial reporting controls, and compliance controls. Operations controls are those needed in managing a firm's activities. Financial reporting controls are those that ensure reliable financial reports. Compliance controls are those that ensure compliance with laws and regulations.

(b) Classification by Risk Aversion

Controls also may be classified according to the ways that they combat the risks to which a firm and its information are exposed. Preventive controls block adverse events, such as errors or losses, from occurring. An example is a manual of processing procedures. Preventive controls tend to be passive in nature. Detective controls discover the occurrence of adverse events. They are more active than preventive controls. An example of a detective control is key verification of data typed onto a magnetic medium by a clerk. Certain detective controls cause further processing to be halted, as when an input error in a transaction is detected. Corrective controls lead to the righting of effects caused by adverse events, usually by providing needed information. For example, information to the effect that the level of an inventory item is too low may trigger a suitable correction—a request that more inventory be ordered. In some instances, corrective controls may anticipate adverse events, as when insurance coverage is prescribed against the theft of assets. Corrective controls are generally more active than detective controls.

(c) Classification by Settings

One of the most useful groupings of controls is in accordance with the elements described in Statement on Auditing Standard (SAS) No. 48, "The Effects of Computer Processing on the Examination of Financial Statements," issued by the American Institute of Certified Public Accountants (AICPA). This statement is further clarified by SAS No. 55. SAS No. 48, which separates controls into general controls and application controls. General controls are those controls that pertain to all activities involving a firm's accounting information system and resources (assets). These controls include those provided by the control environment, plus other control procedures. Application controls relate to specific accounting tasks or transactions; hence, they also may be called transaction controls. Application or transaction controls roughly correspond to the accounting system, as described in SAS No. 55. Another group of controls pertains both to the control environment and to transactions, and does not fit comfortably into either category. These controls, which we shall call security measures, are intended to provide adequate safeguards for access to and use of assets and data records.

These three categories of controls are intertwined, especially in computer-based information systems. An appropriate balance of controls in all three categories is needed for an internal control structure to function effectively.

(d) Classification by System Architectures

As indicated, system architectures include manual systems, computer-based batch processing systems, computer-based on-line processing systems, computer-based database systems, and computer-based data communications systems.

4.7 ORGANIZATIONAL STRUCTURE

A firm's organizational structure represents an underlying control because it specifies the work relationship of employees and units. The central control objective when designing the organizational structure is to establish organizational independence. When properly provided through a careful and logical segregation of assigned duties and responsibilities, organizational independence results in a complete separation of incompatible functions. It involves two or more employees or organizational units in each procedure, who can be assigned to check on the work of one another. Thus, errors made by one employee or unit will be detected by another. No single employee is able to commit a fraudulent act in the normal course of duties and then hide the deed. Fraud under such an arrangement can be perpetrated only by means of collusion. Thus, the chance for fraudulent activities is greatly reduced, since most persons who might consider fraud are afraid of being rejected if they propose the idea to a coworker. Collusion by related persons, such as mother and daughter, can be prevented by employment rules that prohibit nepotism.

Although very important to organizational control, the segregation of duties is usually not sufficient. Most firms also depend on the diligence of independent reviewers as well as internal and external auditors. To be truly effective, these reviewers/auditors must stand apart from the procedures themselves. A typical large- or medium-size firm has several types of reviewers. The higher-level managers, including the board of directors, represent reviewers who have broad perspectives and responsibilities. Lower-level managers, who receive and use the majority of outputs from the AIS, represent reviewers with narrower perspectives. Finally, internal and external auditors represent reviewers who are both expert and objective. A small firm having only a few employees may not be able to afford all these reviewers. However, since it cannot provide adequate segregation of duties, a small firm is in desperate need of review. The answer to this dilemma must be the manager or owner of the firm. He or she should carefully supervise the employees as they perform duties such as processing transactions, either manually or with the aid of computers. In addition, the manager or owner should perform key tasks such as opening mail, writing checks, and reconciling bank statements.

To understand how the concept of organizational independence enhances control, we should review its application in various types of systems by focusing on how the various functions to be performed must be segregated. We will begin with manual systems, since they present the most familiar situations. Then we will apply the concept to differ computer-based environments.

4.8 MANUAL SYSTEMS CONTROL ORGANIZATION

Authorizing, record keeping, and custodial functions should be separated in manual systems. Thus, employees who handle assets, such as cash and inventory, should not authorize transactions involving those assets or keep the records concerning them. For instance, if an accountant is allowed to handle cash receipts and also to keep the accounts receivable records, the accountant can easily conceal a theft. Making sales and cash receipts transactions independent is a logical division of duties. Numerous units are involved in the transactions involving sales, which means greater coordination, but control requires that independence be maintained. The sales order department originates and authorizes sales transactions, while the credit department authorizes the credit terms on which the sales are made; record keeping is performed by the billing and accounts receivable departments; and custodial duties are handled by the warehouse, shipping, and cash receipts departments.

The concept of organizational independence also prohibits the combining of duties in those cases where assets are endangered or adequate checks are not applied. For example:

A clerk who is assigned the duty of handling a petty cash fund should not also handle cash received from customers, since the funds might become commingled and later lost. A buyer who prepares a purchase order should not also approve the prepared form; instead, the purchase order should be signed by the purchasing manager. An accountant who prepares a journal voucher should present the completed form to an accounting manager for signature. An accounting clerk who performs key steps in a procedure, such as posting cash receipts, should not perform a check on the procedure, such as preparing a bank reconciliation.

4.9 COMPUTER-BASED SYSTEMS ORGANIZATION AND CONTROL

Organizational independence also should be maintained in computer-based systems, although adjustments are necessary. As with manual systems, the authorizing, custodial, and record-keeping functions are to be separated. Our discussion of organizational controls in computer-based systems will first consider the needed segregation between user departments and the information systems function; then we will look at needed segregation of responsibilities within the systems function itself.

(a) Segregation of Responsibilities between Departments

The information systems (IS) function has responsibilities relating to processing and controlling data (i.e., record keeping). Thus, it should be organizationally independent of all departments that use data and information, those departments that perform operational and custodial duties, and those persons who authorize transactions. All transactions and changes to master records and application programs should be initiated and authorized by user departments. For instance, sales transactions should be initiated by the sales order department, with the sales orders being processed within the information systems function. Changes to sales application programs should be initiated by sales management. Furthermore, errors in transactions should be corrected by user departments. All assets (except computer and data processing facilities) should reside under the control of designated operational departments; for example, the merchandise needed to fill customers' orders should be stored in a warehouse department.

Sometimes it may appear that complete separation of these functions is not possible. For example, when a computer-based system automatically approves an order from a customer on the basis of credit guidelines built into a sales application program, it may seem that the information systems function is authorizing the transaction. However, the authorizing function is in reality performed by the person, perhaps the credit manager, who established the guidelines and made them part of the software that processes orders from customers.

(b) Segregation of Responsibilities within the IS Function

To achieve organizational independence, it is necessary to subdivide several key responsibilities within the organizational structure of the IS function itself. The IS function has the overall purpose of providing information-related services to other departments within a firm. In those firms having computer-based systems, it has taken over the array of record preparation, record keeping, and processing activities traditionally performed by several accounting departments. That is, the presence of computers centralizes duties that should otherwise be segregated.

The major segregation of responsibilities is between systems development tasks, which create systems, and data processing tasks, which operate systems. The systems development function is concerned with analyzing, designing, programming, and documenting the various applications needed by user departments and the firm as a whole. Not only is it responsible for new computer-based applications, but it also must make changes in existing applications as needed. Furthermore, it can help users via an information center. The data processing function has responsibility for ensuring that transaction data are processed and controlled and the related files and other data sets are properly handled. These two major functions are separated—both organizationally and physically—for a very sound reason. If the same individuals had both detailed knowledge of programs and data and access to them, they could make unauthorized changes. Thus, systems analysts and programmers should not be allowed to operate the computer or to have access to "live" programs or data. Furthermore, computer operators and other data processing personnel should not have access to the documentation concerning programs or to various assets such as inventory and cash.

The IS function also includes other functions, such as technical services and database administration. Technical services has responsibilities with respect to computer-related areas such as data communications, systems programming, and decision modeling. Database administration is concerned with all aspects of the data resources. The database administrator must establish and define the schema of the database, control the use of the database via appropriate security measures, and control all changes in data and programs that use the database. The database administrator should have functional authority over the data library. However, he or she should not have direct access to "live" data or programs. A high degree of segregation is needed to reduce the risks of alteration to "live" data or programs. Without adequate segregation, a computer operator could make changes to personnel records at will and escape detection, or a programmer could alter a computer program and not be caught.

(c) Segregation of Responsibilities within the Data Processing Function

This discussion illustrates how a suitable division of responsibilities provides needed segregation of duties in the course of a batch processing application:

- The data control unit serves as an interface between the various user departments and computer operations. It records input data (including batch totals) in a control log, follows the progress of data being processed, and distributes outputs to authorized users. As a part of its control responsibilities, it maintains the control totals pertaining to master files as well as transaction files, and reconciles these totals with updated totals shown on exception and summary reports. Finally, it monitors the correction of detected errors by the user departments. The data control unit must be independent of computer operations, since it helps to ensure that processing is performed correctly and that data are not lost or mishandled.

- The data preparation unit prepares and verifies data for entry into processing.

- Computer operations processes data to produce outputs. Its duties include loading data into input devices, mounting secondary storage devices such as magnetic tapes and magnetic disk packs, and performing operations as prescribed by run manuals and computer messages. One duty that computer operators should not perform is correcting errors detected during processing, since the corrections may introduce new, undetected errors. Computer operations should be physically as well as organizationally separated from the other units, so that people such as the librarian and data control clerks do not have direct access to the computer.

• The data library unit maintains a storage room, called the library, where the data files and programs are kept. A librarian issues these files and programs to operators when needed for processing and keeps records of file and program usage. Thus the files and programs are better protected when not being used.

In contrast to the division of functions performed in the above batch-processing system, the division of duties is simplified while processing applications on-line. The various users enter the transactions via terminals. The transactions are checked by computer edit programs for accuracy and then are processed against on-line files. Outputs may be printed or displayed on printers, plotters, or terminals located in the departments of the recipients. The data control and data library tasks, as well as data processing, are performed by the computer system hardware and software.

(d) Computer-Based Systems Control

Computer operations are subject to a variety of problems and abuses. For example, operations might be poorly scheduled, with the result that needed computer printouts arrive so late in the purchasing department that out-of-stock parts are not ordered in time to keep the production line running. Sound and well-controlled computer operations are based on close supervision, careful planning, and organized procedures. Thus supervisory personnel, such as the manager of data processing and shift supervisors, should actively observe and review the actions of computer operators. Procedural manuals concerning all aspects of computer operations should be provided to computer operators, together with the appropriate console run books. Data processing schedules should be prepared as far in advance as feasible and revised as necessary. Preventive diagnostic programs should be employed to monitor the hardware and software functions, so that existing or potential problems may be detected. A variety of control reports should be prepared daily or weekly. Suggested reports include computer facilities utilization reports, employee productivity reports, and computer processing run-time reports. To be most effective, these reports should compare actual times against standard times. For instance, the last-named report can compare actual run times, as shown in the console log, against standard times shown in the data processing schedule.

Computer hardware and software checks represent another form of operational control specific to computer-based systems. Although modern computer hardware is generally reliable in operation, malfunctions can occur. Thus a variety of hardware and software checks are built into computer systems. They assure the reliability of computations, manipulations, and transfers of data within the systems. Typical built-in hardware checks include the parity check, echo check, read-after-write check, dual read check, and validity check. Other hardware checks or controls include duplicate circuitry, which allows the arithmetic unit within the central processing unit (CPU) to perform calculations twice and to check the results, and scheduled preventive maintenance, which schedules periodic servicing of the computer system to reduce unexpected system failures and, hence, overall operating costs. Also, certain computers are provided with fault tolerance, the capability to continue functioning even in the face of a partial failure. Fault tolerance usually involves built-in software that constantly verifies the performance of each hardware element, plus the presence of redundant elements. If an element fails, the processing is shifted to an alternative element.

Software checks take a number of forms. Among the controls generally incorporated into operating systems are the label check and the read-write check. The label check automatically notifies the computer operator of the contents of internal labels on storage media such as magnetic tapes and magnetic disks. The read-write check automatically halts a program when reading or writing is inhibited (e.g., when a printer runs out of paper), or initiates an end-of-file routine when no further processing of a file medium is possible (e.g., when the end of a magnetic tape reel is reached). A control procedure involving checkpoints is useful for restarting computer programs when the computer system malfunctions during processing.

The last control objective, concerning accuracy and reliability, is dependent on the transaction processing portion of the AIS. In order to fulfill this objective, such control subobjectives as the following must be accomplished:

- Ensuring that all transactions entered for processing are valid and authorized
- Ensuring that all valid transactions are captured and entered for processing on a timely basis
- Ensuring that the input data of all entered transactions are accurate and complete, with the transactions being expressed in proper monetary values
- Ensuring that all entered transactions are processed properly to update all affected records of master files and/or other types of data sets
- Ensuring that all required outputs are prepared by appropriate rules to provide accurate and reliable information; for example, that financial statements such as income statements are prepared from complete and up-to-date records and in accordance with generally accepted accounting principles

In striving to achieve these objectives, the internal control structure performs a variety of established procedures. For instance, the actual cash on hand and in the bank is matched to the amount reflected in the cash ledger account; the customer number on a remittance advice is matched to the number of an account in the accounts receivable master file.

Control objectives are not easily achieved, however. One difficulty arises from the changes faced by a modern firm, ranging from ever-changing tax laws to rapidly developing technology. Another difficulty derives from the array of risks to which the internal control structure and its firm are exposed. A third difficulty, related to the first, concerns the use of computer technology within the control structure. A fourth difficulty may be traced to the human factor, since control objectives are accomplished through people. Managers may establish policies, procedures, and benchmarks that are unclear or unwise. Employees may not follow procedures consistently or may make incorrect comparisons. A final difficulty relates to the costs of controls.

(e) System Change Procedures

Changes in a computer-based information system most often pertain to application programs or the schema of the database. Both types of changes should follow clearly defined and sound procedures to prevent unauthorized manipulations and possibly well-meaning but injurious errors and mishaps. For instance, a programmer could incorporate into a program a feature that benefits him or her personally or that violates management policy.

If the change pertains to an application program, it should be initiated by a user-department manager, who explains the needed change in writing. The requested change then should be approved by the systems development manager (or by a committee of high-level managers if the modification is sufficiently large). After approval, the change or addition would be assigned to systems personnel, usually a maintenance programmer in the case of an application program. This programmer should use a working copy of the program, rather than the "live" version currently in use. The new or revised design is next tested jointly by systems personnel (including persons not involved in the design) and the user. Documentation should be thoroughly revised to reflect the change or addition. Finally, the documented change or addition and test results should be approved by the systems development manager and should be formally accepted by the initiating user.

(f) New Systems Development Procedures

The design and development of new computer-based applications require controls similar to those needed for system changes. Each request for a new system development should be initiated by either a user-department manager or a higher-level manager, depending on its scope. Assume, for instance, that a new automated credit approval system is desired. The credit manager could initiate the request, which would then be authorized by a computer-system steering committee. The user-department and systems development personnel next would work together to clarify information needs, to define system requirements, and to develop necessary system design specifications. After implementing the designed system, they should jointly test all portions of the system, manual as well as computerized. Finally, the documentation concerning the design and test results would be reviewed and approved by the manager of the user department.

4.10 DOCUMENTATION CONTROLS

An AIS is a complex mixture of procedures, controls, forms, equipment, and users. If the instructions and guidelines for operating such a system are inadequate, the system is likely to function inefficiently. If and when breakdowns occur, the disruptions to operations are likely to be quite harmful. Consider the situation in which a system analyst has designed and installed a computer-based accounting application but has neglected to prepare computer flow charts that describe the programs. If a bug develops in one of the programs, the repairs to the program would be difficult and time-consuming.

Documentation, whether administrative or systems related, is potentially a very useful control tool for effective management. Some controls must be applied to documentation. More about such controls will be said in Chapter 6 dealing with the mechanics of documentation.

4.11 MANAGEMENT PRACTICE CONTROLS

Some of the most severe risk exposures that a firm faces are related to possible deficiencies in management. For instance, an incompetent employee may be hired or an employee may be poorly trained, resulting in excessive errors. Or a bank processing computer program could be changed by a programmer, so that bank funds are diverted into her personal accounts. A wide variety of administrative controls are needed to counteract such management-related risks. Most of the controls are those identified as being a part of the control environment discussed in Chapter 5. These controls are grouped under a category called "management practice controls." This broad category includes the organizational controls discussed above. In addition, management practice controls may be said to include asset accountability control, planning practices, personnel practices, audit practices, system change procedures, new system development procedures, and documentation controls. (See Exhibit 4–1.)

4.12 ASSET ACCOUNTABILITY CONTROLS

A firm's assets are the productive resources that it possesses. These valued assets are subject to theft, pilferage, accidental loss, and damage. Another risk is that the assets will be valued incorrectly in the financial statements, perhaps as a result of miscounting

---

Asset Accountability Controls
Limited access
Periodic verification using:
  Subsidiary ledgers
  Logs and receipts
  Reconciliations/inventories
  Acknowledgment procedures
  Reviews and reassessments

Planning Practices
Budgets
  Develop standards
  Flexible budgeting
  Variance analysis
Schedules
New controls

Personnel Practices
Select competent and trustworthy employees
Train employees adequately
Provide clear job descriptions
Schedule periodic performance evaluations
Require employee bonding
Arrange employee job rotation
Require vacations
Maintain close supervision
Establish clear termination policies

Audit Practices
High-level audit committee
Periodic examinations by external auditors
Ongoing reviews by internal auditors

System Change and New Development Procedures Documentation Control
Administrative
System

Exhibit 4–1. Management practice controls.

the quantities. Thus, one of the objectives of internal control is to protect a firm's assets from these risks. The assets may be safeguarded and accounted for properly by doing the following:

- Permitting access to assets only in accordance with management's authorization
- Comparing the recorded accountability for assets with existing assets at reasonable intervals and taking appropriate action with respect to all differences

Restricting access to assets is achieved through various security measures, which are discussed in Chapters 7 through 13. Assuring that assets are properly valued in the accounting records involves the presence of asset accountability controls. Specific controls that aid in providing proper asset accountability include the use of subsidiary ledgers, logs, receipts, reconciliations/inventories, acknowledgment procedures, reviews, and reassessments. These controls are needed in manual as well as computer-based systems. However, because of the added computational power of computers, controls such as reconciliations can be performed more frequently in computer-based systems.

(a) Accounting Subsidiary Ledgers

Subsidiary ledgers can be maintained for assets such as accounts receivable, inventory, plant assets, and investments. Amounts reflected in these ledgers are based on postings from transaction documents. The total of all balances in a particular subsidiary ledger should be equal to the balance in the corresponding control account in the general ledger. Since the postings are performed independently of each other, the use of a subsidiary ledger provides a cross-check on the correctness of the control account, and vice versa.

(b) Reconciliations

A reconciliation consists of comparing values that have been computed independently. Thus, a comparison of the balance in a control account with the total of balances in a corresponding subsidiary ledger is an example of a reconciliation. Reconciliation also can involve comparisons of physical levels of resources with the quantities or amounts reflected in accounting records. For instance, each item of a physical inventory should be counted periodically. These physical counts then can be reconciled with the quantities shown in the accounting records. If differences appear, they may signal the need to adjust the quantities in the accounting records to reflect the physical realities. Another important reconciliation, the bank reconciliation, compares the balance in the bank account with the cash balance in the general ledger.

In accordance with the principle of organizational independence, reconciliations should be prepared only by employees or managers not otherwise responsible for the processing of related transactions. For instance, no employee involved in the processing or handling of cash receipts or cash disbursements should prepare a bank reconciliation. Instead, it should be prepared by an accounting manager or internal auditor.

(c) Logs and Registers

Receipts, movements, and uses of assets can be monitored by means of logs and registers. For example, cash receipts are logged on remittance listings (i.e., registers). Later, the amounts recorded on deposit slips are reconciled to the amounts of these remittance listings, to ensure that all receipts are deposited intact. Files of data on disks and possibly even magnetic tapes are noted on logs as they are moved from the data library into the computer room, and vice versa. When an employee uses a computer system from a terminal, the access can be recorded on a console log. Logs and registers thus help a firm to account for the status and use of its varied assets.

(d) Reviews and Reassessments

Reviews by outside parties provide independent verification of asset balances and, hence, accountability. For instance, an auditor may verify that the plant assets reflected in the accounts actually exist and are properly valued. A customer who receives a monthly statement will likely verify that the amount owed is correct. Reassessments are reevaluations of measured asset values. For example, accountants make periodic counts of the physical inventory and compare these counts to the inventory records. If necessary, the quantities and amounts in the records may be adjusted downward to reflect losses, breakage, and aging.

(e) Acknowledgment Procedures

In various transactions, employees are called on to acknowledge their accountability for assets. For instance, when merchandise arrives from suppliers, the clerks in the receiving department count the incoming goods, prepare a receiving report, and sign the report. In doing so they acknowledge accountability for the goods. When the merchandise later is moved to the storeroom, the storekeeper recounts the goods and signs for their receipt. Through such an acknowledgment, he or she accepts the transfer of accountability for the goods.

4.13 PLANNING PRACTICES

Another form of management practice controls is organizational planning. Sound planning practices involve activities such as preparing budgets, developing schedules, and approving new controls. Consider, for instance, budget preparation, which is closely allied with the management control system. A budget quantifies the financial objectives of a firm. That is, it establishes both the revenue levels that a firm expects to achieve and the cost levels within which it desires to constrain its operations. Through comparisons with actual revenues and costs, the budgeted amounts can help to detect inefficiencies, losses, and even fraudulent actions.

4.14 PERSONNEL PRACTICES

Sound personnel practices can significantly aid a firm in achieving efficient operations and maintaining data integrity. Trustworthy and competent employees should be sought, screened, and selected to fulfill all positions of responsibility. New employees should be provided with clear-cut job descriptions and be adequately trained concerning their responsibilities. In particular, employees should be made aware of important control requirements, such as the proper use and protection of confidential passwords. Each employee's performance should be evaluated periodically. Employees having access to cash and other negotiable assets should be bonded. A fidelity bond indemnifies a firm when it incurs losses of insured assets due to events such as fraudulent activities of bonded employees. Operational employees such as computer operators should be rotated among jobs and shifts. Also, employees in key positions of trust should be required to take periodic vacations, to subject their activities to review by substitutes. In addition, they should be well supervised, so that they are encouraged to follow established policies and to avoid irregularities. For instance, the manager of data processing and/or shift supervisors should closely observe and review the actions of the computer operators. Finally, employees should be terminated only in accordance with reasonable and well-publicized policies.

4.15 AUDIT PRACTICES

Sound evaluation practices are needed to provide independent checks on the performance of employees, the adequacy of the internal control structure, and the reliability of the accounting records. Evaluation of each employee's performance is normally performed by the employee's supervisor. However, checking computations or other work results is often performed by other employees, as we have discussed. Evaluating the internal control structure and accounting records can best be done by auditors.

Sound audit practices include oversight by audit committees, examinations by external auditors, and reviews by internal auditors. An effective audit committee usually reports directly to the board of directors. It takes an active role in overseeing the firm's accounting and financial reporting policies and practices. It is also a liaison between the board and the external and internal auditors. External auditors should perform periodic independent verifications or audits of the accounting records underlying the financial statements. Internal auditors should be assigned to a permanent organizational function within the firm. Their primary responsibility should consist of evaluating the adequacy and effectiveness of internal control structure policies and procedures. In addition, they may undertake specific verification procedures, such as preparing bank reconciliations and distributing paychecks to employees.

SAS No. 78, "Consideration of Internal Control in a Financial Statement Audit," issued in 1995 by the AICPA, significantly revises the way auditors must perceive organizational internal control in the context of their audits of financial statements.

The newer SAS expands considerably the perception of what is understood to be internal control and explains the relationship between internal control and independent financial audits.

The definition of internal control is much more specific, as seen in paragraph 6 from SAS No. 78:

> Internal control is a process—effected by an entity's board of directors, management, and other personnel—designed to provide reasonable assurance regarding the achievement of objectives in the following categories: (a) reliability of financial reporting, (b) effectiveness and efficiency of operations, and (c) compliance with applicable laws and regulations.

Even though the auditing statement lists the objectives associated with an entity's internal control, it also specifies that not all of these objectives and related controls may be relevant to audits of every entity. The statement goes out of its way to point out the difference in audit requirement for small and midsize firms. It does not insist on using the same yardstick for every entity.

4.16 COMMUNICATION AUDIT IN ACCOUNTING CONTEXT

Accountants or, rather, accounting information systems exist in order to provide information to decision makers. No matter what it is called—decision support, business intelligence, or performance measurement—the goal of providing information is to understand the raw business data the system has collected. By itself data are overwhelming, if not meaningless or even chaotic. To make sense of the raw data, they must be converted into information that can be used by organizational decision makers. The goal for controllers and their departments is the conversion of business data into relevant information that is available to accounting information consumers in a timely manner. But delivering access to financial and other enterprise-asset information on an organization-wide basis is a task that requires ongoing planning, all the more so because the nature of information needed by its users is subject to changes.

The ever-changing environment and technology can require changes in the information sought from the business data being collected. Indeed, the form in which the raw data themselves are collected can change. Gathering data that may be stored in many formats within different databases and across a variety of systems in geographically disparate business units is no longer an impossible dream. But the very availability of such data makes the challenge confronting accountants daunting, since the data themselves are not of use in decision making; rather the information extracted from the data and made available to decision makers in a timely manner is what is important. The challenge is in the fact that decision makers themselves often do not know what they need in the form of information.

The constancy of change and its impact on the kind of information needed by its consumers is what makes the communication audit a very useful tool for accountants, provided they can adapt it to the context of the information system. Section 4.17 deals with communication audits, a tool familiar to those working in the field of corporate communication. By reading it, accountants may be able to acquire a new tool to better accomplish their role as information providers to organizational decision makers.

Specifically, to better realize the goals envisaged by SAS No. 78's focus on communication, communication audits should be adapted to accounting contexts. To do so, accountants must begin at the end, by auditing information consumers. Such accounting department's customers will include executives, line managers, business analysts, and even external business partners as well as the external users of financial statements generated by accounting systems. Knowing the who, what, when, why, and how of their information needs is crucial and, it must be remembered, subject to change due to environmental and technological advances. It is important to know who the information consumers are, what sort of information they need, and the most useful format for providing that information. It is also important to know where the information they need comes from, when they need the information, and for what purpose. Needless to say, on the basis of such knowledge about the information consumers, they can be organized into logical groupings that will make the information flow more useful.

Not every information consumer needs the same information; hence knowing a given information consumer's role can suggest the kind of information needed and the formats in which to deliver it. Upper-level executives may require access to high-level key performance indicators or other exception-driven data measures that deliberately leave out details in favor of end results or even variances from what was planned. For example, the upper-level executive needs to know that the budget is not going to be met as a starter, rather than the bricks and mortar of organizational activities. Senior executives need these data, which are likely to come from various line-of-business systems, to monitor strategic business objectives and make daily business decisions. Graphic presentations in the form of diagrams, charts, and information dashboards can help all information consumers absorb the material presented.

Line managers, in contrast to top executives, need information that helps them perform their responsibilities better. They do not need to know what is taking place everywhere in the organization; they are interested in information that relates only to their operational domain. They do not need the end results but data and information that they can quickly analyze, perhaps with worksheets. Such data are likely to come from one or more specific line-of-business systems and will be required on a daily, weekly, or monthly basis to support tactical decision making.

Another group of information consumers are represented by business planners, information analysts who may require access to a wide array of information summaries and details as well as their sources. They need information as well as the ability to manipulate onscreen drilldowns. This means the ability to navigate from summary to detail data—for example, from a year-to-date balance to a source-transaction debit or credit. A drilldown crosses module boundaries, such as from general ledger to accounts payable to purchase order, and in some cases may cross systems to reach into external databases. The data are likely to come from an enterprise-wide data warehouse and be required on demand in response to unpredictable requests from business managers. Such drilling is possible only due to the tremendous advances in information technology and would have been impossible to accomplish instantaneously less than a decade ago.

Yet another group of information consumers may be business partners—vendors, for example—who may appreciate access to data that relate to their interactions with the business and help them work effectively with an organization. This information may be presented in the form of Web self-service or vendor and customer home pages to allow anytime, anywhere access. Other external consumers of information consist of investors, creditors, and government regulators, whose needs for information must be attended to by accountants.

A communication audit undertaken by accountants will allow them to better know the needs of these customers and to appreciate ongoing changes in their needs. The audit should indicate where the data are located and how they are stored. This phase of the communication audit can be facilitated by asking a question such as: Where are the systems located, both physically and on your network? Even in a small business, often no source can provide everything that must be known to meet the needs of information consumers. The proverbial show boxes that clients bring in to their accountants illustrate the point being made here. Often data is not stored in a formal system or is kept off-line. This range of information sources is likely to be even more confusing in a multinational business with locations all over the planet. Identifying both the physical and the network addresses of the system and its servers is one important purpose of a communication audit, which also can help identify as part of the audit the data that are not systematized or easily accessible across a local or wide area network.

The data information consumers need may come from a single system, such as an enterprise resource planning (ERP) system, or more likely from multiple systems that include sales, financial, human resource, and manufacturing. It is important to identify who is in charge of these systems. Often systems are located and managed by different organizational units.

Another question to ask as part of the communication audit is: What databases are used to store the information? It is critical to know the range of databases used by these systems because it impacts how easily users can extract data from source systems. If all the systems needed run relational databases from leading vendors, the necessary data probably can be retrieved using a single software program that facilitates the retrieval and transformation of data by a target system from a source system. However, if relational, nonrelational, and multidimensional databases are in place, the software used to link them—data-access middleware—will need to be more sophisticated, include data transformation as well as data extraction, and likely be more costly and difficult to set up and maintain.

4.17 WHEN TO CONDUCT A COMMUNICATION AUDIT*

Audits always have a specific purpose in mind. In addition to the primary benefit of being able to establish or clarify goals and objectives set for communication, noted researcher Walter Lindermann also points out these indicators for a communication audit:

- When an organization changes direction—for example, offers new products or services, or merges with or is acquired by another organization
- When there is a change in management
- When a public relations function is being created or restructured
- When the organization continuously finds itself on the defensive, reacting to attacks by inside or outside forces
- When the organization's position is frequently misstated; when its spokespeople are often misquoted
- When the media often fail to query the organization on issues that pertain directly to that organization or its industry
- When issues are forever catching the organization unprepared; when its system for spotting and analyzing issues is not working effectively
- When employees, shareholders, or other recipients of organization materials complain that publications are redundant, poorly written, dull, unprofessional, when there are no quality controls for the organization's communications

*Sections 4.17 and 4.18 are contributed by Michael S. McGraw. Michael S. McGraw, PhD, APR, is a member of the graduate communication faculty at Seton Hall University in New Jersey. As a communications consultant and accredited public relations counselor, he has conducted communication audits for both profit and nonprofit environments. He has also organized presentations on this topic for the Public Relations Society and the Council for the Advancement and Support of Education.

- When target audience groups question the relevance of an organization's overall efforts; when there are no audience studies to demonstrate that the organization's communication efforts are hitting their targets

In "Auditing Communication Practices," a communication expert, Myron Emanuel, indicates that an audit also should be considered when companies experience labor unrest or when there is an economic crisis within the company, such as layoffs or cost-reduction programs.[1]

Generally, a full audit is needed every five years or so, unless there are drastic changes within the company. A mini-audit, done internally, always can provide new and useful information; such an audit should be considered annually. Mini-audits target certain programs and procedures, test them, get feedback from a select audience, and make recommendations regarding changes in communication style, message, flow, or method.

Most communication audits have as their primary construction comprehensive interviews with senior management and other key management constituency groups (board members); a thorough analysis of employee and customer perception; and a complete review of all communication methods, strategies, and tactics.

Specifically, a communication audit looks at the following:

- Face-to-face communication, whether one on one or in groups
- Written communication in the form of letters, memos, and internal reports
- Communication patterns among individuals, sections, and departments
- Communication channels and frequency of interaction (communication work load)
- Communication content, clarity, and effectiveness
- Information needs of individuals, sections, and departments
- Information technology, particularly with respect to the human and organizational aspects of using communication and information technology
- Informal communication (particularly as it affects motivation and performance) and nonverbal communication (i.e., physical layout of work areas, marks of seniority, or norms of dress and manners as they affect the efficiency of the organization)
- Communication climate, or corporate culture

An audit provides a measurement component or a benchmark for this important component of doing business. An audit looks at information flow and how adjustments can be made to improve existing channels as well as develop new strategies for better or different forms of communication. An audit does not necessarily focus on personnel, except to make recommendations related to efficiency or the need to possibly consider personnel additions. It is certainly not designed to evaluate current personnel or identify employees not working at a certain level. That message should be communicated to employees so that there are no misunderstandings about the nature of the communication audit. Their cooperation is vital to the success of the audit.

A communication audit can reenergize the communication function and those working in that function. An audit allows communication specialists to showcase their efforts and helps them position and redefine their area for the future. Objective outcomes tell specialists what needs to be done for effective change, allowing them to learn new ways to deliver messages.

4.18 HOW IS A COMMUNICATION AUDIT ACCOMPLISHED?

A comprehensive communication audit is a diagnostic tool that is constructed in the political arena of the institution. Professionals always should view the process as a positive opportunity, not a witch hunt to find out who is not doing what. Explain to employees that the purpose of an audit is to improve performance, not threaten jobs. A good audit looks at challenges and the ways in which success can be heightened by more effective communication methods.

A communication audit needs a very organized and methodical approach. Everyone who is to be involved should understand the what, when, and why of each step of the audit. The objective nature of the process should be made clear to all, and the communication specialists overseeing the audit should work to have an endorsement from all directly involved. This should be a staff effort; staff should be a part of the process and included in the planning and execution of the audit.

Given the amount of time an audit requires, the timing should be planned carefully so as to avoid conflicts with other major business activities. The audit, once in process, should not be delayed, put off, or rescheduled. Doing this undermines the free-flowing nature of the process.

The communication audit report should be discussed ahead of time. The audit would point out problem areas that need to be corrected. How will results that might bring change be dealt with? Some of the problems could well involve deep-seated traditions and habits. Such an ingrained way of doing things requires one to be in tune with prescriptions associated with change management.

Before going ahead with a communication audit, the decision makers must demonstrate a willingness to implement the recommendations that are likely to be made after the audit. Auditors should remember the practicality of the steps proposed. However, practical considerations must not keep communication auditors from reporting the conditions as they actually exist.

When preparing for the audit, consider the following self-assessment components:

- The stated mission of the organization and how that mission is carried out
- Organizational strengths and challenges
- The constituency base—customers or clients, employees, the business environment, the community
- Past communication methods
- Money and time allowed for communication
- Priorities
- Response mechanism for acting on communication activity

Note any other problem areas in the communications process. Make sure individuals selected for interview have a sense of the larger view of the company. Techniques for an audit are included in Exhibit 4–2.

All participants in the audit should receive a briefing paper, which would provide information on the process, what will be done over the designated time period, information about the auditors, and a schedule of those they will be seeing during the visit.

A comprehensive communication audit will uncover credibility gaps, establish

Type	Time	Cost	Yield	Disruption
1. Observation	Variable	Relatively inexpensive cost of observer	Data from people processes, environment, and task processes	Little if observer remains unobtrusive
2. Interviews	30 to 60 minutes	Expensive; pay interviewers; pay workers for interview time	Perceptions of employees; probing allows in-depth coverage of many topics	Time away from job
3. Questionnaire	20 to 30 minutes	Relatively inexpensive; mass-produced questionnaires can be filled out at will; principal costs are employees' time and analytic time of auditor	Standardized; quantitative data about many topics; general overview of many aspects of the organization	20 to 30 minutes
4. Critical Incidents/Communication Expenses	Usually built in as part of interview or questionnaire	a. Relatively inexpensive b. Depends on whether collected in questionnaire or interview	Specific examples of perceived behavior, but many refuse to give them	Little
5. Network	20 to 30 minutes	Paid time to employees for filling out questionnaire; very expensive to analyze with computers	Structural information	30 minutes
6. Content Analysis	None	Many hours to code and analyze	Kind of information processed through the organization; evaluation of channels	None
7. Communication Diaries	Variable	Expensive; takes worker time to write a report of everything	Interaction networks; content of messages; channel evaluation	Great; most treat it as a nuisance

Exhibit 4-2. Potential audit technologies.

Source: From Cal W. Downs, Communication Audits. Copyright © 1988 by Scott, Foresman and Company. Reprinted by permission of Addison Wesley Educational Publishers Inc.

objectives for communication and a priority list for those objectives, and reveal new ideas and methods for communication.

NOTES

1. M. Emanuel, "Auditing Communication Practices." In *Inside Organizational Communication,* edited by C. Reuss and D. Silvis. New York: Longman Inc., 1985.

CHAPTER 5

THREATS TO THE CONTROL PROCESS

5.1 INTRODUCTION

This chapter continues the study of the organizational control and the ways it is exercised. The focus here is on threats that management control confronts. Managers seek to help organizations realize their goals and objectives, but their objectives are likely to fail if organizational resources are not being deployed in the manner called for by organizational plans, both short term and long term. In order to implement plans and realize objectives, management must be able to control the organization. Internal control seeks to ensure the credibility of financial reports and the safety of the physical resources, the functions traditionally associated with the accounting department. Other forms of controls exist in addition to internal control.

The chapter discusses the threats and risks that confront information systems. Since fraud is a major threat that controls in general and internal controls in particular seek to prevent, the recently issued Statement on Auditing Standard (SAS) No. 82, concerning auditors' responsibilities toward fraudulent financial reporting, is discussed. The SAS makes clear the limited role financial auditors are to play in preventing or discovering internal and external frauds directed against an organization. The chapter concludes with a study of fraud auditing and forensic accounting—disciplines that seek to detect fraud and other threats to the management control of an organization. Fraud auditing and forensic accounting are distinct disciplines, and the discussion here is not meant to be exhaustive. For a more complete understanding of the two emerging disciplines, refer to *Fraud Auditing and Forensic Accounting,* 2d edition, written by G. Jack Bologna and Robert J. Lindquist (New York: John Wiley & Sons, 1995).

5.2 IMPEDIMENTS TO EFFECTIVE CONTROL

Effective control requires ongoing efforts. Impediments to effective managerial control can be caused by a number of factors, individually or in combination. Among them are:

- Exposure to risks
- Technological problems
- Behavioral problems
- Cost-related considerations

Some examples of potential impediments or risks to control are:

- Clerical and operational employees, who process transactional data and have access to assets
- Computer programmers, who prepare computer programs and have knowledge relating to the instructions by which transactions are processed
- Managers and accountants, who have access to records and financial reports and often have authority to approve transactions
- Former employees, who may still understand the control systems and may harbor grudges against the firm
- Customers and suppliers, who generate many of the transactions processed by the firm
- Competitors, who may desire to acquire confidential information of the firm, such as new product plans
- Outside persons, such as computer hackers and criminals, who have various reasons to access the firm's data or its assets or to commit destructive acts
- Acts of nature or accidents, such as floods and fires and equipment breakdowns

Every entity, such as a business firm, faces impediments such as those just mentioned that reduce the chances of it achieving its control objectives. For controls provided by the internal control structure to be adequate, they should counteract all the significant risks to which a firm is exposed. Risk exposures may arise from a variety of internal and external sources, such as employees, customers, computer hackers, criminals, and acts of nature. In order to design sound control systems, accountants and system designers should be able to assess the risks to which a firm is subject. Risk assessment consists of identifying the risks, analyzing the risks in terms of the extent of exposure, and proposing effective control procedures.

5.3 TYPES OF RISK EXPOSURE

Among the system-related risks that confront the typical firm, other than poor decision making and inefficient operations, are:

- *Unintentional Errors.* Errors may appear in input data, such as in customer names or numbers. Alternatively, they may appear during processing, as when clerks incorrectly multiply quantities ordered (on customers' orders) and unit prices of the merchandise items. These errors often occur on an occasional and random basis, as when a clerk accidentally strikes the wrong key on a terminal keyboard. However, errors may occur consistently. For instance, an incorrectly written computer program may produce computational errors each time the program is executed. In any of these situations, the erroneous data will damage the accuracy and reliability of a firm's files and outputs. Unintentional errors often occur because employees lack knowledge owing to inadequate training; they also may occur when employees become tired and careless or are inadequately supervised.
- *Deliberate Errors.* Deliberate errors constitute fraud, since they are made to secure unfair or unlawful gain. These irregularities may appear in input data, during processing, or in generated outputs. For instance, a clerk may increase the amount on a check received from a customer or understate a column of cash receipts. Either type

of error damages the accuracy and reliability of files and/or outputs. Additionally, deliberate errors also may conceal thefts (and, hence, losses) of assets. For example, a manager may enter a misstatement in a report or financial statement. This type of error could mislead and thereby injure stockholders and creditors.

- **Unintentional Loss of Assets.** Assets may be lost or misplaced by accident. For example, newly received merchandise items may be put into the wrong warehouse bins, with the result that they are not found by pickers when filling orders. Data as well as physical assets may be lost. For instance, the accounts receivable file stored on a disk may be wiped out by a sudden power surge.

- **Thefts of Assets.** Assets of a firm may be stolen by outsiders, such as professional thieves who break into a storeroom in the dead of night. Alternatively, assets may be misappropriated through embezzlement or defalcation, that is, taken by employees who have been entrusted with their care. For instance, a cashier may pocket currency received by mail or a production worker may carry home a tool. Employees who embezzle often create deliberate errors in order to hide their thefts. Thus, the cashier who pockets currency may overstate the cash account.

- **Breaches of Security.** Unauthorized persons may gain access to the data files and reports of a firm. For instance, a "hacker" may break into a firm's computerized files via a distant terminal, or an employee may peek at a salary report in an unlocked file drawer. Security breaches can be very damaging in certain cases, as when competitors gain access to a firm's confidential marketing plans.

- **Acts of Violence and Natural Disasters.** Certain violent acts cause damage to a firm's assets, including data. If sufficiently serious, they can interrupt business operations and even propel firms toward bankruptcy. Examples of such acts are sabotage of computer facilities and the willful destruction of customer files. Although violent acts sometimes are performed by outsiders, such as terrorists, they are performed more often by disgruntled employees and ex-employees. Also, violent acts can arise from nonhuman sources, such as fires that engulf computer rooms or short circuits that disable printers.

5.4 DEGREE OF RISK EXPOSURE

To combat these risks effectively, the degree of risk exposure should be assessed. Exposure to risk is caused by factors such as:

- Frequency. The more frequent an occurrence, the greater the exposure to risk. A merchandising firm that makes numerous sales is highly exposed to errors in the transaction data. A contractor that bids on custom projects is exposed to calculating errors. A department store with numerous browsing shoppers has a significant exposure to merchandise losses from shoplifting.

- Vulnerability. The more vulnerable an asset, the greater the exposure to risk. Cash is highly vulnerable to theft, since it is easily hidden and fully convertible. A telephone may be vulnerable to unauthorized use for long-distance calls, especially if it is left untended in a remote office.

- Size. The higher the monetary value of a potential loss, the greater the risk exposure. An accounts receivable file represents a high-risk exposure, since it contains essential information concerning amounts owed and other matters that affect credit customers.

When two or more of the above factors act in unison, the exposure to risk is multiplied. Thus, an extremely high exposure occurs in the case of a firm that conducts numerous sales for cash, with each sale involving a sizable amount. As might be imagined, this situation requires more extensive controls than a situation in which the exposure to risk is slight.

5.5 CONDITIONS AFFECTING EXPOSURES TO RISK

The exposures to risk that a firm faces can be heightened by various internal conditions. Perhaps most serious are weaknesses in one or more of the control systems. Weaknesses may be caused by an inadequate selection of controls. Thus, thefts are abetted when the organizational structure is weakened by an inadequate segregation of duties. Control system weaknesses also may occur because of breakdowns. For instance, an accountant who is responsible for investigating variances from standards may not pursue the exception sufficiently to determine appropriate corrective measures. Other problem conditions involve collusion, lack of enforcement, and computer crime.

(a) Collusion

A frustrating condition of which a firm must be aware is internal collusion, the cooperation of two or more employees for a fraudulent purpose. For instance, an employee who has custody over inventory may remove inventory items from the storeroom, while an employee who keeps inventory records deducts the removed items from the records; the consequence to the employer is lost inventory and covered tracks. Collusion may also involve an employee and a nonemployee. This situation is known as external collusion. Either type of collusion is difficult to counteract, even with soundly designed control systems.

(b) Lack of Enforcement

Still another troubling condition is lack of enforcement. Thus, a firm may have adequate management policies and control procedures but may overlook irregularities. For instance, an employee who has committed embezzlement may not be prosecuted on being detected, perhaps so that the firm can avoid embarrassment over its weak security measures. Such lack of action by a firm may encourage other potential wrongdoers. Management may even actively abet the problem. For example, a higher-level manager might improperly override an installed control procedure, either with the intent of personal gain or to enhance the firm's financial condition.

5.6 FRAUD AND CONTROL PROBLEMS RELATED TO COMPUTERS

Computer systems present special risk exposures and problems of control. After surveying these exposures and problems, we will examine the effects computer systems have on controls. Accountants are becoming increasingly concerned about these controls, since computer-based information systems are rapidly growing in number and complexity. Offenses involving computer-based systems have grown in quantity and seriousness in recent years.

Computer fraud poses very high degrees of risk, since all three factors—frequency, vulnerability, and size—tend to be present. A computer-based system may process hundreds of transactions per hour, with each transaction being subject to error or to fraudulent activity. A computer and its stored data are often vulnerable to unauthorized access as well as to damage. To make matters worse, fraudulent activities—by either authorized or unauthorized persons—are very difficult to detect. Also, a loss from computer fraud tends to be several times larger than the average fraud loss when manual systems are involved. Huge quantities of data and lightning-fast processing speeds magnify the payoff from computer fraud. Individual losses from computer fraud can easily exceed millions. A famous case uncovered as early as 1973 illustrates the magnitude that computer fraud can assume. Equity Funding Corporation, an insurance holding company in Los Angeles, employed its computer system to create over 63,000 fictitious insurance policies with assumed values of hundreds of millions of dollars. In addition to reporting grossly inflated assets in its 1972 year-end financial statements, the firm's higher-level managers embezzled millions of dollars by selling the policies to reinsurers.

5.7 TYPES OF COMPUTER CRIMES

Computer crimes take various forms. Two types already listed are unauthorized access of stored data and sabotage of computer facilities. Other types of computer crimes include the following:

- Theft of computer hardware and software. The latter, known as software piracy, is quite prevalent. It involves making copies of programs and software packages, usually from diskettes.
- Unauthorized use of computer facilities for personal use. This crime may be committed by a hacker, who breaks into a computer system via a remote terminal or microcomputer, or by an employee who runs his or her own programs on the company computer.
- Fraudulent modification or use of data or programs. In most fraud cases the perpetrator intends to steal assets, such as cash or merchandise. For instance, a purchasing agent may enter unauthorized purchase transactions via a terminal and have merchandise sent to his home. A programmer employed by a bank may modify a withdrawal program in a manner that causes withdrawals against her personal account to be charged to an inactive account.

5.8 REASONS UNDERLYING COMPUTER CONTROL PROBLEMS

Computer-based information systems manipulate and transcribe data with impeccable accuracy. In spite of this significant advantage, we have seen convincing evidence that computers do introduce severe problems of control. The major reasons for such problems can be traced to the following inherent characteristics of computer-based systems.

(a) Processing Is Concentrated

In manual systems, the processing is done by clerks in various departments, thereby providing for adequate segregation of duties. Employees can cross-check each other's work, thus detecting processing errors. In computer-based systems, the processing is often concentrated within self-contained computer facilities. Certain organizational units are bypassed during processing operations. Consequently, less opportunity exists for detecting errors and fraudulent events such as unauthorized transactions, changes in programmed instructions, and thefts of assets.

(b) Audit Trails May Be Undermined

Portions of the audit trail are more likely to be fragmented or eliminated in computer-based systems than in manual systems. Source documents may not be used, for instance, when sales orders are received via telephones and entered directly through terminals. Journals or other records may not be maintained when transactions or adjustments are posted directly to ledgers (master files). These shortcuts improve processing efficiency but cause partial losses of the audit trail. One consequence is that fraudulent acts are less likely to leave traces that can be detected.

(c) Human Judgment Is Bypassed

Computers perform programmed instructions blindly; that is, they exercise no judgment. Thus, fewer opportunities exist for people to spot errors and questionable data or to observe processing steps. With no special programmed controls and reviews of processed results, transaction errors and irregularities in data can easily escape detection.

(d) Device-Oriented Data Storage

The stored data are invisible. Although this characteristic does not cause a serious problem, it is necessary for users to take specific steps to retrieve the data in readable form. The necessity for data retrieval increases opportunities for errors and often frustrates users. Another source of problems is that stored data (except for ROM memory) are erasable. Thus, valuable data, such as accounts receivable records, may be lost. Third, data are stored in compressed form. A single disk can hold as much data as several file cabinets. Thus, damage to a single device can cause the loss of a tremendous quantity of valuable data. Finally, stored data are relatively accessible. This condition is particularly acute in the cases of on-line computer systems and computer networks, since people can access data from various points where terminals and on-line microcomputers are located. Thus, knowledgeable but unauthorized persons may gain access to vital files more easily.

(e) Vulnerable Computer Equipment

Computers are increasingly powerful but also complex and vulnerable. As a result of its processing power, a computer-based system can disseminate errors throughout files and reports more quickly. Because of its complexity, a computer system tends to be confusing to many employees, both at the clerical and the managerial levels. Such confusion can cause employees to make errors. It also may lead employees to resist improvements in computer systems, including improved control procedures. Complexity in computer hardware also causes a system to be vulnerable to breakdowns. If the breakdowns are not repaired quickly, serious interruptions to business operations may occur. Furthermore, computer hardware often is placed in fixed locations, thus rendering it vulnerable to disasters such as fires, floods, and vandalism.

5.9 OTHER CONTROL CONSIDERATIONS FOR COMPUTER SYSTEMS

Building an effective and feasible internal control structure is not a simple task. It involves more than assembling all of the controls and security measures that come to mind. Audit, cost, and ethical issues need to be considered, since they too can impede the effectiveness of the controls.

(a) Audit-Related Considerations

A typical accounting information system (AIS) undergoes periodic audits. Normally, the internal control structure receives particularly close scrutiny during such audits. Thus, the internal control structure should be designed to be fully auditable. For instance, certain analyses and reconciliations can be generated on a routine basis for use by the auditors. Generally speaking, auditors should be consulted during the system design phase, so that all of the needed controls are considered beforehand. Adding controls after the system is designed usually tends to be more costly and difficult.

(b) Cost-Benefit Considerations

Incorporating a control into an information system involves a cost. If every conceivable control were included within an internal control structure, the total cost would likely be exorbitant. Thus, a firm should conduct a cost-benefit analysis, in which the following key question is posed: Will the addition of a specific control provide expected benefits that exceed the costs of the control? If the answer is yes, and there is reasonable assurance that the control will achieve specified objectives, then the control is a desirable addition.

The broadest benefit provided by a control usually consists of reducing risk exposures, that is, of reducing the risks of failing to achieve one or more of the objectives pertaining to the internal control structure. Specific benefits may be either quantitative or qualitative in nature, such as reducing the losses due to thefts of assets, improving the reliability of information provided to management, and improving the reputation of the firm.

Costs of a control include one-time costs, recurring costs, and opportunity costs. One-time costs include the installation of security devices and training of clerks; recurring costs may be for supplies and salaries of new employees needed to implement the control. An example of an opportunity cost arises from the reduced efficiency in transaction processing caused by the added control; reduced efficiency translates into lost income.

When the costs of a control exceed its expected benefits, and the control is nevertheless installed, overcontrol exists. For instance, a control might be installed that detects certain errors that are missed by complementary controls. However, the costs deriving from these errors may not be as great as the costs of maintaining the added control.

A cost-benefit analysis includes the following four steps:

1. Assessing the risks to which the firm is exposed, such as losses of vital records.
2. Measuring the extent of each risk exposure in dollar terms. For instance, if the exposure is the possible loss of an asset, the value would be the amount needed to replace the asset.
3. Multiplying the estimated effect of each risk exposure by the estimated frequency of occurrence over a reasonable period, such as a year. The resulting product is the

potential loss that can be incurred by not reducing or avoiding a particular risk. Alternatively, it is the benefit to be gained by avoiding the risk or improving the reliability of information.

4. Determining the cost of installing and maintaining a control that is to counteract each risk exposure. Comparing the benefits against the costs for each control. On a broader level, this comparison should be employed for the group of controls pertaining to individual transaction processing systems and to the activities of the firm as a whole.

Cost-benefit analyses are difficult to apply. None of the factors is easy to measure. Also, in many situations several controls may be needed to mitigate a particular risk. However, new analytical techniques are being developed. For instance, a technique known as reliability analysis calculates reliability by measuring the error probabilities related to a process such as transaction processing.

(c) Ethical Issues

Unfortunately, employees are often subject to negative influences in the workplace. Perhaps their firm gives them strong incentives to engage in questionable behavior. For instance, employees may be pressured to meet unrealistic short-term performance goals, with the consequence that they may "pad" the figures on reports. They also may be affected by appealing temptations. For example, an employee might be tempted to engage in the dishonest act of stealing assets when he or she is aware that controls are missing or penalties are likely to be trivial. Such undesirable behaviors can be reduced or eliminated by removing the incentives and temptations—that is, through an emphasis on ethics and controls.

A strong ethical climate is vital to a firm's well-being, since it contributes to the effectiveness of the component control systems. Thus, management, from the chief executive officer on down, should exhibit high ethical values. The firm should seek and hire employees who are not only competent but also possess integrity. To aid in attracting competent and trustworthy individuals, management should establish enlightened policies. Specific policies might encourage long-term goals, delineate fair human resource practices, and so on.

Ethical standards also might be stated in a written code of conduct and communicated widely to all employees. A sound code of conduct would set out acceptable practices with respect to employee behavior. It might address matters such as conflicts of interest, improper payments, anticompetitive actions, and insider trading. Management should ensure that all employees are as aware of these standards as they are of their assigned job responsibilities. Furthermore, the managers of the firm should strictly follow the standards in their own daily behavior. The internal control structure of a firm is only as effective as the people who create it, operate it, and function within it. One of the primary concerns in designing the structure, therefore, is to provide controls that will influence in a positive manner the behavior of the employees and others who interact with the structure. Consequently, the management of a firm and the designers of the internal control structure must be concerned with employee reactions to controls. If affected employees perceive controls as being weak or unnecessary, the employees may circumvent the controls. Thus, it is highly desirable to inform employees of the purposes of the controls and to instruct them carefully in duties where controls are involved. Supervisors should watch for adverse reactions on the parts of employees, so that this understanding of control objectives can be reinforced. For instance, it can be pointed out to accounting clerks that controls restricting their access to cash are desirable, in that temptation is thus removed from honest employees.

From the foregoing discussion we can conclude that ethical issues and internal controls are closely intertwined. Any internal control structure can be circumvented when the ethical climate is weak, while even a porous internal control structure will be enhanced if the ethical climate is strong.

5.10 FORCES FOR THE IMPROVEMENT OF CONTROLS

At the start of the computer age, many an AIS was deficient with respect to controls and security measures. Often the system was intended primarily to provide the needed day-to-day documents and reports and to satisfy legal obligations. In recent decades, however, various forces have arisen to encourage the improvement of internal control systems. Perhaps the most influential forces have been managements, professional associations, and governmental bodies.

(a) Needs of Management

Managers of most firms have recognized their vital stake in adequate internal control systems. They have become aware of the huge losses and damages that can occur to the costly assets entrusted to their care. Newspapers and other media have publicized the increasing instances of white-collar crime as well as overt thefts of merchandise and other portable assets. Managers have noted that the average loss from each crime also has been rising dramatically. On the other hand, they have grown concerned about the accuracy and reliability of the information they receive. Being primary users of information from their AISs, they appreciate the potential for making poor decisions owing to inaccurate and incomplete information. Furthermore, with the increasing dependence on computer systems, they have realized the seriousness of security breaches.

(b) Ethical Concerns of Professional Associations

Professional accounting associations, such as the American Institute of Certified Public Accountants (AICPA) and the Institute of Internal Auditors (IIA), have established codes of ethics. These codes are self-imposed and self-enforced rules of conduct. Included are rules pertaining to matters such as independence, technical competence, and suitable practices during audits and consulting engagements involving information systems.

5.11 AUDITORS' RESPONSIBILITIES REGARDING FRAUDULENT FINANCIAL REPORTING

Statement on Auditing Standards (SAS) No. 82 has its basis in Section 110 of SAS No. 1, "Responsibilities and Functions of the Independent Auditor," which makes it the responsibility of an auditor to plan and perform the audit in a way that will provide reasonable assurance that the financial statements of the entity being audited are free from material misstatement. SAS No. 82 specifies that the auditor's concern pertains to fraudulent acts that can cause a material misstatement of financial statements. Auditors are to consider the following two types of fraudulent misstatements in the course of auditing financial statements of an entity:

1. Misstatements arising from fraudulent financial reporting
2. Misstatements arising from misappropriation of assets

Fraudulent financial reporting and misappropriation of assets are different from each other. Fraudulent financial reporting is committed, usually by management, to deceive financial statement users; misappropriation of assets is committed against an entity, most often by employees.

The audit statement makes a number of points about fraud. It notes that fraud frequently involves both pressure or an incentive to commit fraud and a perceived opportunity to do so. These two conditions usually are present when fraud occurs. Although fraud usually is concealed, the presence of these risk factors or other conditions should put the auditor on alert. Most times auditors cannot obtain absolute assurance that material misstatements in the financial statements will be detected, because those committing the fraud seek to conceal it. Fraud often involves collusion or falsified documentation, which makes its discovery difficult. Often auditors have to apply professional judgment in the identification and evaluation of fraud risk factors and other conditions. Such a judgment may at times be incorrect, so that an audit—even if properly planned and performed—will not uncover material misstatements resulting from fraud. Because of this, auditors can obtain only reasonable assurance that material misstatements in the financial statements have been detected.

One of the tasks that auditors must perform before carrying out an audit is a fraud risk assessment. Auditors should specifically assess the risk of material misstatement of the financial statements due to fraud and then should consider that assessment when designing the audit procedures to be performed. They also should, through inquiry, obtain management's understanding regarding the risk of fraud in the entity: Ask management if it knows of fraud perpetrated on or within the entity. In making the risk assessment, auditors should consider risk factors relating to fraudulent financial reporting and misappropriation of assets.

Risk factors related to fraudulent financial reporting may be grouped into three categories:

1. Management's characteristics and influence over the control environment. These factors pertain to management's abilities, pressures, style, and attitude toward internal control and the financial reporting process. (For example, there may be a strained relationship between management and the current or predecessor auditor.)
2. Industry conditions. These factors involve the economic and regulatory environment in which the entity operates. (For example, the entity may be part of a declining industry with increasing business failures.)
3. Operating characteristics and financial stability. These factors pertain to the nature and complexity of the entity and its transactions, the entity's financial condition, and its profitability. (For example, there may be significant related-party transactions not in the ordinary course of business or with related entities not audited or audited by another firm.)

Risk factors related to misappropriation of assets may be grouped into the following two categories:

1. **Susceptibility of assets to misappropriation.** These factors pertain to the nature of an entity's assets and the degree to which they are subject to theft. (For example, easily convertible assets, such as bearer bonds, diamonds, or computer chips, are easily stolen.)
2. **Controls.** These factors involve the lack of controls designed to prevent or detect misappropriation of assets. (For example, the auditor may find an accounting system in disarray.)

Although the fraud risk factors suggested here cover a broad range of situations typically faced by auditors, they are only examples. Their significance may vary in entities of different size, with different ownership characteristics, in different industries. It is therefore incumbent upon auditors to use professional judgment when assessing the significance and relevance of fraud risk factors and determining appropriate audit responses to such situations and characteristics.

5.12 FORENSIC ACCOUNTING AND FRAUD AUDITING

Even though SAS No. 82 focuses on fraud at considerable length, it is rather limited in scope, since it talks about fraud mostly in the context of the financial statements that public auditors are called upon to attest. The focus of SAS No. 82 is on financial auditing, which always has been associated with ascertaining whether the presentation of financial reports is in keeping with generally accepted accounting principles (GAAP). Auditing for the compliance with GAAP is not the same as trying to focus exclusively on prevention and detection of fraud or other illegal acts. The expectation gaps with respect to public auditing in the United States is not likely to end with the SAS No. 82. In contrast to the focus on the compliance with GAAP of financial audits, the detection of fraud is more likely to result from the newer disciplines, such as forensic accounting and fraud auditing. The following section explains the differences between financial auditing and fraud auditing. Before that, fraud is defined in order to clarify fraud auditing.

From an accounting and audit standpoint, fraud is an intentional misrepresentation of material facts in the accounting records, which results in financial statements that do not accurately represent income, assets, and liabilities. The misrepresentation may be seeking to misinform external organizational stakeholders such as shareholders, regulators, or creditors. Fraud through misrepresentation also could be aimed at covering up or disguising embezzlement, incompetence, misapplication of funds, and theft. In other words, improper uses of organizational assets by its officers, employees, and agents are being misrepresented.

Frauds of this kind occur most often when the following conditions exist:

- Internal controls are absent, weak, or loosely enforced.
- Employees are hired without due consideration for their honesty and integrity.
- Employees are poorly managed, exploited, abused, or placed under great stress to accomplish financial goals and objectives.
- Management models are themselves corrupt, inefficient, or incompetent.

- A trusted employee has an unresolvable personal problem, usually of a financial nature, brought on by family medical needs or by alcoholism, drug abuse, excessive gambling, or expensive tastes.
- Corruption. The company has fallen on bad times—it is losing money or market share, or its products or services are becoming unacceptable to the public.

Fraud auditors should help define the professional code of conduct and the ethical standards for the company. They should see to it a company has in place an effective corporate code of conduct that has been communicated to all employees. Such codes should provide a clear understanding of management intent and expectations. Such codes must include conflict-of-interest policy guidelines. To ensure that employees are aware of these policies, employees should be asked to sign them. Not only employees but even external vendors should know of such codes. Indeed, vendors should be asked to sign written agreements that allow the company to inspect vendors' records in the normal course of business.

Fraud auditors must have a historical knowledge of fraud possibilities. They should know the kinds of frauds perpetrated in the past and be able to relate this knowledge to the various segments of any accounting systems and organizational environment—for instance, the ability to recognize the symptoms of lapping in the revenue receivable receipt system. The patterns to look for are exceptions and oddities, things that do not fit in an organized scheme because they seem too: large, small, frequent, rare, high, low, ordinary, extraordinary, many, or few, or because they feature odd: times, places, hours, people, and/or combinations. In a word, auditors look for the unusual rather than the usual. Then they go behind and beyond those transactions to reconstruct what may have led to them and what has followed from them.

5.13 FORENSIC AND INVESTIGATIVE ACCOUNTING

In the accounting profession, the term "forensic" refers to the relation and application of financial facts to legal problems. Forensic accounting evidence is oriented to a court of law, whether that court is criminal or civil. Furthermore, with its orientation to courts of law, forensic accountants' work is subject to public scrutiny if the matter at issue goes to trial. The involvement of forensic accountants is almost always reactive; this fact distinguishes forensic accountants from fraud auditors.

Forensic accountants are involved in prevention and detection of criminal acts in a corporate or regulatory environment and are trained to react to complaints arising in criminal matters, statements of claim arising in civil litigation, and rumors and inquiries arising in corporate investigations. The investigative findings of forensic accountants will impact individuals and/or companies in terms of their freedom or a financial reward or loss. Forensic accountants draw on various resources to obtain relevant financial evidence and to interpret and present this evidence in a manner that will assist both parties. Ideally, forensic accounting should allow two parties to resolve more quickly and efficiently the complaint, statement of claim, rumor, or inquiry, or at least reduce the financial element as an area of ongoing debate. The increased business complexities in a litigious environment have enhanced the need for this discipline. The range of application of forensic accounting can be summarized into the following general areas:

(a) Corporate Investigations

Companies react to concerns that arise through a number of sources that might suggest possible wrongdoing within and without the corporate environment. No matter what the source—perhaps an anonymous phone call or letter from disgruntled employees or third parties—these problems must be addressed quickly and effectively to enable the company to continue the pursuit of its objectives. More specifically, the forensic accountant assists in addressing allegations ranging from kickbacks and wrongful dismissals to internal situations involving allegations of management or employee wrongdoing. At times forensic accountants can meet with those people affected by the allegations, rumors, or inquiries; these people may view accountants as independent and objective parties, and thus be more willing to engage in discussion.

(b) Litigation Support

Litigation support includes assisting counsel in investigating and assessing the integrity and amount relating to such areas as loss of profits, construction claims, product liability, shareholder disputes, and breach of contract.

(c) Criminal Matters

White-collar crime consistently has used accountants and auditors in attempts to sort out, assess, and report on financial transactions related to allegations against individuals and companies in a variety of situations, such as arson, shams, fraud, kickbacks, and stock market manipulations. In criminal matters, accountants and auditors as expert witnesses are increasingly important in court cases.

(d) Insurance Claims

Forensic accountants may be required to assess both the integrity and quantum of a claim during the preparation and the assessment of insurance claims on behalf of the insured and insurers. The more significant areas relate to the calculation of loss arising from business interruption, fidelity bond, and personal injury matters. Whereas certain of these cases require financial projections, many need historical analysis on which to base future projections.

(e) Government

Forensic accountants can assist governments to achieve regulatory compliance by ensuring that companies follow the appropriate legislation. Grant and subsidy investigations and public inquiries form a part of this service to government.

In general, forensic accountants are needed when there is a potential perceived or real financial loss or risk of loss.

CHAPTER 6

DOCUMENTING ACCOUNTING INFORMATION SYSTEMS

6.1 INTRODUCTION

This chapter focuses on getting to know the workings of an accounting information system (AIS) and learning tools that can facilitate its documentation. We start by explaining what information is, describing a system, and defining an information system. Then an information system and its components are described in detail, including the various types of information systems, such as management information systems (MIS) and accounting information systems. Then the roles the accounting information system plays within an organization are explained.

Following the description of an AIS is a discussion of the tools, such as flow charts and data flow diagrams, used to analyze and document an information system. Learning the use of such tools is crucial for those charged with the documentation of accounting procedures. Such documentation techniques allow accountants to understand, evaluate, design, and document accounting procedures.

6.2 WHAT IS INFORMATION?

Information is knowledge communicated or received concerning a particular fact or circumstance (a person, place, or thing). Information and data are not the same. Information is data that has been processed or organized into output that is meaningful to those receiving it. Data usually represent observations or measurements of events that can be of importance to potential users upon further processing. Data is the input received by an information system for further processing, after which it converts into information. In contrast to data, information is the processed output that is organized, meaningful, and useful to the person who receives it.

The desirable characteristics of information include:

- Reliability
- Relevance
- Timeliness
- Completeness
- Understandability
- Verifiability

Turning data describing the activities of an organization into information requires the creation of a system, more specifically, an *information* system. Such a system can be defined as a combination of elements or parts forming a complex or unitary whole, an assemblage of a set of correlated members within an organization. In other words, a system is an entity of interrelated components or subsystems that interact to achieve goals. The system's concept requires that alternative courses of action be seen from the standpoint of the system as a whole rather than from that of any of its components or subsystems. The concept of integration is crucial in order for a system to work optimally.

6.3 INFORMATION SYSTEMS

An information system is an organized means of collecting, entering, and processing data. It also is involved with storing, managing, controlling, and reporting information so that an organization can achieve its objectives and goals. The working of an information system therefore may be seen as consisting of four stages: (1) input; (2) processing; (3) storage; and (4) information output. The first three deal with data, while the fourth provides information. There are several ways to classify information systems (IS):

- Formal vs. informal systems. A formal information system is one that has an explicit responsibility to produce information. Accounting, production, and marketing information systems are examples of formal information systems. An informal information system is one that arises out of a need that is not satisfied by a normal channel. The "grapevine" is an example of an informal information system.
- Manual vs. computer-based systems. Manual information systems are those in which the processing tasks are performed by people. Computer-based systems are those in which processing is performed by a computer. The advantages of manual systems are that people are flexible and able to adapt to new situations, but at the same time people can be unreliable and slow. The advantages of computer-based systems are that they are fast and reliable, but they are less flexible and have high initial costs. Furthermore, at a time when technology is changing rapidly, there is a considerable risk of being stuck with a dinosaur of a system when the market provides a more advanced product.
- Mainframe or desktop systems. The systems may be either large or small in scale. Large-scale systems serve many users through a central mainframe computer, while small-scale systems use many personal computers distributed among users. However, thanks to improving technology, personal computers can now be linked to each other and to a common source.

6.4 ROLES PERFORMED BY INFORMATION SYSTEMS

Managers are shooting in the dark without information provided to them from throughout the organization. Individual managers cannot be everywhere, yet they are responsible for what goes on in every niche and corner of their organization. The proverbial buck stops with them. To make up for their inability to be everywhere at the same time, they must rely on information that reports to them the activities and the progress of their organization. By using such a substitute for their physical presence, they can provide surrogate leadership aimed at improving products or services by increasing quality, reducing costs, or adding features. An effective information system can better monitor quality control, improve inventory management, and facilitate the management process.

The ultimate goal of any business is to provide value to its customers. It can do so by enhancing any or all of the value activities that comprise a firm's value chain. In other words, the output of a firm, in the form of goods made or services provided, emerges after going through several stages. At each stage, the work in process assimilates greater value. At the end of the process, having gone through all the intervening steps, the finished product is potentially most valuable. A cake made for a customer becomes most valuable once it is mixed, baked, decorated, and delivered to the customer.

In the following paragraph, a typical organizational value chain is outlined and followed up with a list that supports activities needed for it to function in an optimum manner.

The value chain itself and the necessary support activities correspond to line and staff functions, in the more traditional vocabulary. Five primary value activities in the value chain:

1. Inbound activities—deal with receiving, storing, and distribution of resources.
2. Operation activities—transform raw materials or partially finished goods into final products.
3. Outbound activities—involve distribution of products or services to customers.
4. Marketing and sales activities—meant to ensure that customers learn about the value they will receive by buying given products or services. Customers will not rush to buy if they have no knowledge of the value they will be purchasing.
5. Service activities—deal with repair and maintenance for the products sold. They involve follow-up and learning from the customers how to improve the product or the service.

Four support activities in the value chain:

1. Firm infrastructure—includes the information system
2. Human resources
3. Purchasing—procurement activities related to inbound activities
4. Technology—includes research and development, new computers, and product design

Information systems can provide value in many ways. The more value an information system provides for a given cost to the users, the more likely it is to help the firm stay healthy or overcome its competition. The failure to keep up with rivals can lead a firm to go the way of carrier pigeons.

6.5 LIMITATIONS OF INFORMATION SYSTEMS

Not all information systems are equally good. Such systems can provide better information on a more timely basis, but not all of them do. Among the reasons responsible for the failure of information systems is the tendency to see them only in technical terms. Information systems also must be understood in terms of the organizational contexts within which they operate. The degree of ambiguity fostered by an organization as well as its design cannot but impact the working of an information system. The success of an information system is also dependent on factors such as human relations, social psychology, and cognitive styles of those affected by and in turn affecting the information system.

The failure of information systems to deliver is fostered by the failure to think about the way individuals within an organization actually use the information provided to them by the system. It is also caused by simplistic explanations of the way decisions are made within an organization. The notion promoted in business courses that human beings driven by self-interest will make rational decisions is not always true; too many managers and employees often make seemingly irrational decisions. All too often, decisions get made first and justified later. Such irrational acts occur because the world of an organization is not well planned, nor is the environment within which it works very predictable. Yet the assumptions driving an information system often are based on predictability in a well-defined world.

Information users and producers could learn a lot from the rules governing language-based communication. Language must contend with what is commonly known as denotation and connotation of words. Red is just a color, but it can cause one to think about, among other things, communism. Different individuals see a given event differently. Language-based communication also must grapple with establishment of communicational links between senders and receivers: Speakers must use the language of the listeners in order to be understood. Listeners' comprehension is enhanced if the message they receive happens to be relevant to their concerns. Such linguistic and communicational truisms must be understood by those involved with the design and operations of information systems. Information can mean different things to different individuals; for example, budgets and variance analysis can have different meanings for different individuals within the same organization. Information systems will have greater impact if the output they disperse is understandable, meaningful, and relevant to those receiving it.

6.6 COMPONENTS OF AN INFORMATION SYSTEM

An information system is made of many distinct elements, described as follows.

(a) Objectives

A system cannot be everything to everyone; therefore it should be provided with objectives. Such objectives are related to key financial and operational variables that impact managerial decision making.

(b) Inputs and Outputs

A system receives inputs from throughout the organization, which are then converted into outputs. The input may be time cards of the employee, while the output may be the payroll checks prepared for distribution to employees. Outputs are reports that the system provides after it has converted the data it received from throughout the firm. Output that is later reentered into the system as input is called feedback. Such feedback can take the form of variance analysis, which points out the difference between the budgeted and the actual costs of production, thus helping managers take care of problems preventing the realization of budgetary goals.

(c) Stored Data

In addition to providing periodic reports, a system also builds up its memory, which then allows managers to compare past performance with current activities. The stored data is akin to organizational archives or an individual's memory. When the new inputs are received, an updating of stored data takes place. Such updating is called file maintenance.

(d) Processor

This is the part of the system where inputs are converted to outputs using the technology provided by the system hardware and software. It is the computer, in other words. It is important to remember that a processor's effectiveness is dependent on software packages, without which a computer is no more than inert metal and wires.

(e) Instructions and Procedures

To ensure that the system works as designed, those connected with it must follow instructions and carry out the correct procedures. Otherwise, the integration of the system will fail, and the system will not run as a well-oiled machine.

(f) Boundaries and Constraints

These are the limits within which an information system must operate. Boundaries divide a system from its environment, while constraints are factors, such as capacity, that govern speed and efficiency of the system.

(g) Users

An information system exists in order to satisfy managers' needs for information. While simpler systems have a limited number of users, the same is not true of the more complex systems. Such complex systems must be capable of providing information reports that help a variety of users. Not all managers have the same needs, so an information system must be capable of satisfying their diverse needs. Furthermore, external users of organizational information have needs that are unlike the needs of the internal users.

(h) Security Measures

An information system is a valuable resource both for its technical machinery and for the information that is contained in its files. Steps must be taken to ensure the safety of the machines and what they contain.

(i) Subsystems

Increasingly, systems are becoming very complex. They can be asked to tackle, at the same time and often on an immediate, on-line basis, more than one set of users' needs. This has led to the emergence of systems that combine several subsystems. An example of an information system that contains more than one subsystem is the integrated accounting system, which may contain separate elements to deal with inventory, accounts receivable, and payroll subsystems.

(j) Information Interfaces

These are the shared boundaries at which information passes from one (sub)system to another.

6.7 TYPES OF INFORMATION SYSTEMS

Given the great diversity of information systems, there have evolved many ways to classify them:

- Management information systems (MIS) collect and process data needed to produce information for planning and controlling activities of an organization at all levels of administration.
- Accounting information systems (AISs) are subsets of the MIS that collect and process financial data. An AIS is often the largest subsystem of the MIS; in many organizations, it may be the only formal information system.
- Decision support systems (DSS) help users to make decisions in unstructured environments where there is a high degree of uncertainty. DSSs typically are used on an ad hoc, rather than an ongoing, basis.
- Executive information systems (EISs) provide executives with the information they need to make strategic plans, to control and operate the company, to monitor business conditions in general, and to identify business problems and opportunities. An EIS accepts data from many sources and then combines and summarizes the data so that they can be displayed in an easy-to-understand way. The objective of an EIS is to filter and condense information.
- Expert systems (ESs) support users with the expertise needed to solve specific problems in a well-defined area.
- Office automation systems (OASs) are systems designed to enhance the productivity of information workers through a variety of technologies, including word processing, spreadsheets, databases, and so on.
- End-user systems (EUSs) are information systems developed by users to enhance their personal productivity.

6.8 ACCOUNTING INFORMATION SYSTEMS

While it has all the attributes of an information system, an accounting information system usually is only one among several information systems within an organization. The concern with financial transactions and reporting differentiates an accounting information system from other systems within an organization. However, since very few transactions taking place within an organization lack monetary implications, an AIS can become a means to track almost all of the activities taking place within an organization. While more will be said about AIS throughout the book, here we will describe the system in terms of its users' needs. The accounting information system serves two subsets of users, the internal and the external. We talk about the needs of external users an accounting system must satisfy, then we talk about the needs unique to internal users. The collection of information directed at external users is financial accounting, while that directed at internal users is managerial accounting. Following are two lists that summarize external and internal users and their needs.

External Information Users and Their Needs
- Customers need information about:
  a. account status
  b. discounts available
  c. date payments are due
- Suppliers need information about:
  a. items desired
  b. quantities desired
- Stockholders need information about:
  a. past performance to predict future performance
  b. routine information about dividends and stock transactions
- Employees need information about:
  a. wages, salaries, deductions, etc.
  b. fringe benefits
- Lenders need information about:
  a. ability to meet present obligations
  b. prospects for future success
- Governments need information about:
  a. taxes due
  b. wages paid
  c. regulatory matters

Internal Information Users and Requirements
- Marketing management needs answers to questions about:
  a. pricing of products
  b. discounts, credit terms, and warranty policy
  c. how much to spend on advertising
- Purchasing and inventory control management needs answers to questions about:
  a. how much inventory to purchase
  b. when to purchase inventory
  c. which vendors to use
- Production management needs answers to questions about:
  a. what to produce
  b. when and how much to produce
- Human resource management needs answers to questions about:
  a. how much to pay and deduct from each employee
  b. skill experience of employees
  c. turnover, efficiency, etc.
- Financial managers need answers to questions about:
  a. amount and timing of cash inflows and outflows
  b. planned capital expenditures (amount and timing)

There are two principal differences between internal and external information supplied:

1. Most of the information supplied to external users is mandatory or essential. In contrast, most of the information provided to internal users is discretionary. External reports also must follow a prescribed form and be in keeping with generally accepted accounting principles.

2. Most managerial decisions require more detailed information than is needed for external reporting. Managers need the information as it develops. External reports are prepared long after the transactions being reported in an aggregate form actually occurred.

While there have been calls for separate systems for internal and external users, currently the needs of both are met by the same systems, even though it means the needs of internal users are given a lower priority.

6.9 SUBSYSTEMS OF ACCOUNTING INFORMATION SYSTEMS

Since an AIS can be quite complex, it is best to approach it in terms of its subsystems. We have chosen to divide it into the following elements to better illustrate the roles performed by the accounting information systems:

- Revenue cycle (sales)
- Resources management cycle
- Expenditure cycle
- Financial reporting cycle

Of these elements, the last cycle is unique in that it integrates the financial consequences of the transactions taking place throughout the firm. The activities that are carried out by the firm to raise revenue, procure resources, convert them into products for profitable sales, market them, and reimburse workers all become part of the information flow received and processed by the financial reporting subsystem. Consequently, those people charged with financial reporting are also given the charge of directing the financial aspects arising from a firm's other activities. Establishing credit policies, paying vendors, and reimbursing employees are activities carried out by the accounting department, whose principal task remains the production of financial statements.

6.10 DOCUMENTATION TOOLS AND TECHNIQUES

This section focuses on the tools and techniques used to analyze, develop, document, and evaluate accounting information systems. Such techniques consist of graphical representations as well as narrative descriptions.

Common systems documentation tools are:

- Flow charts
- Data flow diagrams (DFDs)
- Decision tables

- Structured English
- HIPO (hierarchy plus input, process, and output) charts
- Structure charts
- Prototyping
- Narrative/manuals

Accountants and those in charge of writing procedures manuals need to understand these tools because they add value by reducing the time needed to develop, evaluate, and document systems. Data models provide a static view of the data used by a firm. By contrast, flows of data through procedures present a dynamic view. Narrative descriptions often are used to document procedural data flows. Many firms maintain system manuals that are full of such descriptions. While they are useful, narratives should be supplemented by visual representations. Two very suitable techniques for depicting data flows are system flow charts and data flow diagrams, but a variety of other techniques are in use. They range from the very basic to the very detailed.

Visual representations of the greatest interest to accountants are system flow charts—diagrams that pictorially portray the physical flows of data through sequential procedures. They highlight relationships among the elements within transaction processing systems. That is, they provide answers to questions such as:

- What inputs are received and from where?
- What outputs are generated, and what is their form?
- What are the steps involved in the processing sequence?
- What files and accounting records are affected by the processing carried out?
- What type of accounting and organizational controls are employed?

6.11 VARIETIES OF VISUAL REPRESENTATIONS

System flow charts and diagrams can be adapted to emphasize one or more aspects of a transaction processing system. A process flow chart emphasizes the procedural steps. It is therefore useful to systems analysts when they review present procedures for possible improvements. A document flow chart emphasizes the hard-copy inputs and outputs and their flows through organizational units. It is often used by auditors and accountants when analyzing a current system for weaknesses in controls and reports. A computer system flow chart focuses on the computer-based portions of transaction processing systems, including computer runs or steps and accesses of on-line files. The most important use of a computer system flow chart is to document a current procedure or a proposed new or improved procedure.

6.12 FLOW-CHARTING SYMBOLS

The building blocks for a system flow chart are a set of symbols, most of which are generally accepted by accountants and analysts. Exhibit 6–1 displays the set of symbols to be used in this book. These symbols may be grouped as input-output symbols, processing symbols, storage symbols, flow symbols, and miscellaneous symbols. All of the symbols in the exhibit can be drawn with the assistance of a flow-charting template, which is

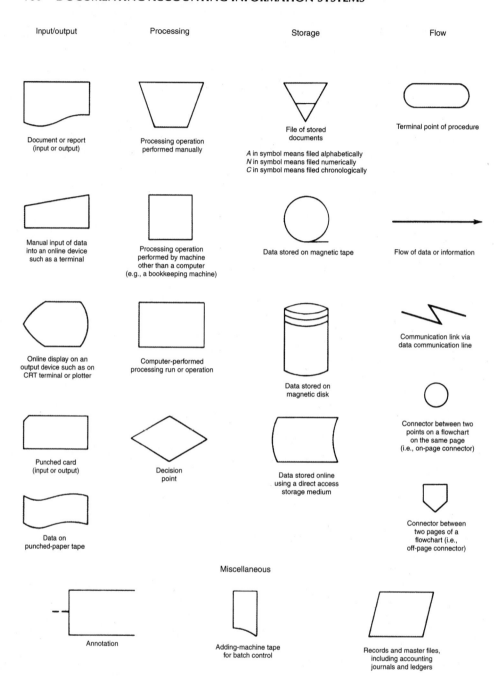

Input/output	Processing	Storage	Flow

Document or report (input or output)

Processing operation performed manually

File of stored documents

A in symbol means filed alphabetically
N in symbol means filed numerically
C in symbol means filed chronologically

Terminal point of procedure

Manual input of data into an online device such as a terminal

Processing operation performed by machine other than a computer (e.g., a bookkeeping machine)

Data stored on magnetic tape

Flow of data or information

Online display on an output device such as on CRT terminal or plotter

Computer-performed processing run or operation

Data stored on magnetic disk

Communication link via data communication line

Punched card (input or output)

Decision point

Data stored online using a direct access storage medium

Connector between two points on a flowchart on the same page (i.e., on-page connector)

Data on punched-paper tape

Connector between two pages of a flowchart (i.e., off-page connector)

Miscellaneous

Annotation

Adding-machine tape for batch control

Records and master files, including accounting journals and ledgers

Exhibit 6–1.　Set of symbols for system flow charting.

Based on American National Standards Institutes, *Standard Flowchart Symbols and Their Use in Information Processing (X3.5)* (New York: ANSI, 1971) and on other sources. Adapted from J. Wilkinson, *Accounting Information System: Essential Concepts & Applications,* 2nd ed. (New York: John Wiley & Sons, 1993).

readily available, or software packages can do it. The following list provides an explanation of the symbols contained in the exhibit:

(a) Input-Output Symbols

The top symbol in the leftmost column represents data on source documents or information on output documents or reports. The second and third symbols reflect the entry of data by keyboards or other on-line means and the display of information on terminal screens or other on-line devices. The term "on-line" refers to devices that are connected directly to a computer system. The last two symbols in the column, involving punched cards and punched paper tape, are seldom used in modern systems.

(b) Processing Symbols

Symbols are available to indicate the processing of data by clerks (trapezoid), noncomputerized machines (square), and computers (rectangle). The decision symbol (diamond) is used to indicate when alternative processing paths exist. For instance, in a flow chart showing sales transaction processing, a decision symbol may be placed at the point just after a credit check. If an ordering customer's credit is found to be satisfactory, one path may lead to continued processing of the order. If the credit is not satisfactory, another path might lead to the writing of a rejection letter.

(c) Storage Symbols

The top symbol (a triangle) is used to show documents and/or records being stored in an off-line storage device, such as a file cabinet or hold basket. Remaining symbols are available to show data being stored on computerized media. The bottom symbol pertains to any on-line storage device, including a magnetic disk.

(d) Data and Information Flow Symbols

The five symbols in the rightmost column provide direction throughout a flow chart. The oval terminal symbol marks a beginning or end point within the flow chart being examined, such as the receipt of an order from a customer. Often a beginning or end point is also a link to an adjoining procedure. The flow line shows the flow of data or information, usually in written form. The communication link symbol (the one that looks like a lightning bolt) represents the electronic flow of data from one physical location to another. Finally, two connector symbols are available to provide further linkages. The on-page connector (circle) is used within a single page of a flow chart, while the off-page connector (like homeplate) links two pages of a multipage flow chart.

(e) Miscellaneous Symbols

The annotation symbol (open-ended rectangle) can be connected to any symbol within a flow chart; its purpose is to provide space for a note concerning the procedure. For instance, it could indicate how often a particular processing step takes place, or who performs it. The remaining two symbols are useful in flow charts portraying transaction processing through the accounting cycle. The parallelogram, for instance, is a specialized symbol that adds clarity to journalizing and ledger posting steps.

6.13 FLOW-CHARTING A PROCESS

To help illustrate flow-charting, we will demonstrate it by using it to visually represent a common accounting procedure. The process begins with the following narrative describing the purchasing procedure for the Easybuy Company.

A clerk in the accounting department periodically reviews the inventory records in order to determine which items need reordering. If the quantity on hand for a particular item has fallen below a preestablished reorder point, the clerk prepares a prenumbered purchase requisition in two copies. The original is sent to the purchasing department, where a buyer (1) decides on a suitable supplier by reference to a supplier file and (2) prepares a prenumbered purchase order in four copies. The original copy of the purchase order is signed by the purchasing manager/supervisor and mailed to the selected vendor. The second copy is returned to the inventory clerk in the accounting department, who pulls the matching requisition copy from a temporary file (where it has been filed chronologically), posts the ordered quantities to the inventory records, and files the purchase requisition and order together. The third copy is forwarded to the receiving department, where it is filed numerically to await the receipt of the ordered goods. The fourth copy is filed numerically, together with the original copy of the purchase requisition, in an open purchase order file. When the invoice from the supplier arrives, this last copy will be entered into the accounts payable procedure.

Several features of this procedure should be noted. It involves manual processing of transactions, which moves among three departments and generates documents having several copies. A system flow chart can present all these features in a clear manner by blending the features of a document flow chart with those of a process flow chart. Such a blended flow chart can be called a document system flow chart.

In order to plan a flow chart of this type, we begin by deciding that three organizational units are to be involved in the procedure. Then we section a sheet of paper into three columns, which we label "Accounting Department," "Purchasing Department," and "Receiving Department." Next, we select those symbols that pertain to manual processing, which will be combined in strict accordance with the sequence of the narrative.

For convenience, the work is subdivided into four key steps or functions. Each is discussed and then visually represented in Exhibits 6–2, 6–3, 6–4, and 6–5, respectively.

(a) Preparation of the Purchase Requisition

The first step is the preparation of a purchase requisition. It consists of the following steps:

1. As the beginning segment shows, the flow-charted procedure begins in the accounting department with a terminal symbol.
2. This symbol is connected by a flowline to a clerical or manual processing symbol.
3. Inserted inside this second symbol is a notation that briefly states the actions taken by the inventory clerk.
4. To explain the basis on which the clerk prepares the document labeled "Purchase requisition," an annotation symbol is also attached to the manual processing symbol.

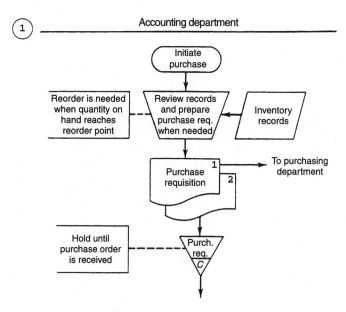

Exhibit 6–2.   Diagram depicting the preparation of the purchase requisition.
Adapted from J. Wilkinson, *Accounting Information System: Essential Concepts and Applications,* 2nd ed. (New York: John Wiley & Sons , 1993).

5. Another flowline connects an accounting record symbol, labeled "Inventory records," to the manual processing symbol. This connection from the inventory records to the manual processing symbol denotes that inventory data on file are used during the preparation of the purchase requisition.

6. A flowline from the manual processing to the document symbol indicates that a purchase requisition, in two copies, is an output from the processing step. Note that when multiple copies of a form are prepared, they are numbered and shown in an offset manner.

7. The final function of this flowchart segment is to show the disposition of the two copies of the purchase requisition. A flowline pointing to the right directs copy 1 to the purchasing department, whereas a downward flowline indicates that copy 2 is filed in a folder. The letter C in the file symbol means that copy 2 is arranged chronologically (by date) within the file. Note that it is not necessary to show a processing symbol that specifies a filing action between the document and the file.

(b) Preparation of a Purchase Order

The second step in the process consists of preparing a purchase order. To do so, the following steps are undertaken:

1. The activity in the second segment also centers on a manual processing symbol. Two flowlines lead to this processing symbol, one from the first copy of the purchase requisition and the other from the supplier file.

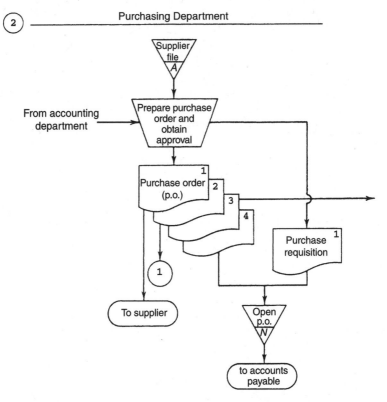

Exhibit 6–3.   Diagram depicting the preparation of the purchase order.

Adapted from J. Wilkinson, *Accounting Information System: Essential Concepts and Applications,* 2nd ed. (New York: John Wiley & Sons, 1993).

2. Based on data from these two sources, a buyer in the purchasing department prepares a purchase order in four copies. Again, a flowline pointing from the processing symbol to the document symbol(s) designates the latter as being an output.

3. Another "output" flowing from the processing symbol is copy 1 of the purchase requisition. Since it entered the processing symbol, as noted by the flowline from the accounting department, it also must leave the processing symbol. As the segment shows, it is then deposited in the open purchase order file. An important rule of flow-charting is to show the final disposition of every copy.

4. The remainder of this flow chart segment depicts the disposition of the four purchase order copies.

   a. Copy 1 is mailed to the supplier. Since this mailing ends the treatment of copy 1 (as far as the flow chart is concerned), this is dictated by means of a terminal symbol. (Alternatively, we could have added a column on the flow chart labeled "Supplier" and shown the flow of copy 1 to that column. However, a column is necessary only if processing steps are to be shown within the column.)

   b. Copy 2 terminates with an on-page connector labeled "1." The next segment will continue the disposition of copy 2.

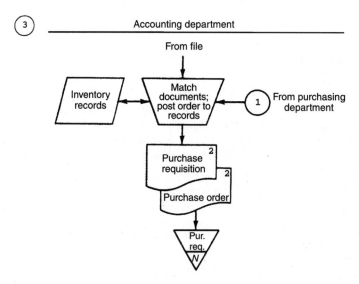

Exhibit 6–4.   Diagram depicting the process of updating the inventory record.

Adapted from J. Wilkinson, *Accounting Information System: Essential Concepts and Applications,* 2nd ed. (New York: John Wiley & Sons, 1993).

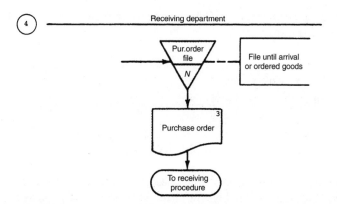

Exhibit 6–5.   Diagram depicting the process of filing of receiving department's copy of the purchase order.

Adapted from J. Wilkinson, *Accounting Information System: Essential Concepts and Applications,* 2nd ed. (New York: John Wiley & Sons, 1993).

    c. Copy 3 is directed to the receiving department.

    d. Copy 4 is filed together with copy 1 of the purchase requisition.

5. The terminal symbol below the file indicates that the filed copies will be used in the accounts payable procedure. Note that a column has not been allotted on this flow chart for the accounts payable department, since the department is not involved in the processing being portrayed.

6. One additional flow-charting convention is illustrated in this segment. When flow-lines cross, a symbol called a "jumper" denotes the crossover.

(c) Updating the Inventory Records

The third stage in the process consists of updating the inventory records, which in turn depends on the following steps.

1. This flow-chart segment, like the first segment, is located organizationally in the accounting department. Both copy 2 of the purchase requisition and copy 2 of the purchase order enter into the processing. The former is pulled from the file folder, while the latter arrives from the purchasing department. Note that the on-page connector in effect links to the on-page connector shown in the previous segment.

2. Processing is performed by the inventory clerk, who matches the documents, accesses the proper inventory records, posts the ordered quantities, and then replaces the posted inventory records within the inventory file. A bidirectional flowline (i.e., one with arrowheads on both ends) symbolically represents these accessing, posting, and replacing actions.

3. As the last step in this segment, the two documents leave the processing symbol and flow into a file. Note that when two or more documents move together, a single flowline is sufficient to represent both.

(d) Filing Receiving Department's Copy of the Purchase Order

The last stage of the process consists of disposal of the third copy of the purchase order. To do so, the following steps are taken:

1. In this brief segment, copy 3 of the purchase order is placed temporarily into a file maintained in the receiving department.

2. On the arrival of the ordered inventory goods, the copy is withdrawn (pulled) and entered into the receiving procedure.

3. Since the receiving procedure is shown on a different flow chart, a terminal symbol is employed to denote the interface with that procedure.

Exhibit 6–6 combines the four segments just described into a system flow chart of the purchases procedure. A variation of this flow chart, which omits the columns for organizational units, appears in Exhibit 6–7. Between them the various figures show the diversity of visual representations using flow diagrams.

6.14 GUIDELINES FOR PREPARING FLOW CHARTS

Given that different experts can draw a given process differently, it is imperative to have some guidelines. Good flow charts result from sound practices consistently followed. Sound practices should be grounded on the following six guidelines:

1. Carefully read the narrative description of the procedure to be flow-charted. Determine from the facts the usual or normal steps in the procedure, and focus on these steps when preparing the flow chart.

2. Choose the size of paper to be used. Either use letter size (8 1/2 × 11 in.) or a larger size. Then gather materials such as pencils, erasers, and a flow-charting template.

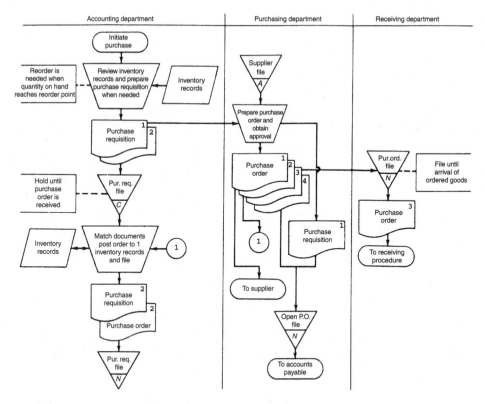

Exhibit 6–6.   Document flow chart of a manually performed purchases procedure.

Adapted from J. Wilkinson, *Accounting Information System: Essential Concepts and Applications,* 2nd ed. (New York: John Wiley & Sons, 1993).

3. Select the flow-charting symbols to be used. The variety of symbols used should be limited for clarity.

4. Prepare a rough flow chart sketch as a first draft. Attempting to draw a finished flow chart during the first effort usually results in a poorer final product.

5. Review your sketch to be sure that the following have been accomplished:

   a. The flows begin at the upper left-hand corner of the sheet and generally move from left to right and from top to bottom.

   b. All steps are clearly presented in a sequence or a series of sequences. No obvious gaps in the procedure should be present.

   c. Symbols are used consistently throughout. Thus, the symbol for manual processing (an inverted trapezoid) should appear each time that a clerk performs a step in the procedure.

   d. The dispositions of all documents and reports are shown. In fact, the final "resting place" of every copy of every prepared document should be specified. Typical dispositions include placing documents in files, sending documents to outside parties such as customers, forwarding documents to connecting procedures (i.e., a general ledger procedure), distributing reports to managers, and even destroying documents.

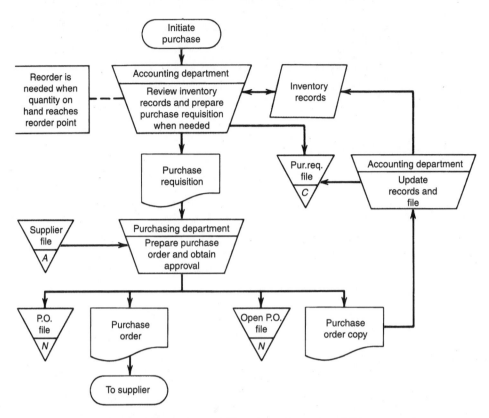

Exhibit 6–7.   Variation of the document flow chart shown in Exhibit 6–6.

Adapted from J. Wilkinson, *Accounting Information System: Essential Concepts and Applications,* 2nd ed. (New York: John Wiley & Sons, 1993).

e. The "sandwich" rule is consistently applied. This rule states that a processing symbol should be sandwiched between an input symbol and an output symbol.

f. When a document crosses an organizational line within the flow chart, the document is normally pictured again in the new organizational unit. However, the repetition is not necessary in some instances if the organizational units are adjacent.

g. All symbols contain brief but specific labels written inside the symbols. For instance, "Sales invoice" might appear inside a document symbol. Do not simply write "Document" inside a document symbol, since the shape of the symbol indicates its nature. When lengthy labels are needed, draw the symbols large enough to contain the labels completely. That is, the size of a symbol may vary without affecting its meaning.

h. Multiple copies of documents are drawn as an overlapping group and are numbered in the upper right-hand corners; these numbers remain with the copies during their flows through the procedure.

i. Added comments are included within annotation symbols and are attached to appropriate symbols, such as the processing symbols to which the comments relate.

j. Ample connections (cross-references) are provided. The symbols used in forming the connections depend on the situation. Thus, if two sheets are needed to contain the flow chart, the flows between pages are formed by off-page connector symbols. In those cases where the procedure being flow-charted links to an adjoining procedure, the connection can be formed by a terminal symbol.

k. Exceptional occurrences, such as backorders, are clearly noted. They may appear as: (i) comments within annotation symbols, (ii) separate flow charts, with references to the main flow chart, or (iii) decision branches.

l. Special presentation techniques are adopted when their use increases both the content and clarity of the procedure. An apt illustration of this rule is the portrayal of batch control totals in computer-based batch processing systems. Batch control totals generally are computed from key data in each batch of transactions prior to processing runs. Then during each processing run the totals are recomputed and compared to the precomputed totals. These run-to-run comparisons may be performed at the direction of the computer processing programs, and the results may be shown on printed exception and summary reports. If the results show differences in the totals, the differences must be located before processing can continue. This batch control procedure may be diagrammed with the help of dashed lines that depict the run-to-run comparisons with the precomputed totals.

6. Complete the flow chart in final form. A finished flow chart should be neatly drawn and uncrowded. Normally it also should contain a title, the date, and the name(s) of the preparers.

6.15 DATA FLOW DIAGRAMS

Unlike flow charts, data flow diagrams emphasize the logical view of data rather than the physical view. That is, they focus on what happens rather than on the mechanics of how it happens. While both are visual representations of procedures used within an organization, differences exist between them: DFDs emphasize the flow of data, while flow charts emphasize the flow of documentation. DFDs concentrate on *what happens,* but flow charts focus on *how* the processing of data into information occurs. DFDs use only four basic symbols, but flow charts use many more. DFDs leave out the timing or sequence of data processing steps; in contrast, flow charts show both the timing and the sequence of steps that occur during the process.

A system flow chart clearly indicates how data are being processed, for example, manually or with the aid of computers. It also specifies certain physical aspects. For instance, a flow chart may portray the storage media as being file cabinets or magnetic disks and the input method as being documents on hard copy or data entry screens. In contrast, a data flow diagram emphasizes the specific data and what is being done to that data. The diagram reveals the content of data flows, the processes involving data, the stores of data, and the sources and destinations of data. Because of this simplified focus, only four symbols are needed.

The two techniques also differ with respect to their roles. A system flow chart is mainly used to document the physical elements of an AIS, either the system that is currently in use or a newly designed system. However, a data flow diagram is better suited for analyzing a processing system. That is, it allows systems analysts and accountants to visualize the essential flows and processes without being concerned about the physical design features.

The four symbols used to draw data flow diagrams include rectangles, circles, pairs of parallel lines, and curved lines with arrowheads. The rectangle represents an entity that is a source or destination of data residing outside the system being diagrammed. Examples of sources (and also destinations) are customers, suppliers, banks, and managers. The circle (also called a bubble) represents a process that transforms data inflows into data outflows. An example is the process of handling incoming cash receipts. A pair of parallel lines represents a data store, that is, a place where data can be kept. An example is a file of cash receipts transaction data. A curved line having an arrowhead represents a data flow. It may connect together any of the above symbols, but at least one end of the flow generally is connected to a process, shown as a circle.

6.16 ILLUSTRATING DATA FLOW DIAGRAMS

A data flow diagram is in reality a hierarchical set of diagrams. Each diagram in the set is a decomposition (in effect, an "explosion") of the preceding diagram. In other words, each succeeding diagram provides a greater degree of detail concerning a process. Data flow diagrams within a set may delve deeper and deeper until extremely detailed views appear.

The example of a sales process will consist of only two levels, as depicted in Exhibits 6–8 and 6–9. The diagram in the former is called a context diagram. It is the top level of a set of data flow diagrams, since the process is encompassed within a single circle. The four entities shown in the diagram are outside the scope of the process being documented. Two of the entities (the customer and credit department) serve as both sources and destinations with respect to data involved in the sales process. One of the entities (the

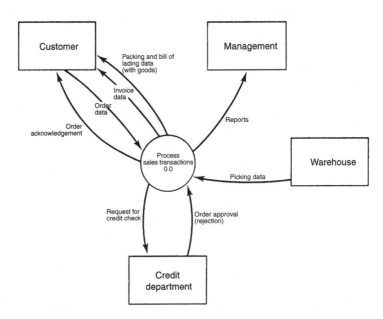

Exhibit 6–8.   Context diagram depicting the process of a sales transaction.

Adapted from J. Wilkinson, *Accounting Information System: Essential Concepts and Applications,* 2nd ed. (New York: John Wiley & Sons, 1993).

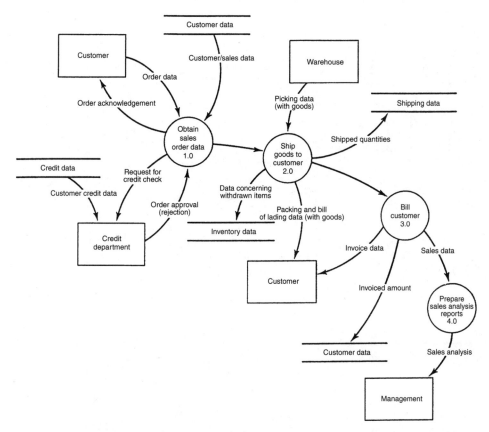

Exhibit 6–9. Data flow diagram (level 1) of the four major subactivities in processing sales transactions.

Adapted from J. Wilkinson, *Accounting Information System: Essential Concepts & Applications,* 2nd ed. (New York: John Wiley & Sons, 1993).

management) is only a destination (i.e., a recipient of data and information) from the process. Yet another (the warehouse) is only a source. Notice that the type of data involved in each flow is written along the flowline. Also note that no data stores appear on this diagram, since they are incorporated within the process itself.

The second data flow diagram, Exhibit 6–9, shows certain details of the sales process. It contains four subprocesses, numbered 1.0, 2.0, 3.0, and 4.0. Because of the zeros following the decimal points, this level just below the context diagram is called the level-zero data flow diagram. Included with the subprocesses are four data stores (customer, inventory, shipping, and credit data) and a variety of data flows.

Additional data flow diagrams can be prepared to show more details concerning each process. For instance, a level 1 diagram of the "obtain sales order data" would include sub-subprocesses shown by circles coded 1.1, 1.2, 1.3, and so on; level 2 diagrams would show sub-sub-subprocesses detailing each of these sub-subprocesses. An illustration showing the context diagram, level 0 and level 1 of the registration process in a college, is shown in Exhibit 6–10.

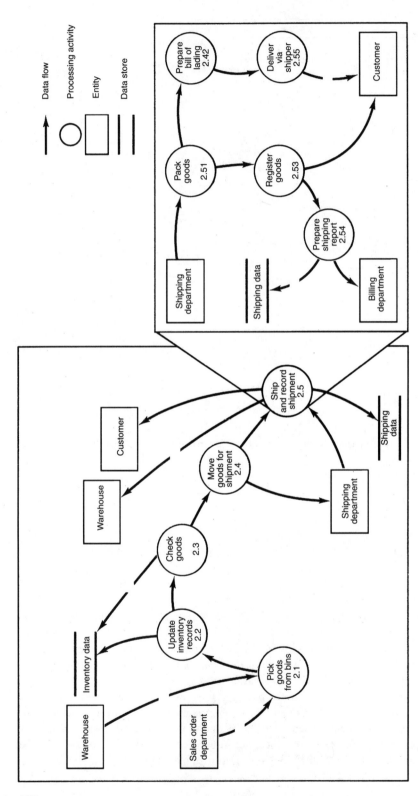

Exhibit 6–10. Two levels of data flow diagrams.

Adapted from a transparency for use with J. Wilkinson, *Accounting Information System: Essential Concepts & Applications*, 2nd ed. (New York: John Wiley & Sons, 1993).

To summarize, the data flow diagrams are a logical representation of data flows that focuses on a process. A variation of this type of representation, called a physical data flow diagram, specifies where or by whom the processes are performed. It also may indicate how the processing is performed.

6.17 GUIDELINES FOR PREPARING DATA FLOW DIAGRAMS

Effective data flow diagrams also require established guidelines. The exhibits used to illustrate data flow diagrams follow several guidelines that should be helpful when you prepare data flow diagrams:

1. Begin with a context diagram that shows the interactions of the selected process with the outside entities. Include all interactions as separate data flowlines, even though there may be more than one flow from the process to an outside entity, or vice versa. Include in the context diagram only those outside entities that are directly involved in data flows to or from the process.

2. Then break the context diagram into a data flow diagram at the zero level. Verify that the data flows are balanced between the context diagram and the level-zero diagram. That is, make sure that all of the data flows in the context diagram also appear in the level-zero diagram.

3. "Explode" the subprocesses in the level-zero diagram into successively more detailed sub-subprocesses in level-1 diagrams, level-2 diagrams, level-3 diagrams, and so on. Continue the balancing of data flows between successive levels, for example, between the level-zero diagram and its set of "exploded" diagrams at level 1. To check that the diagrams are balanced, first verify that all of the outside entities have been carried to the lower level, such as from level zero to level 1. Then count the data flows between each outside entity and the subprocesses in the diagrams.

4. Do not incorporate too many details into any single diagram. For instance, limit each detailed diagram to only a few circles, probably no more than six or seven.

5. Code the sub-subprocesses carefully in each detailed diagram, so that they can be identified easily with their "parent" subprocess. For instance, if three subprocesses are coded as 1.0, 2.0, and 3.0, the sub-subprocesses for 1.0 would be 1.1, 1.2, 1.3, and so on; the sub-subprocesses for 2.0 would be 2.1, 2.2, 2.3, and so on; and the sub-subprocesses for 3.0 would be 3.1, 3.2, 3.3, and so on. In turn, those for 1.1 would begin as 1.11, 1.12, and 1.13.

6. In instances where multiple entities function in the same manner, use a single encompassing label to represent all. For instance, the reference to "customer" in the example means all customers.

7. Where multiple entities function differently, use separate boxes. For instance, assume that a process involves both credit and cash customers, and that the processing steps relating to credit customers are different from those for cash customers. Separate boxes, labeled "credit customer" and "cash customer," should be employed.

8. Do not allow data flowlines to cross over each other. To avoid crossovers, repeat an entity box or data store symbol as necessary in a single data flow diagram.

9. Show only normal processing sequences in a single data flow diagram. That is, avoid exceptional situations or show them as a separate set of data flow diagrams.

10. Show process circles that progress generally from left to right and from top to bottom in a single data flow diagram. The first circle (1.0) appears near the upper left and the last circle (4.0) appears near the lower right.

These guidelines are further illustrated in the exhibits. They carry the analysis to more than one level.

6.18 ADDITIONAL TECHNIQUES

This section takes a brief look at some of the newer documentation tools that have emerged to ameliorate some of the difficulties encountered while working with flow charts.

Decision tables are a tabular alternative to a program flow chart, and can help further clarify a given process. There are four parts to a decision table:

1. The condition stub contains a row for each logical condition for which the input data will be tested.

2. The condition entry consists of a set of vertical columns that specify a pattern of yes, no, or not relevant for the set of tests in the condition stub.

3. The action stub lists the actions to be taken.

4. The action entry links which actions should be taken with the pattern specified in the condition entry.

A fairly basic example of a decision table is given in Exhibit 6–11. In Exhibit 6–12 an alternative to a decision table is exemplified.

Sometimes called pseudocode, structured English is a narrative alternative to a program flow chart. It can be used by systems designers to communicate with programmers, since it is easy to understand. It reduces the time required to code a program. A fairly basic example of structured English is given in Exhibit 6–13.

HIPO charts are yet another tool. HIPO is an acronym for *h*ierarchy plus *i*nput, *p*rocess, and *o*utput. It shows the modular design of a system and its components. HIPO

Purchase Discounts Allowed	1	2	3
Purchase > $10,000	Y	N	N
Purchase $5,000 to $10,000		Y	N
Purchase < $5,000			Y
Take 5% discount	1		
Take 3% discount		1	
Pay full amount			1

Exhibit 6–11.   Decision table showing purchase discount procedures.

Adapted from J. Burch and G. Grudnitski, *Information Systems,* 5th ed. (New York: John Wiley & Sons, 1989).

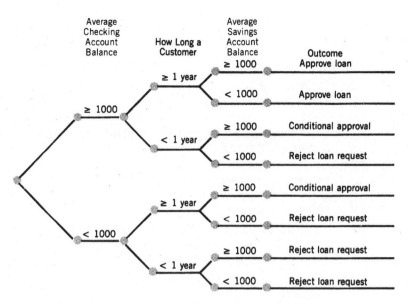

Average Checking Account Balance	How Long a Customer	Average Savings Account Balance	Outcome
	≥ 1 year	≥ 1000	Approve loan
		< 1000	Approve loan
≥ 1000	< 1 year	≥ 1000	Conditional approval
		< 1000	Reject loan request
	≥ 1 year	≥ 1000	Conditional approval
		< 1000	Reject loan request
< 1000	< 1 year	≥ 1000	Reject loan request
		< 1000	Reject loan request

Exhibit 6–12.   Decision tree describing the loan approval process.

Adapted from J. Burch and G. Grudnitski, *Information Systems,* 5th ed. (New York: John Wiley & Sons, 1989).

charts are another alternative to program flow charts. There are two advantages to such use of HIPO charts. First, they are easy to create and understand because they focus more on the logic rather than the mechanics of what is to be accomplished. They also focus on the process and how its various components are related to each other. Doing this allows one to see the trees as well as the forest. An illustration is in Exhibit 6–14.

Structure charts display the structure of systems application. Exhibit 6–15 is a good example of a structure chart describing the payment of accounts payable. Prototyping is another technique that seeks to represent perceived users' requirements. If the first set of requirements is not acceptable, then another set is drawn up. The process continues until an acceptable prototype emerges. Exhibit 6–16 describes prototyping.

6.19 NARRATIVE DOCUMENTATION OF INFORMATION SYSTEMS

In addition to flow charts and data flow diagrams, an information system needs further documentation. Such documentation consists of manuals and other means of describing the information system and its operations. It also should include those aspects of a firm that have an impact on the system, such as policy statements, organizational charts, and job descriptions. Ordinarily, the documentation of a manual accounting information system should be the same as accounting procedures documentation. However, since very few accounting systems in use by organizations of any substance are totally manual anymore, a major segment of documentation is devoted to describing the technical aspects of the system. Here the documentation refers to technical aspects of the accounting system and not to the documentation of accounting procedures, the subject of this book. It is important to recognize, however, that similar considerations govern both kinds of documentation.

```
ORDER ENTRY:
*Process customer and item file;
  FOR ALL orders
      Access CUSTOMER record;
      IF CUSTOMER NUMBER is valid
          Access ORDER form;
      ELSE
          Issue "invalid customer code" message;
          STOP ORDER ENTRY;
      ENDIF;
      FOR ALL items ordered
          Access ITEM record;
          IF ITEM NUMBER is valid
              IF QUANTITY ON HAND GE QUANTITY ORDERED
                  Enter ORDER;
                  Decrease QUANTITY ON HAND by
                      QUANTITY ORDERED;
              ELSE
                  Access BACKORDER form;
                  Write BACKORDER;
              ENDIF;
          ELSE
              Issue "invalid item code" message;
          ENDIF;
      ENDFOR;
      Access SHIPPING DOCUMENT form;
      Enter shipping data;
      Print documents;
  ENDFOR;
EXIT ORDER ENTRY.
```

Exhibit 6–13.   Example of order entry procedure using structural English.
Adapted from J. Burch and G. Grudnitski, *Information Systems,* 5th ed. (New York: John Wiley & Sons, 1989).

System documentation also can be an important cog in the internal control structure pertaining to an information system. Auditors are able to examine the internal control system more quickly and thoroughly. Consequently, a general control objective is to prepare complete and clear system documentation and to maintain it in an up-to-date condition. It helps employees to understand and interpret policies and procedures. Data processing clerks are more likely to perform their appointed tasks correctly and consistently if they know what they are. Systems analysts and programmers can redesign transaction processing systems more easily and reliably, especially when the original designers have left the firm.

A description of the typical documentations needed by manual and computerized systems follows. Each has different needs, while they also have a great deal in common.

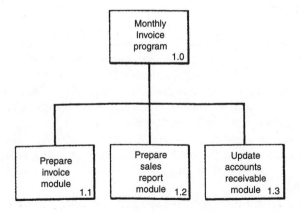

Exhibit 6–14. HIPO visual table of contents.
Adapted from J. Burch and G. Grudnitski, *Information Systems,* 5th ed. (New York: John Wiley & Sons, 1989).

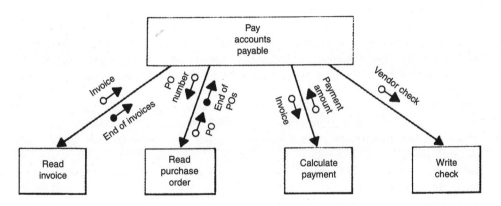

Exhibit 6–15. Structure chart.
Adapted from J. Burch and G. Grudnitski, *Information Systems,* 5th ed. (New York: John Wiley & Sons, 1989).

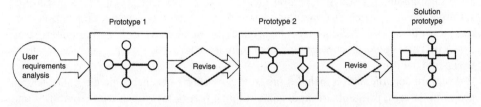

Exhibit 6–16. Flow chart showing prototype iteration until acceptable prototype is achieved.
Adapted from J. Burch and G. Grudnitski, *Information Systems,* 5th ed. (New York: John Wiley & Sons, 1989).

6.20 MANUAL SYSTEMS

Documentation for manual systems should include all of the usual components associated with accounting systems: source documents, journals, ledgers, reports, document outputs, charts of accounts, audit trail details, procedural steps, record layouts, data dictionaries, and control procedures. Numerous examples should be provided, such as typical accounting entries and filled-in source documents. Procedures should be documented by narrative descriptions, system flow charts, and data flow diagrams.

Equally necessary are those elements related to the effective operation of the system. Clear policy statements encourage employees to adhere to management's policies. An organization chart and job descriptions inform employees of their roles and responsibilities with respect to data processing.

Since a manual system does not have to reckon with the mechanics of computer-based processing, its documentation is simpler. Indeed, it is no different from basic accounting manuals containing procedures and policies in effect. But once computers are introduced, additional documentation specific to the computers and the constraints they impose is required.

6.21 COMPUTER-BASED SYSTEMS

All of the documentation appropriate to manual systems is needed in computer-based systems. Even the most automated system contains some manual processing steps and involves interactions with human users and clerks. However, additional documentation is needed because complex hardware and nonvisible programs are used.

Computer-related documentation concerns the computer system itself and the people who interface with it. In the former category are the overall system standards, system application documentation, program documentation, and data documentation. In the latter category are operating documentation and user documentation. Although the contents of each type of documentation will differ as circumstances dictate, the following descriptions represent a reasonable coverage. Exhibit 6–17 itemizes the array of documentation needed in a computer-based system.

System standards consist of policy statements pertaining to systems development and other system-related matters. For instance, a systems development standard might describe suitable methods and procedures for analyzing, designing, and implementing information system modules. One firm's standard might specify, for example, the use of techniques such as data flow diagrams and entity-relationship diagrams.

System application documentation includes the purpose of the application and descriptive materials such as computer system flow charts, input-output descriptions, error procedures, and the components needed for manual as well as computer-based systems. This type of documentation is of primary interest to systems analysts, systems users, and auditors.

Program documentation includes program flow charts or other logic diagrams, source program listings, printouts of inputs and outputs, record layouts or data structures, and information pertaining to operations, testing, changes, and errors. Program documentation is usually organized around individual programs and packaged into run manuals. In the case of applications programs, program documentation may be combined with system application documentation. It is of primary interest to programmers; however,

System Standards Documentation
Systems development policy statements
Program testing policy statements
Computer operations policy statements
Security and disaster policy statements

System Application Documentation
Computer system flow charts
Data flow diagrams
Narrative descriptions of procedures
Input/output descriptions, including filled-in source documents
Formats of journals, ledgers, reports, and other outputs
Details concerning audit trails
Charts of accounts
File descriptions, including record layouts and data dictionaries
Error messages and formats
Error-correction procedures
Control procedures

Program Documentation
Program flow charts, decision tables, data structure diagrams
Source program listings
Inputs, formats, and sample filled-in forms
Printouts of reports, listings, and other outputs
Operating instructions
Test data and testing procedures
Program change procedures
Error listings

Data Documentation
Descriptions of data elements, including names, field sizes, and so on
Relationships of specific data elements to other data elements

Operating Documentation
Performance instructions for executing computer programs
Required input/output files for specific programs
Setup procedures for specific programs
List of programmed halts, including related messages and required operator actions,
    for specific programs
Recovery and restart procedures for specific programs
Estimated run times of specific programs
Distribution of reports generated by specific programs

User Documentation
Procedures for entering data on source documents
Checks of input data for accuracy and completeness
Formats and uses of reports
Possible error messages and correction procedures

Exhibit 6–17. Table of types of documentation needed in computer-based systems.

Adapted from J. Wilkinson, *Accounting Information System: Essential Concepts and Applications,* 2nd ed. (New York: John Wiley & Sons, 1993).

Element or Activity	Manual System Characteristics	Computer-Based System		
		Characteristics	Risk Exposures	Compensating Controls
Data collection	Data recorded on paper source documents	Data sometimes captured without use of source documents	Audit trail may be partially lost	Printed copies of source documents prepared by computer system
	Data reviewed for errors by clerks	Data often not subject to review by clerks	Errors, accidental or deliberate, may be entered for processing	Edit checks performed by computer system
Data processing	Processing steps performed by clerks who possess judgment	Processing steps performed by CPU "blindly" in accordance with program instructions	Errors may cause incorrect results of processing	Outputs reviewed by users of computer system; carefully developed computer processing programs
	Processing steps spread among various clerks in separate departments	Processing steps concentrated within computer CPU	Unauthorized manipulation of data and theft of assets can occur on larger scale	Restricted access to computer facilities; clear procedure for authorizing changes to programs
	Processing requires use of journals and ledgers	Processing does not require use of journals	Audit trail may be partially lost	Printed journals and other analyses
	Processing performed relatively slowly	Processing performed very rapidly	Effects of errors may spread rapidly throughout files	Editing of all data during input and processing steps
Data storage and retrieval	Data stored in file drawers throughout the various departments	Data compressed on magnetic media (e.g., tapes, disks)	Data may be accessed by unauthorized persons or stolen	Security measures at points of access and over data library
	Data stored on hard copies in human-readable form	Data stored in invisible, erasable, computer-readable form	Data are temporarily unusable by humans and might possibly be lost	Data files printed periodically; backups of files; protection against sudden power losses
	Stored data accessible on a piecemeal basis at various locations	Stored data often readily accessible from various locations via terminals	Data may be accessed by unauthorized persons	Security measures at points of access
Information generation	Outputs generated laboriously and usually in small volumes	Outputs generated quickly and neatly, often in large volumes	Inaccuracies may be buried in impressive-looking outputs that users accept on faith	Reviews by users of outputs, including the checking of amounts
	Outputs usually in hard copy form	Outputs provided in various forms, including soft copy displays and voice responses	Information stored on magnetic media is subject to modification (only hard copy provides permanent record)	Backups of files; periodic printing of stored files onto hard copy records
Transmission of data and information	Usually transmitted via postal service and hand delivery	Often transmitted by communications lines	Data may be accessed or modified or destroyed by unauthorized persons	Security measures over transmission lines; coding of data; verification of transmitted data
Equipment	Relatively simple, inexpensive, and mobile	Relatively complex, expensive, and in fixed locations	Business operations may be intentionally or unintentionally interrupted; data or hardware may be destroyed; operations may be delayed through inefficiencies	Backup of data and power supply and equipment; preventive maintenance of equipment; restrictions on access to computer facilities; documentation of equipment usage and processing procedures

Exhibit 6–18.   Table of control problems caused by computerization.

Adapted from J. Wilkinson, *Accounting Information System: Essential Concepts and Applications*, 2nd ed. (New York: John Wiley & Sons, 1993).

database administrators have concerns with respect to data manipulation language verbs that alter data. Auditors also may need to review program documentation to detect unauthorized changes to programs, as reflected in program listings and printouts of outputs.

Data documentation includes the descriptions of data elements stored within the firm's database, including their relationships. This type of documentation, usually incorporated within a data dictionary, is of particular importance to database administrators and auditors. It is also of interest to application programmers, but only insofar as it relates to the data elements required by the programs that they develop or change.

Operating documentation includes all of the performance instructions needed to execute computer programs, plus instructions for distributing the outputs. Operating documentation, generally organized into console run books, is of primary interest to computer operators, since they need very explicit directions. Note, however, that operating documentation does not contain program flow charts and listings, since operators should not be informed of the detailed logic of the programs that process data.

User documentation includes instructions for entering data on source documents, information relating to the formats and uses of reports, and procedures for checking for and correcting errors in data. User documentation is of primary interest to user-department clerks and managers.

6.22 ADDITIONAL DOCUMENTATION NEEDED

The system documentation also must address problems caused by the introduction of computers within the accounting systems. Such problems could occur in the context of collections, processing, storage, and retrieval of data as well as the generation and transmission of information. Alternatively, problems could occur because of the equipment itself.

The existence of documentation allows these problems to be addressed more effectively. The fact is, no system is immune to such problems. What can go wrong eventually will go wrong, but dealing with the unpleasant or unexpected is easier if documentation anticipating the problems exists.

Exhibits 6–18 and 6–19 suggest the documentation needed if a system is to be ready for the unforeseen. The first is a listing of control problems caused by computerization; the second lists selected security measures needed to protect the system resources from an assortment of dangers.

6.23 CONCLUSION

This chapter examined the nature of an accounting information system and studied the tools that help to analyze and document the system. To better appreciate and communicate the working of an accounting information system, and in fact to better design one, it is helpful to ask a series of questions pertaining to how the system works and what it supplies, namely information. Such questions can be: Why is information needed? Where does that information come from? Who decides what information is relevant for a particular purpose? How is such a decision made? Who is going to use the information, and who is going to develop it? What steps are required in order to obtain the relevant information

Purpose of Security Measures	Physical Noncomputer Resources in Both Manual and Computer-Based Systems	Hardware Facilities of Computer-Based Systems	Data in Computer-Based Systems
1. Protect from theft or access by unauthorized persons	Security guards Fenced-in areas Burglar alarms Television monitors Safes and vaults Locked cash registers Lockboxes Close supervision Insurance coverage Logs and registers	Security guards Television monitors Locked doors Locked terminals Inaccessible terminals Employee badges Passwords Segregated test terminals	Locked doors, terminals, stacks of blank forms Off-line data library On-line data and program storage partitions Encoded data Paper shredders Passwords Limited terminal functions Automatic lockouts Callback procedures
2. Protect from natural environment or disasters	Sprinkler systems Fireproof vaults	Air-conditioning Humidity controls Fireproof vaults Halon gas spheres Auxiliary power supplies Insurance coverage Prudent locations Disaster contingency plans	
3. Protect from breakdowns and business interruptions	Preventive maintenance Backup equipment Insurance coverage	Preventive maintenance Backup hardware systems Graceful degradation Insurance coverage	
4. Detect attempted access or change			Access logs Control logs System and program change logs
5. Protect from loss or alteration			Read-only memory Tape file protection rings External file labels Internal file labels Library log Transaction logs Batch control logs Lockouts
6. Reconstruct lost files			Backup procedures Reconstruction procedures Rollback and recovery procedures

Exhibit 6–19.   Table of selected security measures for physical resources, computer facilities, and data.

Adapted from J. Wilkinson, *Accounting Information System: Essential Concepts and Applications,* 2nd ed. (New York: John Wiley & Sons, 1993).

and make it available to users? What resources are consumed in obtaining the information and making it available? Is the value of the information worth the cost of producing it? How can the organization ensure that the information is available on a timely basis, and is accurate and reliable? The posing of such questions and the documenting of the answers received is facilitated by the discussions in this chapter.

CHAPTER 7

THE WORKING OF ACCOUNTING INFORMATION SYSTEMS

7.1 INTRODUCTION

In this chapter the focus is on the actual working of an accounting information system, in other words, the bricks and mortar that makes up an AIS. The chapter starts by providing an overview of the accounting system and follows it by describing the ways in which data resulting from various transactions throughout the organization flow into the accounting system and are processed. Given the large number of transactions that need to be tracked and then processed, a variety of tools are used to facilitate the processing of such transactions. One approach classifies the transactions into different cycles. Another tool uses codes to help classify data. Both are described in the chapter.

7.2 BRICKS AND MORTAR OF ACCOUNTING INFORMATION SYSTEMS

Business organizations must routinely process a vast quantity of data in an orderly and efficient manner to accomplish the following:

- Provide financial statements on a timely basis.
- Pay bills in a timely manner.
- Ensure that resources in the right quantity are available to do business with customers.
- Ensure that the issue of invoices to customers and checks to employees are conducted in an orderly and purposeful manner.
- Provide reports required by the government or regulatory agencies properly and in a timely manner.

These objectives can be accomplished by orderly and efficient processing of account data by the accounting system.

The basic accounting system is the manual system with one journal and one ledger. This basic system is generally used by very small businesses. However, as a business grows, its number of business transactions will also grow, and the company looks for ways to speed up the accounting process by developing its accounting system.

An accounting system can be defined as a set of records (journals, ledgers, work sheets, trial balances, and reports) plus the procedures and equipment regularly used to process business transactions. To be effective, accounting systems should:

- Provide for the efficient, cost-effective processing of data.
- Be accurate.
- Allow for control to prevent theft or fraud and for managerial efficiency.
- Provide room for growth within the system to keep up with the growth of the business.

Accounting systems consist of a set of record-keeping tools: ledgers, journals, work sheets, trial balances, and statements. This discussion begins with the most basic forms of such tools.

A ledger is the collection of all the accounts of a company. The accounts are used to record the changes occurring in the financial values of a firm's assets, liabilities, owner's equity, revenues, and expenses. It is best visualized in the form of the letter "T," and such a visualization is the source of the word "T-account," used to describe the various elements of an accounting ledger. Accounts can have debit or credit balances. Assets, expenses, and dividends have debit balances, while the liabilities, revenue, and owner's equity accounts will have credit balances. The debit accounts are increased by means of debits and decreased by means of credits. The credit accounts, on the other hand, are increased by means of credits and decreased by means of debits.

The revenue and expense accounts, also called nominal accounts, are closed out at the end of each accounting period. Such closing of those accounts is needed to measure the income earned for the accounting period. The balances, if carried over to the next period, will distort the firm's performance expressed in terms of income, the difference between revenue and expenses for a period.

The ledger accounts list only the increases and decreases in the account balances. They do not reveal how those changes came about. To track those changes, a journal is needed. A journal is a chronological record of business transactions expressed in monetary terms. It lists all the internal and external transactions that occur in the course of business in the form of a journal entry. After transactions have been recorded in the journal, the information they contain gets transferred to the various ledger accounts. This step, called "posting," is undertaken periodically.

A journal entry is a representation of a transaction, expressed in terms of the monetary changes the transaction will bring to a company's assets, liabilities, revenue, or owner's equity. A given entry consists of a debit and a credit—which translates as changes in various accounts. If a transaction is going to represent the payment of an amount owed, say $1,000 by a customer to a business, it will be represented by means of a debit and a credit to the two accounts that will be affected. Cash paid to the firm will increase its cash balance; hence cash account will be debited. At the same time accounts receivable will decrease, since a customer is paying the amount owed. The amounts owed to a firm are listed in the account called accounts receivable.

In an accounting universe governed by the logic of double-entry bookkeeping, there cannot be a debit without a credit. There is no such thing as an immaculate debit or credit in the accounting world. Consequently, at any point in time the balances in debit accounts will equal the balances in credit accounts, unless some mistakes were made in record keeping.

In addition to regular journal entries, there exists adjusting entries. Accountants make adjusting entries as part of accounting transaction processing in order to document information on an activity that has occurred but has not yet been documented. Such absence of documentation is most likely due to two causes: It is more convenient to wait until the end of the accounting period to record the activity, or the source documents concerning the particular activity have not yet reached those in charge of documenting it. One way to explain adjusting entries is by a reference to the way people mark their birthdays. Even though we grow older every second, we do not put aside everything in order to mark advancing age in very small fractions of time; instead, we conveniently defer the passing of time until a "birthday," at which time we suddenly grow, in a legal sense, a year older. Birthdays are like adjusting entries. The same holds for economic activities involving assets and liabilities that can live with periodic adjustments in their values as listed in accounting records, such as marking depreciation within accounting books.

There are also entries that pertain to the end of the accounting period. Such closing entries are needed to close out the nominal accounts in order to prepare the financial statements.

7.3 IMPACT OF COMPLEXITY ON ACCOUNTING INFORMATION SYSTEMS

One journal and one ledger is adequate if a business is small and needs to process only a very limited amount of information. To process a large quantity of information efficiently an accounting system must adapt itself to the type and quantity of information needed. The large number of transactions that occur in a typical business organization requires the use of subsidiary ledgers and special journals.

(a) Subsidiary Ledgers

A subsidiary ledger is a grouping of related accounts, such as receivables or payables, showing the details of the balance of a general ledger control account. Subsidiary ledgers are segregated from the general ledger to simplify record keeping and eliminate a lot of details from the general ledger. The subsidiary ledger tracks accounts receivable, and lists the amounts owed by each customer. In effect, this system lets each customer have its own space. This subsidiary ledger can be used to bill customers. Similarly, the subsidiary ledger for payables can be used to pay vendors and suppliers.

While relieving the general ledger of the details, it is still a good idea to keep a summary account within the general ledger, representing receivables and payables for control purposes. In this "control account" the balance should equal the sum of all balances in the subsidiary accounts.

The general ledger has backup subsidiary ledgers for accounts in addition to the accounts receivable account. Some examples of accounts that frequently have backup subsidiary ledgers are those for office equipment, delivery equipment, and store fixtures. The number of subsidiary ledgers maintained by a company varies according to the company's information requirements. Control accounts and subsidiary ledgers generally are set up when a company has many transactions in a given account and detailed information is needed about these transactions on a continuing basis.

(b) Special Journals

As the transactions of a company increase, the first step in altering the manual accounting system usually is to use special journals along with the original general journal. Each special journal records one particular type of transaction, such as sales on account, cash receipts, purchases on account, or cash disbursements.

The following advantages are obtained from the use of special journals:

- Time is saved in journalizing. Only one line is used for each transaction; usually a full description is not necessary. The amount of writing is reduced because it is not necessary to repeat the account titles printed at the top of the special column or columns.
- Time is saved in posting. Many amounts are posted as column totals rather than individually.
- Detail is eliminated from the general ledger. Column totals are posted to the general ledger, and the detail is left in the special journals.
- Division of labor is promoted. Several persons can work simultaneously on the accounting records. This specialization and division of labor pinpoints responsibility and allows for more rapid location of errors.
- Management analysis is aided. The journals themselves can be useful to management in analyzing classes of transactions, such as credit sales, because all similar transactions are in one place.

Special journals, then, are designed to systematize the original recording of major recurring types of transactions. The number and format of the special journals actually used in a company depend primarily on the nature of the company's business transactions. The special journals usually used are the sales, cash receipts, purchases, and cash disbursements journals:

- The sales journal is used to record all sales of merchandise on account (on credit).
- The cash receipts journal is used to record all inflows of cash into the business.
- The purchases journal is used to record all purchases of merchandise on account (on credit). Merchandise refers to items of inventory that are available for sale to customers.
- The cash disbursements journal is used to record all payments (or outflows) of cash by the business.

The general journal is not eliminated by the use of special journals; it is used to record all transactions that cannot be entered in one of the special journals. All five of these journals are books of original entry. If a transaction is recorded in a journal, it will be posted and is part of the accounting records. Therefore, if a transaction is recorded in a special journal, it should not be recorded in the general journal because this would record the transaction twice. Since the journals are posted to ledger accounts, the posting reference column in the ledger should indicate the source of the posting, and it should be posted in both the control and the subsidiary ledgers.

7.4 TRANSACTION PROCESSING CYCLES

Even though subsidiary ledgers and special journals help process transactions more efficiently and speedily, their usefulness is limited. Additional sophistication is realized by using a cycle approach to transaction processing. A transaction processing cycle combines one or more types of transactions having related features or similar objectives. It groups together recurrent, cyclically occurring activities. Any such groupings are arbitrary and subject to overlapping. Nonetheless, the groupings are useful, and the following groups will be used in this book: revenue cycle, expenditure cycle, resource management cycle, and financial reporting cycle. Following this chapter, each group of transactions is examined in greater detail in Chapters 8 through 13.

The revenue cycle facilitates the exchange of products or services with customers for cash. The transactions involved span the activities from the point the customer order is received to the point at which the payment is received.

The expenditure cycle seeks to facilitate the payments to vendors for the goods and services provided to the firm. This cycle covers the span between the time the need for an order to vendor(s) is felt and the time the payment is disbursed for the acquired services and products.

The resources management cycle consists of all activities pertaining to the operation of the business. This could include obtaining the capital to invest in the business; acquiring and maintaining the plant and other fixed assets used by the business; selling and marketing; and, lastly, human resource management. This particular cycle can be seen as encompassing a series of self-contained cycles. Given their relative independence, the subcycle can be grouped in a variety of ways. For instance, the cash receipts from customers and cash disbursements could be removed from those cycles and could be included with the funds resource cycle. However, this would truncate those cycles. Thus, we will define the funds cycle to include only the funds acquired from bank loans, bond issues, stock issues, contributions from owners and others, and disposal of plant assets.

The resources management cycles can be defined in other ways. Alternate descriptions are the financial cycle (those transactions relating to funds received from owners and facilities acquired with those funds), the administrative cycle (those transactions relating to cash receipts and disbursements as well as to the acquisition of facilities), and the inventory cycle (those transactions relating to acquiring, maintaining, and selling inventory).

At the center of the aforementioned cycles is the general ledger and financial reporting cycle. This cycle is unique in that the processing of individual transactions is not its sole or even its most important function. Its primary inflows arise as outputs of a variety of transaction processing systems. In addition, the cycle processes the relatively few nonroutine transactions that arise during each accounting period and the adjustment type transactions that occur at the end of each period.

The transaction processing cycles described above pertain only to merchandising firms. Many other types of organizations exist, however. Although all organizations employ most of the cycles just discussed, some significant differences appear. Thus, certain types of organizations can dispense with certain key cycles. For instance, the typical governmental agency does not make sales and therefore does not need a revenue cycle. More often, though, organizations require added cycles that are unique to them. A manufacturing firm requires a product conversion cycle. A bank requires demand deposit and installment loan cycles. Health care, insurance, and transportation firms also require special cycles. All of these special cycles display certain peculiarities not found elsewhere. Nevertheless, they exhibit many features that are very similar to those of the basic transaction processing cycles.

7.5 COMPUTER TRANSACTION PROCESSING APPROACHES

Transaction processing typically involves three stages: data entry, file processing, and output preparation. Processing may be performed either manually or with the use of computers. Although we will contrast these alternative means of processing, our main focus is on the latter. The two basic computer-based transaction processing approaches are batch processing and on-line processing. One or the other of these approaches must be selected by a firm for each of its transaction processing applications. For instance, a firm might decide to employ the batch processing approach for its payroll application and the on-line processing approach for its sales application. The choice of one approach over the other depends on which attributes—such as efficiency, timeliness, economy, accuracy—are most critical for a particular application.

7.6 BATCH PROCESSING APPROACH

Batch processing involves the periodic processing of data from groups of like transactions. Transactions are collected and stored temporarily until a sufficiently large number is accumulated or until a designated time arrives. Then the batch of transactions is processed to post the transaction data to one or more files. This approach is most frequently employed to process routine transactions that occur in relatively large volumes. In addition to payroll transactions, batch processing can be applied to applications such as general ledger accounting, cash disbursements, cash receipts, and student registration transactions. Batch processing also is used to extract information from a file. Thus, the quantity of items on order could be extracted from an inventory file and listed on an inventory status report. Often posting and extracting/reporting are combined.

Since time is required to collect transactions into batches, batch processing is marked by delays. Periods of time—days, weeks, months—elapse between successive processings. Hence, this approach sometimes is referred to as delayed processing, and the periods of time between successive processings are called processing cycles.

Most batch processing applications involve sequential file access and off-line data entry. Sequential file access consists of processing transactions one after the other, according to the order in which they have been sorted. Off-line data entry consists of entering batches of data onto computer-readable media by off-line input devices. For instance, a data-entry clerk may key transaction data from a batch of source documents onto magnetic tape via a key-to-disk system. A batch processing application can alternatively involve direct file access and on-line data entry.

(a) Sequential Batch Processing Application

Exhibit 7–1 diagrams the steps in a typical sequential batch processing application. Major steps in the application consist of off-line data entry, sequential file access processing, and printed output preparation. For purposes of discussion, we will assume that the application pertains to sales transactions for a merchandising firm.

Data entry begins when the source documents (i.e., sales invoices) are gathered into a batch and one or more batch totals are computed. For instance, the sales amounts shown on the invoices might be totaled. This batch total will be used as a key accounting control over the accuracy of the processing step. Next, the sales transaction data are converted (transcribed), by an off-line device such as a key-to-tape encoder, to magnetic tape. The data elements transcribed by a clerk from each sales invoice source document, such as customer number and name, are arranged on a magnetic tape to form a record. To increase processing efficiency, the records are grouped into blocks within the created file of sales transactions. Each block of transaction records is then entered into the computer proces-

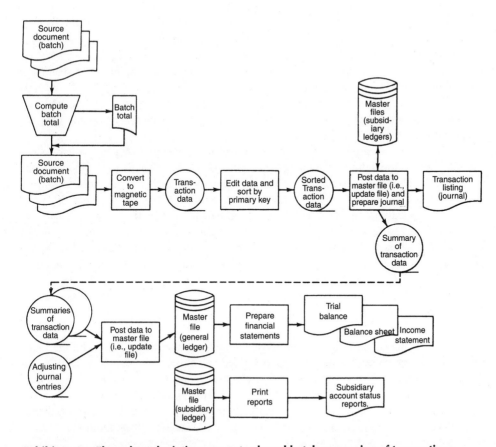

Exhibit 7–1.   Flow chart depicting computer-based batch processing of transactions.

Adapted from J. Wilkinson, *Accounting Information System: Essential Concepts and Applications,* 2nd ed. (New York: John Wiley & Sons, 1993).

sor, using a magnetic tape drive. On being entered, the transaction data are validated by an edit procedure within the sales application program. Any program function performed within a computer and affecting a batch of transactions is called a run. This editing procedure is generally the first run performed in a computer-based application, since it is important to check the input data for correctness and completeness.

File processing in this application involves accessing a file in which the records are arranged sequentially. Thus, it begins with the sales transactions being sorted into the same order as the records in the file that is to be posted. This sorting step is performed by reference to a sort key, the data element by which the records are to be rearranged. For sales transactions, the sort key is likely to be the customer number, since records in the accounts receivable master file are generally arranged according to customer numbers. In a computer-based system the accounts receivable master file is, in effect, the subsidiary ledger.

A critical step in transaction processing is to post data from the batch of transactions to one or more master files. This step is called updating. With respect to sales transactions the two master files of concern are the accounts receivable file and the general ledger. These master files are shown as being stored on magnetic disks (designated by the cylindrical symbols). Since the transaction records have been sorted according to customer numbers, the accounts receivable master file is updated first. In updating the file, the processing program starts at the beginning accounts receivable record and reads every record in the file, changing (updating) each record affected by a transaction. Summary data from the updated transactions are copied onto a magnetic tape. Periodically, the daily totals from the summary tapes are combined with those from other types of transactions and with adjusting journal entries. Then these summary data are posted to the affected accounts within the general ledger.

Various reports—outputs—are generated from the application. A listing of the sales transactions is printed during the file updating run. This transaction listing is, in effect, the sales journal. The total amount that it shows as being added to the accounts receivable account balances should be compared with the predetermined batch total to verify the accuracy of the updating. In addition, the account balances from the general ledger are arranged periodically to produce trial balances, balance sheets, and income statements. Also, status reports of the subsidiary ledger, such as an accounts receivable aging report, are generated. These outputs are provided as needed by users, whether weekly, monthly, or at the end of each accounting period.

7.7 CONTRASTS WITH MANUAL BATCH PROCESSING

Accounting systems before the advent of the computer traditionally employed the batch processing approach. As a result, the computerized batch processing and its manual counterpart have much in common. Exhibit 7–2 portrays manual batch processing in a flow chart that parallels the computer-based batch processing shown in Exhibit 7–1. By comparing these two flow charts, it is easy to see both similarities and differences between manual batch processing and computer-based batch processing. Key similarities are as follows:

- Both involve the same essential steps, such as computing batch totals, sorting transactions, posting to subsidiary and general ledgers, and preparing financial outputs.
- Both generate the same outputs—trial balances, financial statements, status reports—that are similar in terms of content and printed formats.
- Both rely on batch totals to provide an important control over the accuracy and completeness of processing.
- Both employ processing cycles of constant lengths.

Major differences include:

- Computer-based batch processing steps are performed more rapidly and accurately than those in manual batch processing applications.
- In computer-based batch processing applications the transaction data and master files are stored on magnetic media and thus not readable by humans; in manual batch processing applications the data and files are stored on hard-copy records.
- In computer-based batch processing applications, the journal is produced as a by-product of the posting step rather than during a prior step in the processing sequence. In fact, the primary value of a journal in a computer-based system is to provide a visible human-readable link in the audit trail.

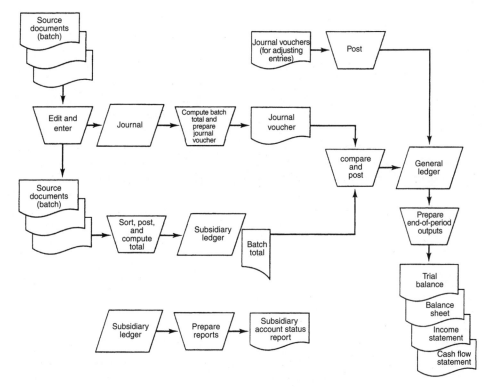

Exhibit 7–2.   Flow chart depicting batch processing of transactions by a manual system.
Adapted from J. Wilkinson, *Accounting Information System: Essential Concepts and Applications,* 2nd ed. (New York: John Wiley & Sons, 1993).

- In computer-based batch processing applications many of the processing steps are combined and performed by the system itself; in a manual system all of the steps are performed by human clerks, who are located in separate organizational units. Thus a computer-based system performs the validation (edit) checks customarily performed by human clerks.

Given the similarities between manual and computerized batch transactions processing, it's possible to argue that accountants using computers were simply using faster tools to do the same things they did before. This is not the most optimum use of technology. But advances are being made in the world of accounting, where information technology is starting to have an impact on the nature of functions performed by accountants, such as payment made to vendors.

7.8 ADVANTAGES AND DISADVANTAGES OF BATCH PROCESSING

Computer-based batch processing provides several advantages. First, it is relatively simple and requires less complex and expensive hardware and software than the on-line processing approach. Second, because it normally involves sequential processing, the batch processing approach is relatively efficient, especially when large batches are accumulated. Third, this approach facilitates the use of controls such as batch totals and thorough audit trails. Fourth, it was similar to the way things were before the advent of computers, which made the change easier.

The main disadvantage of the batch processing approach is that the records in the master file become out of date very quickly. Consequently, most reports from a batch processing application are tied to the processing cycles. Another drawback is that errors detected in transaction data cannot be corrected easily at the time of entry; they must be corrected and reentered, either in a separate "run" or during the next processing cycle. A third disadvantage is that the processing step of sorting must be performed before a master file can be updated. Finally, all records in the master file must be read during the updating step, thus increasing the processing time when relatively few records are affected.

(a) Variations in Batch Processing Applications

Sequential batch processing applications may be modified with respect to data entry, data storage and posting, and report preparation.

(i) Transaction Data May Be Entered into the Computer System by On-Line Devices Such as Terminals.   In this variation, the data would be validated (edited) as entered. Then it would be accumulated temporarily on an on-line storage medium, such as magnetic disks, until time for processing as a batch.

(ii) Direct Access May Be Used for File Processing.   Instead of processing a batch of transactions sequentially against the entire master file, each transaction could be posted directly to the particular record in the master file that it affects.

(iii) Data Could Be Captured on Scannable Documents.   Credit card transaction slips could contain information that could then be read with scanners.

(iv) Outputs Could Be Spooled.   Instead of printing the reports directly onto hard copy, the information could be stored temporarily on a magnetic tape or disk. The reports could be printed off-line at a later time, thus making more efficient use of the computer processor.

7.9 COMPUTER-BASED ON-LINE TRANSACTION PROCESSING

On-line processing consists of processing each transaction as soon as it is captured and entered. A flow chart of such processing is shown in Exhibit 7–3. Data from each transaction are entered via an on-line device and posted immediately and directly to the affected record in one or more master files. Thus, the stored data in the master files, which are continuously on-line, are kept up-to-date. Also, the application software or programs that direct the transaction processing are continuously on-line and are available for use. Often this type of processing is called immediate or direct processing, since it so obviously exhibits these characteristics. An on-line processing system is also called an interactive processing system, since it involves direct interactions between people and a computer-based system.

As shown in Exhibit 7–3, steps needed for an on-line approach consist of data entry and edit, file processing, file inquiry, and report generation. For purposes of illustra-

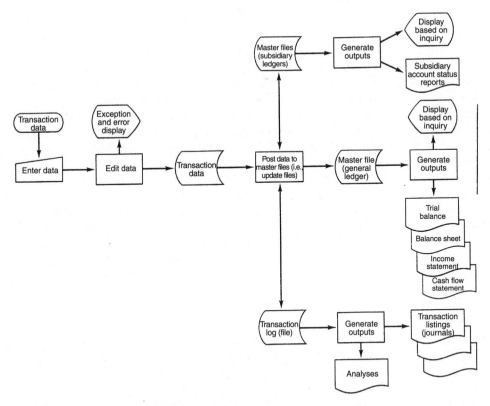

Exhibit 7–3.   Flow chart depicting computer-based on-line processing of transactions.
Adapted from J. Wilkinson, *Accounting Information System: Essential Concepts and Applications,* 2nd ed. (New York: John Wiley & Sons, 1993).

tion, we again assume that the application involves sales transaction processing. To simplify the application, we will further assume that sales orders are billed as soon as they are received.

The need for data entry arises when a sales order clerk receives an order from a customer. The sales transaction data may be recorded on a source document, such as a sales order. Alternatively, the data may be acquired without benefit of a source document. For instance, the sales clerk may receive sales orders by phone. To begin the interactive data entry procedure, the sales order clerk accesses the system via an on-line device, such as a terminal. The specific steps taken depend on the method of assistance provided by the system software. If the dialogue prompt method is employed, the clerk would key the code SO (for sales order transaction) when the system prompts: "What is the transaction type code?" If the menu method is used, the clerk would key numbers that lead to the option for sales order data entry. Under either method the clerk's response causes the sales order application program to be activated, that is, loaded into the primary storage unit and initialized. The data entry portion of this program aids the clerk in entering the sales data (perhaps by means of a preformatted screen) and edits the data. If errors or omissions are found by the edit routine, the edit routine notifies the clerk by some type of message displayed on the screen. After all errors and omissions are corrected, the data are accepted and readied for processing.

File processing consists mainly of updating the affected files immediately and directly. In the sales application, it also involves calculating the amount of the sale from the sales order. First, the proper customer's account in the accounts receivable master file (subsidiary ledger) is posted to reflect the amount of the sale. Second, the accounts receivable and sales accounts in the general ledger also are posted to reflect the debit and credit effects of the transaction. Finally, the transaction data are added to a transaction log, generally just following the most recently posted transaction. Note that in a typical on-line processing system, various types of transactions may be entered in the order received. Thus, a sales transaction may be preceded by a purchase or cash receipts transaction. Inquiries of up-to-date information in files may be made at any time. One may inquire about a particular sale or a customer's account in the accounts receivable file. Responses to the inquiries would be displayed on terminal screens.

The same reports and other outputs provided by a batch processing procedure can be generated by an on-line processing system. The sales application program might generate status reports concerning accounts receivable, sales summaries, and also sales invoices. A general ledger program would periodically generate trial balances, balance sheets, income statements, and cash flow statements. Other programs might produce the transaction listings. If desirable, these listings could be analyzed by type of transaction and in other ways.

7.10 CONTRASTS WITH COMPUTER-BASED BATCH PROCESSING

On-line processing is similar to computer-based batch processing in that both approaches generate the same basic outputs and employ the same data records. The two approaches exhibit significant differences, however. Batch processing generally involves sequential processing of transactions, whereas on-line processing always employs direct processing. In the batch processing approach, the transaction data either may be prepared off-line or may be entered via an on-line device as received. In the on-line processing approach, the data are always entered via an on-line device. Batch processing focuses a separate program within a particular application on all the transactions comprising a batch. In contrast, on-line processing employs a single application program to perform all the processes for each transaction before beginning the processing of the next transaction. Although batch processing applications may on occasion employ magnetic tape to store master files, on-line processing applications use magnetic tape to store the backup files and records. Finally, batch processing applications are relatively unintegrated, whereas individual on-line processing applications tend to be highly integrated with related applications.

7.11 ADVANTAGES AND DISADVANTAGES OF ON-LINE PROCESSING

The major advantage of on-line processing is better service to users. Since records are updated immediately and are directly accessible, up-to-date information is available in a timely manner. Also, data are accurate and complete, since transactions are checked thoroughly on capture and detected errors are corrected. Since processing is performed in a direct manner, no sorting or transcribing is necessary. Finally, because on-line processing applications are integrated, fewer duplicates of files are required, and the informational needs of users can be satisfied more fully.

These advantages greatly affect a variety of applications. Many firms have found the sales order application to be an apt example, especially if it is integrated with an on-line inventory system. An integrated system of this type allows a sales clerk to determine if adequate inventory is available to fill a sales order when received. Other suitable candidate applications for on-line processing include airline reservations, job order manufacturing, hospital patient care, and materials management.

The main disadvantage of the on-line processing method is its complexity relative to batch processing. Not only must the operating system handle varied users and diverse functions, but the data entry routines in the application programs usually are expected to provide more user guidance and perform more elaborate checks. Also, the needed hardware, such as terminals and direct-access storage devices, is more expensive than the hardware needed in batch processing. Furthermore, transaction data processed by the on-line processing method cannot be supported by controls such as batch totals. In addition, reliable and thorough audit trails are more difficult to maintain. Finally, the entry of data is slower, since the system must wait for the clerks to key in the data and to respond to error messages.

(a) Variations in On-line Processing Applications

The variations in on-line processing applications are relatively limited. The data must be entered on-line, and direct access storage devices must be employed. The five options essentially concern: (1) whether to use source documents as the basis for data entry; (2) whether to enter transactions individually or in batches; (3) which type of on-line input device to use; (4) which method of interactive assistance to provide to users; and (5) which mode of output to provide (e.g., soft-copy display, hard-copy report, voice response).

A major alternative is to convert the on-line processing system into a real-time system, a support system that provides information in a sufficiently timely manner to control a process. Real-time systems may control physical processes or transaction-oriented business processes. For instance, the physical process of cold-rolling steel sheets is often controlled by a real-time system through the use of process control computers. As another example, a transaction-oriented real-time system is activated each time a consumer purchases merchandise with a credit card and the clerk makes an on-the-spot credit check.

7.12 FILE PROCESSING AND MANAGEMENT

Traditionally a firm's data have been stored in a variety of files. A file of data may be defined as a collection of data elements that have been organized into records. All applications involving transaction processing require one or more files. Therefore, accountants should be keenly aware of the characteristics and types of files as well as the nature of file storage and the several functions of file management. In addition, accountants should recognize the alternative file structures that may be used for organizing and accessing data.

7.13 NATURE OF FILE STORAGE

Before delving into the details of file management, let us clarify the differences between data storage in manual and computerized systems and between logical storage and physical storage. In a manual information system, the file data are generally stored in folders, tubs, in/out baskets, and file drawers throughout the departments of a firm. Often the same data are duplicated in multiple copies of a form and stored in several places. Certain data may be abbreviated or even omitted on forms, since such shortcuts are understandable to experienced clerks. In general, an air of informality permeates the storage and management of files. In computer-based information systems, the data comprising files are stored on magnetic or optical media. File storage and management require formalized procedures that must be strictly followed. The identity and location of each item of data stored in a computerized system must be precisely specified. Each step in file storage must be carefully planned. But the rewards of such planning comes from the ease of access and the compactness of storage: A small disk replaces volumes of bulky ledgers.

Data used in processing transactions are stored in logical records within files. In turn, the logical records and files are stored on physical media (e.g., magnetic disks) in the form of physical records and files. Logical files include data files—such as master, transaction, history, reference, and nondata (i.e., program, text, and index files) files. In logical terms, data files consist of records, data elements, and characters. Each record is organized into a series of fields, either fixed or variable in length. Data elements, whose values are placed within the fields, reflect attributes of entities or events. Data elements also may serve as primary or secondary keys within the records. Three major functions of file management are file storage, file maintenance, and retrieval of stored records. Files may be arranged sequentially or may be random. Records within files may be accessed either by following a specified sequence or by means of a direct method. Three widely used methods of physical file organization are sequential files, indexed sequential files, and random files. Indexed sequential files may be updated sequentially, but their records may be accessed directly. Random files cannot be updated sequentially, but their records may be accessed very quickly. Each file organization method is selected for particular circumstances by reference to such measures as activity ratio, volatility, and required response time.

In summary, a random file (on a direct-access storage medium) is most suitable when up-to-dateness and fast response times are important, the activity ratio is low, file volatility is high, and the file is relatively limited in size. A sequential file (on magnetic tape) is most suited to the opposite set of conditions. An indexed sequential file (on a direct-access storage medium) is a good choice when both processing efficiency and rapid accessibility are important.

7.14 CLASSIFICATION AND CODING OF DATA

Coding is critical to the efficient storage and processing of data. Thus, an important step when creating a database is to devise codes suited to the various types of data needed by a firm in its transaction and information processing activities. This section examines the relationships of coding to classification, the major coding systems, and the attributes of sound codes.

Classification is the act of grouping into classes. In the context of an information system, classification refers to the grouping of data and information. For instance, transaction data may be grouped according to the accounts to which they pertain, such as the sales account. Sales data may be classified or grouped according to the sales offices making the sales, the product lines sold, and the dates of the sales.

Classification plans or schemes are designed with certain objectives in mind. Consider, for example, a chart of accounts, the basic financial classification plan of every organization. The chart of accounts has the primary purpose of satisfying key internal and external information needs. If it is well designed, a chart of accounts enables useful financial statements and other reports to be prepared. Not only should such financial statements and reports aid managers in controlling operations, but they should assist external parties in making investment decisions.

Coding is the assignment of symbols, such as letters and numbers, in accordance with a classification plan. A coding system provides unique identities for specific events and entities. For instance, the coding system of a firm may assign the letter code "CS" to identify a credit sales transaction; the number code "711" to identify the sales invoice issued in a particular credit sales transaction; the number code "1346" to identify the customer John Henry Johnson of Akron, Ohio; and the alphanumeric code "XQ7" to specify a particular item that it sells. As can be seen, codes are much briefer than the events or entities for which they stand. A coding system therefore can ease the entry of data, enhance processing efficiency and accuracy, speed the retrieval of data from files, and aid the preparation of reports.

7.15 CODING SYSTEMS

A variety of coding systems have been devised. Familiar examples are bar codes, such as those used to identify merchandise items; color codes, such as those used to distinguish copies of multicopy forms; and cipher codes, such as those used to protect confidential messages. However, the codes most widely useful to business firms are based on alphabetic, numeric, and alphanumeric characters.

Four coding systems that use these characters are mnenomic, sequence, block, and group coding systems.

(a) Mnemonic Coding System

A code of this type provides visible clues concerning the objects it represents. For instance, AZ is the code for Arizona and WSW-P175R 14 represents a white sidewall radial tire of a specific size. Thus, a mnemonic code is relatively easy to remember. However, its applications are more limited than those of the other three coding systems.

(b) Sequence Coding System

The simplest type of coding system is the sequence code, which assigns numbers or letters in consecutive order. Sequence codes are applied primarily to source documents such as checks and sales invoices. A sequence code can facilitate document searches, such as a search for a particular sales invoice. Furthermore, a sequence code can help prevent the loss of data, since gaps in the sequence signal missing documents. Sequence codes are inflexible, however. New entities or events can be added only at the end of the sequence. Moreover, a sequence code generally is devoid of logical significance. For instance, a specific sequence code assigned to a customer does not identify the sales territory within which he or she resides, nor the customer class to which he or she belongs.

(c) Block Coding System

A third coding system partially overcomes these drawbacks. A block coding system assigns a series of numbers within a sequence to entities or events having common features. Consequently, a block code designates the classification of an individual entity or event. Block codes have varied applicability within a firm. Customer numbers, for instance, may be blocked by sales territory. To illustrate, customers in the southern sales territory may be assigned numbers ranging from 1 to 4999, whereas customers in the northern sales territory may be assigned numbers from 5000 to 9999. In other applications, products may be blocked by product line, employees by department. An important use of block codes is to designate blocks of numbers for the major account groupings within charts of accounts. While a block is reserved for individual codes, it is not necessary to assign every possible number within a block. In fact, one advantage of a block code is that unassigned numbers are usually available to be assigned to new objects (e.g., products) as they are added to the firm's scope of activity.

(d) Group Coding System

The group code is a refinement of the block code, in that it provides added meaning to the users. That is, a group coding system reveals two or more dimensions or facets pertaining to an object. Each facet is assigned a specific location, called a field, within the code format. Code segments (i.e., subcodes) appear within the respective fields, thus identifying the facets pertaining to a particular object.

An example of a group code for an entity should clarify this description. Raw materials stored for use by a metal products manufacturer may be coded by means of a six-digit code, where the first digit may represent the type of material, the next two represent the storage location, while the last three define the size of the material. A particular raw material item could therefore be coded 573201 or 5–73–201 for greater clarity, where 5 stands for the type of material (steel rod), 73 represents seventh row and third bin, and 201 represents a 20 by 1 square inch material.

Group codes are extremely versatile. They may be expressed as hierarchical structures. For instance, the leftmost field in the code of a plant asset may designate the major or broad classification, the fields to the right designating increasingly detailed classifications. They may include block, sequence, or other types of codes. For instance, the employee code may be assigned sequentially as each employee is hired, with the department code being added as a suffix. Although this combinational feature of group codes tends to make them relatively lengthy and cumbersome, it also packs such codes with much useful information. For instance, a code that captures relevant features of a transaction can provide the basis for key analyses and reports. Thus, a variety of sales analyses can be prepared when a group code of the following format is employed to record sales transactions:

ABBBBCCDDDEEE or A-BBBB-CC-DDD-EEE

In this code, the first letter, A, represents the class of customer to whom a sale is made. The next four letters, BBBB, stand for the customer's account number. The following two letters, CC, represent the sales territory where the sale is made. The following three letters, DDD, represent the code of the salesperson making the sale. The last three, EEE, represent the type of product (product line) sold. From an accounting perspective, coded charts of accounts are of immense help, since transaction processing is very cumbersome without the coded ledger accounts. In the appendix following Chapter 8, a coded chart of accounts for a midsize company is provided.

7.16 CODING AND COMPUTERS

Computer-based systems also dictate certain attributes. For example, they require that codes be fixed in length. In addition, they encourage the use of numeric codes, since numeric sorting can be performed more easily. However, the presence of computers should not discourage the application of sound design principles. Thus, alphabetic codes provide twenty-six choices for each character position of a code. Their use can therefore aid conciseness.

Certain codes are peculiar to computer-based systems. Two such codes, the user code and the cipher, relate to security and access to the system. Two other computer-oriented codes are the transaction code and the action code. Transaction codes identify types of transactions to the computer system. Such codes designate the specific application programs to be used in processing the various transactions entered into the system. By specifying a particular transaction code, a user informs the computer system of which accounts to debit and credit and which data elements to update in which files. In effect, a transaction code is a concise replacement for the familiar journal entry format used in manual processing systems.

Action codes identify specific operations pertaining to file maintenance or data retrieval. For instance, they may specify the addition of new master records, the deletion of current master records, or the display of stored records. Action codes are employed primarily with on-line processing systems. Often they are entered with the aid of menu screens.

7.17 ATTRIBUTES OF CODES

A sound coding system furthers the primary purpose of a classification plan, which is to satisfy certain informational needs of users. In addition, each of its codes:

- Uniquely identifies objects, such as customers and sales.
- Is concise and simple, so it is easy to remember and apply and economical to maintain.
- Allows for expected growth, so that it will not need to be changed in the foreseeable future. For instance, a growing firm with nine product lines should allow two digits (assuming a numeric code) for the product line coding system.
- Is standardized throughout all functions and levels within a firm, so that reporting systems can be fully integrated.

7.18 CONCLUSION

The transaction processing systems of an organization comprise activities that focus on particular economic events. They may be grouped to form transaction cycles, such as the revenue cycle, expenditure cycle, resources management cycle, and general ledger and financial reporting cycle.

Transaction processing typically involves three stages: data entry, file processing, and output preparation. Processing can be performed either manually or with the use of computers. The two basic computer-based transaction processing approaches are batch processing and on-line processing. Batch processing generally consists of accumulating groups of like transactions, computing batch totals, entering the data for processing on magnetic media, sorting the data by appropriate sort keys, posting the transaction data to the sequentially organized records in master files, and generating printed outputs.

Computerized batch processing is similar in most respects to manual processing of transaction data, although the benefits of computers are realized and the journal is produced as a by-product of the posting step. Whether it is performed with the aid of computer, or manually, batch processing offers two advantages: (1) relatively efficient processing and (2) the important control known as batch totals. Its major drawback is that the records in the master files become out of date between processing cycles.

On-line processing consists of entering single transactions via on-line input devices, posting the transactions directly to the records in the master files, and generating outputs as needed. This immediate and direct type of processing offers the important advantage of up-to-date records that are readily accessible to users. It also allows data to be edited and corrected as soon as they are entered and eliminates the need for sorting transaction records. The major drawbacks of on-line processing are the added complexity and cost of software and hardware as well as the lack of the batch total control.

Sound classification and coding techniques can improve the efficiency of data storage and processing. Four coding systems that use alphanumeric characters are the mnemonic, sequence, block, and group coding systems. A sound coding system satisfies the information needs of users, employs unique identifiers, allows for expected growth, and is concise and simple. Two codes peculiar to computer systems are transaction and action codes.

CHAPTER 8

GENERAL LEDGER AND FINANCIAL REPORTING CYCLE

8.1 INTRODUCTION

This chapter describes the objectives and functions of the general ledger and financial reporting cycle and its relationship with other business transaction cycles. In addition, the data sources, inputs, files, data sets, data flows and processing, accounting controls, and outputs pertaining to the general ledger system are all identified and discussed. The chapter also considers the nature of financial statements and the characteristics of the responsibility accounting system, and provides additional exposure to account coding and charts of accounts.

Chapter 7 discussed the transaction cycles used to facilitate the transactions having related features or similar objectives. In this chapter, and the next five, we discuss the various accounting cycles in more detail. Exhibit 8–1 summarizes the transaction cycles pertaining to revenues, expenditures, resources management, product conversion, and the general ledger and financial reporting. We begin our coverage of transaction cycles with the general ledger and financial reporting cycle, since it provides an overview of the objectives associated with the accounting information system and leads into the remaining transaction processing cycles and systems. As Exhibit 8–2 shows, transactions from component transaction processing systems flow into the general ledger. The information appears in the form of a data flow diagram, in order to show more clearly the logical data flows among entities (e.g., customers, suppliers, banks), data stores (e.g., customer records, inventory records), and processes (e.g., order receiving process, cash receipt process). Beyond updating the general ledger, the transaction flow permits the system to prepare financial reports.

8.2 OBJECTIVES AND FUNCTIONS

The general ledger and financial reporting cycle—to be called the general ledger system—represents the very core of an accounting information system. After discussing the objectives associated with this cycle, we go on to cover other topics associated with the cycle, such as data sources and inputs, data flows and processing, the database itself, accounting controls, charts of accounts, and reports relating to this particular cycle. Both manual and computer-based systems are discussed.

As stated earlier, the overall objectives of the general ledger system are to gather together all of the transactions and then to provide information for the array of reports concerning an entity (e.g., a business firm, a governmental agency). The following attributes will allow a general ledger system to function in an optimum manner:

Cycle	Typical Included Events
Revenue	Sales of products or services
	Cash receipts from credit sales of products or services
Expenditure	Purchases of materials or services
	Cash disbursements in payment of acquired materials or services
Resources management	Acquisition, maintenance, and disposal (or disbursement) of funds, facilities, and human (e.g., employee) services
Product conversion	Conversion of raw materials into finished goods through the use of labor and overhead
General ledger and financial reporting	Compilation of accounting transactions from the remaining transaction cycles Generation of financial reports

Exhibit 8–1.   Table of common transaction cycles.

Adapted from J. Wilkinson, *Accounting Information System: Essential Concepts and Applications,* 2nd ed. (New York: John Wiley & Sons, 1993).

- Records all accounting transactions promptly and accurately
- Posts transactions to the proper accounts
- Maintains an equality of debit and credit balances among the accounts
- Allows for needed adjusting of journal entries
- Generates reliable and timely financial reports pertaining to each accounting period

In order to achieve these objectives, a general ledger system performs several functions. The manner in which these functions are performed depends in part on the extent and type of computerization employed. However, all general ledger systems must perform the following:

- Collect transaction data. Transactions arise from a variety of sources, such as sales and purchases. The more numerous types of transactions are grouped by component processing systems. These component systems then interface with and feed their summarized data to the general ledger system. Other daily transactions are recorded individually, generally on specially designed forms and journal vouchers. In addition, varied adjusting entries are posted at the end of each accounting period.
- Process transaction inflows. Collected transaction data undergo several processing steps before coming to rest in the general ledger. First, they are checked to see that debit amounts equal credit amounts, that eligible account names are used, and so on. Also, individual transactions may be verified to see that they are in conformity with generally accepted accounting principles. Then the transactions are posted to the general ledger accounts. Proof listings of the posted transactions may be prepared.

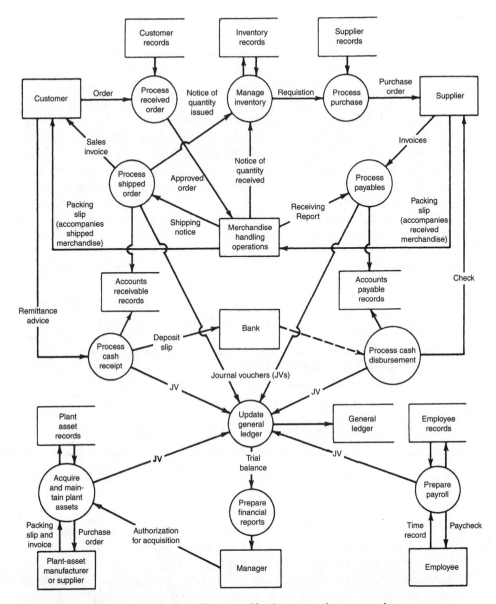

Exhibit 8–2.   Overview data flow diagram of basic transaction processing systems.
Adapted from J. Wilkinson, *Accounting Information System: Essential Concepts and Applications*, 2nd ed. (New York: John Wiley & Sons, 1993).

- Store transaction data. The general ledger and various subsidiary ledgers reflect account balances. Thus, they represent master files within a firm's database. If the balances in the accounts of the general ledger "master file" are to be kept current, they must be updated through the posting of transaction data.
- Assist in maintaining controls. The general ledger system is an integral part of the accounting system. It incorporates a number of controls. Indeed, the general ledger

itself represents a form of control, since the credit account balances must constantly equal the total of the debit account balances. Other controls range from checks or edits of the transaction data as they are entered into the system as well as reviews of the financial reports by managers and other recipients.

- Classify and code transaction data and accounts. Underlying the maintenance of the general ledger system are adequate classification and coding systems. Classification is necessary in assigning the effects of transactions to various accounts within the general ledger. Coding is desirable for identifying accounts, transactions, files, and other elements that have an impact on the general ledger.

- Generate financial reports. The most familiar financial reports generated by the general ledger system are the income statement and the balance sheet. However, a wide variety of other beneficial reports may be prepared. Some of these reports aid in the verification of the general ledger accounts while other reports, such as operating budgets, aid managers in planning and control responsibilities.

8.3 DATA SOURCES AND INPUTS

As should be clear by now, the general ledger system receives inputs from a wide variety of sources. Exhibit 8–3 illustrates this variety by showing the source documents of the various component or feeder transaction processing systems being entered into special journals. Summary totals from these entries are posted to the general ledger as well as to any subsidiary ledgers that are maintained. Other data entered into the general ledger usually are recorded in a general journal or on journal vouchers. Regardless of the source, transaction data should include elements such as the date, accounts affected and amounts, and an authorization code or initials.

The types of transactions that affect the general ledger of a firm can be summarized as follows:

- Routine external transactions that arise during an accounting period from exchanges with independent parties who are in the environment of the firm. An example is a credit sale.

- Routine internal transactions that arise during an accounting period from internal activities of the firm. An example is the transfer of raw materials inventory to work-in-process inventory within a manufacturing firm.

- Nonroutine transactions that arise, usually on an occasional basis and externally, during an accounting period from nonroutine activities. An example is the donation of public land to the firm or even the purchase of a business in exchange for company stock. Company X will buy company Y and pay for it through its stocks.

- Adjusting entries that usually occur on a recurring basis at the end of accounting periods although they may be nonrecurring and take place at any time. Four types of adjusting entries are accruals, deferrals, revaluations, and corrections.

  a. Accruals are recurring entries that arise from the passage of time and that reflect accumulated amounts as of the end of accounting periods. For instance, a firm may provide services that are not billed or paid by the end of an accounting period. The adjusting entry would show a debit to accrued fees receivable and a credit to service fees revenue.

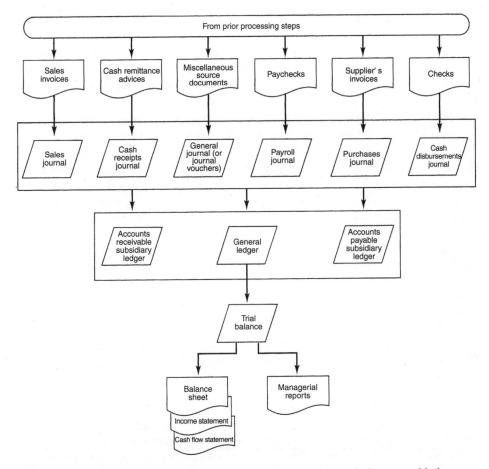

Exhibit 8–3. Diagram of sources of inputs and their flows through the general ledger system.

Adapted from J. Wilkinson, *Accounting Information System: Essential Concepts and Applications,* 2nd ed. (New York: John Wiley & Sons, 1993).

b. Deferrals are recurring entries that also arise from the passage of time, but they represent the amount not yet due or earned. For instance, a firm may receive revenue for which services are still unearned at the end of the accounting period. At the time of the receipt, the entry would show debit to cash and a credit to the liability account named unearned service fees. The adjusting entry at the end of the accounting period, to reflect the portion earned, would show a debit to unearned service fees and a credit to service fees revenue.

c. Revaluations are nonrecurring entries that arise when the value of a physical asset is found not to correspond to the values reflected in the accounting records, or when an accounting measurement method is changed. An example of the former is the adjustment of the merchandise inventory account to reflect a shrinkage in the physical inventory. An example of the latter is a change in inventory cost flow assumptions from the First In First Out (FIFO) to the Last In First Out (LIFO) method.

d. Corrections are entries that reverse the effects of errors, thus restoring affected accounts to proper balances.

- Reversing entries that are entered at the beginning of accounting periods in order to reverse the effects of adjusting entries made at the end of the previous periods. An example is the entry on January 1, 2001, that reverses the accrual of payroll expense made on December 31, 2000.
- Closing entries that transfer the amounts in all temporary accounts to the appropriate owners' equity account, leaving the temporary accounts with zero balances.

The general ledger can be manual or computer-based. Although computer-based processing is gaining in popularity, it is best to include a discussion of a manual system.

The primary source document used as an input to the general ledger system is the general ledger journal voucher, which has largely replaced the general journal sheet. A journal voucher is a document that lists the details of a single transaction. It is typically prepared for each nonroutine, adjusting, reversing, and correcting transaction. A journal voucher is also often prepared to summarize the results of a batch of routine transactions that have been manually entered into special journals. For instance, after entering checks written today into the check register, a clerk may prepare a journal voucher that reflects the total of the cash disbursements.

Although the journal voucher remains the primary input to the general ledger in computer-based systems, its form will likely vary from that employed in manual systems. Three variations worth noting are the individual journal entry form, the batch entry form, and the on-line screen.

The journal voucher for entering individual transactions most likely contains columns for entering account descriptions and numbers as well as columns for debit and credit amounts. After the data pertaining to an individual transaction have been manually written onto this form, data entry clerks key the data onto transaction files stored on magnetic tape or disk.

The batch entry forms are similar to journal voucher forms. They have replaced the special journal in computer-based systems and are used to record and process the miscellaneous transactions. Data are entered manually onto the batch entry form and then are keyed onto tape or disk transaction files. Often the entered data are then listed on a hard-copy printout, to provide a permanent record of the journal.

A data entry screen can be used to record transactions when the general ledger system employs on-line files. Transactions are entered interactively with the aid of a computer terminal that is preformatted to exhibit a journal voucher. Either individual transactions or batches of transactions may be entered in this manner. It may be preceded by a hard-copy authorization form, which has been signed by a data entry clerk and supervisor. Alternatively, the authorization may be indicated by an on-screen code, as provided by a supervisor. The screen can have provision for several debits and credits; also, running totals are computed and shown on the screen by the application program. There are several advantages to on-line data entry:

- A preformatted screen aids the proper entry of data.
- The application software performs Automatic data entry (e.g., date) and calculations (e.g., total debit amount and credit amount).
- Extensive use of codes reduces input strokes.
- Main and detailed level menus allow easy access to the preformatted screen.

On-line data entry also can provide other assistance. On-line help is available as built-in editing features such as validity checks.

8.4 DATABASE USED FOR GENERAL LEDGER SYSTEM

The database for the general ledger and financial reporting system contains a variety of master, transaction, and history files and data sets. In addition to financial data concerning past events and current status, the database contains budgeted data that relate to planned future operations and status. Although their exact contents and composition will vary from firm to firm, the following set of files is representative.

(a) General Ledger Master File

Each record of the general ledger master file contains data concerning one general ledger account. In effect, the general ledger master file is the computerized version of the general ledger maintained in hard-copy form in a manual system. Taken together, the records in the general ledger master file constitute the complete chart of accounts for the firm and the current status of all account balances. Thus, the primary key is the account number.

(b) Current Journal Voucher File

This transaction file contains all of the significant details concerning each transaction that has been posted to the general ledger during the current month. In addition to individual nonroutine transactions, it contains summary vouchers pertaining to daily routine transactions and adjusting entries. Included for each record would be the journal voucher number, date of the transaction, accounts debited and credited and the corresponding amounts, and a description of the transaction. Alternatively, in on-line processing systems, a transaction code may replace the chart of account numbers for amounts debited and credited. In effect, this file is a summary of all of the journals for the current month. Its primary key is the journal voucher number, which also provides the audit trail for transaction data. In the case of batch entries, the audit trail is provided by the batch number. In a database system, the journal voucher records can be linked to the appropriate accounts in the general ledger master file. For a database having a relational structure, the common linking columns in the transaction and master tables would contain the transaction codes.

(c) General Ledger History File

The general ledger history file contains the actual balances of general ledger accounts for each month for several past years. It is used to provide financial trend information.

(d) Responsibility Center Master File

The responsibility center master file contains the actual revenues and costs for the various divisions, departments, work centers, and other responsibility centers within a firm. It is used in the preparation of responsibility reports for managers.

(e) Budget Master File

The budget master file contains the budgeted amounts of assets, liabilities, revenues, and expenses allocated to the various responsibility centers of the firm. The budgeted values may be broken down on a monthly basis for the next year, whereas the budget period may extend for five or more years into the future. Together with the responsibility center master file, the budget file provides the basis for the preparation of responsibility reports.

(f) Financial Reports Format File

This file contains the information necessary for generating the formats of the various financial reports. Included are factors such as the report headings, column headings, side labels (i.e., descriptions of accounts and subtotal and total lines), spacing and totaling instructions, and the like.

In addition to the above-mentioned files, a firm will need a journal voucher history file for past months and years. It also will need detailed transaction files that support the current and historical journal voucher files. Certain firms also need various reference files, such as a cost allocation file that contains factors for allocating incurred costs (e.g., administrative costs) to responsibility centers and other segments within the firm. Systems in which transaction codes are employed will need reference files that link the specific accounts to debit and credit with each transaction code analyses, financial statements, and managerial reports. Exhibit 8–4 portrays the variety of outputs that may be generated from the files. Although several output preparation programs may be necessary to produce the displayed outputs, the exhibit summarizes the relationship between files and outputs and previews the specific types of reports to be discussed later.

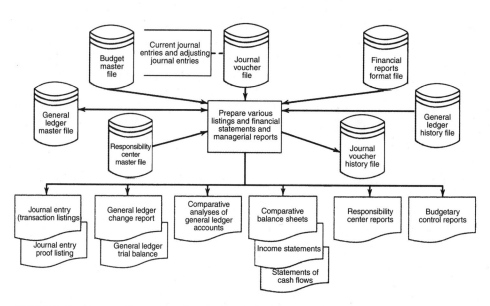

Exhibit 8–4.   System flow chart showing period-end preparation of outputs related to the general ledger.

Adapted from J. Wilkinson, *Accounting Information System: Essential Concepts and Applications,* 2nd ed. (New York: John Wiley & Sons, 1993).

8.5 DATA FLOWS AND PROCESSING

In the traditional manual system, transaction data flow into journals and are posted to subsidiary ledgers; then the total amounts are posted to the general ledger. Data from source documents involving high-volume transactions, such as sales and cash disbursements, are entered into special journals. Columns in the journals are summed to generate batch totals. These totals are entered on journal vouchers. After the source documents are posted to the appropriate subsidiary ledgers, the posted totals are compared with the totals on the journal vouchers. Then the total amounts from journals are posted to the general ledger. Various financial statements and reports are periodically prepared from the general ledger and subsidiary ledgers.

In computer-based systems, the transaction data are entered from the source document forms described earlier. While there are systems that input on-line to the database, resulting in immediate file maintenance, most systems are on-line and batch processing. Periodically, the individual transactions are processed to update the master files (known as subsidiary ledgers), and their summarized amounts are processed to update the general ledger. If the transaction data are stored on magnetic tapes, they are sorted by account numbers and then processed sequentially against the general ledger accounts. If the transaction data are stored on magnetic disks, they will likely be processed directly to the general ledger accounts.

Many general ledger processing systems are a combination of on-line processing and batch processing. Exhibits 8–5 and Exhibit 8–6 show one likely combination.

Exhibit 8–5 shows the on-line processing of transaction data during an accounting period. The sales, cash receipts, purchases, cash disbursements, payroll, plant asset, and application procedures process volumes of transaction data daily. In the course of their processing, the application programs accumulate and summarize the transaction amounts. Since the general ledger is on-line, these application programs also can post the summary amounts to the respective general ledger accounts. In fact, the general ledger postings can be done concurrently with, and as a by-product of, the updating of the various subsidiary ledgers (master files). As nonrecurring special transactions arise, they are entered by accountants via computer terminals from manually prepared journal vouchers. Each day the general ledger system generates a journal entry listing and a trial balance. These outputs enable the accountants to verify the correctness and accuracy of the postings. For instance, they can trace the summary amounts on the journal entry listing back to predetermined batch totals for each of the types of transactions. The journal entry listing also may serve as an integral part of the audit trail. Other outputs (not shown) can be generated as well. Thus, prenumbered journal vouchers that reflect the summary amounts can be printed, thereby strengthening the audit trial. In addition, an error listing of all transactions in error can be printed, so that users can be monitored in correcting detected errors or omissions.

Exhibit 8–6 shows a batch computer system for processing adjusting journal entries at the end of each accounting period. The system begins with the entry of the journal entry data onto a transaction file. Standard adjusting journal entries, which are stored in an on-line file, are transferred to the journal entry data file by a special end-of-period program. Nonrecurring adjusting journal entries are entered via a computer terminal, using manually prepared journal voucher coding forms prepared by accountants. The entered adjusting entries are edited for mistakes. After being accepted by the system, the adjusting journal entries are merged with the standard recurring adjusting entries. Then the entries

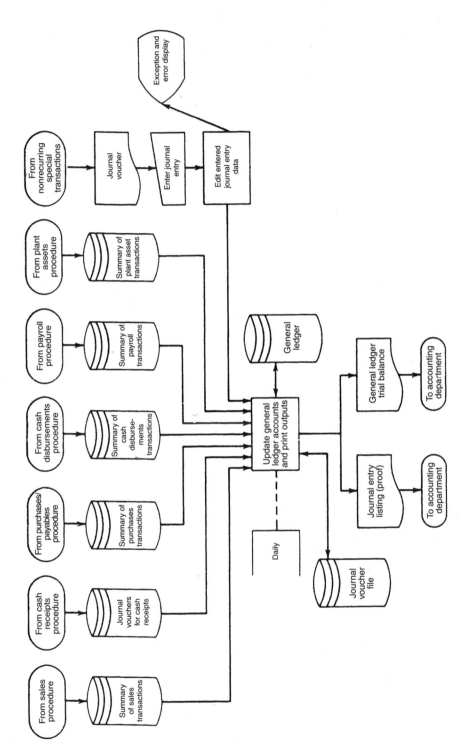

Exhibit 8–5. Computer-based general ledger processing procedure.

Adapted from J. Wilkinson, *Accounting Information System: Essential Concepts and Applications*, 2nd ed. (New York: John Wiley & Sons, 1993).

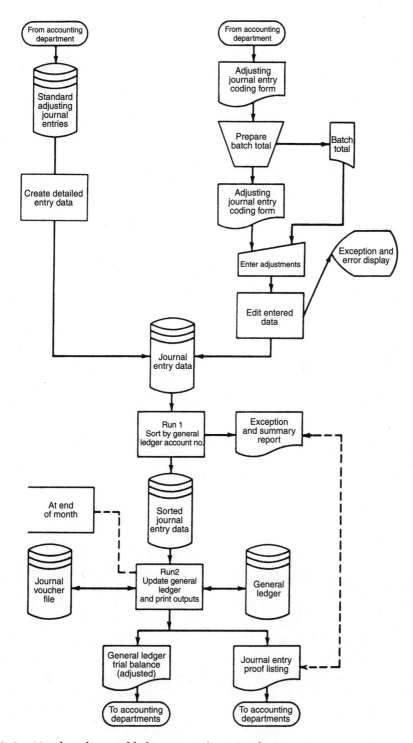

Exhibit 8–6.   Month-end general ledger processing procedure.

Adapted from J. Wilkinson, *Accounting Information System: Essential Concepts and Applications,* 2nd ed. (New York: John Wiley & Sons, 1993).

are split, with each portion being tagged by its identifying journal entry number. In computer processing run 1, the split entries are sorted into the general ledger account number sequence. In run 2 the general ledger accounts are updated, and two printed outputs are generated. One output is a journal entry proof listing, whose totals are compared with the run-to-run totals on the exception and summary report from run 1. The other output is an adjusted trial balance. After accountants review the outputs for correctness, an end-of-period program produces and posts closing entries and prepares a postclosing trial balance and financial statements. Individual firms may use some variation of the processing illustrated in Exhibit 8–6.

8.6 ACCOUNTING CONTROLS

The general ledger system is expected to provide reliable financial reports for a variety of users. To do so, it must independently check on the component transaction processing systems, carefully monitor the array of nonroutine transactions that it accepts, and accurately record and post data from all transactions. A general ledger system faces a number of risks that can keep it from providing reliable reports.

The first step in providing reliable reports is to determine the risks to which the general ledger is exposed. Among the risks that exist in the maintenance of the general ledger are the following:

- Journal entries may be improperly prepared.
- Journal entries may be left unposted.
- Total debit balances and total credit balances in the accounts in the general ledger may become out of balance.
- Control account balances in the general ledger may become out of balance with the totals of balances in subsidiary ledgers.
- Unauthorized people may gain access to data in the general ledger.
- The audit trail that links the general ledger with source documents may become obscured.
- Data pertaining to the general ledger and source documents may be lost or destroyed.

These risks lead to exposures such as inaccurate financial statements and related reports. For instance, assets and liabilities may be valued incorrectly; they could be either overstated or understated. The risks also can lead to "leaks" of important financial data to competitors and added costs in locating or reconstructing needed transaction data. Adequate general and transaction controls are necessary to counteract such risk exposures.

(a) General Controls

Suitable general controls include the following:

- Organizationally, the function of posting journal vouchers to the general ledger should be separated from the functions of preparing and approving journal vouchers and from the function of preparing the trial balances of the general ledger.

- Documentation should consist of a fully descriptive chart of accounts plus a manual of general ledger process in effect.
- Operating practices should be clearly established, including period-end schedules and the preparation of control reports.
- Security should be maintained (in the case of on-line systems) by such techniques as (a) requiring that clerks enter passwords before accessing the general ledger file, (b) employing special terminals for the sole entry of journal voucher data, (c) generating audit reports (access logs) that monitor entries, and (d) dumping the general ledger onto magnetic tape backups.

(b) Transaction Controls

The following control procedures relating directly to general ledger accounts and processing are generally adequate:

- Prenumbered journal vouchers are prepared in the appropriate departments. For example, a journal voucher that reflects the declaration of a dividend may be prepared in the treasurer's office. These prepared journal vouchers are then approved by responsible managers.
- The data in journal vouchers, such as the account numbers, are checked for accuracy in order to provide assurance that errors and omissions are detected before processing. In manual systems, general ledger clerks perform the checks. In computer-based systems, the checks are mainly performed by computer edit programs. Exhibit 8–7 lists several suitable programmed checks that are employed to detect errors and omissions in transaction data being entered for processing. Any errors detected by the programs are either listed in exception reports or are signaled on data entry screens, depending on the type of processing system being used.
- Detected errors in journal entries are corrected before the data are posted to the general ledger.
- Approved journal vouchers are posted by specially designated persons who are not involved in their preparation or approval:
  - **a.** In manual systems, the journal vouchers are posted by general ledger clerks directly to the general ledger sheets.
  - **b.** In batch computer-based systems, the journal vouchers are keyed by data entry clerks onto a magnetic medium; then the batches of entries are sorted by general ledger account numbers and posted during computer runs to the accounts. Exhibit 8–8 lists various checks that should be made during the posting or updating run to provide assurance that processing errors are detected.
  - **c.** In on-line computer-based systems, the journal vouchers are entered directly into the system with the aid of preformatted screens on terminals; then the entries are posted by the computer system to the accounts.
- The equality of debits and credits for each posted journal entry is verified.
- The totals of amounts posted from batched journal entries to general ledger accounts are compared with precomputed control totals.
- Adequate cross-references are included to provide a clear audit trail. For instance, the journal voucher number and general ledger account numbers are shown in printed

Type of Edit Check	Typical Transaction Data Items Checked	Assurance Provided
1. Validity check	General ledger account numbers; transaction codes	The entered numbers and codes are checked against lists of valid numbers and codes stored within the computer system.
2. Field check	Transaction amounts	The amount fields in the input records are checked to see if they contain the proper modes of characters for amounts (i.e., numeric characters). If other modes are found, such as alphabetic characters or blanks, an error is indicated.
3. Limit check	Transaction amounts	The entered amounts are checked against preestablished limits that represent reasonable maximums to be expected. (A separate limit is set for each account.)
4. Zero-balance checks	Transaction amounts	The entered debit amounts are netted against the entered credit amounts, and the resulting net amount is compared to zero. (A nonzero net amount indicates that the debits and credits are unequal.)
5. Completeness check	All entered data items	The entered transaction is checked to see that all required data items have been entered.
6. Echo check	General ledger account numbers and titles	After the account numbers pertaining to the transaction are entered at a terminal, the system retrieves and "echoes" back the account title; the person who has made the entry can visually verify from reading the titles that the correct account numbers were entered.

Exhibit 8–7. Table of programmed checks that edit and validate journal entry data. *Note: When entered data do not match or otherwise meet the expected conditions or limits, alert messages are displayed by the edit program on the screen in the case of an on-line data-entry system.*

Adapted from J. Wilkinson, *Accounting Information System: Essential Concepts and Applications,* 2nd ed. (New York: John Wiley & Sons, 1993).

listings of the general journal, and the source page number of the general journal or journal voucher number is shown in each posting to the general ledger. Also, transaction numbers on source documents may be carried to transaction listings and into proof reports such as listings of account activity.

- Journal vouchers are filed by number, and the file is checked periodically to make certain that the sequence of numbers is complete.
- Standardized adjusting journal entries (including accruals and reversing entries) are maintained on preprinted sheets (or on magnetic media) to enhance the posting step at the end of each accounting period. Standardized journal entries are those that are prepared to reflect period-end adjustments of a recurring nature.
- Trial balances of general ledger accounts are prepared periodically, and differences between total debits and credits are fully investigated.

Type of Edit Check	Typical Transaction Data Items Checked	Assurance Provided
1. Internal label check		The internal header label of the file to be updated (posted to) is checked before processing begins to ascertain that the correct general ledger master file has been accessed for processing.
2. Sequence check	General ledger account numbers	The transaction file, which has been sorted so that the amounts in the various journal vouchers are ordered according to account numbers, is checked to see that no transaction item is out of sequence.
3. Redundancy matching check	General ledger account numbers and titles	Each transaction debit and credit is checked to see that its account number matches the account number in the general ledger record it is to update. Then the account titles in the transaction record and master file record are also matched, thus providing double protection against updating the wrong file record.
4. Relationship check	Transaction amounts and account numbers	The balance of each general ledger account is checked, after the transaction has been posted, to see that the balance has a normal relationship to the account. If the balance in an account balance that normally exhibits a debit balance (e.g., accounts receivable) appears as a credit, the abnormality will be flagged by the check.
5. Posting check	Transaction amounts	The after-posting balance in each updated account is compared to the before-posting balance, to see that the difference equals the transaction amount.
6. Batch control total checks	Transaction amounts	The amounts posted are totaled and compared to the precomputed amount total of the batch being processed; also, the total number of transaction items processed is compared to the precomputed count of the transactions.

Exhibit 8–8. Table of programmed edit checks that validate batched data during posting (updating) runs.

Adapted from J. Wilkinson, *Accounting Information System: Essential Concepts and Applications,* 2nd ed. (New York: John Wiley & Sons, 1993).

- General ledger control account balances are reconciled periodically to totals of balances in subsidiary ledger accounts.
- Special period-end reports that help correct mistakes are printed for review by accountants and managers.
- Accountants and managers perform periodic review of journal entries and financial reports, while internal auditors may check the procedures being used.

8.7 FINANCIAL AND MANAGERIAL REPORTS

The financial reports generated by the general ledger system may be classified as general ledger analyses, financial statements, and managerial reports. A wide variety of examples are found in each category.

(a) General Ledger Analyses

Most general ledger analyses are prepared as control devices. That is, they are intended to aid accountants in verifying the accuracy of postings. Two examples are the general journal listing and the general ledger change report. Other analyses related to general ledger processing may contain the following:

- Listings of all transactions posted during an accounting period, arranged by account numbers
- Allocations of expenses to the respective cost centers
- Comparisons of account balances for the current period with those for the same period last year and comparisons of year-to-date account balances for this year with those for last year

(b) Financial Statements

The most visible financial statements are the balance sheet, income statement, and cash flow statement. These statements, which are based directly on information in the general ledger, are provided to various parties outside the firm. Since a major reason for getting these reports prepared and disseminated is due to legal obligations, the accounting information system must incorporate rules and procedures that ensure that financial statements and derivative reports will conform with generally accepted accounting principles. Furthermore, since the array of financial reports include income tax returns and other tax reports, the AIS also must comply with federal, state, and local tax regulations.

Often the financial statements are accompanied by additional information that is useful to recipients. For instance, they may be accompanied by comparative statements for previous years, by budgetary amounts, and by detailed schedules. Variances also may be computed and reported.

(c) Managerial Reports

Numerous reports based on the general ledger may be prepared for the use of the firm's managers. Most of these managerial reports are generated from the same data used to prepare the financial statements. However, financial statements for managers tend to be much more detailed than those provided to outside parties. For instance, analyses based on individual general ledger accounts are often prepared. Examples are analyses of sales, broken down by products or sales territories or markets; analyses of cash, broken down by type of receipts and expenditures; analyses of receivables, broken down by customers and ages of amounts due.

For managerial control and performance evaluation, comparative financial statements are also useful to managers. To be genuinely useful, though, the comparative information must be detailed and performance-oriented. Consequently, financial reports have been incorporated into reporting systems that focus on managerial responsibilities and segment profits. They enable managers to exercise more precise control over cost centers, profit centers, investment centers, products, sales territories, and so on. These responsibility-oriented reports are derived largely from the same information used in preparing financial statements.

A responsibility accounting system compares actual financial performance results with planned budgetary amounts for the various responsibility centers of a firm. In its report the focus is on controllable versus noncontrollable costs. Managers cannot be held responsible for costs they do not control. Controllable costs are usually those pertaining to direct materials, direct labor, supplies, and the like. Controllable costs are those that the manager heading the cost center can affect. Every cost is controllable at some level within the organization.

8.8 CODING OF ACCOUNTS

A sound coding system is critical to the success of a responsibility accounting system. Costs must be gathered and coded by responsibility centers (as must revenues for those centers having profit responsibilities). Exhibit 8–9 illustrates responsibility center codes based on a hierarchical group coding scheme. For instance, all costs coded 1333 will be compiled for the report to be received by the foreperson of production unit 3. If the code 761 is the general

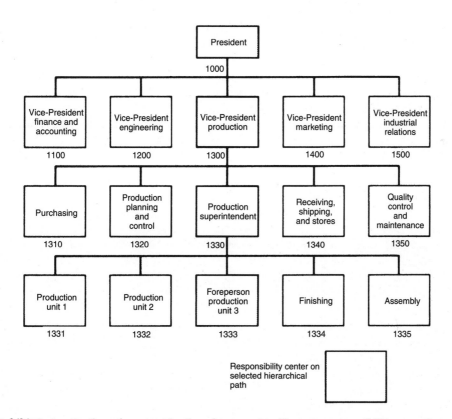

Exhibit 8–9.   Portion of an organization chart used to illustrate responsibility reporting.
Adapted from J. Wilkinson, *Accounting Information System: Essential Concepts and Applications,* 2nd ed. (New York: John Wiley & Sons, 1993).

ledger account code for direct labor, the code 761–1333 attached to a cost of $200 would identify the cost as being direct labor incurred by cost center 1333. All costs having the same code for a month would be totaled and listed as one of the items on the foreman's report.

8.9 CHARTS OF ACCOUNTS

We should not leave the general ledger system without discussing the chart of accounts, the AIS component around which the general ledger is organized. A chart of accounts is a coded listing of the asset, liability, owners' equity, revenue, and expense accounts pertaining to a firm. Taken together, these accounts facilitate the preparation of needed financial statements and reports. As an aid in its use, the chart of accounts also should describe accurately (but concisely) the contents of each account. For instance, it might identify the specific transactions that will affect a particular account, such as all purchases of merchandise and purchase returns will affect the purchases account (assuming that the periodic inventory method is to be employed).

The chart of accounts is closely related to the general ledger and subsidiary ledgers as well as to the financial statements. Each record in the general ledger is identified by one of the accounts listed in the chart of accounts. Details of the transactions affecting the accounts are reflected in the records of the general ledger. Certain accounts in the chart of accounts are control accounts, since the corresponding records in the general ledger contain balances that equal the total of balances in subsidiary ledgers. An example is the accounts receivable control account in the general ledger that controls the balances in the accounts receivable subsidiary ledger. It must be emphasized that the financial outputs dictate the composition of the chart of accounts as well as the accounting records. This explains why managers find systems set up to meet external financial reporting needs inadequate for internal managerial decision making.

Having described the place of the chart of accounts within the system, let us examine more closely its account classifications and coding systems.

(a) Account Classifications

As noted previously, financial statements and reports are needed by a wide variety of external as well as internal users. Thus, the listing of accounts should include all accounts required by law and by tax regulations and other legal obligations. For instance, public utilities are required to have specific accounts prescribed by the Federal Power Commission and by state utility regulatory bodies.

The accounts also are affected by the activities and customs of the industries within which firms operate. Thus, firms that manufacture goods need three inventory accounts and one supplies account (at least), whereas firms that provide services need only supplies accounts. Service firms, however, must focus on the performance and pricing of services. Not-for-profit organizations differ from both manufacturing and service firms in that they are more concerned with costs than with revenues.

With respect to the internal users such as managers, the accounts should be sufficiently detailed to aid in planning and control functions. For example, the revenues of an automobile dealer could be separated into accounts for new car sales, used car sales, parts sales, and repairs services. To provide sufficient details for managers, the number of accounts maintained within a chart of accounts is generally greater than the items appearing in the financial statements.

Although a chart of accounts pertains directly to asset and equity accounts (including revenues and expenses), it is closely tied to a firm's organizational structure and segments. As we have noted, an expense account within the chart of accounts can be linked to responsibility centers. We consider this expanded view of the chart of accounts in the discussion of account coding.

(b) Account Coding

The coding system used to form the broad framework within a chart of accounts is usually of the block type. For instance, current assets may be assigned numbers from 100 to 199, noncurrent assets from 200 to 299, liabilities may be 300 to 399, while revenues could be 500 to 599, product expenses may be 600 to 699, 700 to 899 could be operating expenses, while 900 to 999 may be the nonoperating expenses. Each block may contain subordinate blocks. Consider the operating expenses, which are blocked from 700 through 899. Within this broad block could be subordinate blocks representing the functional categories of expenses such as administrative travel. The particular accounts and the details they represent are based on the various needs of internal and external users.

A group coding system can provide added meaning to individual account codes. The leftmost digit can represent a major category (e.g., asset), the middle digit an intermediate classification (e.g., plant assets), and the rightmost digit a minor classification (e.g., the type of plant asset). For example, the account code 112 may refer to the type of plant asset known as buildings. This example of a code is similar in construction to the hierarchical group code employed with responsibility centers. Also, it is interesting to observe the close relationship between block and group codes.

Group codes are often used as the coding structure for general ledger accounts, since they allow several facets to be incorporated. For instance, direct labor expense in a production department might be coded 761–1333. Other coding fields might be added, relating to subsidiary ledgers, locations, and products. Group codes that capture these facets of transactions aid the preparation of useful analyses.

An illustrative group code having fields pertaining to general ledger accounts, subsidiary ledger accounts, and responsibility centers would appear as follows:

AAA-BBBB-CC

A sales transaction coded according to this format could show a code 121–563–00 to identify the debit and the code 820–1738–08 to identify the credit. The 121 and 820 refer to the general ledger accounts entitled accounts receivable and sales. The 5634 refers to the customer account against which the credit sale is charged, and the 1738 refers to the salesperson whose account is credited in the commissions payable ledger. The 08 refers to the sales region (responsibility center) where the sale is made. Finally, the 00 indicates that accounts receivable are general in nature and not applicable to a particular responsibility center.

The appendix to this chapter represents a coded chart of account for a midsize firm. Through it one can gain further understanding of how ledger accounts are coded.

8.10 CONCLUSION

General ledger systems are involved in collecting, classifying, coding, processing, storing transaction data, maintaining accounting controls, and generating financial reports. The general ledger system is also called the general ledger and financial reporting cycle, which is at the center of such transaction-oriented cycles as the revenue, expenditure, and resources management.

The general ledger system receives routine recurring and nonrecurring transactions, nonroutine transactions, adjusting entries, reversing entries, and closing entries. The inputs are normally on general ledger journal vouchers, which in computer-based systems may be transferred to batch entry forms or to data entry screens. The entered data, in journal entry form, are then posted to the general ledger to update the accounts during the accounting period. At the end of each accounting period standard and nonstandard adjusting journal entries are posted. The exact methods of processing vary, depending on whether the processing is performed by manual or computer-based systems. The database includes files such as the general ledger master file, general ledger history file, responsibility center master file, budget master file, financial reports format file, current journal voucher file, and journal voucher history file.

A variety of general and transaction controls are needed to offset a number of risks to which the general ledger is exposed. These controls include adequate documentation, organizational segregation, data security, carefully designed and prepared journal vouchers, and periodic trial balances. Financial reports typically generated by the general ledger system include analyses of general ledger accounts, financial statements, and managerial reports such as sales analyses and responsibility reports. Many of the managerial reports involve comparisons between budget and actual amounts.

The chart of accounts is a coded listing of all of the classified accounts of a firm. Charts of accounts vary widely among firms, since they must satisfy the needs of both external and internal users.

APPENDIX: TOTAL QUALITY APPLIANCE CORPORATION—CLASSIFICATION OF ACCOUNTS

BALANCE SHEET ACCOUNTS
Current Assets
10100 Petty Cash
10200 Cash in Bank
11100 Accounts Receivable—Customers
11100A Allowance for Uncollectible Accounts
11200 Accounts Receivable—Officers and Employees
11300 Sales/Representative's Drawing Accounts
11400 Notes Receivable
11400D Notes Receivable Discounted
11500 Accrued Interest Receivable
12000 Merchandise Inventories
12100 Kitchen Appliances
12200 Laundry Appliances
12300 Other Appliances
13100 Prepaid Rent—Outside Warehousing
14100 Office Supplies

14200 Warehouse and Shop Supplies

Property, Plant, and Equipment
15000 Land
16100 Building
16100A Allowance for Depreciation—Building
16200 Warehouse Equipment
16200A Allowance for Depreciation—Warehouse Equipment
16300 Delivery Trucks
16300A Allowance for Depreciation—Delivery Trucks
16400 Service Shop Equipment
16400A Allowance for Depreciation—Service Shop Equipment

Current Liabilities
17100 Vouchers Payable—Appliance Suppliers
17200 Vouchers Payable—Other
17300 Accrued Payroll
17500 Notes Payable
17600 Bank Loans
17700 Accrued Interest Payable
17800 Dividends Payable
18100 Accrued Payroll Taxes
18200 Withholding Tax Deducted
18300 Federal Income Tax Accrued
18400 Accrued Real Estate Taxes
18500 Accrued Personal Property Taxes
18600 Accrued Sales Tax—Illinois

Reserves
18900 Reserve for Warranty

Long-Term Liabilities
19000 Mortgage Payable

Net Worth
19500 Capital Stock
19600 Retained Earnings
19900 Profit and Loss

INCOME STATEMENT ACCOUNTS
Sales and Purchases
21000 Sales and Service Income
21100 Sales of Kitchen Appliances and Parts

21200 Sales of Laundry Appliances and Parts

21300 Sales of Other Appliances

21400 Service Income—Inside

21500 Service Income—Outside

21600 Service Contracts

21700 Labor Used on Service Contracts (debit)

22000 Sales Returns and Allowances

22100 Kitchen Appliances and Parts

22200 Laundry Appliances and Parts

22300 Other Appliances

23000 Purchases

24000 Freight In

25000 Purchase Returns and Allowances

Administrative Expenses

30000 Administrative Expenses Control

31100 Administrative Salaries

31900 Overtime Premium

32100 FICA Tax Expense

32200 Unemployment Insurance Expense

33100 Stationery and Office Supplies

34100 Repairs to Office Furniture and Equipment

36100 Postage

36200 Telephone and Telegraph

36500 Donations

37000 Travel

38000 Unclassified

39100 Rentals of Office Equipment

39300 Insurance—Office Furniture and Equipment

39400 Taxes—Office Furniture and Equipment

Selling Expenses

40000 Selling Expenses Control

41100 Sales Supervisory Salaries

41300 Outside Salespeople

41400 Commissions

45100 Newspaper and Magazine Advertising

45200 Dealer Aids

45300 Convention Expense

45400 Advertising Allowances to Dealers

46100 Association Dues

46200 Professional Services

46300 Freight Out

Receiving, Warehousing, and Shipping Expenses

50000 Receiving, Warehousing, and Shipping Expenses Control

51300 Truck Drivers and Helpers

51900 Overtime Premium

53100 Packing Supplies

54100 Repairs to Warehouse Equipment

54300 Gasoline and Oil

59500 Insurance—Inventories

59600 Insurance—Trucks

59700 Taxes—Warehouse Equipment

59900 Taxes and Licenses—Trucks

CHAPTER 9

THE REVENUE CYCLE

9.1 INTRODUCTION

This chapter provides an understanding of the working of the revenue cycle of a firm as well as the documentation used to carry out the functions associated with it. Furthermore, since realizing revenue involves the entire organization in various roles, this chapter outlines the involvement of various departments with respect to the functions performed during the revenue cycle and the information needs of those involved. Key activities and data processing operations included in the revenue cycle are also detailed. The flow-charting of data and information flows in typical sales order processing systems is highlighted, along with information that prepares managers and accountants to evaluate and recommend control policies and procedures for a sales order processing system. In addition, this chapter discusses data files used for the cycle, typical accounting entries used, and coding used to facilitate processing.

The revenue cycle of an organization seeks to facilitate transactions that exchange products or services for cash. Most organizations depend on the revenue they raise through such transactions for their survival. The functions related to revenue generation, either through providing services or products, comprise the revenue cycle of an organization.

Specifically, the revenue cycle for a business includes: soliciting customer orders, executing sales transactions, and delivering products or services to the customers. The revenue cycle also involves the following data processing operations: sales order processing, billing, updating inventory records, and maintaining customer account records. Additionally, one of the business cycles interfaces with the general ledger and financial reporting system. Information about the revenues earned is a major component of the financial reports periodically issued by a firm.

In other words, the revenue cycle consists of both transaction-related and data-related functions. But the efforts needed to earn revenue cannot be limited to elements specifically related to the revenue cycle. Indeed, the entire organization has to be involved if the business is to continue, and every function affects the continued ability of a firm to earn revenue. While showing how the involvement of the entire organization results in revenue may be difficult, we describe the involvement of some of the departments in the revenue cycle and the information needs of those involved.

9.2 ORGANIZATIONAL CONTEXT

One department that plays a major role in the revenue cycle is the marketing staff. Marketing managers usually are charged with functions such as establishing policies with respect to base prices, discounts, credit terms, return policies, and warranties. In addition, they participate in staff decisions such as those pertaining to advertising and new product development. They also have to review and evaluate the performance of marketing personnel. Their time is taken up, to a large extent, with allocating key resources, such as people and funds, to achieve marketing goals both strategic and operational.

These functions are facilitated by the information available to them. To perform their duties, marketing managers usually need information pertaining to the following: economic trends, competitors' prices, national and international sociopolitical developments, sales forecasts, market research data, product costs, and costs of returns, credit, and warranties.

Sales personnel are also heavily involved in the revenue cycle. Their duties include: establishing standards and quotas (with the help of others such as marketing managers), selecting effective distribution channels, and reviewing and evaluating performance of sales personnel. Sales managers need information pertaining to: sales forecasts; sales analyses (breakdown of sales by category); profitability analyses (showing marginal contribution to profit); operational data on individual salespeople, including information about sales calls made and ratio of calls made to sales concluded; and inventory availability.

The advertising and promotion department is also heavily involved in the revenue cycle of a business. Their duties include: creating advertising campaigns, establishing dealer incentives, and managing other promotional activities. Key information needed by the advertising and promotion department to perform those duties are: sales forecasts, profitability analyses, surveys of customer attitudes, advertising costs, and measures of advertising effectiveness.

The department of product planning also affects the revenue function. Its duties include: planning characteristics of product lines, styling and packaging, and introducing new products and reviewing performance of existing products. The information needed to perform those duties includes: sales analyses, profitability analyses, product costs, and customer attitudes.

Finally, customer service affects the ability to keep earning revenue. Those involved in customer service are concerned with: setting policies and making decisions relating to customer needs, providing retailers with product availability and pricing data, providing customers with warranty information, and dealing with complaints. Key information needed to perform those duties includes some knowledge of customer attitudes as well as costs of servicing customers.

Judging from this survey, it is clear that the revenue cycle requires the involvement of a variety of departments. In order for managers in such departments to make better decisions, both accounting and nonaccounting information is needed. To provide such information, a great deal of data pertaining to revenue function must be made available. This is the function of accounting information systems.

Given the number of steps involved, it is better to treat the revenue cycle as made up of three interrelated subcycles: credit sales, cash receipts, and accounts receivable maintenance. Such is the case in this book. We also differentiate between the manual and computerized systems pertaining to the three above-mentioned subsets of the revenue cycle.

9.3 DOCUMENTATION OF THE REVENUE CYCLE

In this section, the documentation needed for a manual revenue cycle is described. The revenue cycle source documents typically found in firms that employ manual processing and make product sales include the following:

(a) Customer Order

Often the customer order is the customer's purchase order, and thus not a document prepared by the selling firm. However, it may be a form prepared by the salesperson that lists information that identifies the customer as well as the items ordered, together with their unit prices and discounts provided, if any. The form also identifies the person taking the order.

(b) Sales Order

Although similar to the customer order, a sales order has significant differences. First, it is often a more formal, multicopy form that is prepared from the customer order. Second, it is prenumbered for more effective control. Finally, it often contains price and extension columns, so that it can be completed to serve as the invoice. In some firms the sales order is called the shipping order, since it provides authorization for the shipping action.

(c) Order Acknowledgment

Usually the order acknowledgment is a copy of the sales order, although it may be a separate form. Sometimes the customer also requires that the selling firm return a signed acknowledgment that has been prepared by the customer.

(d) Picking List

In some cases, a copy of the sales order is sent to the warehouse for use in picking the ordered goods from the bins. Alternatively, a separate picking list document may be prepared. This document specifies the goods to be picked and authorizes their removal. The ordered product data often are arranged in a picking list in accordance with the bin locations in the warehouse. Thus, the picking can be done more efficiently.

(e) Packing List or Slip

The packing list is enclosed with the goods when they are packaged. It is generally a copy of the sales order, or it may be the picking list.

(f) Bill of Lading

A document such as a bill of lading is relatively uniform from firm to firm. It is intended for the agents of the common carrier that is to transport the products, informing them that goods are legally on board the carrier, that the freight has been paid or billed, and that the consignee is authorized to receive the goods at the destination. In addition to the carrier, both the shipping department and the customer receive copies. Another copy may serve as the freight bill (invoice) and be forwarded to the traffic department (if any) of the customer or seller, depending on who is paying.

(g) Shipping Notice

Often a copy of the sales order, when duly noted by the shipping manager, serves as proof that the goods were shipped. When a common carrier is involved, a copy of the bill of lading can serve this purpose. In other cases a separate prenumbered shipping notice, also called a shipping report, may be prepared by the shipping department. This notice is forwarded to the billing department and is to be used for completing the invoice sent to the customers.

(h) Remittance Advice

The remittance advice is a counterpart to the sales invoice, since it contains the amount of the cash receipt from the customer and the payor's name. It can be described as a turn-around document, since it represents a portion of the sales invoice that is returned by the customer with the cash. If the customer does not include a cash remittance, the firm must prepare one for use as the posting medium.

(i) Deposit Slip

Deposits of cash in the bank must be accompanied by deposit slips. A deposit slip usually contains imprints of both the firm name and the bank name. Coding at the bottom of the slip refers to the account number and the bank code.

(j) Backorder

A form called a backorder is prepared when insufficient quantities are in inventory to satisfy sales orders. It should be prenumbered and contain data concerning the customer for whom the backorder is being placed, the original sales order number, the quantity needed, and the date requested. If the original order is partially filled and the remaining quantities are backordered, the backorder number and relevant data should be entered on the sales invoice. These backorder data have also likely been posted to the inventory records. When the backordered items are received from the supplier, they will be shipped to the customer immediately and the notation will be removed from the inventory records. A new sales invoice also will be prepared for the backordered items and mailed to the customer.

(k) Credit Memo

Before ordered goods can be returned or before allowances can be granted, a prenumbered credit memo must be prepared and approved. When filled in, it will state that a customer's account balance will be credited by an indicated amount (e.g., $100). On receipt by the customer, it will serve that firm as the posting medium to reduce the balance in the accounts payable account. A credit memo relating to a return should be approved only on the basis of clear-cut evidence, such as a sales return notice, that lists the physical count of returned goods by the receiving department.

(l) Other Documents

A new-customer credit application is useful when customers apply for credit. It should include all of the data pertaining to the applicant's current financial condition and earning level. A salesperson call report may be used to describe each call on a prospective customer and to indicate the result of the call. A delinquent notice may be sent to customers who are past due on their credit account balances. A write-off notice or form is a document prepared by the credit manager when an account is deemed to be uncollectible. A journal voucher is prepared as the basis for each posting to accounts in the general ledger. For instance, a journal voucher may be prepared to reflect one or more account write-offs.

Finally, retail firms that make cash sales use receipted sales tickets or cash register receipts to reflect cash received.

9.4 DOCUMENTATION FOR COMPUTER-BASED SYSTEMS

All of the above-mentioned hard-copy documents also may be used in computer-based systems. If so, they should be designed to speed the entry of data into the computer system with few errors. Preformatted screens may be used to expedite data entry pertaining to sales orders, sales returns, and cash receipts transactions. Such screens may be designed to handle individual transactions or batches of transactions. They do not differ greatly in format from hard-copy forms. With slight changes, for instance, hard-copy forms could be employed as preformatted screens. Also, on-line computer systems may generate hard copies of documents after data have been entered via preformatted screens.

The on-line entry of data is becoming increasingly common. Note that the underlying computer program aids data entry by performing several functions automatically. Thus, the date and batch number are entered when the preformatted screen is accessed. Similarly, data for a number of fields may be retrieved from the open sales invoice and customer files, which the program searches by reference to the entered customer and invoice numbers. Also, the total of all payment amounts entered is computed and placed in the field designated on the screen. In addition, the entered total and previously computed control total are compared by the program, and the difference is displayed.

9.5 JOURNAL ENTRIES USED FOR THE REVENUE CYCLE

Sales transactions give rise to their share of general entries. Each sale results in an invoice, and every invoice leads to entries into a sales journal as well as to individual customer accounts in the accounts receivable subsidiary ledger. Periodically, summary totals in the sales journal are posted to the general ledger accounts as follows:

1. Dr. Accounts Receivable XXX

Cr. Sales XXX

To record the total of credit sales.

If the inventory is maintained on a perpetual basis, the following entry would be recorded on a journal voucher to accompany each daily sales entry:

2. Dr. Cost of Goods Sold XXX

Cr. Merchandise Inventory XXX

To record the costs of those goods sold during this date.

If necessary, journal vouchers are prepared to reflect sales returns and allowances or write-offs via the following entries:

3. Dr. Sales Returns and Allowances XXX

Cr. Accounts Receivable XXX

To adjust customer account balances to reflect returns and allowances on previous sales.

4. Dr. Allowance for Doubtful Accounts XXX

Cr. Accounts Receivable XXX

To write off those customers' account balances that are deemed to be uncollectible (assuming that the allowance method for establishing bad debt expense is used).

The flow of cash receipts is also a source of transactions flowing through the accounting cycle. Checks received from customers initiate most cash receipts transactions. The amounts of the checks are entered from accompanying remittance advice into a cash receipts journal and are posted to the accounts receivable subsidiary ledger. Periodically, totals from the journal are posted to the general ledger by the following entry:

1. Dr. Cash XXX

Cr. Accounts Receivable XXX

To record daily cash receipts.

Cash may be received from sources other than customer accounts. If so, it may be recorded as a part of the above entry, or it may be reflected in a separate entry like the following:

2. Dr. Cash XXX

Cr. Notes Payable XXX

Cr. Interest or Dividend Income XXX

To record cash received from sources other than customers.

9.6 TRANSACTION CODING

Codes are essential for identifying key aspects of sales and cash receipts transactions. Codes may be assigned to customers, sales territories, salespeople, and product types when recording sales transactions. Codes such as these reduce the quantity of data entered and provide unique identifiers. They also facilitate the preparation of sales analyses. Based on the above-mentioned example, sales analyses could show amounts of sales made to customers within each sales territory and amounts of sales made of the various products by each salesperson.

Codes that describe transactions should be group codes, since they encompass several characteristics. In turn, the code for each characteristic could incorporate several features. For instance, a particular customer code might be R9174248, based on the format ABBC-CCCD, where:

- A represents the class or type of customer.
- BB represents the year the customer became active.
- CCCC represents the specific customer identifier.
- D represents a self-checking digit.

On-line computer system codes that identify transactions are often used. For instance, transaction codes may be entered together with the remaining data for transactions, so that the system knows which application program to employ. Transaction codes may be developed for sales, sales returns or allowances, and other prospective types of transactions. These other transaction codes may not be needed if preformatted screens are accessed via menus, since menu-driven systems designate the suitable application programs through the menu selections.

9.7 DATABASE FILES

The database for the revenue cycle contains master files, transaction files, open document files, and other types of files. If appropriate database software is available, it may also contain data structures. Two likely master files employed within the revenue cycle pertain to customers and accounts receivable. If a firm has product sales, a third file is the merchandise inventory master file. It will not be needed if the firm offers services only. The content of these files will vary from firm to firm, depending on factors such as types of customers and markets, variety of desired managerial reports, and degree of computerization. Our survey of these files is necessarily brief.

(a) Customer Master File

A customer master file contains records pertaining to individual credit customers. Generally, its primary and sorting key will be the customer number. Each record of this file contains customer data such as the shipping and billing addresses, telephone number, past payment performance, credit rating, trade discount allowed, and sales activity. These data items (i.e., elements) are useful in preparing sales invoices and monthly statements as well as in determining the credit limit.

(b) Accounts Receivable Master File

The records in an accounts receivable master file also relate to credit customers. They represent the computerized counterpart to the accounts receivable subsidiary ledger sheets in a manual system. Two data items are essential: the customer identification (usually the customer account number) and the current account balance. Other data items are optional, and they may include: credit limit, balance at the start of the year, year-to-date sales, and year-to-date payments. For firms using the open invoice method, data concerning specific unpaid invoices are also needed.

The data from both of the above-mentioned files are needed for preparing outputs such as customer monthly statements. If desired, however, the added items could be moved to the customer file. Alternatively, all data items pertaining to a customer, including all transactions for this year, could be consolidated into the accounts receivable file. The most important reason for separating the customer and accounts receivable files is to reduce the size of records during updates and, hence, the processing run times.

(c) Merchandise Inventory Master File

A merchandise file (or finished goods file) is relevant to the revenue cycle for a firm that sells products. Data items that might appear in a record layout include the product (inventory item) number, description, warehouse location code, unit of measure code, reorder point, reorder quantity, unit cost, quantity on order, date of last purchase, and quantity on hand. If inventory is maintained on the perpetual basis, the current balance also will be included. The primary and sorting key is usually the product or inventory item number.

(d) Transaction and Open Document Files

Transactions in the revenue cycle involve sales orders, sales invoices, shipping reports, credit memos, backorders, and cash receipts. Each of the records in related transaction files would contain roughly the data shown in the documents discussed earlier. Three of the major transaction files require closer attention: sales order file, sales invoice transaction file, and cash receipts transaction file.

(i) Sales Order File. The content of the sales order files is similar to the data elements contained in accounts receivable master file. When stored in a record on a computerized medium, however, elements such as the customer name and product descriptions may be omitted. They may be drawn from the customer and merchandise inventory files when preparing sales invoices. The record may allow for repeating line items such as product numbers and quantities ordered. Alternatively, these line items may be placed in a separate line item file and cross-referenced. If this file consists of orders that have not yet been shipped and billed, it is known as an open sales order file. The sorting and primary key of the file is usually a preassigned order number. When an order is shipped and billed, it is usually transferred to a closed orders file.

(ii) Sales Invoice Transaction File. In a manual system, a sales invoice file consists of a copy of each current sales invoice. Records in this file provide the details of sales transactions posted to the accounts receivable record. By maintaining them in a separate file, the size of the accounts receivable records can be reduced. In a computer-based system, a printed copy may or may not be filed. The record stored on magnetic media essentially contains the sales date, customer number, sales order number, terms, product codes, unit prices, quantities, and transaction amount. It likely omits customer names and product data, since the data are available in other files. The primary (and sorting key) is likely the sales invoice number. Each record remains in an open sales invoice file until payment is received from the customer (or until the end of the period if the balance forward method is used).

(iii) Cash Receipts Transaction File. In a manual system, a cash receipts transaction file likely consists of a copy of each current remittance advice. In a computer-based system, the record layout on magnetic media may contain the customer's account number, the sales invoice number against which the payment is being applied, date of payment, and amount of payment. It also includes a code to identify the record as a cash receipt transaction, and it may be assigned a transaction number.

(e) Other Files

In addition to files described above, some systems may have a shipping and price data reference file. This reference file may contain such shipping data as freight rates, common carrier routes and schedules, current prices of all products, trade discounts, and so on. Another reference file, especially in manual systems, is a credit file, used to check and approve the credit of customers. Additionally, systems also may have files to track sales history and accounts receivable details.

(i) Sales History File. A sales history file contains summary data from sales order invoices. In a computer-based system, the records pertaining to sales orders and invoices are trans-

ferred to this file when they are removed from the open files. These records are retained in the history file for a reasonable period. For instance, a firm may decide to maintain a history file for the five years past. Records older than five years would be purged from the file. However, the firm that employs computer-based processing may retain printed copies of sales orders and invoices for a longer period. Data from this file are used to prepare sales forecasts and analyses. If desired, a cash receipts history file could also be maintained.

(ii) Accounts Receivable Detail File. In addition to creating separate sales invoice and cash receipts transaction files, the application program may accumulate records of the transactions in a detail file. Since it is restricted to the current period's transactions, it is not a replacement for the history files. Instead, its main purpose is to facilitate the preparation of monthly statements for customers. Also, it can serve as an audit trail.

9.8 WORKING OF THE REVENUE CYCLE

For the sake of convenience, the data flows and processing steps of a revenue cycle are divided into three major subsets: processing of sales transactions, processing of cash receipts transactions, and maintenance of the accounts receivable ledger. Exhibit 9–1 depicts these subdivisions and lists related documentation. We will take up the three subsets of a manually processed revenue cycle and then discuss their counterparts in a computer-based system. Understanding the work flows in a manual system will help make clear the processing steps performed by computer.

9.9 CREDIT SALES PROCEDURES IN MANUAL PROCESSING SYSTEMS

To help readers get oriented with the procedures involved in the manual processing system for the revenue cycle, Exhibit 9–2 presents a document flow chart of procedures involving the credit sales of products. Since the processing is performed manually, the emphasis is on the flows of source documents and outputs. Although the flow chart is detailed and appears to be quite complex, it provides an overall view of a sound sales procedure.

1. The receipt of an order by the order department leads to the preparation of a sales order, which should be prenumbered. Customer orders can be received by telephone, mail, sales agent, and electronically. This sales order form gets distributed across many departments. To facilitate such distribution, a sales order can have several copies. Here the form is assumed to consist of seven copies. While preparing the document, the sales order clerk will refer to the customer master file to obtain pertinent information such as credit history.

2. Credit check is the next step. A copy (#6) of the sales order is sent to the credit department. For long-standing customers this is done by utilizing a credit limit check, while for new customers, or for sales above the limit, formal credit approval is needed. If the credit is approved, the sale is authorized. The copy of the sales order is sent back to the sales order department. Copies of the sales order are then distributed as follows:

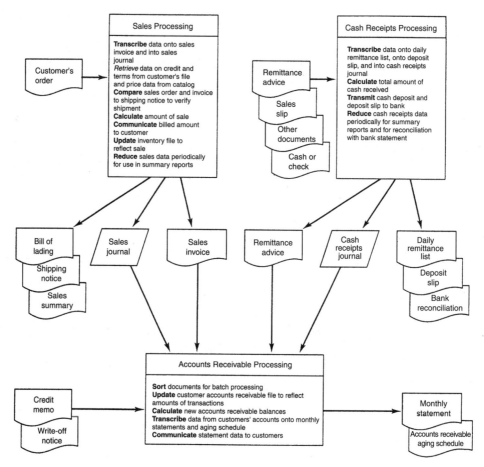

Exhibit 9–1. Diagram depicting processing steps and related documents for the revenue cycle.

Adapted from J. Wilkinson, *Accounting Information System: Essential Concepts and Applications,* 2nd ed. (New York: John Wiley & Sons, 1993).

A. Copies #1, 2, and 3 are sent to the billing department to await the notice of shipment before additional steps can be taken with respect to their subsequent use.

B. Copy #4 is sent to shipping to allow them to anticipate the arrival of goods from the warehouse.

C. Copy #5 of the sales order is sent to warehouse, where it will lead to the preparation of a picking list.

D. Copy #6 is made a part of the customer order file.

3. Shipping of ordered goods. This is initiated at the finished goods warehouse, which has custody of the merchandise. After getting the copy #5 of the sales order, the staff in the warehouse will assemble the order. They may use the copy of the order itself or another document, the picking list, to put together the goods needed for the order. If some of the ordered goods are not available, that absence is noted on the order. Subsequently, the merchandise and the copy #5 are delivered to the shipping department. In the shipping department, they will compare the goods delivered to them, copy #5, and copy #4 of the sales order. After such checking, the order is shipped to the customer together with copy #4 of the sales order. In some cases the shipping also will adjust the inventory record, although it is not usually feasible in a shipping department, given the nature of their environment. The shipping department also prepares the shipment-related documentation, such as the bill of lading. The bill of lading can have several copies. Here it is a document with three copies. The copy #1 is for the customer, #2 is for the carrier, and #3 is for the shipping department's records.

4. Billing for goods sold and shipped. After the goods are shipped, the shipping department notifies the billing department. There a clerk will compare the quantities shipped with the quantities ordered and enter onto the invoice the unit prices from a current pricing list. At times this may be checked by another individual for accuracy. A third individual may then complete the amounts to be billed and then accumulate enough invoices to form a batch and compute the batch totals. The batch of sales invoices is then sent to the accounts receivable department for posting. There a journal voucher is prepared for posting to the ledger. This procedure is further explained in the section "Accounts Receivable Maintenance Procedure."

5. Receipt of the order by the customer. The customer receives the goods shipped together with a packing slip, actually a copy of the sales order, as well as a copy of the bill of lading. Prior to the receipt of the order itself, customers usually receive a copy of the sales order, which confirms the order placed. Some time after receiving the shipment, the customer will receive an invoice proper listing the amount owed to the seller. It is usual for the customer to compare the invoice, the packing slip, and the receiving report prepared by the customer's receiving department after the shipment arrived.

Before leaving this subset, it may be helpful to understand the disposal of the sales order copies. This will also serve as a useful review of an involved process:

1. Copies #1, 2, and 3 get sent to billing. After additional processing there, #1 becomes the sales invoice and goes to the customer, #2 becomes the sales invoice file copy and remains in the closed orders file, while #3 becomes the sales invoice ledger copy and is sent to accounts receivable.

2. Copy #4 is sent to shipping, often becomes a packing slip, and goes to the customer with the order.

3. Copy #5 goes first to the warehouse (stock request copy), then goes back to the billing department and finally to the inventory control department.

4. Copy #6 goes to the credit department and then becomes part of the customer order file.

5. Copy #7 goes to the customer as an acknowledgment of the order received.

There can be variations. The invoice received by the customer, copy #1, could itself have a copy that the customer can keep for his or her records.

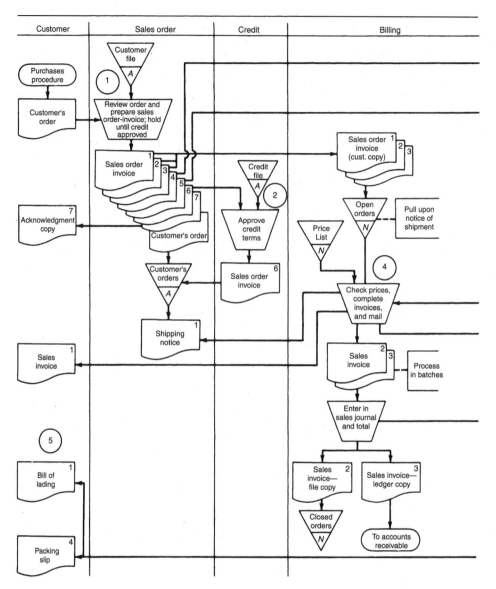

Exhibit 9–2.   Document system flow chart of a manual credit sales transaction processing procedure.

Adapted from J. Wilkinson, *Accounting Information System: Essential Concepts and Applications,* 2nd ed. (New York: John Wiley & Sons, 1993).

9.10 CASH RECEIPTS PROCEDURE

As noted earlier, cash receipts are seen as an independent subset of the revenue cycle. Exhibit 9–3 shows a flow chart of a procedure involving the receipts of cash related to sales. The principal control points involve the receipt of cash, the processing of the cash deposit, and the posting of cash amounts to the ledgers.

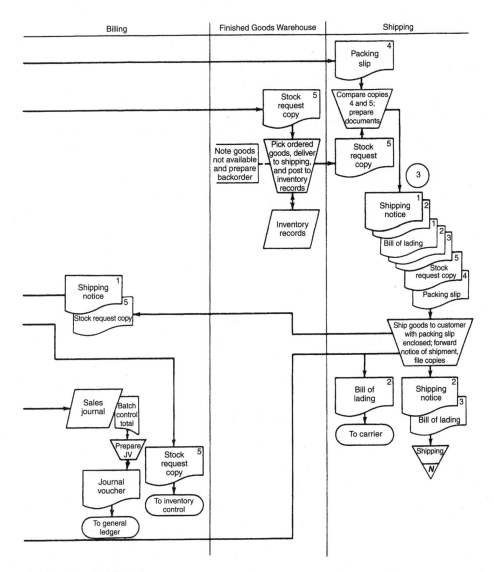

Exhibit 9–2.   Continued.

1. **Receipt of cash.** The cash receipts procedure begins with the daily receipt of mailed cash and remittance advices from customers. An authorized person, such as a mailroom clerk, compares the checks with the remittance advices and prepares advices when none are received. Then the clerk endorses/stamps the checks "For Deposit Only," enters their amounts on a prenumbered remittance list, and computes a total of the batch received. One copy of the remittance list (also called a prelist) is sent to the cashier with the checks; a second copy is sent to the internal audit department (if any) for later reviews; the third copy is filed.

2. **Processing of the cash deposit.** A person who is authorized to handle the cash, such as the cashier, prepares a deposit slip in triplicate. All checks from cus-

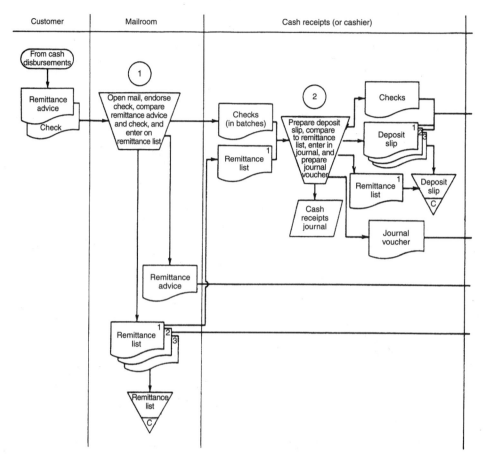

Exhibit 9–3.   Document system flow chart of a manual cash receipts transaction processing procedure.

Adapted from J. Wilkinson, *Accounting Information System: Essential Concepts and Applications,* 2nd ed. (New York: John Wiley & Sons, 1993).

tomers, plus cash received from other sources that day, are listed on the deposit slip. After the cashier compares the computed deposit total with that shown on the remittance list, he or she delivers the deposit to the bank intact. A cash receipts clerk then enters the total amount of receipts in the cash receipts journal. The clerk prepares a journal voucher, which is sent to the general ledger department for posting. The internal audit department receives an authenticated copy of the deposit slip, which has been stamped and initialed by a bank teller and delivered directly by the bank. This deposit slip is compared to the remittance list, as well as to the deposit slip in the cashier's office and to the general ledger posting.

3. Posting of cash amounts. After preparing the remittance list, the mailroom clerk forwards the remittance advices to the accounts receivable department for posting. The cashier sends a journal voucher to the general ledger department.

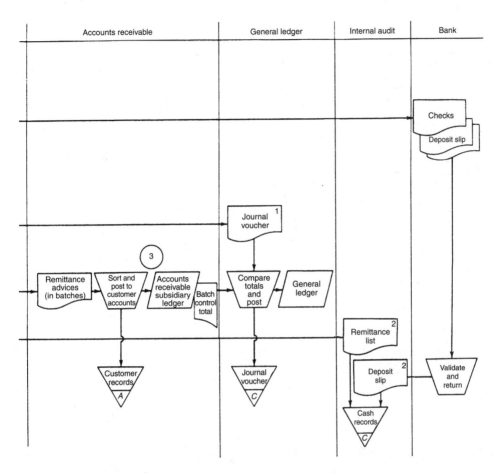

Exhibit 9–3. Continued.

9.11 ACCOUNTS RECEIVABLE MAINTENANCE PROCEDURE

The third subset of the revenue cycle pertains to updating accounts receivable. The accounts receivable subsidiary ledger is the link between the sales and cash receipts procedures. Exhibit 9–4 illustrates the steps related to posting sales transactions to the accounts receivable ledger. It parallels the figure describing the cash receipts subset. Both figures include the posting step to the general ledger. In addition, Exhibit 9–4 shows the procedures relating to sales returns and allowances and write-offs.

- Posting to accounts receivable accounts. On receiving copies of the sales invoices from the billing department, a clerk in the accounts receivable department posts the credit sales amounts to the customers' accounts. Another clerk verifies the posting and obtains a total of the amounts posted. This clerk then forwards customers' accounts. Sales postings need verification of their accuracy, as do the total of the amounts posted. The batch total is then forwarded to the general ledger department.
- Posting to general ledger accounts. In the general ledger department, a clerk compares (for each type of transaction) the total posted to the precomputed batch total

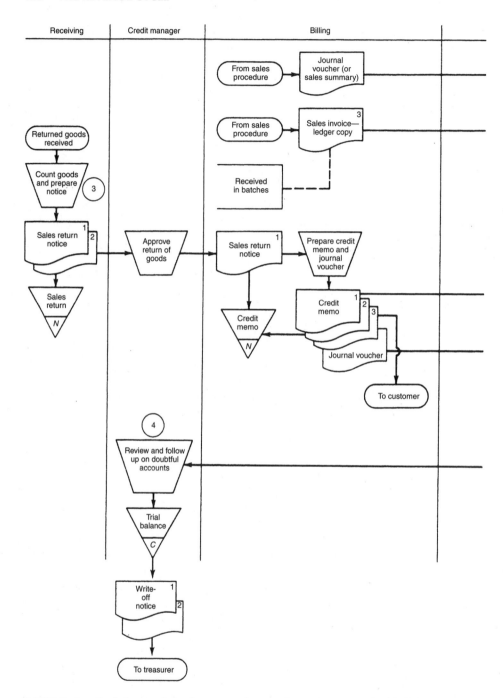

Exhibit 9–4.   Steps for posting sale transactions to the accounts receivable ledger.
Adapted from J. Wilkinson, *Accounting Information System: Essential Concepts and Applications,* 2nd
ed. (New York: John Wiley & Sons, 1993).

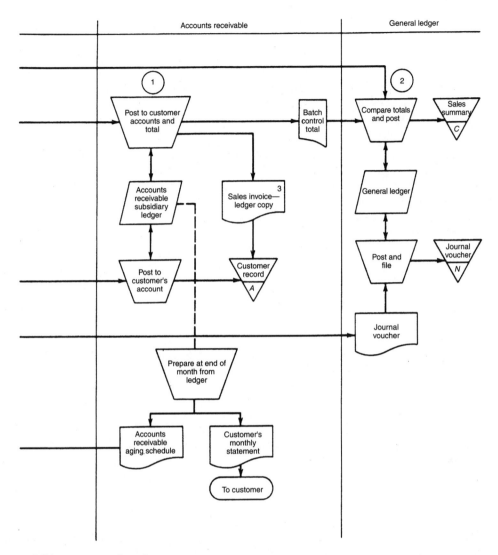

Exhibit 9–4. Continued.

amount, as shown on a summary journal voucher. If they agree, the clerk posts the totals to the general ledger accounts. If they disagree, the clerk locates discrepancies, corrects the errors, notifies the accounts receivable clerk of posting errors, and then completes the general ledger postings.

- Processing of sales return and allowances. When goods are returned from customers or if customers are to be given allowances, a manager must authorize the transaction. If a return of merchandise previously sold is involved, it is received in the receiving department, where a clerk counts and lists them on a sales return notice. If there was no prior authorization for the return, the receiving department will forward a copy to the credit manager for approval. The approved notice (or a return notification, if issued) is transmitted to the billing department, where the prices are checked against the original sales invoice. Then a prenumbered credit memo is prepared, with copies being sent to the accounts receivable department for posting and to the customer. A clerk in the billing department also prepares a journal voucher for the general ledger department, which posts the sales return transaction. Allowances on sales amounts are granted for damaged goods, shortages, or similar deficiencies. In such cases the sales order department or salesperson settles the amount, which is approved by the credit manager. Sales allowances are then processed in the same manner as sales returns.

- Processing of account write-offs. Another type of accounts adjustment is the write-off of customer account balances. After reviewing account balances and other available evidence, the credit manager makes a decision concerning the collectibility of accounts. As a result of the review, a write-off notice is prepared. After the treasurer or other designated manager approves the notice, it is processed in the same manner as sales returns and allowances.

9.12 COMPUTER-BASED PROCESSING SYSTEMS

When computers are used to process sales and cash receipt subcycles, transactions may be processed by a batch approach, an on-line approach, or a combination of the two. In the batch approach, the transaction data are keyed onto magnetic tape or disk, are sorted according to customer account numbers, and are posted sequentially to the accounts receivable master file. In the on-line approach, the transaction data are entered via a terminal and are posted individually to the master file. In the combined approach, the transaction data are entered via a terminal; however, they are gathered into a batch before being processed, either sequentially or directly, to the master file. The combined approach, described next, is popular, since it aids data entry and editing while retaining batch total controls.

9.13 CREDIT SALES PROCEDURE IN COMPUTERIZED SYSTEMS

Exhibit 9–5 presents a system flow chart of the on-line batch sales processing procedure. The flow chart logically divides into three segments: order entry, shipping, and billing.

1. Order entry. Each customer's order is entered when received by means of a terminal in the sales order department. The edit program validates the accuracy of the data, performs the credit check, and verifies that adequate merchandise is available to fill the order. If insufficient quantities of goods are available, the sales order clerk may specify to the computer system that a backorder is to be prepared. If the credit limit is not exceeded, the order is accepted and is placed in the open order file. When the order is ready to be filled (which may be immediately), the order entry program prints the acknowledgment to the customer, a picking list, and a backup file copy.

2. Shipping. After the ordered goods have been picked in the warehouse, the picking list is initialed by the picker and is amended to show any changes (e.g., items out of stock, substitutions). The goods are moved to the shipping department, where a clerk counts the goods and enters the quantities ready for shipment from the picking slip. A shipping program prepares the necessary documents for the shipment. When the goods are packed, they are delivered to the carrier for shipment. A shipping no-

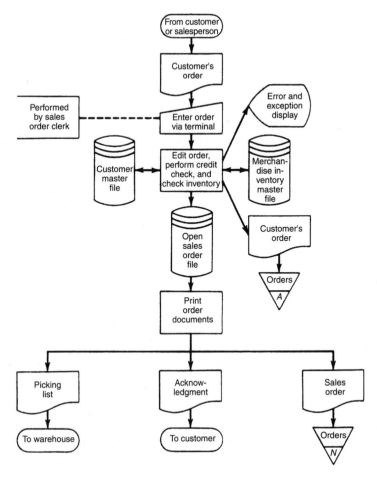

Exhibit 9–5.   System flow chart of an on-line/batch computer-based credit sales transaction processing procedure. (*a*) Order entry.

Adapted from J. Wilkinson, *Accounting Information System: Essential Concepts and Applications,* 2nd ed. (New York: John Wiley & Sons, 1993).

tice (which is, in effect, a copy of the bill of lading) is generated on the billing department's printer concerning the shipment. It shows not only quantities shipped but also the shipping routes, freight charges, and other needed shipping data.

3. Billing. Upon receiving the shipping notices for the day, a billing clerk prepares and enters the batch total of quantities shipped. The same clerk also converts each order into an invoice by viewing the order on the terminal screen, selecting product prices, and so on. All entered data are validated by an edit program. Then the data for all the readied invoices are stored temporarily in a billing file until processed. At that time: (a) the invoices are printed; (b) each customer's account is debited; (c) the inventory records are reduced by the quantities shipped; (d) the sales order is closed to the sales history file; (e) a new record is created in the sales invoice file; (f) a sales invoice register and a summary of accounts receivable are printed; and (g) the total amounts affecting the sales and accounts receivable accounts are posted to the

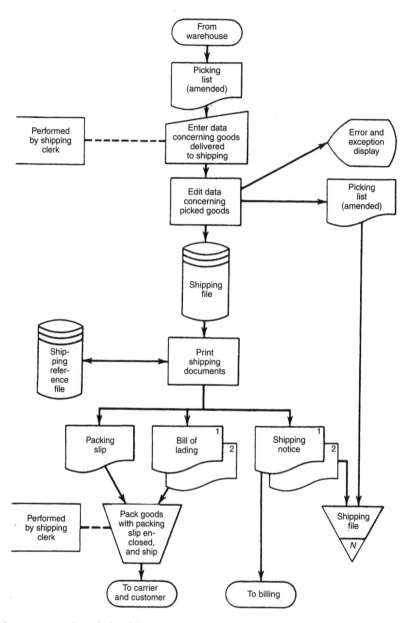

Exhibit 9–5. Continued. (b) Shipping.

general ledger accounts. Finally, the accounts receivable clerk verifies that the postings to the accounts receivable ledger agree with the batch total.

Other features not shown in the flow chart may be incorporated. The billing file could be sorted by customer number before posting to the accounts receivable master file. Sales returns may be processed together with sales, so that credit memos are produced. An accounts receivable detail file may also be maintained, to serve as an audit trail. If desired,

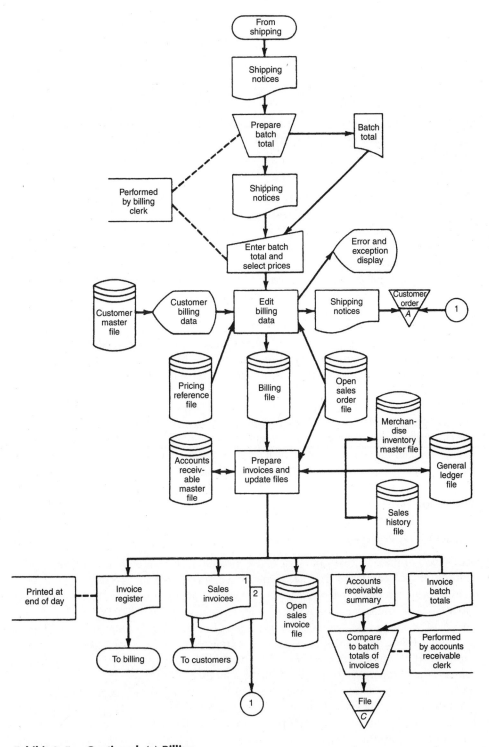

Exhibit 9–5. Continued. (c) Billing.

the general ledger processing could be maintained as a separate application. In that case, the billing application would generate a summary entry for later posting to the general ledger.

9.14 CASH RECEIPTS PROCEDURE IN COMPUTERIZED SYSTEMS

Exhibit 9–6 presents a system flow chart of the on-line cash receipts procedure. It is divided into two segments: (a) entry and deposit and (b) end-of-day processing.

(a) Entry and Deposit

As checks and remittances are received, one mailroom clerk endorses the checks and prepares a batch total. In place of the batch total the clerk could prepare a remittance list and add up the amounts of remittances. Another clerk enters the batch total and the data (amount, customer number, and sales invoice number) for each payment. If the indicated sales invoice pertaining to an amount is unpaid, and if the customer number is correct, the amount is accepted by the system. If the total of all the individual amounts entered, when computed by an edit program, is shown equal to the precomputed batch total, the batch is accepted. Following this, the application program credits the accounts receivable records for the customers remitting payments, documents that the affected sales invoices are paid, and closes the sales invoices to the sales history file. As in the case of sales transaction processing, the batch of cash receipts could be sorted by the application program prior to the posting step. After the processing is completed, the mail clerk sends the remittance advices to the accounts receivable department and the checks to the cashier. The cashier compares the checks to deposit slips prepared by a print program. In order to verify that all received checks are listed on the deposit slips, the cashier also may (1) receive a computer-prepared listing of cash remittances, or (2) access via a terminal the record of cash receipts for the day. When satisfied that the deposit slips are accurate and complete, the cashier has the checks and deposit slips delivered to the bank. The remainder of the deposit procedure corresponds to the steps in a manual system.

(b) End-of-Day Processing

At the end of the day, two summaries are prepared: a summary of accounts receivable activity and a remittance list (i.e., a cash receipts journal for the day). These summaries, which contain the batch total of receipts, are compared with the remittance advices. This comparison, performed by an accounts receivable clerk, verifies the accuracy of posting to the accounts. As another end-of-day step, a summary journal entry pertaining to the day's total cash receipts is transferred to the general ledger transaction file. If the open invoice method is employed for posting payments from customers, the foregoing procedure might be modified as follows: Instead of entering payments into the computer system, the mailroom clerks would prepare a remittance listing manually. They would then forward a copy to the accounts receivable department. An accounts receivable clerk would then enter the batch total and payment data via an on-line terminal. During the entry of each payment, the clerk would match the cash payments directly against specific sales amounts in the appropriate customer's account.

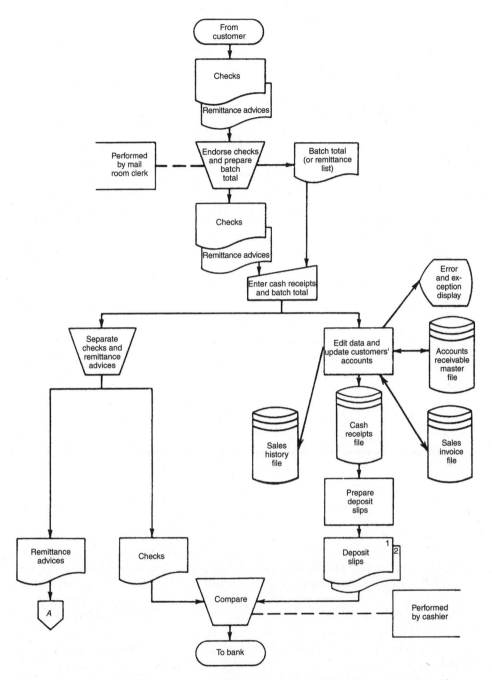

Exhibit 9–6.   System flow chart of an on-line computer-based cash receipts transaction processing procedure. (a) Entry and deposit.

Adapted from J. Wilkinson, *Accounting Information System: Essential Concepts and Applications,* 2nd ed. (New York: John Wiley & Sons, 1993).

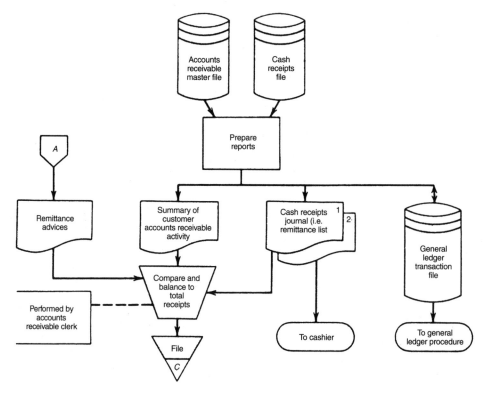

Exhibit 9–6.   Continued. (b) End-of-day processing.

9.15 ADVANTAGES OF COMPUTER-BASED PROCESSING SYSTEMS

Computer-based processing of revenue cycle transactions has several advantages, especially when on-line systems are employed. Processing efficiency is greater, since the relevant files are integrated and can be updated concurrently. Data in the files can be kept more up-to-date and can be retrieved easily when needed. Processed data are likely to be more accurate, since the transaction data are validated as entered. Also, batch totals can be employed, regardless of whether processing is performed directly or performed sequentially. Furthermore, a greater variety of control reports and summaries can be prepared automatically by the application programs as a by-product of processing steps. Finally, needed and useful outputs can be produced more easily. For instance, monthly statements for customers can be generated from data in on-line files. Analyses and reports for managers, such as the accounts receivable aging schedule, can likewise be printed as often as desired.

9.16 CONTROLS NEEDED FOR THE REVENUE CYCLE

Transactions within the revenue cycle are exposed to a variety of risks. Exhibit 9–7 lists representative risks and consequent exposures due to these risks. For example, one risk is that payments from credit customers may be lapped when the accounts receivable records are posted. Lapping is a type of embezzlement that involves the theft of cash and its con-

Risk	Exposure(s)
1. Credit sales made to customers who represent poor credit risks	1. Losses from bad debts
2. Unrecorded or unbilled shipments	2. Losses of revenue; overstatement of inventory and understatement of accounts receivable in the balance sheet
3. Errors in preparing sales invoices (e.g., showing greater quantities than were shipped or showing unit prices that are too low)	3. Alienation of customers and possible loss of future sales (when quantities are too high); losses of revenue (when unit prices are too low)
4. Misplacement of orders from customers or unfilled backorders	4. Losses of revenue and alienation of customers
5. Incorrect postings of sales to accounts receivable records or postings to wrong accounting periods	5. Incorrect balances in accounts receivable and general ledger account records (e.g., overstatement of Mary Smith's balance), overstatement of revenue in 1992 and understatement in 1993
6. Excessive sales returns and allowances, with certain of the credit memos being for fictitious returns	6. Losses in net revenue, with the proceeds from subsequent payments by affected customers being fraudulently pocketed
7. Theft or misplacement of finished goods in the warehouse or on the shipping dock	7. Losses in revenue; overstatement of inventory on the balance sheet
8. Fraudulent write-offs of customers' accounts by unauthorized persons	8. Understatement of accounts receivable; losses of cash receipts when subsequent collections on written-off accounts are misappropriated by perpetrators of the fraud
9. Theft of cash receipts, especially currency, by persons involved in the processing; often accompanied by omitted postings to affected customers' accounts	9. Losses of cash receipts; overstatement of accounts receivable in the subsidiary ledger and the balance sheet
10. Lapping of payments from customers when amounts are posted to accounts receivable records	10. Losses of cash receipts; incorrect account balances for those customers whose records are involved in the lapping
11. Accessing of accounts receivable, merchandise inventory, and other records by unauthorized persons	11. Loss of security over such records, with possibly detrimental use made of the data accessed
12. Involvement of cash, merchandise inventory, and accounts receivable records in natural or man-made disasters	12. Losses of or damages to assets, including possible loss of data needed to monitor collection of amounts due from previous sales

Exhibit 9–7.   Table of risk exposures within the revenue cycle.

Adapted from J. Wilkinson, *Accounting Information System: Essential Concepts and Applications,* 2nd ed. (New York: John Wiley & Sons, 1993).

cealment by a succession of delayed postings to customers' accounts. A clerk who undertakes lapping first cashes a check from a customer and keeps the cash. Since the check has not been recorded, the customer's account is in error and is overstated. To cover his or her tracks, the clerk credits the customer's account on receiving a check for an equal or larger amount from another customer. Then the clerk credits the second customer's account with the proceeds from the check of still another customer. This falsifying process continues indefinitely, unless the clerk decides to return the embezzled funds. The major risk exposure to the firm from lapping is clearly a loss of funds received from customers. Another risk exposure, however, is that certain accounts will be overstated, making the amount shown in the balance sheet for accounts receivable overstated.

To minimize the dangers accruing from the kind of risks listed in Exhibit 9–7, various forms of controls may be put in place. In order to have effective measures that counteract its risk exposures, a firm must first clarify the most important control objectives. With respect to the revenue cycle, several key control objectives are to ensure that:

- All customers who are accepted for credit sales are creditworthy.
- All ordered goods are shipped or services are performed by dates that are agreeable to both parties.
- All shipped goods are authorized and accurately billed within the proper accounting period.
- All sales returns and allowances are authorized and accurately recorded and based on actual returns of goods.
- All cash receipts are recorded completely and accurately.
- All credit sales and cash receipts transactions are posted to proper customers' accounts in the accounts receivable ledger.
- All accounting records, merchandise inventory, and cash are safeguarded.

To fulfill these control objectives, the firm must then specify and incorporate adequate general controls and transaction controls.

9.17 GENERAL CONTROLS

General controls that particularly concern the revenue cycle include those involving organizational independence, documentation, practices and policies, and security measures.

(a) Organizational Independence

With respect to sales transactions, the units having custodial functions (i.e., the warehouse and shipping department) should be separate from each other and from those units that keep the records (i.e., billing department, accounts receivable department, inventory control department, general ledger department, data processing department). Also, the sales order and credit departments, whose managers authorize credit sales transactions as well as account adjustments and write-offs, should be separate from all the above-mentioned units. For cash receipts transactions, the mailroom and cashier (who handles cash) should be separate from each other and from the accounts receivable department, general ledger department, and data processing department.

(b) Documentation Controls

Complete and up-to-date documentation should be available concerning the revenue cycle, including copies of the source documents, flow charts, and record layouts. In addition, details pertaining to sales and cash receipts, and edit and processing programs should be organized into separate packages that are meant for use by programmers, computer operators, and systems users. Furthermore, management policies concerning credit approvals, account write-offs, and so forth should be in written form so that all employees have knowledge of them.

(c) Operating Practices

Practices relating to operational matters such as processing schedules, control summaries and reports, and personnel should be clearly established and soundly based. For instance, all employees who handle cash are required to be bonded and are subject to close supervision.

(d) Security Measures

Security should be maintained (for on-line systems) by techniques such as (1) requiring that clerks enter assigned passwords before accessing accounts receivable and other customer-related files; (2) employing terminals with restricted functions for the entry of sales and cash receipts transactions; (3) generating audit reports (access logs) that monitor accesses of system files; and (4) dumping the accounts receivable and merchandise inventory master files onto magnetic tape backups. Security measures for manual and computer-based systems include the use of physically restricted warehouses (for protecting goods) and safes (for holding cash receipts). Also, a lockbox collection system may be considered, where feasible. A lockbox is a postal address that is used solely to collect remittances, which are removed and processed by the firm's bank.

9.18 TRANSACTION CONTROLS

The following controls and control procedures are applicable to revenue cycle transactions and customer accounts. They are arranged by input, processing, and output categories.
  Input controls include:

- Prenumbered and well-designed documents relating to sales, shipping, and cash receipts.
- Validation of data on sales orders and remittance advices as the data are prepared and entered for processing. In the case of computer-based systems, validation is performed by means of programmed checks built into the system.
- Correction of errors that are detected during data entry. Detected errors should be corrected by an error-correction procedure that is appropriate to the processing approach being employed.
- Batch control totals that are precomputed from sales invoices (or shipping notices) and remittance advices. These precomputed batch control totals are compared with totals computed during postings to the accounts receivable ledger and during each processing run. In the case of cash receipts, the total of remittance advices also is compared with the total on deposit slips.

Processing controls include:

- Issuance of multicopy sales orders and/or invoices on the basis of valid authorization, such as credit approved customer orders.
- Movement of ordered goods from the finished goods warehouse and shipment on the basis of written authorizations, such as picking lists or stock request copies.
- Invoicing of customers only on notification by the shipping department of the quantities that have been shipped.

- Issuance of credit memos and write-off notices only on the basis of prior approvals by designated managers. In the case of sales returns, approval is not granted until the goods being returned have been received.

- Verification of all data elements and computations on sales invoices by a billing clerk other than the preparer or by a computer program before mailing. Another verification consists of comparing the sales invoices against shipping notices and open sales orders, to ensure that the quantities ordered reconcile with the orders shipped and backordered.

- Verification that total postings to the accounts receivable master file accounts agree with the total postings to the general ledger accounts (in the case of a computer-based batch processing system).

- Deposit of all cash receipts with a minimum of delay. This step eliminates the possibility of cash receipts being used to pay employees or to reimburse petty cash funds. It also preserves the audit trail.

- Reconciliation of accounts in the accounts receivable subsidiary ledger with the accounts receivable control account in the general ledger.

- Correction of errors made during processing steps. All such corrections consist of reversing erroneous postings to accounts and reentering correct data. The audit trail concerning accounts being corrected should show the original error, the reversal, and the correction.

Output controls include the following:

- Preparation of monthly statements, which are mailed to all credit customers. Since a customer will likely complain if overcharged, this practice provides control over accidental and fraudulent acts.

- Filing of copies of all documents pertaining to sales and cash receipts transactions by reference to their preassigned numbers, with the sequence of numbers in each file being checked periodically to see if gaps exist. If transactions are not supported by preprinted documents, as often is the case in on-line computer-based systems, numbers are assigned to the documents and they are stored in a transaction file.

- For computer-based systems, preparation of printed transaction listings, such as the cash receipts journal and account summaries, on a periodic basis to provide an adequate audit trail. Also, various outputs that aid control, such as exception and summary reports, should be prepared.

- Reconciliation of all bank accounts should be done monthly by someone not involved in the revenue cycle processing activities. New bank accounts are to be authorized by designated managers.

9.19 MANAGERIAL REPORTS

The revenue cycle database can provide a wealth of information to aid managers in making decisions. One example already listed is the accounts receivable aging schedule, which is useful for decision making as well as operational control. Several other useful reports and analyses are worth noting.

(a) Performance Reports

These reports reflect results in terms of key measures, such as average dollar value per order, percentage of orders shipped on time, and the average number of days between the order date and shipping date.

(b) Sales Analyses

Analyses of sales reflect the relative effectiveness of individual salespeople, sales regions, product lines, customers, and markets. One possible report shows a sales analysis that compares the actual sales for three of the above-mentioned factors against established quotas.

(c) Cash Flow Statements

These reports show the sources and uses of cash for an accounting period, classified by operating profit-directed activities, financing activities, and investment activities. They provide the basis for developing cash forecasts and budgets. Hence, they aid the process of managing the all important cash resource.

Other useful reports are open orders reports, backorders reports, sales analyses by product, and unbilled shipments reports.

9.20 CONCLUSION

The revenue cycle permits a firm to trade its products or services for cash. The cycle contains the following steps: receiving orders from customers, checking customers' creditworthiness, processing the orders, obtaining the merchandise from the warehouse, packing and shipping orders to customers, billing customers, receiving and depositing the payments, maintaining the customers' accounts, posting transactions to the general ledger, and finally, informing decision makers by preparing pertinent reports, which could be about products sold, sales force performance, and status of accounts receivable and other elements of the revenue cycle.

The revenue cycle is not a localized affair. It directly or indirectly involves every department in the organization. To ensure that the information needs of each department are met and to maintain adequate records, documentation unique to revenue cycle is necessary. This may include sales orders, packing lists, shipping notices, invoices, and credit memos. In the Information Age, preformatted screens are replacing the forms and other types of documentation used in manual transaction processing. The forms or the preformatted screens both feed data into the revenue cycle database, which includes files related to customer accounts, order status, sales history, and other aspects of the cycle.

The revenue cycle also confronts an assortment of risks. A firm's exposure to these risks can be minimized through different forms of control. The cycle is represented by various accounting entries. Given the volume of such transactions, involving both customers and employees is essential to ensure proper procedures and accurate coding.

CHAPTER 10

THE EXPENDITURE CYCLE

10.1 INTRODUCTION

This chapter describes the expenditure cycle's objectives, functions, and relationships to other organizational units. This is done by identifying data sources, forms of input, and accounting entries. The database used for the cycle is outlined, as are the steps and approaches used in processing its transaction data flows. The cycle must be safeguarded from a variety of risks, and steps that can be taken to minimize such risks are described.

An organization has expenditures for goods and services. Goods may consist of merchandise, raw materials, parts, subassemblies, supplies, and plant assets. Services may include those provided by outside parties, such as telephone and legal services, as well as the labor provided by the organization's employees. Because the expenditure cycle involves the outflow of funds, it is the counterpoint to the revenue cycle, which provides inflows of funds.

Most acquired goods and services represent resources to the organization. For instance, merchandise, raw materials, and supplies are materials resources; plant assets are facilities resources; and hours worked by employees are human service resources. All such resources also fall within the resources management cycle, which is closely related to the expenditure cycle. This chapter focuses on the goods involved in the materials resources, plus outside services, while the next two chapters examine resources such as employee services and facilities.

The major purpose of the expenditure cycle is to facilitate the exchange of cash with suppliers for needed goods and services. When goods (i.e., merchandise, supplies, or raw materials) are purchased, the functions of the expenditure cycle consist of recognizing the need for the goods, placing the order, receiving and storing the goods, ascertaining the validity of the payment obligation, preparing the cash disbursement, maintaining the accounts payable, posting transactions to the general ledger, and preparing needed financial reports and other outputs. In the case of services, the functions of receiving and storing the goods are replaced by the function of accepting the ordered services. In the case of direct payments by cash (as is done through a petty cash fund), the function of maintaining the payable records is unnecessary. These groups of functions are pictured in Exhibit 10–1.

Exhibit 10–2 presents a data flow diagram that includes the several functions performed as part of the cycle. Each function in the diagram is viewed as a logical process that is linked to other processes and to entities and data stores. The diagram emphasizes the critical role played by each activity within the cycle, while Exhibit 10–3 provides additional insight by depicting relationships within the expenditure cycle.

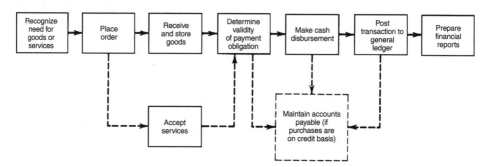

Exhibit 10–1.   Diagram depicting typical functions of an expenditure cycle.
Adapted from J. Wilkinson, *Accounting Information System: Essential Concepts and Applications,* 2nd ed. (New York: John Wiley & Sons, 1993).

In addition to the functions listed above, some related functions performed by the cycle must be mentioned. These other related functions include payroll disbursements, expense distribution, purchase returns and allowances, miscellaneous cash disbursements, and petty cash disbursements.

10.2 ORGANIZATIONAL CONTEXT OF THE EXPENDITURE CYCLE

The above-mentioned expenditure cycle functions are typically achieved under the direction of the firm's inventory management and finance/accounting organizational units. The expenditure cycle therefore involves both the inventory management information system and the accounting information system (AIS). Moreover, the results attained and information generated by the expenditure cycle further the objectives of these organizational units.

The inventory management function in a merchandising firm is concerned with managing the merchandise that the firm acquires for resale. In addition to planning responsibilities, the function is responsible for purchasing, receiving, and storing the merchandise. In some firms, for example, manufacturing firms, inventory management can be viewed as the major subfunction within a broader logistics function. Also included in the logistics function might be the production and distribution functions. Alternatively, distribution may be assigned to the marketing/distribution function.

Purchasing focuses primarily on selecting the most suitable suppliers or vendors from whom to order goods and services. It makes the selections on the basis of factors such as the unit prices charged for the goods or services, the quality of the goods or services offered, the terms and promised delivery dates, and the supplier's reliability. Together with inventory control, purchasing also ascertains the quantity of goods to acquire. The optimal order quantity is determined by a formula that includes factors such as the expected demand for the goods, the carrying cost, and the ordering cost. However, this formula normally is applied only to high-cost or high-volume goods. Order quantities for low-cost or low-volume goods are more likely to be determined on a rough basis that seeks to avoid stockouts. In some cases a good buying opportunity or a price break determines the quantities to order.

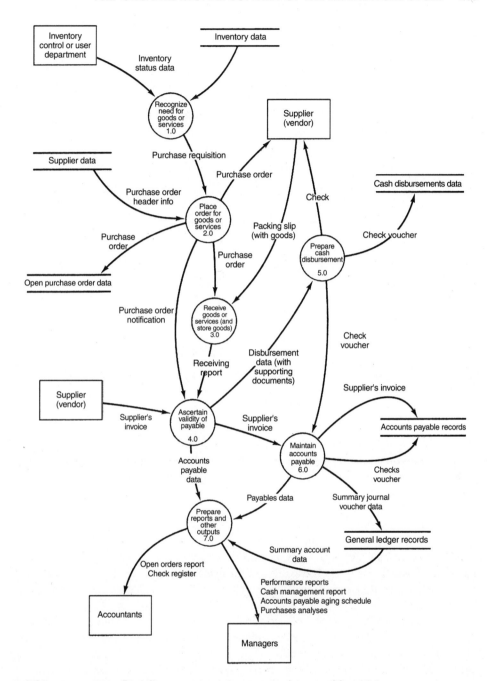

Exhibit 10–2.   Data flow diagram pertaining to accounts payable activity.

Adapted from J. Wilkinson, *Accounting Information System: Essential Concepts and Applications,* 2nd ed. (New York: John Wiley & Sons, 1993).

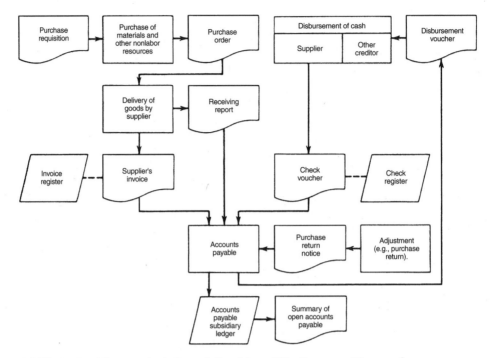

Exhibit 10–3.   Diagram depicting relationships within the expenditure cycle.

Adapted from J. Wilkinson, *Accounting Information System: Essential Concepts and Applications,* 2nd ed. (New York: John Wiley & Sons, 1993).

Receiving has the responsibilities of accepting only those goods that were ordered, verifying their quantities and condition, and moving the goods to the storeroom. Storing, or stores, has the responsibility of safeguarding the goods from theft, loss, obsolescence, and deterioration. The storeroom is also charged with getting the goods together and delivering them when properly authorized requisitions are presented to the staff in charge of the storeroom. Inventory control maintains the records pertaining to inventory balances and initiates the reordering of goods.

The second major player in the expenditure cycle is the team of the accounting department and financial managers. The essence of the cycle relates to a firm spending money to acquire resources, goods, and services. Both accounting and finance have a lot to say about the availability and disbursement of money. The objectives of financial and accounting management relate broadly to funds, data, information, planning, and control over resources. With respect to the expenditure cycle, the objectives are limited to cash planning and control, to data pertaining to purchases and suppliers' accounts, to inventory control, and to information pertaining to cash and purchases and suppliers.

The senior financial managers are often the vice-president of finance, the treasurer, and the controller. One important manager reporting to the treasurer is the cashier. The treasurer's responsibilities include cash disbursements, whereas the controller's responsibilities include accounts payable, inventory control, and the general ledger. Between them, they take care of the actual disbursements pertaining to expenditure cycle. Cash disbursements, a part of the cashier's department, prepares checks for disbursement and maintains the related records. Accounts payable maintains the records of individual suppliers and approves their invoices for payment. General ledger maintains control over all asset, equity, expense, and income accounts.

10.3 MANAGERIAL DECISION MAKING

Three department managers having key responsibilities with respect to the expenditure cycle for goods are the inventory manager, the treasurer, and the controller. They must make decisions that influence the way purchases are made and cash is disbursed. To a large extent, the decisions pertaining to expenditures rely on the information that is a by-product of processing within the expenditure cycle. The inventory manager (or logistics manager in some firms) depends on the inventory management information system to provide needed information for decision making. No matter what the source of information, specific questions requiring answers of the inventory manager (or subordinate managers) of a merchandising firm include the following:

- What levels of inventory should be stocked?
- When should particular inventory items be reordered?
- What quantities of particular inventory items should be reordered?
- When should long-term purchase contracts be obtained for particular inventory items?
- From which suppliers should particular inventory items be ordered?
- What procedures should be followed in receiving and storing merchandise inventory?
- What organizational units are to be included in the inventory management and logistics functions?
- What logistics plans and budgets are to be established for the coming year?

Like the inventory managers, those working for the controller and treasurer make decisions pertaining to expenditures. Among the questions requiring answers of the controller and treasurer (or subordinate managers) are:

- What policies concerning purchase terms and discounts should be established?
- What level of services should departments be allowed to acquire?
- What accounts payable records are to be maintained concerning amounts owed to suppliers?
- What financial plans and budgets are to be established for the coming year?
- What sources of funds are to be employed?

In order to make sound decisions in the context of the expenditure cycle, the senior managers need the assistance of accountants, purchasing analysts, auditors, and systems developers. Managerial accountants aid in developing appropriate decision models and in determining what information is needed. Purchasing analysts are specialists who aid in making purchases and inventory decisions and in analyzing their effects. Auditors examine and evaluate the controls incorporated in the expenditure cycle; they also review the financial statements and related financial outputs for reliability. Systems developers participate in the analysis and design of the systems used to process purchases and cash disbursements transactions; thus, they aid in specifying outputs that provide information to managers.

10.4 DOCUMENTATION NEEDED FOR THE CYCLE

Documentation used in the expenditure cycle is based mainly on inputs from the inventory records and from suppliers. The inventory records are the primary source of most purchase transactions, whereas suppliers invoices are the source of payable/disbursement transactions. Other sources are the records of department heads, buyers, supplier history files, receiving and stores departments, and (for manufacturing firms) the production departments. If payroll disbursements are included within the expenditure, such sources as the personnel and payroll records are to be added.

10.5 DOCUMENTATION FOR MANUAL SYSTEMS

The expenditure cycle source documents typically found in firms that employ manual processing include the following:

(a) Purchase Requisition

The initiating form in the expenditure cycle is the purchase requisition. It both requests and authorizes the purchasing department to place an order for goods or services. Key items of data that it conveys are the quantities and identifications of the goods to be purchased, plus the date needed, the name of the requestor and department, and the approver's name or initials. Optional data include the suggested supplier (vendor), suggested unit prices, and shipping instructions. After approval by the purchasing department on the confirmation copy, the request is returned to the requester.

(b) Purchase Order

This is the formal request, signed by an authorized buyer or purchasing manager, to an outside supplier. If the supplier agrees to all stated terms and conditions on the order, it is binding on the issuing firm. In addition to the signature area at the bottom of the form, a typical purchase order has two sections: a heading and a body. The heading contains the supplier's name and address as well as shipping instructions. The body contains one or more line items, with each line item pertaining to a single item of merchandise or material being ordered. Although unit prices for the various line items are included, cost extensions are not normally provided because the unit prices are tentative.

(c) Receiving Report

A prenumbered document prepared by a clerk in the receiving department is called a receiving report (or record, memorandum, or ticket). This document states that the listed quantities of goods have been received and indicates their overall condition. It can be used to reflect the receipt of any goods, including goods on consignment or goods returned by a dissatisfied customer. However, most receipts of goods—and receiving reports—relate to issued purchase orders. A copy of the receiving report usually accompanies the goods to the storeroom and then is forwarded to accounts payable.

(d) Supplier's Invoice

To the buying firm, a supplier's (vendor's) invoice is a response to a previously issued purchase order. To the supplier, it is a sales invoice. The invoice is the source document used as the posting medium into the accounting cycle. Neither the purchase order nor the receiving report can serve this purpose, since neither reflects the amount of the obligation incurred.

(e) Disbursement Voucher

This document, also called a payment voucher, authenticates a liability for an expenditure and authorizes payment. It is prepared when the widely popular voucher system is used. A voucher is generated when one or more invoices are received from a supplier. It is entered in a voucher register, which serves as a journal. Then the voucher may be used as the medium for posting to the accounts payable ledger, if one is maintained. Summary totals from the voucher register are posted to the general ledger. A disbursement voucher offers several advantages. It allows several invoices to be accumulated, thereby reducing the number of checks to be written. Because it is prenumbered, the voucher provides numerical control over the payment. Finally, it provides a convenient means for grouping the vouching documents together in a package and reflecting the approval for its payment.

(f) Check Voucher

A disbursement check is the final document in the expenditure cycle. Usually the check has an attachment, which in effect is a copy or abbreviated version of the voucher. In some systems the check voucher is prepared in lieu of the disbursement voucher. The check is signed by an authorized signer. In some instances, as when the amounts are large, it may be countersigned. Then a copy of the check, containing the attached voucher section (and hence called the check voucher), is entered in a cash disbursements journal or check register.

(g) Debit Memorandum

When a purchasing firm decides to reject received goods or desires to obtain adjusted terms, it first requests that the selling firm authorize a return or allowance. When granted, the purchasing firm prepares a debit memorandum. In effect, this document notifies the selling firm and the accounts payable department.

(h) Additional Documents

A new supplier (vendor) form is useful in the selection of new suppliers. It contains data such as prices or rates, types of goods or services provided, experience, credit standing, and references. A request for proposal (RFP), or for quotation, is a form used during a competitive bidding procedure. It lists the various goods or services needed and provides columns in which the bidding suppliers enter their proposed prices, terms, and so on. A bill of lading generally accompanies received goods. Finally, a journal voucher is prepared as the basis for each posting to the general ledger. For instance, a journal voucher is prepared by reference to debit memoranda that have been issued during a period.

10.6 DOCUMENTATION NEEDED BY COMPUTER-BASED SYSTEMS

All of the aforementioned hard-copy documents also may be used in computer-based systems. In some cases, however, they may be generated automatically upon the entry of data via computer. Moreover, the source documents can be designed to aid the entry of data into the computer system with fewer errors. Preformatted screens may be used to enter data concerning purchases, payments, purchase returns, and cash disbursement transactions. These screens, like simplified entry forms, may be designed to handle individual transactions or batches of transactions.

10.7 ACCOUNTING ENTRIES

In a manual system, data from a supplier's invoice are entered into a purchases journal and posted to individual supplier accounts in the accounts payable subsidiary ledger. Otherwise, invoices are used to prepare a disbursement voucher, which then becomes the source of input into the voucher register. Periodically, the summary total from the journal or register is posted to the general ledger. Under a periodic inventory system, this particular entry will be a debit to purchases and a credit to accounts payable. Under a perpetual inventory system, the entry will be a debit to inventory and a credit to accounts payable.

Entries also must be made to reflect purchases returns and allowances. Usually journal vouchers are prepared to reflect such returns and allowances, and the entry made involves a decrease in the accounts payable through a debit entry with a credit to purchase returns account. Exhibit 10–4 shows the flow of purchases transactions through the accounting cycle, beginning with the supplier's invoice.

Exhibit 10–5 portrays the flow of cash disbursements through the accounting cycle. Checks are prepared for suppliers for their invoices or disbursement vouchers. Copies of such checks provide the amounts and other details to be entered into the cash disbursement journal and then posted to individual supplier records in the accounts payable subsidiary ledger. Periodically, totals from the cash disbursements journal are posted to the

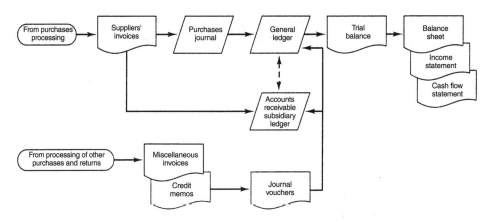

Exhibit 10–4. Diagram describing the transactions resulting from purchases flowing through the accounting cycle.

Adapted from J. Wilkinson, *Accounting Information System: Essential Concepts and Applications,* 2nd ed. (New York: John Wiley & Sons, 1993).

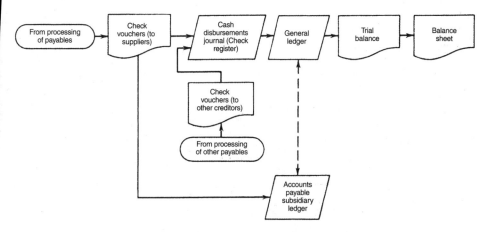

Exhibit 10–5.   Diagram depicting the flow of cash disbursements through the accounting cycle.

Adapted from J. Wilkinson, *Accounting Information System: Essential Concepts and Applications,* 2nd ed. (New York: John Wiley & Sons, 1993).

general ledger as a debit to accounts payable and credit to cash. If there are any cash discounts involved for prompt payments, they will form a part of the entry as credit.

The entries just discussed could be different if the payment was recorded under the net value method instead of the gross value method. In such a case, the entry will be different if the discount criteria were not met. The discounts lost will be added to the purchase price.

Cash can be expended for reasons other than purchase of merchandise. In such cases, the entries will be a debit to the given account, with credit going to cash. Certain purchased goods and services are consumed over the course of more than one accounting period. At the end of each period the consumed portion should be reflected in the accounts. In the case of supplies, which were set up in accordance with the perpetual method when acquired, an end-of-period adjustment would be a debit to supplies expense account and credit to supplies inventory. The notation for such an adjusting entry will explain that the entry records the amount of supplies used during the period.

10.8 TRANSACTION CODING

Since codes were discussed in detail in Chapter 8, which dealt with the general ledger cycle as well as the accounting system, the discussion here will be very brief. Codes can aid the entry of purchases and cash disbursements transactions. In addition to codes for general ledger accounts, codes can be entered for suppliers, purchase orders, products, buyers, purchase contracts, and so on. When such codes are used, various purchase analyses can be performed. Group codes are useful when recording transactions such as purchases, since they encompass several dimensions. They also may be used to represent entities such as products, suppliers, and buyers. A product code for a battery sold by a retail chain, for instance, might include these fields: the coded item is numbered 28-B-485-34-D, with 28 representing the product line, such as auto accessories; B representing the product subgroup, in this case a battery; 485 referring to the vehicle for which the battery is to be used; 34 denoting the size of the battery; and D representing the battery type, such as dry cell.

10.9 DATABASE FOR THE EXPENDITURE CYCLE

The database for the expenditure cycle contains master files, transaction files, open document files, and other types of files. If appropriate database software is available, it may also contain data structures.

(a) Master Files

Two likely master files employed within the expenditure cycle pertain to suppliers and accounts payable. If a firm purchases merchandise for resale, a third file is the merchandise inventory master file. The content of these files will vary from firm to firm, depending on factors such as types of suppliers and sources of services, variety of desired managerial report, degree of computerization, and structure of the database.

(i) Supplier (Vendor) Master File.   A supplier master file is vital to the expenditure cycle, since it specifies where the checks for suppliers are to be mailed. In many firms, it also serves as the accounts payable subsidiary ledger by showing the amount currently owed to each supplier. The data elements that may usefully appear in a supplier file include account number, supplier name, mailing address, phone number, fax number, credit terms, year-to-date purchases, year-to-date payments, and the current account balance. Generally, the primary and sorting key of the file is the supplier number. An important concern with this file, as with the inventory master file, is keeping the records up-to-date. When a supplier obtains a new mailing address, for instance, this change must be quickly reflected in the record. When a new supplier is added to the approved supplier list, a new record should appear in the file; when a supplier is dropped, the corresponding record should be deleted also. These changes can be made during the processing of invoices, or they may be made at other times as they arise.

(ii) Accounts Payable Master File.   The records in the accounts payable master file also relate to suppliers. Two data elements are essential: the supplier identification (usually the supplier account number) and the current account balance. If this file is used, the account balance would be removed from the supplier master file. A separate accounts payable master file is useful, since records containing fewer fields can be processed faster during file update runs.

(iii) Merchandise Inventory Master File.   The merchandise inventory master file is essentially the same file discussed in Chapter 9 for revenue cycle. If the firm is a manufacturer, the file will be called the raw materials inventory master file. Some firms also maintain a separate supplies inventory master file.

(b) Transaction and Open Document Files

Transactions in the expenditure cycle involve purchase requisitions, purchase orders, receiving reports, suppliers' invoices, debit memos, and cash disbursements. If a voucher system is in effect, vouchers also are included. Each of the records in related transaction files contains roughly the data shown in the documents discussed earlier. Three major transaction files deserve closer attention.

(i) Purchase Order File. The content of the purchase order file is similar to the content of a purchase order, discussed earlier. When stored on a computerized medium, the data often are separated into two records: a header record and one or more detailed line item records. The header record consists of the purchase order number, supplier number, purchase order date, and expected delivery date. Each line item record contains the purchase order number, line item number, inventory item number, quantity ordered, and expected unit price. If the supplier's product number differs from the inventory item number, the former should also be listed. Other data elements, such as the supplier's name and address, can be obtained from the supplier's master file when preparing vouchers and checks. The purchase order records pertaining to purchases not yet approved for payment are stored in an open purchase order file. The sorting and primary key of the file is the preassigned order number. When an order is approved for payment, its record is usually transferred to a closed orders file.

(ii) Suppliers Invoice Transaction File. In a manual system, a supplier's invoice file consists of a copy of each current supplier's invoice. Records in this file provide the details of purchases transactions posted to the accounts payable records. In practice, the file may be separated into two files: a pending invoice file of those invoices not yet vouched and an open invoices file of those invoices not yet paid. Each invoice also may be assigned a new number, or the supplier's number may be used for reference. If a voucher system is in use, the open invoices file may be replaced by an open vouchers file. In a computer-based system, only a few key data elements would be stored on magnetic media. For a voucher, the data elements would include the voucher number (the sorting key), each invoice number and date, each invoice amount, and the payment discount date. All of the associated invoices would be linked to the voucher record and would cross-reference the related purchase order, requisition, and receiving report. Records in the open documents file are closed when payments are made

(iii) Check Disbursements Transaction File. In a manual system, this file consists of a copy of each current check voucher, arranged in check number order. In a computer-based system, the record layout on magnetic media may contain the supplier's account number, related purchase order number(s), date of payment, and amount of payment. It also may include a code to identify the record as a cash disbursement transaction.

(c) Other Files

The supplier reference and history file is one of the other files used. Considerable data are needed concerning suppliers, so that buyers can make informed decisions when placing purchases. Such information can be maintained in a reference file. The accounts payable detail file is another useful file. In addition to creating separate suppliers' invoice and cash disbursement transaction files, the application program may accumulate records of the transactions in a detail file. Since it is restricted to the current period's transactions, this detail file is not a replacement for the history files. Instead, its main purpose is to facilitate the preparation of purchases reports and analyses. Also, it can serve as an audit trail.

10.10 DATA FLOWS AND PROCESSING FOR MANUAL SYSTEMS

Within the expenditure cycle, data flows and processing steps can be divided into three major subsets: (1) processing of purchases transactions, (2) establishment of accounts payable, and (3) processing of cash disbursements. Each of these subsets can be examined through system flow charts for manual and computer-based processing procedures.

(a) Manually Processed Purchases System

Exhibit 10–6 presents a document flow chart of a procedure involving the purchases of goods on credit. Since the processing is performed manually, the emphasis is on the flows of source documents and outputs. Although the flow chart is detailed and appears to be quite complex, it provides an overall view of a sound purchases procedure. The flow chart, together with the following narrative, will present a clear picture of the data flows and processing. Also, an understanding of the document flows will clarify the processing steps performed by computer-based systems.

The narrative description will be assisted through the use of reference numbers, which have been placed on the flow chart at key spots. These numbers designate several control points within the purchases procedure.

1. **Determination of a need for goods.** The procedure for purchasing goods usually begins in the inventory control department. There an accounting clerk refers to the inventory ledger records to locate those items whose on-hand quantities are below a preestablished reorder point. Those items that need to be reordered are listed on a prenumbered and well-designed purchase requisition form. For each item the clerk specifies a precomputed economic order quantity. On approval of the requisition, perhaps by the inventory manager, copies are sent to the purchasing department and receiving department.

2. **Preparation of the purchase order.** When the purchase requisition is received in the purchasing department, a buyer is assigned by the purchasing manager to handle the purchase transaction. No purchasing action can take place without authorization by a requisition. If the goods or circumstances are nonroutine, competitive bids are obtained. If the needed goods are routine or after bids have been evaluated, the buyer selects the most suitable supplier from an approved supplier file and prepares a prenumbered purchase order. When the purchase order has been checked for prices and terms and signed by an authorized person, such as the purchasing manager, the copies are distributed. Two copies are mailed to the supplier. Other copies are forwarded to the inventory control, receiving, and accounts payable departments. The copy sent to inventory control (which may actually be an amended copy of the requisition) is used to post ordered quantities to the inventory records. The copy for the receiving department (which has the quantities blanked out, i.e., is "blind") is used later to verify the authenticity of the received goods. Thus it serves an important control purpose. The copy sent to accounts payable provides prior notification that an invoice is soon to be received. The last copy is filed in the open purchase order file to await the arrival of the invoice.

3. **Receipt of ordered goods.** When the ordered goods arrive at the receiving dock, the "blind" copy of the purchase order is matched to the packing slip, in order to verify that the goods were ordered. Next, the receiving clerk inspects the goods for damage

and counts the quantities received. Then he or she prepares a prenumbered receiving report on which the findings are recorded. The original copy of this report accompanies the goods to stores, where the storekeeper or warehouse person signs the copy (to acknowledge receipt) and forwards it to accounts payable. Other copies of the receiving report are sent to the purchasing department (to update the open purchase order) and to the inventory control department (to update the inventory ledger records).

4. Receipt of the supplier's invoice. When the supplier's invoice arrives shortly after the ordered goods, it is routed to the purchasing department for comparison with the documents relating to the purchase. If found to be proper and complete, the invoice is forwarded to the accounts payable department for more extensive processing. Invoices pertaining to services are first routed to the using departments, where they are approved for payment by the managers responsible for incurring the expenditures. Then they are forwarded to accounts payable.

(b) Manually Processed Accounts Payable Procedure

Since accounts payable is an accounting department not directly involved in purchasing and receiving goods, it is the most suitable department to examine the supplier's invoice and to trace its content to the supporting documents (i.e., to vouch the invoice). Exhibit 10–7 illustrates the vouching step and the processing steps that follow. On receiving a supplier's invoice in the accounts payable department, a clerk pulls the supporting documents from a file. Then the clerk performs the various comparisons and checks that constitute vouching. These verifications are intended to determine that (1) the purchase has been authorized, (2) the goods or services listed in the invoice have been duly ordered, (3) the goods or services have been received in full, (4) the unit prices applied are in conformity with the purchase order, or are satisfactory to the purchasing department, (5) the terms and other specifications are in agreement with the purchase order, and (6) all computations are correct. After finishing, the clerk initials an audit box (stamped either on the invoice or on another document, such as a voucher) to acknowledge that the verifications have been performed and that the supplier's invoice is approved for payment. Any differences must be settled, however, before a supplier's invoice can be approved for payment. For instance, if only part of the order is received, the purchase order should be so marked and returned to the file.

Assuming that the voucher system is used, a disbursement voucher is prepared on the basis of one or more approved suppliers' invoices. Then the voucher is entered in a voucher register. Batch control totals are computed from the columns in the voucher register, including the total amount of payment, the total merchandise cost, the total selling expense, and so on. A journal voucher is prepared from the totals.

A clerk posts the vouchers to the suppliers' accounts in the accounts payable subsidiary ledger. Batch totals are computed of the posted credits. Also, copies of the vouchers are forwarded to accounting departments that maintain the ledgers relating to the various expenditures (e.g., inventory control). Clerks in these departments post debits to inventory, supplies, plant assets, selling expense, and administrative expense ledgers. Batch totals are computed of the posted debits. Then the batch totals of the posted debits and credits are compared with the journal voucher previously prepared. If all amounts agree, the entry is posted to the accounts in the general ledger.

Finally, the originals of the vouchers, together with the supporting documents, are filed in a file arranged by payment due dates, that is, a "tickler" file. There the unpaid vouchers remain until ready for use in cash disbursements processing.

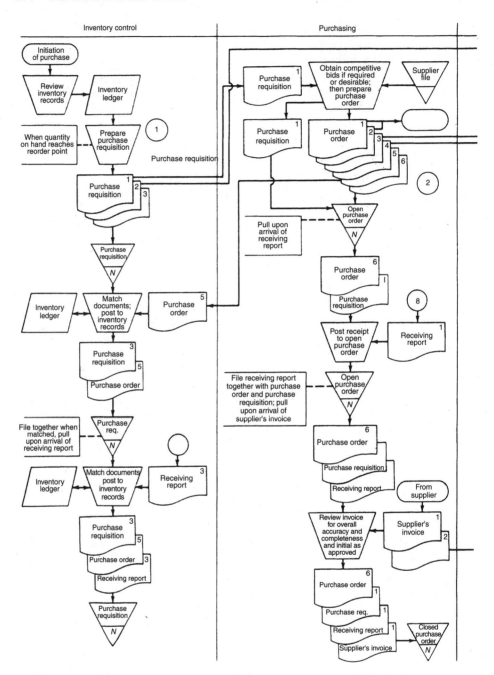

Exhibit 10–6.   Flow chart of a manual purchases transaction processing system.

Adapted from J. Wilkinson, *Accounting Information System: Essential Concepts and Applications,* 2nd ed. (New York: John Wiley & Sons, 1993).

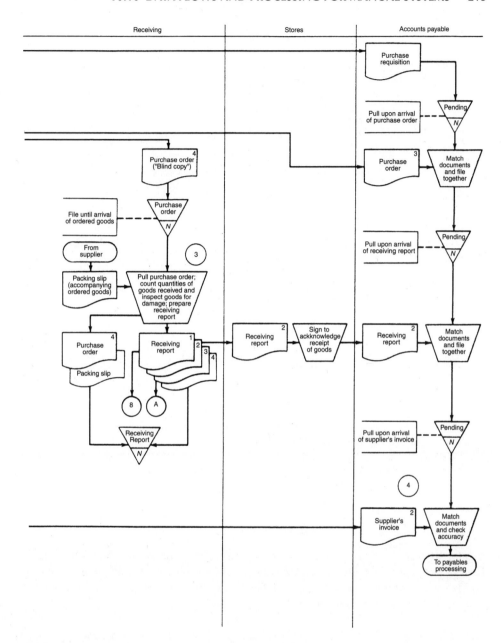

Exhibit 10–6.   Continued.

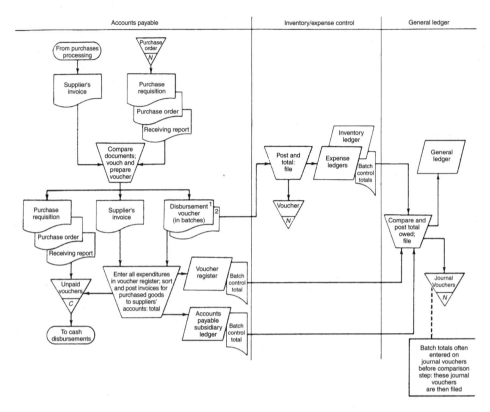

Exhibit 10–7.   System flow chart of a manual payables processing procedure, with an emphasis on document flows.

Adapted from J. Wilkinson, *Accounting Information System: Essential Concept and Applications,* 2nd ed. (New York: John Wiley & Sons, 1993).

(c) Manually Processed Cash Disbursements Procedure

Exhibit 10–8 shows a flow chart of a procedure involving the disbursements of cash related to purchases on credit. The principal control points involve assembling the unpaid vouchers, preparing the checks, signing the checks, processing the cash disbursement records, and posting the cash amounts.

1. Assembly of the unpaid vouchers. The cash disbursements procedure begins in the accounts payable department with the unpaid voucher file. Each day a clerk extracts the unpaid vouchers due to be paid. She or he reviews each voucher "package" to see that it contains all of the supporting documents including the suppliers' invoices. After computing the total amount to be paid and posting the payment amounts from the vouchers to the appropriate suppliers' accounts, the clerk forwards the vouchers and supporting documents to the cash disbursements department.

2. Preparation of the checks. A cash disbursements clerk inspects each voucher for completeness and authenticity and then prepares a prenumbered check. When fin-

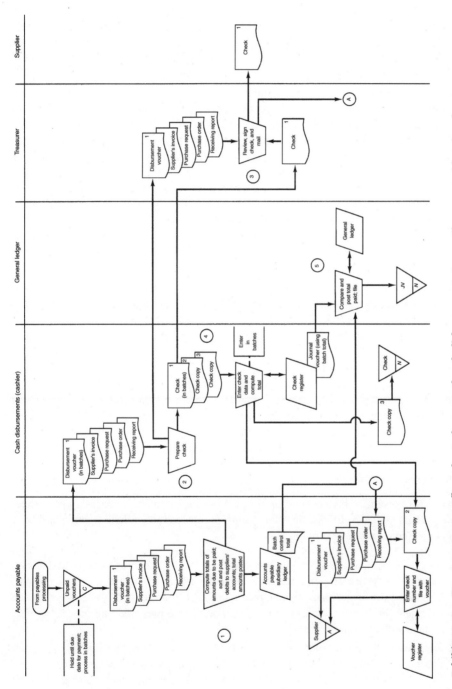

Exhibit 10-8. Document system flow chart of a manual cash disbursements transaction processing procedure.

Adapted from J. Wilkinson, *Accounting Information System: Essential Concepts and Applications*, 2nd ed. (New York: John Wiley & Sons, 1993).

ished, the clerk forwards the original checks to an authorized check signer, together with the supporting documents. Then the check copies are entered into the records.

3. Signing of the checks. In many firms, the authorized check signer is the treasurer, although the cashier may be authorized to sign checks below a designated amount. The signer first reviews the supporting documents. Then he or she signs each check that is properly supported and sends the checks directly to the mailroom. From the mailroom the checks are delivered to the post office.

4. Processing of the cash disbursement records. The amounts and other key data concerning the checks are entered in a check register, and the total of the paid amounts is computed. One copy of the check voucher is filed in the cash disbursements department numerically. The other copy of the check voucher is stapled to the supporting documents, which are stamped as paid. The number of each check and the date are entered in the voucher register, and the package is filed alphabetically by supplier in the accounts payable department. Firms that process large volumes of invoices often find that the bulky voucher packages consume much storage space and are awkward to retrieve. Thus, they may decide to microfilm the documents after processing and then destroy the documents. The microfilm images may be arranged by voucher number and cross-referenced to supplier names.

5. Posting of cash amounts. A journal voucher is prepared on the basis of the total of prepared checks and sent to the general ledger department. If the amount in the journal voucher agrees with the total debits posted to the accounts payable ledger, the entry is posted to the accounts in the general ledger.

10.11 COMPUTER-BASED PROCESSING SYSTEMS

When computer-based systems are used, purchases and cash disbursements transactions may be processed by the batch approach, by the on-line approach, or by a combination of the two approaches. In our examples, the on-line approach is used for purchases, the combined approach for payables, and the batch approach for cash disbursements.

(a) Purchases Procedure

Exhibit 10–9 presents a system flow chart of the on-line purchases processing procedure. The flow chart logically divides into three steps: inventory requisitioning, purchase order processing, and purchase approving.

1. Inventory requisitioning. In the first step the inventory records are checked to find those items whose on-hand quantities have been drawn below their reorder points. This step may be performed when batches of sales transactions are being processed to update the inventory master file. If backorders are prepared and processed, they could also be an input to this step.

2. Purchase order processing. The output from this first step is an inventory reorder list, which is, in effect, a batch of purchase requisitions. After being approved by an inventory control manager, the list is sent to the purchasing department. Buyers are assigned the various items on the list. By making inquiries of an on-line supplier reference file containing evaluation data, the buyers select suitable suppliers and enter them on the list. Then they enter the data needed to prepare purchase orders into

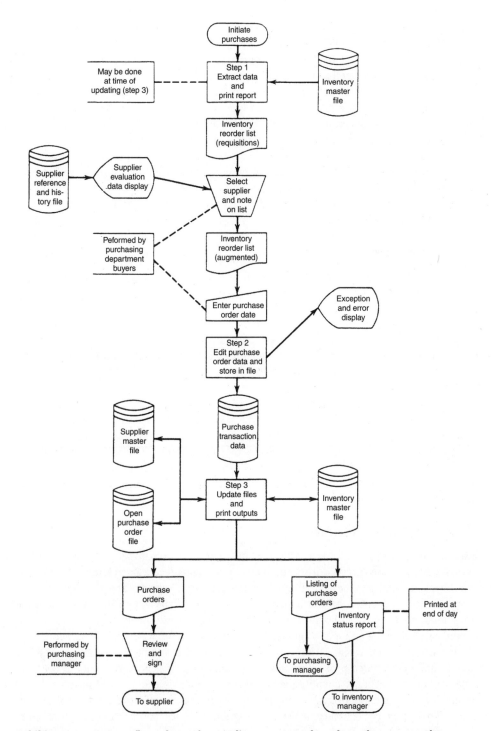

Exhibit 10–9. System flow chart of an on-line computer-based purchases procedure.

Adapted from J. Wilkinson, *Accounting Information System: Essential Concepts and Applications,* 2nd ed. (New York: John Wiley & Sons, 1993).

their video display terminals. On being validated by an edit program, the purchase order data are stored temporarily in a purchase transaction file.

3. Purchase approving. In this step a purchase order is printed, using data from the transaction file as well as the supplier and inventory master files. Also, the computer system automatically assigns a number to the purchase order and dates it. A copy of the purchase order is placed in the on-line open purchase order file, and a notation of the order is placed in the appropriate record(s) of the inventory master file. The purchasing manager, or other authorized signer, reviews the purchase order. When he or she approves and signs the order, it is mailed to the supplier. If revisions are necessary, the buyer retrieves the purchase transaction data via the terminal, makes the changes, and prints a revised purchase order. At the end of the day a listing of the day's purchase orders is printed. Other reports, such as an inventory status report, also may be generated.

(b) Receiving Procedure

Exhibit 10–10 shows a system flow chart of an on-line receiving procedure. A clerk in the receiving department first counts and inspects the received goods. Then he or she keys the count and inventory item numbers into a departmental terminal, together with the related purchase order number listed on the packing slip. A receiving program checks the entered data against the on-line open purchase order file. Any differences between the ordered quantities and the counted quantities are displayed on the terminal screen. Also, if no matching purchase order number is found in the on-line file, an alerting message is displayed.

Assuming that the goods are accepted, the program prints a prenumbered receiving report. A copy of this report accompanies the goods to the stores department, is signed, and is forwarded to the accounts payable department. The receiving program also (1) updates the inventory master file, increasing the on-hand quantity and eliminating the quantity on order, (2) notes the quantity received in the open purchase order file, and (3) notes the date of receipt in the supplier history file. If a backorder is involved, the backorder record is flagged.

(c) Accounts Payable Procedure

Exhibit 10–11 portrays a system flowchart of a combined on-line/batch payable procedure. As invoices are received from suppliers, an accounts receivable clerk performs a visual check for completeness, pulls the related receiving reports, and then computes a batch control total based on the invoice amounts. He or she enters into a terminal the batch total, plus key data elements from each invoice. An edit program validates the entered data, checks the quantities against those in the open purchase order file, recomputes the batch totals, and displays any differences. Then the vouched transaction data are stored until a designated processing time (e.g., the end of the day). When the processing time arrives, an accounts payable posting program updates each record in the supplier master file (i.e., accounts payable subsidiary ledger) that is affected by a supplier's invoice. No sorting is necessary, since the program accesses and retrieves each supplier record directly from its location in the file. Then the program adds the amount of the supplier's invoice to the balance in the account. If all of the quantities pertaining to the related purchase order have been received, it also closes the purchase order and transfers its record to the supplier history file.

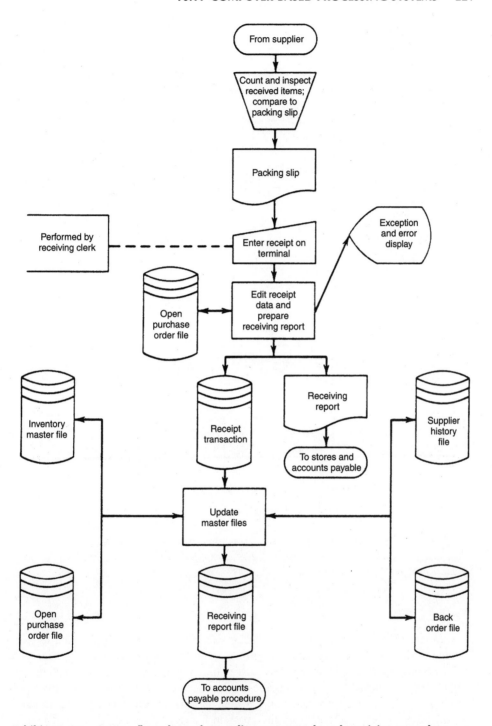

Exhibit 10–10. System flow chart of an on-line computer-based receiving procedure.

Adapted from J. Wilkinson, *Accounting Information System: Essential Concepts and Applications,* 2nd ed. (New York: John Wiley & Sons, 1993).

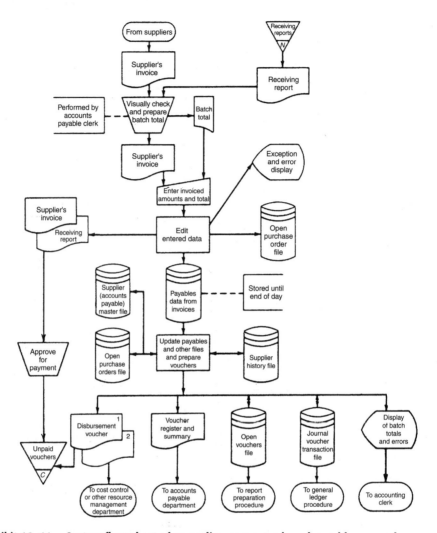

Exhibit 10–11. System flow chart of an on-line computer-based payables procedure.

Adapted from J. Wilkinson, *Accounting Information System: Essential Concepts and Applications,* 2nd ed. (New York: John Wiley & Sons, 1993).

A variety of outputs are generated during this posting of the supplier master file. Prenumbered disbursement vouchers are printed, with one copy being filed together with the supporting documents in an unpaid vouchers file. A voucher register is printed to provide a key part of the audit trail. Summaries of the vouchers are added to the on-line open vouchers file. The debits from the summary vouchers are accumulated by account number; the totals are then compiled by the program into a sequentially numbered journal voucher and added to the journal voucher transaction file or posted immediately to the accounts in the general ledger. A total of the invoice amounts is also computed by the program and displayed on a terminal in the accounts payable department. A clerk verifies that this total agrees with the precomputed batch total.

(d) Cash Disbursements Procedure

Exhibit 10–12 shows a system flow chart of a batch cash disbursements procedure. Our illustrated procedure begins with the approved disbursement vouchers that have been printed during the payable procedure and filed with the supporting documents. This procedure has been widely used, and it provides a contrast to the on-line procedures discussed above. Also, it facilitates the prior computation of batch control totals and the review of documents by the check signer. However, it is important to recognize that the alternative on-line procedure offers significant benefits. For instance, it can use as transaction data the open vouchers stored in an on-line file, thereby omitting the need to key data from the vouchers. The vouchers in that file are sorted by due date at the end of each day, and the vouchers due to be paid on the next payment date are extracted.

The batch procedure shown in the flow chart can be described as follows. On each payment date, the vouchers due to be paid are pulled from the unpaid vouchers file. As in all batch processing procedures, the first step is to compute one or more batch control totals. Then the data needed for preparing checks are keyed from the vouchers onto a magnetic disk. The data are edited, either during the keying or during a separate edit run. Next, the data are sorted, in run 1 by supplier account numbers. Finally, in run 2 the voucher amounts are posted to the accounts payable ledger. The program also prints the checks and a check register as well as a summary of disbursements. It removes the paid vouchers from the open vouchers file (if one is maintained on-line) and adds the data concerning disbursements to the supplier history file. Finally, it accumulates the amounts disbursed and prepares a sequentially numbered journal voucher, which it adds to the journal voucher transaction file.

The person authorized to sign reviews the checks and supporting documents. After signing, he or she forwards the checks to the mailroom. Alternatively, the checks may be signed automatically by the program in run 2, using a signature plate. If this is done, the checks are later reviewed to see that they pertain to authorized obligations.

Computer-based processing of expenditure cycle transactions offers several advantages, especially when on-line systems are employed. Processing efficiency is greater, since the relevant files are integrated and can be updated concurrently. Data in the files can be kept more up-to-date and can be retrieved easily when needed. Processed data are likely to be more accurate, since the transaction data are validated when entered. Also, batch totals can be employed regardless of whether processing is performed directly or performed sequentially. Furthermore, a greater variety of control reports and summaries can be prepared automatically by the application programs as a by-product of processing steps. Finally, needed and useful outputs can be produced more easily.

10.12 CONTROLS NEEDED FOR THE EXPENDITURE CYCLE

Like transactions within other cycles, those within the expenditure cycle are also exposed to a variety of risks. Exhibit 10–13 lists representative risks and consequent exposures due to these risks. An adequate set of general and transaction (application) controls is necessary to counteract risks due to the above-mentioned exposures and to realize the objectives of the expenditure cycle.

Typical risks, for example, are that goods may be ordered that are not needed, or more goods may be ordered than are needed. Goods that are not ordered may be received or,

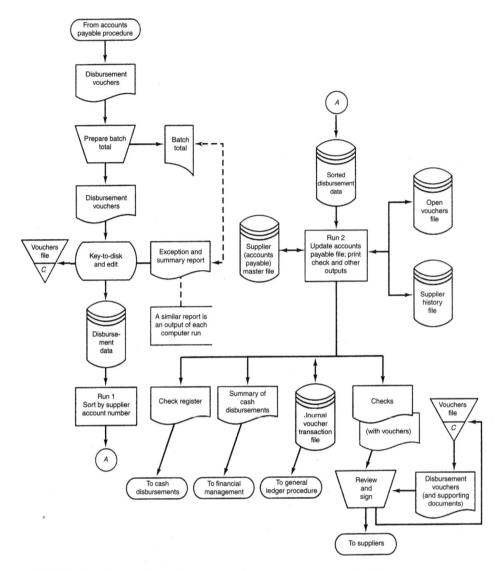

Exhibit 10–12.   System flow chart of a batch computer-based cash disbursements procedure.

Adapted from J. Wilkinson, *Accounting Information System: Essential Concepts and Applications,* 2nd ed. (New York: John Wiley & Sons, 1993).

conversely, goods may be ordered that are not received. These risks expose the acquiring firm to excessive inventory and storage costs or to possible losses due to goods being unavailable for sale. Another risk is that checks may be kited. Kiting is a type of embezzlement that involves transfers of checks among bank accounts. The purpose is generally to cover cash shortages or to inflate the assets. Transfers typically take place near the end of the month, so that float causes the checks not to be recorded until the following month. Such activity, besides causing the loss of cash through embezzlement, can lead to an overstating of cash balances in the financial statement.

10.13 CONTROL OBJECTIVES

In order to counteract exposures to the kind of risks listed in Exhibit 10–13, a firm must first clarify the control objectives that the management sees as crucial. With respect to the expenditure cycle, several key control objectives may be as follows:

Risk	Exposure(s)
1. Orders placed for unneeded goods or more goods than needed	1. Excessive inventory and storage costs
2. Receipt of unordered goods	2. Excessive inventory and storage costs
3. No receipt of ordered goods	3. Losses due to stock-outs
4. Fraudulent placement of orders by buyers with suppliers to whom they have personal or financial attachments	4. Possibility of inferior or overpriced goods or services
5. Overcharges (with respect either to unit prices or to quantities) by suppliers for goods delivered	5. Excessive purchasing costs
6. Damage of goods en route to the acquiring firm	6. Possibility of inferior goods for use or sale (if undetected)
7. Errors by suppliers in computing amounts on invoices	7. Possibility of overpayment for goods received
8. Erroneous or omitted postings of purchases or purchase returns to suppliers' accounts payable records	8. Incorrect balances in accounts payable and general ledger account records
9. Errors in charging transaction amounts to purchases and expense accounts	9. Incorrect levels (either high or low) for purchases and expense accounts
10. Lost purchase discounts due to late payments	10. Excessive purchasing costs
11. Duplicate payments of invoices from suppliers	11. Excessive purchasing costs
12. Incorrect disbursements of cash, either to improper or fictitious parties or for greater amounts than approved	12. Losses of cash and excessive costs for goods and services
13. Improper disbursements of cash for goods or services not received	13. Excessive costs for goods or services
14. Fraudulent alteration and cashing of checks by employees	14. Losses of cash
15. Kiting of checks by employees	15. Overstatement of bank balances; possible losses of deposited cash
16. Accessing of supplier records by unauthorized persons	16. Loss of security over such records, with possibly detrimental use made of data accessed
17. Involvement of cash, merchandise inventory, and accounts payable records in natural or man-made disasters	17. Loss of or damage to assets, including possible loss of data needed to monitor payments of amounts due to suppliers within discount periods

Exhibit 10–13.   Table of risk exposures within the expenditure cycle.

Adapted from J. Wilkinson, *Accounting Information System: Essential Concepts and Applications,* 2nd ed. (New York: John Wiley & Sons, 1993).

- All purchases are authorized on a timely basis when needed and are based on economic order quantity calculations.
- All received goods are verified to determine that the quantities agree with those ordered and that they are in good condition.
- All services are authorized before being performed and are monitored to determine that they are properly performed.
- All suppliers' invoices are verified on a timely basis with respect to accuracy and conformance with goods received or services performed.
- All available purchase discounts are identified so that they may be taken if economical to do so.
- All purchase returns and allowances are authorized and accurately recorded and based on actual returns of goods.
- All cash disbursements are recorded completely and accurately.
- All credit purchases and cash disbursements transactions are posted to proper suppliers' accounts in the accounts payable ledger.
- All accounting records and merchandise inventory are safeguarded.

To fulfill these control objectives, the firm must specify and incorporate adequate general controls and transaction controls.

General controls that particularly concern the expenditure cycle include those involving organizational independence, documentation, practices and policies, and security measures. Each is briefly discussed below.

1. Organizational Independence. With respect to purchases transactions, the units having custodial functions (i.e., the warehouse or receiving department) should be separate from each other and from those units that keep the records (i.e., inventory control department, accounts payable department, general ledger department, data processing department). Also, the purchasing department, whose manager authorizes purchases and returns, and the user departments, whose managers authorize services, should be separate from all the above-mentioned departments. Of course, this separation is not always possible with respect to services, since every department requires some types of services. For cash disbursements, the cash disbursements department and treasurer (who prepare and sign checks) should be separate from the accounts payable department, general ledger department, and data processing department.

2. Documentation. Complete and up-to-date documentation should be available concerning the expenditure cycle, including copies of the documents, flow charts, record layouts, and reports available. In addition, details pertaining to purchases and cash disbursements edit and processing programs should be organized into separate books or "packages" that are directed to programmers, computer operators, and system users. Furthermore, management policies concerning purchase discounts, purchase returns, and so forth should be in written form.

3. Operating Practices. Practices relating to such operational matters as processing schedules, control summaries and reports, and personnel should be clearly established and soundly based. For instance, all employees who handle cash should be required to be bonded and subjected to close supervision.

4. Security Measures. Security should be maintained (in the case of on-line systems) by techniques such as (1) requiring that clerks enter assigned passwords before accessing supplier and inventory files, (2) employing terminals with restricted functions for the entry of purchases and cash disbursement transactions, (3) generating audit reports (access logs) that monitor accesses of system files, and (4) dumping the supplier and inventory files onto magnetic tape backups. Security measures for manual and computer-based systems include the use of physically restricted stores areas (for protecting goods) and safes (for holding stocks of blank checks).

(a) Transaction Controls

The following controls and control procedures are applicable to expenditure cycle transactions and supplier accounts. They are arranged by input, processing, and output categories.

Input controls include the following:

- Prenumbered and well-designed documents relating to purchases, receiving, payable, and cash disbursements.
- Validation of data on purchase orders and receiving reports and invoices as the data are prepared and entered for processing. In computer-based systems, validation is performed by means of the kinds of programmed checks listed in Exhibit 10–14. When data are keyed onto a computer-readable medium, key verification is also recommended.
- Correction of errors that are detected during data entry. Detected errors should be corrected by an error correction procedure that is appropriate to the processing approach being employed.
- Use of control totals (when feasible) that are precomputed from amounts on suppliers' invoices and vouchers due for payment. These precomputed batch control totals are compared with totals computed during posting to the accounts payable ledger and during each processing run. In the case of cash disbursements, the precomputed total of vouchers is also compared with the total of the check register.

Processing controls include the following:

- Issuance of multiple-copy purchase requisitions, purchase orders, disbursement vouchers, checks, and debit memoranda on the basis of valid authorizations:
- Verification of all data elements and computations on purchase requisitions and on purchase orders by persons other than the preparers. Another verification consists of counting the quantities received and comparing the counted quantities against the ordered quantities.
- Vouching of all data elements and computations on suppliers' invoices, including comparisons with the corresponding purchase orders and receiving reports (in the case of goods) by an accounts payable clerk or computer program.
- Monitoring of all open transactions, such as partial deliveries and rejected goods. Also, all transactions in which one or more supporting documents are missing are investigated.

Type of Edit Check	Typical Transaction Data Being Checked		Assurance Provided
	Purchases	Cash Disbursements	
1. Validity check	Supplier account numbers, inventory item numbers, transaction codes	Supplier account numbers, transaction codes	The entered numbers and codes are checked against lists of valid numbers and codes that are stored within the computer system.
2. Self-checking digit	Supplier account numbers	Supplier account numbers	Each supplier account number contains a check digit that enables errors in its entry to be detected.
3. Field check	Supplier account numbers, quantities ordered, unit prices	Supplier account numbers, amounts paid	The fields in the input records that are designated to contain the data items (listed at the left) are checked to see if they contain the proper mode of characters (i.e., numeric characters). If other modes are detected, an error is indicated.
4. Limit check	Quantities ordered	Amounts paid	The entered quantities and amounts are checked against preestablished limits that represent reasonable maximums to be expected. (Separate limits are set for each product.)
5. Range check	Unit prices	None	Each entered unit price is checked to see that it is within a preestablished range (either higher or lower than an expected value).
6. Relationship check	Quantities received	Amounts paid	The quantity of goods received is compared to the quantity ordered, as shown in the open purchase orders file; if the quantities do not agree, the receipt is flagged by the edit program. When an amount of a cash payment is entered as a cash disbursement transaction, together with the number of the voucher or invoice to which the amount applies, the amount in the open vouchers (or invoices) file is retrieved and compared with the entered amount. If a difference appears, the transaction is flagged.
7. Sign check	None	Supplier account balances	After the amount of a cash disbursement transaction is entered and posted to the supplier's account in the accounts payable ledger (thereby reducing the account balance of the supplier), the remaining balance is checked. If the balance is preceded by a negative sign (indicating a debit balance), the transaction is flagged.
8. Completeness check[a]	All entered data elements	All entered data elements	The entered transactions are checked to see that all required data elements have been entered.
9. Echo check[a]	Supplier account numbers and names, inventory item numbers and descriptions	Supplier account numbers and names	After the account numbers for suppliers relating to a purchase or cash disbursements transaction (and also the product numbers in the purchase transaction) have been entered at a terminal, the edit program retrieves and "echoes back" the related supplier names (and product descriptions in the case of purchase transactions).

Exhibit 10–14.   Table of programmed edit checks useful for validating data entered into the expenditure cycle.

Adapted from J. Wilkinson, *Accounting Information System: Essential Concepts and Applications,* 2nd ed. (New York: John Wiley & Sons, 1993).

- Issuance of debit memoranda only on the basis of prior approval of the purchasing manager.
- Reconciliation of accounts in the accounts payable subsidiary ledger and the expense ledgers (if any) with control accounts in the general ledger.
- Verification that total posting to the accounts payable master file accounts agree with the totals posted to the general ledger accounts (in batch processing systems).

- Monitoring of discount terms relating to payments, to ensure that all purchase discounts are taken (if economical).
- Review of evidence supporting the validity of expenditures and the correct posting of amounts prior to the signing of checks.
- Use of check protectors to protect the amounts on checks against alteration before the checks are presented to be signed.
- Countersigning of checks over a specified amount by a second manager.
- Verification of all inventories on hand by physical counts at least once yearly, and reconciliation of the counted quantities with the quantities shown in the inventory records. The inventory taking should be performed under close supervision, and adjustments should be made when necessary to reflect the actual quantities on hand.
- Use of an imprest system for disbursing currency from petty cash funds, with the funds being subject to surprise counts by internal auditors or a designated manager.
- Establishment of purchasing policies that require competitive bidding for large and/or non-routine purchases and that prohibit conflicts of interest, such as financial interests by buyers in current or potential suppliers.

Output controls include the following:

- Establishment of clear-cut receiving and payable cutoff policies, so that the balances for inventories and accounts payable are properly measured at the end of each accounting period.
- Establishment of budgetary control over purchases, with periodic reviews of actual purchase costs and key factors such as inventory turnover rates.
- Comparison of monthly statements from suppliers with the balances appearing in the suppliers' accounts in the accounts payable ledger.
- Filing of copies of all documents pertaining to purchases and cash disbursements by number, including voided documents such as checks. The sequence of numbers in each file should be checked periodically to see if gaps exist. If transactions are not supported by preprinted documents, as often is the case in on-line computer-based systems, numbers are assigned to generated documents and the documents are stored in transaction files.
- In the case of computer-based systems, preparation of transaction listings (e.g., check registers) and account summaries on a periodic basis to provide an adequate audit trail.
- Reconciliation of all bank accounts monthly by someone who is not involved in expenditure cycle processing activities. New bank accounts should be authorized by designated managers only.

10.14 REPORTS AND OTHER OUTPUTS

Outputs generated by the expenditure cycle include financial and nonfinancial reports, purchases-related and cash-related reports, daily and weekly and monthly reports, and hard-copy and soft-copy reports. These reports are classified as operational reports, managerial reports, and inquiry screens.

(a) Operational Reports

Various registers and journals help to maintain the audit trail. The invoice or voucher register is a listing of invoices received from suppliers or a listing of the vouchers prepared from the invoices. The check register is a listing of all the checks issued. It is sometimes called a cash disbursement journal. Each day's listing is accompanied by a summary of the gross amount of payable reduced, the discounts taken, and the net amount paid.

Another group of reports deals with so-called open documents. The open purchase order report shows all purchases for which the related invoices have not yet been approved. The open invoice report lists invoices approved but not yet paid. Another report is the inventory status report, which lists quantities received, shipped, and on hand for each merchandise item. The receiving register contains a listing of all incoming shipments. The overdue deliveries report pinpoints those purchases that are yet to be received.

(b) Inquiry Screens

If part or all of the expenditure cycle is on-line, a variety of reports can be produced interactively within seconds. Many programs have software packages that permit inquiries to be made of the system concerning orders, vendors, payments, order receipts, and other elements of the expenditure cycle.

(c) Managerial Reports

The expenditure cycle database contains considerable information that can aid managers in making decisions. This information can be used to generate a number of reports, some of which, such as the cash flow statement, overlap with the revenue cycle, while others focus on purchases, suppliers, and disbursements. Purchase analyses are useful reports that show the levels of purchasing activity for each supplier, inventory item, and buyer. For instance, a typical analysis may show the number and dollar amount of purchases placed with each supplier this year as well as the average dollar expenditure. This analysis shows the degree to which purchases are concentrated with certain selected suppliers. An analysis of the number of purchases placed by each buyer indicates the relative productivity of the buyers. The most important report relating to suppliers is known as a vendor performance report. This report describes the performance of suppliers (vendors) in terms of on-time shipments, quality of goods, unit prices, level of service, and condition of goods delivered. Discounts on purchases are important to most firms. Thus, a purchase discounts lost report can highlight the relative effectiveness of a firm in paying invoices promptly.

10.15 CONCLUSION

The expenditure cycle facilitates the exchange of cash with suppliers for needed goods and services. Functions of the cycle (in the case of goods) are to recognize the need, place the order, receive and store the goods, ascertain the validity of the payment obligation, prepare the cash disbursement, maintain the accounts payable, post transactions to the general ledger, and prepare needed financial reports and other outputs. These functions often are achieved under the direction of the inventory management as well as finance and accounting managers.

Most of the documentation used in the cycle arises from suppliers' or inventory records. Documents typically employed are the purchase requisition, purchase order, receiving report, supplier's vendors invoice, disbursement voucher, and check voucher. Preformatted screens may be used in on-line systems to enter purchases and cash disbursements data. The database includes files such as the supplier (vendor) master file, merchandise inventory master file, open purchase order file, cash disbursements transaction file, and supplier reference and history files. The expenditure cycle is exposed to a number of control risks. Steps can be taken to minimize such risks through organizational independence, segregation of duties, and written procedure documentation, among other controls.

CHAPTER 11

THE RESOURCES MANAGEMENT CYCLE: EMPLOYEE SERVICES

11.1 INTRODUCTION

This chapter and the next two introduce readers to the treatment of organizational resources within the accounting information system. For reasons of convenience, resources management activity will be viewed as being a single cycle, consisting of four subcycles or systems: employee services management, facilities management, inventory management, and funds management. We deal with the first, employee services management in this chapter, while inventory management is treated in Chapter 12. Facilities management and funds management are dealt with together in Chapter 13.

11.2 RESOURCES MANAGEMENT: AN OVERVIEW

An organization is a composite of its resources, such as employees, facilities, and inventories. On the surface, an organization is no more than the sum of its resources, but the synergy resulting from effective organizational management can make it into something much more than the sum of its parts. The survival, not to mention the success and ongoing prosperity, of every organization depends on the manner in which it manages the resources available to it in the context of an ever-changing environment. Every organization uses resources that may be categorized as inventory, human and technical services, facilities, funds, and data. Each type of resource must be managed.

11.3 OBJECTIVES OF EMPLOYEE SERVICES MANAGEMENT SYSTEM

Employee services are the major component of the human services resource employed by organizations. In certain organizations, such as service-oriented firms and governmental agencies, this resource is responsible for the largest share of the operating expenditures. In other organizations, such as manufacturing firms, this resource can be a major cost in the conversion of raw materials into finished goods. Given the increasing automation in the industrial and service sectors, the complexity of products being manufactured, and changing demographics, labor-related costs are starting to represent something less than a prime share of the total product costs, even while the so-called manufacturing overhead increases its share.

Functions related to employee services include hiring, training, transferring, terminating, classifying, adjusting pay levels, establishing safety measures, maintaining employee benefits programs, reporting to governmental agencies, and payroll. The major purpose of the employee services management system is to facilitate the exchange of cash with employees for needed services. Because it centers on payments to employees, it is also known as the payroll system. The label is not fully descriptive of what management of human resources entails, and, for this reason, we will not use it here. Nevertheless, the key discussions here pertain largely to payroll functions.

Employee services functions discussed here deal with establishing pay status, measuring and recording the services rendered, preparing paychecks, issuing and distributing paychecks, distributing labor costs, and preparing required reports and statements. Exhibit 11–1 presents a data flow diagram that includes the several functions just described. Each function is viewed in the diagram as a logical process that links to other processes and to entities and data stores. The diagram emphasizes the parallel flows involving the distribution of paychecks and distribution or allocation of payroll-related costs. It also shows the several recipients of information based on employee services activity and pay-related reports.

11.4 ORGANIZATIONAL CONTEXT OF EMPLOYEE SERVICES

The functions described in Exhibit 11–2 typically are performed under the direction of the personnel and finance/accounting organizational units of the firm. The employee services management system therefore involves the interaction of the personnel information system and the accounting information system (AIS). In addition, every department or other organizational unit is involved, since the employees are located throughout the organization. Exhibit 11–2 shows the relations between key departments and the system functions.

(a) Personnel Management's Role

Personnel management has the primary objective of planning, controlling, and coordinating the issues pertaining to employees—the internally employed human resource—within an organization. The personnel function itself may be under the direction of a vice-president of personnel, while managers who might report to this senior officer are those in charge of employment and personnel planning, safety and benefits, industrial relations, employee development, and human resource administration. Employment and personnel planning is concerned with recruiting and testing prospective employees, hiring selected employees, assuring sound promotion and termination procedures, and determining future personnel needs (in terms of both skills and management levels). Safety and benefits is responsible for employees' safety and health and for providing pleasant working conditions. The industrial relations unit is responsible for dealing with unions and other labor-related organizations. The employee development unit is concerned with training employees and with the improvement of executive skills in managers. Human resource administration is responsible for salary compensation plans, group insurance, and related programs; it also administers and maintains the records of all employees and related personnel actions. Thus, the human resource administration unit, at times called personnel administration, is the most closely related to the payroll activity and of most concern in this chapter.

(b) Finance/Accounting

The objectives of financial and accounting management relate broadly to funds, data, information, planning, and control over resources. Organizational units that are within this function and are involved in the management of employee services include timekeeping, payroll, accounts payable, cash disbursements, cost distribution, and general ledger. Time-

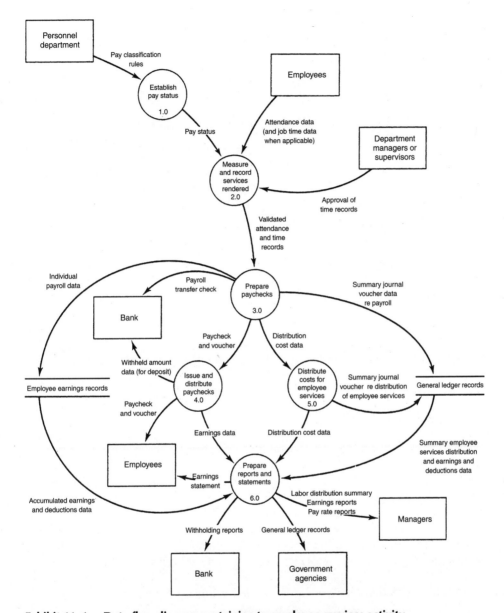

Exhibit 11–1.   Data flow diagram pertaining to employee services activity.

Adapted from J. Wilkinson, *Accounting Information System: Essential Concepts and Application,* 2nd ed. (New York: John Wiley & Sons, 1993).

keeping maintains control over the time and attendance records of hourly employees. Payroll prepares paychecks, maintains the payroll records, and prepares required reports and statements. Accounts payable, in the context of employee services, approves the disbursement voucher pertaining to employee services. Cash disbursements, together with the cashier, signs and distributes the paychecks. Cost distribution maintains the records reflecting detailed costs of employee services, as allocated to responsibility centers and products.

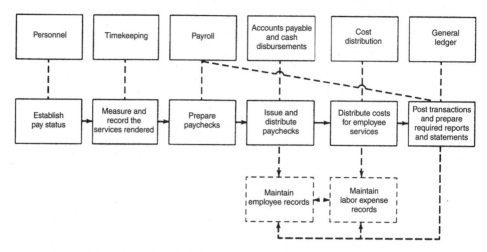

Exhibit 11–2.   Flow chart of typical functions and related organizational units of an employee services system.

Adapted from J. Wilkinson, *Accounting Information System: Essential Concepts and Applications,* 2nd ed. (New York: John Wiley & Sons, 1993).

General ledger maintains control over all asset, equity, expense, and income accounts. Note that the timekeeping and cost distribution units are more typically found in manufacturing firms than in other types of organizations.

(c) Managerial Decision Making

Three managers who have key responsibilities with respect to the employee services management system are the personnel manager, the treasurer, and the controller. They must constantly make and remake decisions that influence acquiring, managing, and paying employees and keeping them motivated. The personnel manager depends most heavily on the personnel information system to provide needed information for decision making. Many of the decisions are not based, even in part, on routine accounting transactions. However, some of the payroll-related decisions do draw on information from the AIS. Some of the typical decisions most closely bound to the payroll activity are:

- What organizational units are to be included within the personnel function?
- Which applicants should be hired as new employees?
- Which employees should be promoted, transferred, given pay raises, or terminated?
- What benefits of financial value should be made available to employees?

The controller and treasurer depend primarily on the AIS for needed decision-making information. Much of the information is a by-product of processing within the employee services management system. Among the decisions requiring answers of these managers (or their subordinates) are:

- What employees' earnings records are to be maintained concerning amounts paid to employees?

- Which payroll deduction plans, for example, United Way, are to be made available to employees?
- What type of payroll bank accounts are to be established?
- Who is to sign paychecks, and how are pay amounts to be distributed to employees?
- What pay periods (e.g., weekly, biweekly) are to be established?

Among the information needed to make these decisions are qualifications of applicants, evaluations of employees, wage and salary scales (both for the firm and for the industry), expected costs of benefit plans, and educational and work experience histories of employees.

11.5 DOCUMENTATION NEEDED FOR EMPLOYEE SERVICES

Source documents typically used in the management of employee services include the following:

(a) Personnel Action Form

A personnel action form serves to notify interested parties of actions concerning employees. These actions may pertain to hiring, changing of status, evaluating job performance, and so on. A personnel action form notifies the payroll department of a situation or change affecting the status of an employee's pay. Another category of personnel actions concerns deductions. Some of these forms are issued by the firm and some by government agencies. An example of the latter is the W4 Form, Employee Withholding Allowance Certificate, provided by the Internal Revenue Service and informing the employer about the number of exemptions being claimed by the employee. Other documents provide employees with the total amount of taxes withheld from their earnings during the fiscal year.

(b) Time and/or Attendance Form

The time card, also known as a clock card, documents the actual hours spent by hourly employees at their work locations. It contains an employee's name and number, plus the dates of the applicable pay period. Usually the bottom of the card has a space for the supervisor's signature attesting that the hours recorded are accurate. Attendance forms and other forms of time cards are not limited to hourly employees; time sheets are also used by salaried employees, such as those working for public accounting firms.

(c) Job-Time Ticket

In contrast to the time card, which focuses on attendance at the work site, the job-time ticket focuses on specific jobs or work orders. Each time an hourly employee, such as a production worker, begins and ends work on the job, he or she records the time on the card. As in the case of the time card, the means of entering the times may be a time clock or terminal. If appropriate to the employees' tasks, spaces are provided for entering the productivity in terms of pieces completed during the elapsed periods.

(d) Paycheck

A paycheck, with voucher stub, is the final supporting document in the employee services management cycle. The stub shows all necessary details, including overtime pay and deductions.

11.6 ACCOUNTING ENTRIES

Exhibit 11–3 shows the flow of payroll transactions through the accounting cycle. The transactions begin with records reflecting times worked by employees. These source documents, when expressed in dollar terms after applying rates of pay, are used in the two steps comprising payroll processing. As the first step, the data from these source documents are entered into a summary that distributes the costs for employee services to activities such as selling goods, performing administrative tasks, and manufacturing goods. The totals from this summary are posted to the general ledger accounts as follows, to record the gross payroll costs of employee services for the period:

> Dr. Selling Expense Control XXX
> Dr. Administrative Expense Control XXX
> Dr. Direct Labor or Work-in-Process XXX
> Dr. Manufacturing Overhead Control XXX
> Cr. Wages and Salaries Payable XXX

Details also can be posted to appropriate expense subsidiary ledgers for manufacturing overhead control, selling expense control, and administrative expense control, if such ledgers are maintained.

The second step consists of using the time data to prepare payroll checks. Copies of these paychecks, together with attached earnings statements, are the source documents from which pay data are entered into the payroll register. They also are used as the basis for posting the same data to the earnings records of individual employees. Totals from the payroll register are then posted to the general ledger accounts as follows, to record the payroll for the period:

> Dr. Wages and Salaries Payable XXX
> Cr. Federal Income Taxes Withholding Payable XXX

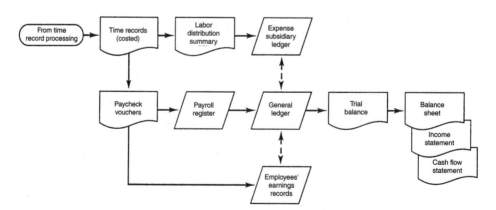

Exhibit 11–3.   Diagram showing the flow of payroll transactions through the employee services system.

Adapted from J. Wilkinson, *Accounting Information System: Essential Concepts and Applications,* 2nd ed. (New York: John Wiley & Sons, 1993).

Cr. FICA Tax Payable XXX

Cr. Other Accrued Deductions Payable XXX

Cr. Cash XXX

A payroll clearing account may be used in place of the wages and salaries payable account, since the effect is to clear the costs of employee services. Either account also can serve as a control over the total of the gross amounts of pay for all employees.

11.7 TRANSACTION CODING

Codes are useful for identifying data needed in payrolls and labor cost distributions. In addition to codes for general ledger accounts, codes can be used to identify employees, departments, production jobs, and skills. Many firms use an employee's social security number, since it is unique and familiar to the employees. Other firms may use group codes that include factors such as pay category (i.e., hourly or salaried), department number, skill, date of hire, and self-checking digit.

11.8 DATABASE NEEDED FOR EMPLOYEE SERVICES

A considerable amount of data are needed in order to process the payroll and to take care of other functions associated with employee services. To facilitate the use of such data, they are arranged in assorted files. Among the files needed in managing employee services are the employee payroll master, personnel reference and history, time record transaction, paycheck transaction, compensation reference, and personnel planning files. These are described below.

(a) Employee Payroll Master File

An employee payroll master file contains the earnings records of the employees. It is updated to show the amounts received from paychecks at the end of each pay period. Typical items listed in this file are: employee's name, identification number, marital status, number of exemptions claimed, department where employed, pay classification, pay rate, overtime rate, deduction rate, year-to-date withholding, and year-to-date gross pay. Generally, the primary and sorting key is the employee number. The accumulated amounts shown in the record serve various purposes. For instance, the year-to-date gross pay has the purpose of determining the maximum levels for deductions pertaining to unemployment benefits and social security.

A major concern with respect to this file is keeping the records and their permanent data up-to-date. If an employee marries and obtains a new last name, for instance, this change should appear quickly in her record. When a new employee is hired, a record must be established before the end of the pay period. On the other hand, when an employee is terminated, the record should not be discarded until after the end of the year. Certain year-end reports require data concerning all employees who were active during any part of the year.

(b) Personnel Reference and History File

As the main source of personnel data in the firm, the personnel reference and history file complements the payroll master file. It contains a variety of nonfinancial data as well as financial data concerning each employee. For instance, it might contain the employee's address, skills, job title, work experience, educational history, performance evaluations, and even family status. This file may be consolidated and maintained in the personnel department. Alternatively, it may be split into several reference files, which may be located in the payroll and/or data processing departments as well as the personnel department. A related file is the skills file, which provides an inventory of job capabilities required by the firm and the employees who currently possess each skill. This type of file enables a firm to locate qualified candidates when an opening or new need arises.

(c) Time Record Transaction File

A time record transaction file consists of copies of all the time cards or sheets for a particular pay period. In computer-based systems they are likely stored on magnetic media for use in processing the payroll.

(d) Paycheck Transaction File

In a manual system the payroll transaction file consists of a copy of each current paycheck, arranged in check number order. In a computer-based system the record layout on magnetic media may appear similar to a record in the check disbursements transaction file.

(e) Compensation Reference File

A table of pay rates and salary levels for the various job descriptions serves as a compensation reference file.

(f) Personnel Planning File

In order to provide the basis for planning for future personnel needs, a firm may maintain a collection of information relating to current and past trends as well as projections. It might show the number of employees in each department during the past ten years, for instance, as well as the turnover for each department.

11.9 DATA FLOWS AND PROCESSING FOR MANUAL SYSTEMS

Exhibit 11–4 presents a document flow chart of a procedure involving the payment of hourly operations-type employees (e.g., production employees) who also work directly on specific jobs. The numbers on the flow chart designate the various control points within the procedure and parallel the functions described earlier.

1. Establishment of pay status. This beginning function takes place in the personnel department, where all of the personnel actions and changes are prepared and then transmitted to the payroll department.
2. Measurement of the services rendered. The time records are prepared in the operational (e.g., production) departments and timekeeping areas. Employees clock in and clock out under the eye of a timekeeper. The job-time tickets are available right at the work site. Employees either punch the tickets on a clock or mark them manually under the eye of their supervisor. At the end of each day, the job-time tickets are collected and approved by the employees' supervisor. Then the supervisor forwards

the tickets to the timekeeper. At the end of the pay period the timekeeper compares the total hours shown on each employee's job-time ticket with the total hours shown on his or her attendance time card. If the two sets of total hours are approximately equal (allowing for breaks, lunch, etc.), the time records are said to be reconciled. Then the timekeeper sends the attendance time cards to the payroll department (together with the total of hours worked) and the job-time tickets to the cost distribution department.

3. Preparation of the paychecks. In the payroll department, a clerk prepares a paycheck and voucher stub for each employee, based on data from the time card and from the employee's payroll reference file. Next, the clerk enters the relevant information from the paycheck and voucher stub (i.e., gross pay, deductions, net pay, overtime premium) on the payroll register. Another clerk then posts the information to the employee's earnings record (i.e., the payroll master). Still another clerk verifies that the hours used in preparing the payroll register equal the total hours on the time cards and that the total payroll amount entered into the register equals the total amount posted to all employees' earnings records. The paychecks and attached voucher stubs are sent, in a batch, to the cash disbursements department (or cashier).

4. Issuance and distribution of the paychecks. On receiving a copy of the payroll register, an accounts payable clerk verifies its correctness and then prepares a disbursement voucher. A clerk in the cash disbursements department draws a check on the firm's regular bank account and gives it to the cashier for signing. The signed check is delivered to the bank and deposited in the special imprest payroll account. Then the cashier signs all the paychecks. A paymaster (a designated person not otherwise involved in personnel or payroll procedures) distributes the paychecks.

5. Distribution of the labor costs. Meanwhile, a clerk in the cost distribution department spreads or distributes the costs of services incurred by the operational personnel (e.g., production employees) to the various jobs in progress. The clerk next reports the costs, via a labor distribution summary or a journal voucher, to the general ledger department. Then the general ledger clerk debits the amounts to the various labor-related accounts (e.g., direct factory labor) and credits a payroll control account (e.g., wages and salaries payable). Subsequently, the general ledger clerk clears the payroll clearing account by reference to the disbursement voucher (or related journal voucher) prepared by accounts payable. That is, he or she debits the payroll clearing account and credits the cash account and the accounts with liabilities for payroll deductions. Since the total of gross pay from both sources (labor cost distribution and disbursement voucher) should be equal, the payroll clearing account will be cleared to zero if processing has been correct. Note that this clearing procedure is a partial substitute for the computation of formal batch totals in the timekeeping department. When attendance time records are not accompanied by time records related to jobs, it is highly desirable to compute batch totals at the point where the time records are assembled.

6. Preparation of required outputs. Numerous payroll-related reports and statements and other outputs are prepared. The only outputs shown in the flow chart are the labor distribution summary (mentioned in the previous step) and the payroll register. Additional reports can also be extracted from the data available.

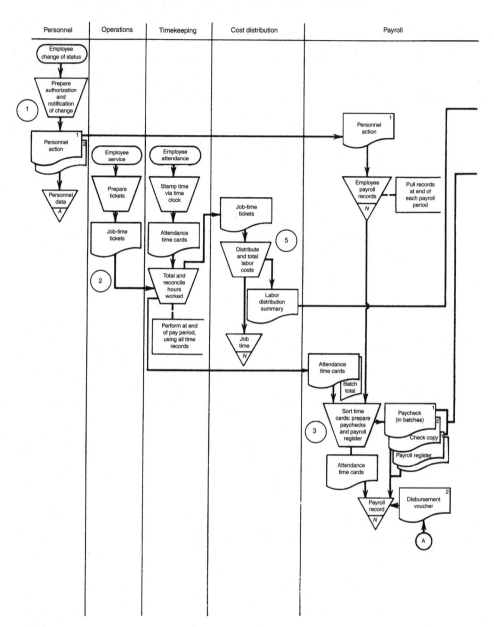

Exhibit 11–4.   Document system flow chart of a manual employee payroll transaction processing procedure.

Adapted from J. Wilkinson, *Accounting Information System: Essential Concepts and Applications,* 2nd ed. (New York: John Wiley & Sons, 1993).

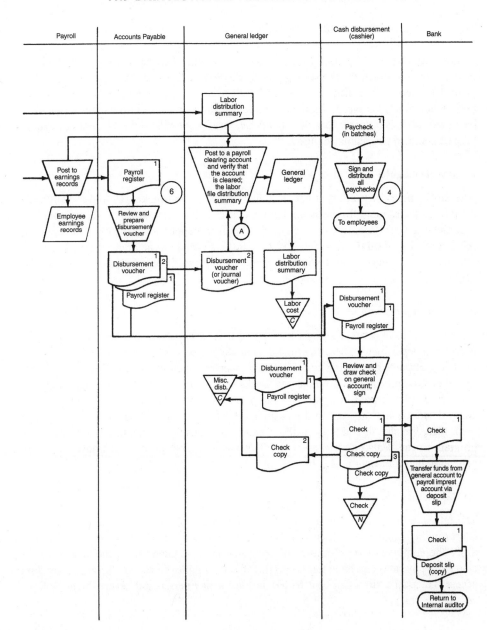

Exhibit 11–4. Continued.

11.10 COMPUTER-BASED PROCESSING SYSTEM

Although the on-line approach may be used in computer-based processing, the batch approach is better suited to the payroll procedure. Since all of the records in the employee payroll master file are affected, sequentially accessing and updating the records is the more efficient alternative. Exhibit 11–5 therefore shows a system flow chart in which the batch approach is applied. The flow chart has three segments: time data entry, paycheck preparation, and pay status changes.

(a) Time Data Entry

Attendance time cards are first gathered in a batch by the timekeeper and transmitted to the payroll department. In the system being described, the employees do not prepare job-time tickets. Therefore, to enhance control the timekeeper (or a payroll clerk) computes batch totals based on the time records. One total is based on the hours worked, a second total is based on the employee numbers, and a third total is based on a count of the time cards.

(b) Paycheck Preparation

The batch of time cards, prefaced by a batch transmittal sheet, is forwarded to the data processing department. There the time data are keyed onto a magnetic disk and edited. In the first computer processing run the data are sorted by employee numbers. In run 2 the time data are processed to produce paychecks (and voucher stubs). The program also updates the employee payroll master file and prints the payroll register. The paychecks and a copy of the register are sent to the cashier, where the paychecks are signed and distributed. (The transfer of funds from the regular account may be included if desired.) The program in run 2 also adds a journal voucher concerning the payroll transaction to the general ledger transaction file.

(c) Pay Status Changes

The left side of the flow chart portrays changes made in the pay status of employees. Clerks in the personnel department enter all personnel actions via departmental terminals. Since the employee payroll master file is stored on a magnetic disk, the actions (e.g., a change in pay rate) can be entered into the affected employee records promptly by direct access. Thus, all actions can be effected during the pay period and before the payroll processing begins.

11.11 CONTROLS NEEDED FOR EMPLOYEE SERVICES

Transactions within the employee services system are exposed to a variety of risks. Exhibit 11–6 lists representative risks and consequent exposures due to these risks. With respect to the employee services system, several key objectives are to ensure that:

- All services performed by employees, including hours worked on specified tasks such as production jobs, are recorded accurately and in a timely manner.
- All employees are paid in accordance with wage contracts or other established policies.

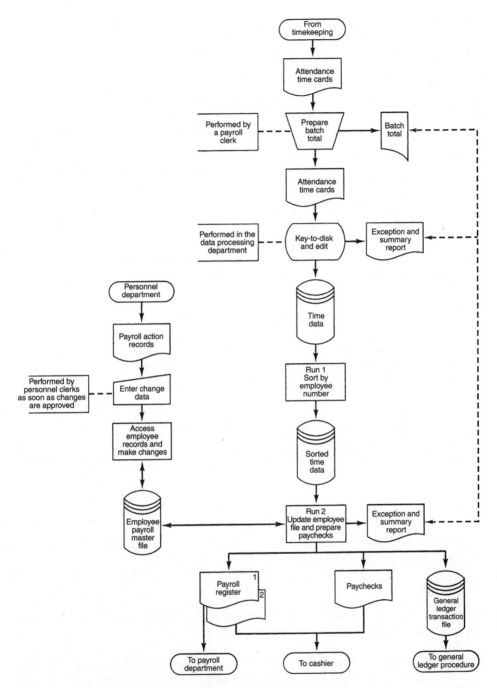

Exhibit 11–5.   System flow chart of a batch computer-base employee payroll transaction processing procedure.

Adapted from J. Wilkinson, *Accounting Information System: Essential Concepts and Applications,* 2nd ed. (New York: John Wiley & Sons, 1993).

Risk	Exposure(s)
1. Employment of unqualified persons	1. Lessened productivity and higher training costs
2. Employment of larcenous persons	2. Possibility of loss of assets and circumvented policies and controls
3. Errors or omissions in time records	3. Incorrect payroll records and labor distribution summaries
4. Errors in payments to employees	4. Possibility of overpayments and/or adverse effects on employee morale; erroneous quarterly statements sent to federal and state agencies
5. Incorrect disbursements of paychecks to fictitious or terminated employees, or diversions of valid paychecks to unentitled employees	5. Excessive wage and salary costs
6. Errors in charging labor expenses or in stating payroll liabilities	6. Incorrect levels for expense and liability accounts
7. Violation of government regulations and laws with regard to payments or reporting requirements	7. Possibility of penalties and fines being assessed

Exhibit 11–6.   Table of risk exposures within the employee services management system.
Adapted from J. Wilkinson *Accounting Information System: Essential Concepts and Applications,* 2nd ed. (New York: John Wiley & Sons, 1993).

- All paychecks are calculated accurately, with due allowance for authorized payroll deductions and approved benefit programs.
- All costs for employee services are distributed to accounts in accordance with clearly established accounting policies.
- All required reports are prepared accurately and completely in accordance with prescribed laws and regulations and submitted by their scheduled dates.

To fulfill these control objectives, the firm must then specify and incorporate adequate general controls and transaction controls.

(a) General Controls

General controls include those involving organizational independence, documentation, security measures, and practices and policies.

- Within the organization, the persons and units that have custodial functions (i.e., the cash disbursements department, cashier, and paymaster) should be separate from those units that keep time records (i.e., timekeeping) and that prepare the payroll documents (i.e., the payroll department). Also, the personnel department, which authorizes personnel actions, and the departmental supervisors, who approve the time records, should be separate from all the above-mentioned units.
- Complete and up-to-date documentation should be available concerning the management of employee services.

- Security should be maintained (in on-line systems) by such techniques as (a) requiring the clerks enter assigned passwords before accessing employee payroll files; (b) employing terminals with restricted functions for the entry of personnel actions; (c) generating audit reports (access logs) that monitor accesses of system files; and (d) dumping the employee files onto magnetic tape backups. Physical security measures include the use of safes for holding stocks of blank paychecks and signature plates.
- Operating policies and practices relating to processing schedules, reports, changes in programs, and other matters should be clearly established.

(b) Transaction (Application) Controls

The following controls and control procedures are applicable to employee services transactions and employee records:

- Documents relating to payables and cash disbursements are prenumbered and well designed. Also, time cards and job-time tickets, where applicable, are preprinted with the employees' names and numbers.
- Data on time records are validated (and key-verified if suitable) as the data are prepared and entered for processing. In the case of computer-based systems, validation is performed by means of programmed checks such as (a) validity checks on employee numbers, (b) limit checks on hours worked, (c) field checks on key identification and amount data, and (d) relationship checks on employee numbers and related departments to which employees are assigned.
- During payroll processing, the results, such as net pay, are validated. In the case of computer-based systems, validation is performed by means of programmed checks, such as the sign check and cross-foot balance check. Thus, the net-pay field of each paycheck is verified by the former to see that the sign is positive and by the latter to see that the amount equals the gross pay, less all deductions.
- Errors detected during data entry or processing are corrected as soon as possible by means of an established error-correction procedure. A part of this procedure may involve the printing of suitable exception and summary reports during edit runs. In the case of the payroll application, processing of paychecks may be delayed until all transaction data errors and discrepancies have been corrected.
- Personnel actions (such as new hires and pay rate changes) and paychecks are issued promptly on the basis of valid authorizations.
- Time cards and job-time tickets, where applicable, are approved by the employees' supervisors.
- Where job-time tickets are used, the hours that they reflect for each employee are reconciled with the hours shown on the attendance timecards.
- Batch control totals are precomputed on hours worked, as reflected by time cards, and on net pay amounts, as shown in the payroll register; these batch totals are compared with totals computed during paycheck preparation and during postings to the employee payroll master file, respectively.
- Paychecks are drawn on a separate payroll-imprest bank account.
- Voided paychecks are retained, in order that all paycheck numbers can be accounted for.

- Unclaimed paychecks are traced back to the time records and employee payroll master file, to verify that they belong to actual, current employees.
- In the case of computer-based systems, a preliminary payroll register is reviewed before the paychecks are printed, to determine that all errors have been corrected. Payroll account summaries are also printed periodically to enhance the audit trail.

In addition, all controls pertaining to cash disbursements also apply to the issuance of paychecks.

11.12 REPORTS AND OTHER OUTPUTS

The reports made available to managers and other users can be used to meet operational needs or to help managerial decision making.

(a) Operational Reports

One of the most used outputs is the payroll register. In essence, it is the journal in the payroll procedure, and it lists the key payment data concerning each employee for a single pay period, ranging from gross pay to net pay. A related output is the deduction register, which provides a detailed breakdown of the deductions for each employee. The cumulative earnings register shows amounts earned year-to-date, and possibly quarter-to-date, for each employee. Various control reports are also needed. One example is a report that shows the number of checks printed and the total amounts of the checks.

Required governmental reports include those pertaining to withholdings of social security and federal income taxes, plus a variety of others. Some are due during the month following the end of each quarter; others are due during the month following the end of each year.

(b) Managerial Report

Various analyses are of interest to managers, such as those pertaining to absenteeism, overtime pay, turnover, sales commissions, and indirect labor costs. One useful analysis is a projection of salaries for the upcoming months of the year. Other reports that often are helpful include surveys of average pay rates per occupational category, compared with similar firms, and personnel strength reports, showing levels of staffing and changes during the past month.

The labor distribution summary can serve two purposes: as the basis for accounting entries and as an analysis for management. In essence, the summary shows the amounts of employee services costs to be distributed to various accounts. However, it also can include details concerning the costs incurred by individual employees and responsibility centers for various tasks. For instance, it might show that Ray Valdez incurred $350 this week with respect to Production Job 301 and $420 with respect to Production Job 318. In addition, it separates the costs between direct labor and indirect labor.

11.13 CONCLUSION

Resources allow an organization to function, and they must be managed. The employee services function consists of hiring, training, assigning, compensating, evaluating, and when needed, terminating employees. The focus of the chapter is on compensating employees, or payroll function, even though employee services or human resources comprise much more. Functions surveyed include establishing pay status, measuring the services rendered, preparing paychecks, issuing and distributing paychecks, distributing employee service costs, and preparing required reports and statements. This system involves the personnel, timekeeping, payroll, accounts payable, cash disbursements, cost distribution, and general ledger units. Key inputs are the personnel action form, time record, job-time ticket, and paycheck. The database includes the employee payroll master and personnel reference and history files. Outputs include the payroll and other registers, plus analyses of labor cost components.

CHAPTER 12

THE RESOURCES MANAGEMENT CYCLE: INVENTORY MANAGEMENT

12.1 INTRODUCTION

This chapter continues the coverage of systems within the resources management cycle by surveying inventory management. Inventory refers to goods held for the purpose of sale. The goods held in the inventory by a merchandiser like Sears are sales-ready, finished products. But in the case of a manufacturer of automobiles, like Ford, it will include raw materials, work in process, finished goods, component parts for factory machines, and supplies. Inventory represents a firm's reason for being. Both manufacturers and merchandisers are in business to sell, and without inventories there will be nothing to sell. Furthermore, inventories can represent a major portion of a firm's working capital. Not only do inventories tie up capital, but their storage and safekeeping also consumes considerable resources.

The discussion of inventory management is split into two sections: Inventory management for merchandisers is discussed first, followed by a discussion of inventory management for manufacturers. The discussion of the merchandise inventory system is relatively brief, since various facets concerning the inventory management system for a merchandising firm were included in the earlier discussions of interfacing cycles and systems. For example, Chapter 9, which focused on the revenue cycle, discussed the system considerations governing the sale of inventory, while Chapter 10, on the expenditure cycle, dealt with payments for the merchandise acquired. In Chapters 9 and 10, the emphasis was on those firms that acquire merchandise for resale. Given this, the discussion of merchandise inventory in this chapter will fill in the gaps. After discussing the inventory resource for merchandisers, we will go on to discuss inventory management for firms that manufacture products.

12.2 MERCHANDISE INVENTORY MANAGEMENT SYSTEM

The major purpose of the merchandise inventory management system is to facilitate the inflows, storage, and outflows of the merchandise needed by a firm that obtains revenues from the merchandise's resale. Key objectives within this purpose are to (1) assure that an adequate quantity of merchandise is available to meet the demands of customers, (2) reflect accurate values for the merchandise on hand, (3) safeguard the merchandise from theft and other various losses, and (4) handle returns and other adjustments in a prompt and judicious manner.

Major functions related to merchandise inventory consist of acquisition, receipt and storage, shipment, and adjustment. In each of these functions, the merchandise inventory

251

management system tracks the flows of inventory items and generates information to aid in making decisions. We have already referred to most of the concerns and actions that pertain to the management of merchandise inventory. However, to help readers better visualize the central place of the inventory resource in such firms, we provide an overview of the merchandise inventory management system in this section. Exhibit 12–1 presents a data flow diagram that includes the major functions related to merchandise inventory: acquiring inventory, receiving and storing it, shipping it to purchasers, and adjusting inventory valuation. These functions are discussed below.

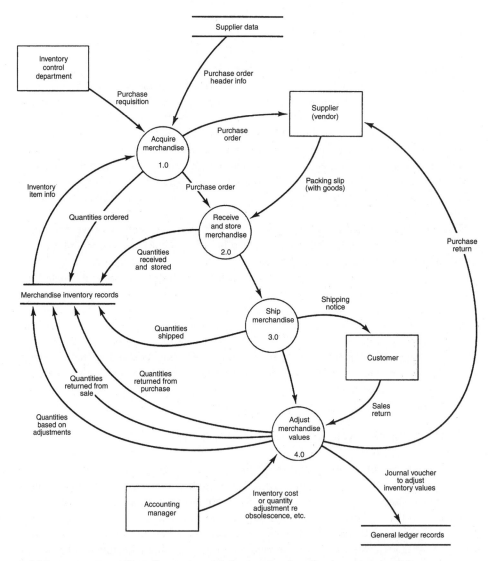

Exhibit 12–1.   Data flow diagram pertaining to merchandise inventory activity.

Adapted from J. Wilkinson, *Accounting Information System: Essential Concepts and Applications,* 2nd ed. (New York: John Wiley & Sons, 1993).

(a) Acquiring Merchandise

In order to restock merchandise, a firm must first determine when and how much to reorder. This information is often provided by reference to a reorder point and reorder quantity, whose values are computed in accordance with inventory control principles described in Chapter 10. The information concerning reorders may be provided by a purchase requisition. Alternatively, it may appear on a merchandise reorder report, if one is available.

Data concerning the various items of merchandise inventory are typically maintained in merchandise inventory ledger records. In a manual system, these records usually are kept on ledger cards, one card per merchandise inventory item. Included on a ledger card will likely be a header data, such as the item number, the description of the item, its unit cost, and its location in the warehouse. The body of the ledger card will show the data for each transaction, plus the balances after each transaction.

Before leaving this function, we should observe its effects on a computer-based inventory processing system. As Exhibit 12–2 shows, the ordering procedure might consist of entering data from the merchandise reorder report, via a terminal, into the system. Purchase orders are printed, with a copy being stored in the on-line open purchase orders file. Also, the merchandise inventory master file is updated to reflect the ordered quantity. This merchandise inventory item record, which corresponds to the merchandise inventory ledger card in a manual system, contains a quantity on-order field.

(b) Receiving and Storing Merchandise

When ordered merchandise items arrive, the quantities received are posted to the merchandise inventory ledger records, leading to an increase in the quantities on hand. Exhibit 12–2 shows this posting for a computer-based system. It also indicates that the related purchase order is removed from the open purchase orders file upon its receipt and a copy of the receiving report is added to the receipts transaction file. If a portion of the received quantities are to be allocated to particular customers, perhaps because of backorders, the affected quantities should be noted.

For tracking inventory, most firms that have computer-based inventory systems employ the perpetual method. Under this method, the merchandise inventory account in the general ledger is debited when the payable relating to a purchase has been established. If the inventory account in the general ledger is to be used as a control account, costs pertaining to the various items comprising the purchase also must be posted to the merchandise inventory item records. In a subsequent section, we discuss the basics of inventory costing. The amount posted to each inventory item record is roughly equal to the unit cost of the item times the quantity received. However, allowance may need to be made for costs pertaining to freight and handling.

(c) Shipping Sold Merchandise

When merchandise is sold, it is normally shipped a short time later. Then the quantities sold are removed from the affected inventory records. If the perpetual method is used, the value of the inventory sold on a given day, for instance, April 1, would be posted to the inventory account in the general ledger (after billing) by the following entry, to record the value of inventory sold on April 1, 20XX:

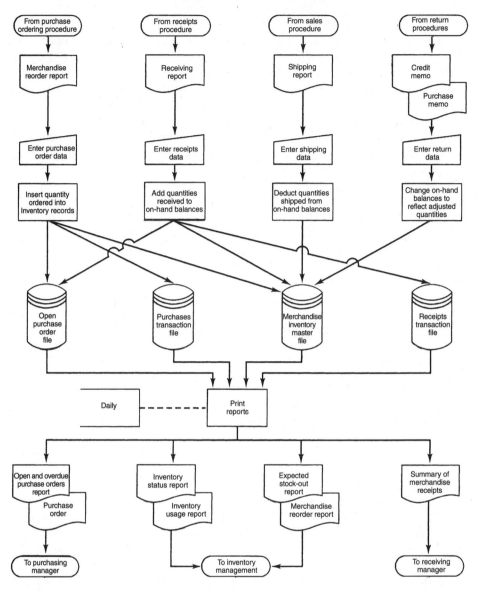

Exhibit 12–2.   System flow chart of an on-line computer-based inventory management system.

Adapted from J. Wilkinson, *Accounting Information System: Essential Concepts and Applications,* 2nd ed. (New York: John Wiley & Sons, 1993).

| Dr. Cost of Goods Sold | XXX |
| Cr. Merchandise Inventory | XXX |

The measured cost valuation of each inventory item involved in a sale also must be reduced. In determining the amounts to be reduced, the firm multiplies the quantity sold of each item times its unit cost. The unit cost, in turn, is based on the particular inventory valuation method employed by the firm.

(d) Adjusting Value of Merchandise

A firm may accept returns of merchandise it has sold, and it also may return merchandise to its suppliers. A firm also may write down the recorded value of stored inventory, due to obsolescence, pilferage, or other reasons. Such adjustments, which are quite frequent, are posted to the merchandise inventory master file, as Exhibit 12–2 shows.

12.3 INVENTORY VALUATION METHODS

Before discussing inventory valuation methods, it is best to clarify the various costs associated with inventory. The costs directly related to inventory are:

- Purchase costs refer to the value of the inventory itself. This is the amount paid to the vendor in exchange for the goods purchased.
- Ordering costs define the managerial and clerical expenses incurred to prepare the purchase order, or in the case of manufacturing firms, the production order.
- Carrying costs are those incurred for inventory's storage, handling, insurance, pilferage, spoilage, obsolescence, taxes, and the opportunity cost of capital tied in the inventory. The last one, opportunity cost, does not appear in the accounting statements, but managers who ignore it are putting their firm's future in danger.
- Stockout costs are incurred when the needed item is not in stock. It may take the form of lost sales revenue, the cost of delayed production, or penalties incurred for not meeting customers' deadlines. Again, this is included as a part of the accounting reports.
- Setup costs occur because different products require equipment to be reset to meet the specific needs of each batch of the product. In addition to equipment setups, making a batch of product different from the one previously made involves obtaining the raw materials from the warehouse, moving out the previous stock at the workstations, and filing paperwork. While setups are being changed, workers involved in operating the equipment may be idle, though they are still being paid. The setup costs are non–value-adding to the firm; they can be minimized by redesigning the production process and simplifying the product design.

The value of inventory on hand must be determined periodically, along with the value of other assets, to enable a company to determine its cost of goods sold and to state the firm's financial position. The basis used for inventory valuation has a significant effect on the costs and earnings reflected in the operating statements and on the asset value shown on the balance sheet.

A variety of methods can be used to value inventory. Income tax computation, accounting principles, ease of application, management reporting, and control considerations all influence the approach used. From a management point of view, the evaluation method that is selected should take advantage of benefits that may affect the operating statement but also should be easy to use.

The principal methods of cost determination for financial statement preparation begin with standard costs and/or average costs. The development of standard or average unit costs allows the extension of physical units by these costs to determine the ending inventory value, which, when subtracted from the beginning inventory plus materials purchases and conversion expenses for the period, equals the cost of goods sold for the period. Ending inventory values and, correspondingly, costs of goods sold may be further adjusted by the use of FIFO (first in, first out), LIFO (last in, first out), or cost-of-specific-lot methods. For retail and distribution companies, which do not incur conversion costs, the gross margin retail method is the commonly accepted valuation method.

(a) Standard Costs

A simply administered technique for determining inventory cost is provided by standard costs. To facilitate its use, standard costs representing the expected costs of purchase and conversion must be established for materials, labor, and other expenses directly related to each inventoried unit. Those manufacturing expenses (overhead or burden) not directly identified with a product or inventory item usually are assigned to each unit of production on a realistic basis. Thus, supervision might be assigned on the basis of the labor hours required to make a product, whereas depreciation, insurance, and taxes might be on the basis of machine hours required to make a product.

When actual costs are not equal to the standards, variances result and must be recorded. If these variances are substantial, they are accumulated and reallocated to all the production of the period and the inventory on hand. If the variances are minor, they generally are taken as an expense as they occur. To remain accurate and effective, standard costs must be revised at least annually by correcting for changes in costs and methods; otherwise, the values derived lose validity either for valuing inventory or for controlling purchasing or operations.

(b) Average Cost

Many companies use an average unit cost to determine inventory value. Two methods are used for this purpose: an average calculated by dividing the total cost of beginning inventory and purchases by the total number of units represented, and a moving average, calculated after each new purchase is made. Where the time lapse between valuations is long or price changes are rapid, the two methods produce somewhat different results. It is important to note that the moving average requires the maintenance of perpetual records, while the weighted average may be computed periodically. In either case, the use of averaging tends to spread the effect of short-range price changes and level their effect on profit determination.

(c) FIFO

The FIFO method assumes that the goods are sold in the order in which they were received or manufactured. With the use of FIFO it is not necessary to identify lots or physically segregate items in the order of purchase. Under this method, the final inventory is priced by determining the costs of the most recent purchases or using the most recent standard costs. Generally this is done by working back from the most recent invoices of units manufactured until the quantity on hand has been covered.

(d) LIFO

The LIFO method assumes that the last goods received or manufactured were sold first. In a period of rising prices, this method reduces profits and postpones tax payments because the highest-cost items are used to compute the cost of sales. This method assumes that all items in inventory, or in a segment of inventory, are homogeneous. This assumption allows the use of price indices to convert the final inventory priced at current prices to the same inventory priced in terms of the base year (the year in which LIFO was adopted).

The LIFO method allows a firm to postpone the payment of taxes and thus receive an "interest-free" loan from the government. Generally, any company with the following characteristics should adopt the LIFO method: inventories that are significant relative to total assets (a manufacturer or distributor); inventory costs that are increasing; an effective tax rate that is not expected to increase significantly; and/or inventory levels that are expected to remain stable or increase. Conversely, if inventory levels or unit costs are expected to decline or the tax rates increase, a company should not use the LIFO method because LIFO could increase rather than decrease the company's future tax liability.

(e) Cost of Specific Lots

For capital-goods industries and some other industries, it is usually desirable to maintain the identity and actual costs of specific lots or items. This is done by recording the actual raw materials purchase price and conversion costs for each lot or item in inventory. The application of this method usually is limited to inventories containing high-value, low-quantity items or to those situations where such records are practical or mandatory.

(f) Gross-Margin Method

The gross-margin method of pricing inventory has been developed in the distribution and retailing industries to facilitate inventory valuation by having items in inventory priced at an adjusted selling price rather than cost. The basis for computing this ratio is an established average margin, or markup, which is added to the cost to arrive at the selling price. Assuming that the goods in inventory are representative, in terms of their markup, of goods purchased during the recent operating period, their cost is easily determined by using the ratio to recompute the inventory value. Using this method, the ending-inventory value is determined by extending the physical units by their selling prices and then reducing the extended amount by the average markup percentage. As with other methods, cost of goods sold is calculated by subtracting the ending-inventory value from beginning inventory plus purchases.

(g) Selecting a Method

The size, age, and type of inventory must be considered in selecting the method used for valuation. The techniques chosen should provide for the requirements of financial and tax reporting as well as relate to the methods used by management for measuring its performance in inventory management and control. For consistency in financial reporting, it is mandatory that the method of inventory valuation remain constant. If at any time a change in method is made, the effect on the financial results must be clearly stated.

12.4 ORGANIZATIONAL CONTEXT OF INVENTORY MANAGEMENT

While specific managers within a firm are directly responsible for the inventory management function, inventory-related functions have impact throughout the organization. Indeed, the functions of the inventory management system overlap with the revenue and expenditure cycles, and span organizational units such as inventory management (or logistics), marketing, finance, and accounting. Departments typically involved are inventory control, purchasing, receiving, sales order, credit, shipping, billing, and general ledger. Collectively those involved with inventory seek to answer questions such as: What should be ordered? Whom should it be ordered from? Where should it be delivered? When should it be ordered? How much should be ordered? In addition, the inventory managers also need to keep track of what has been ordered and received.

(a) What Should Be Ordered?

The inventory to be ordered or manufactured depends on sales forecasted. In the case of merchandisers, the quantities of various items to be ordered are unrelated to each other: The number of appliances to keep in stock is not related to the number of shirts on hand. This is described as independent demand. On the other hand, for a manufacturer, the number of tires to be ordered is related to the number of automobiles being manufactured. When goods ordered are so related, their demand is called dependent.

While a manufacturer is more likely to order goods that have dependent demands, it also can order items that are independent of the decision to manufacture a certain quantity; the amount of supplies and the number of machine parts ordered may not be directly related to the number of cars being made.

(b) Whom Should It Be Ordered From?

In the past, the job of purchasing managers was to shop around among a large sample of vendors for the best value. But old ways are changing. A manifestation of this change involves the trend toward bypassing the middle link in the chain—the wholesalers—in favor of suppliers. This thinking means that the number of suppliers that buyers deal with can be much smaller. It also has meant long-term, close relationships with a few vendors. Vendors are expected to be more quality conscious and make deliveries on time. In return, they are assured business.

One consequence of the new thinking has been a reduction in ordering costs. Advances in information technologies, combined with fewer, more reliable vendors, has allowed changes in accounts payable procedures: Payments are made faster with less paperwork, and the clerical staff that processes purchase orders and receiving reports has been reduced. Bar codes allow arriving shipments to be identified sooner; such identification of shipments received can then allow automatic bank transfers to vendors' accounts.

(c) Where Should It Be Delivered?

For manufacturers, the need for reducing inventory on hand has led to having vendors deliver goods directly to work centers on the factory floor as needed. However, not everyone is able to do this, since the production facilities may not have been built to accommodate such deliveries. In any case, manufacturers may be able to have material delivered to the factories, but retailers have more of a problem, since their warehouses and stores may be far apart. Instead of storing inventory in their facilities, mega-retailers can have the vendors deliver merchandise to their stores directly. This trend is increasing in popularity.

(d) When Should It Be Ordered

The issue of when to order inventory is handled differently, depending on whether the goods are demand independent or dependent. For dependent-demand goods, the issue revolves around a certain point in time when desired goods must be ordered or, in many cases, reordered. That point in time is described as the reorder point. For most firms, the reorder point is reached when the quantity on hand of a certain item falls below a certain level. At this level there is still some quantity on hand, termed safety stock, to last until the reordered stock reaches the warehouse. The quantity of safety stock is dependent on the lead time needed for stock ordered to be delivered. The reorder points, when drawn graphically, resemble the teeth of a saw; hence they are called the sawtooth model.

One measure of change in retailing has come about through the point of sales computers that link the sales registers to the vendors, alerting them to items that need to be replaced. Such electronically determined reorder points can be of benefit to both the vendors and the buyers.

(e) How Much Should Be Ordered?

In the past, quantities being ordered were related not only to the sales projected but also to a decision to have safety stock on hand. Managers provided safeguards for variation in the deliveries of goods ordered and took advantage of the economies of purchasing in bulk. More recently, the rules of the game dictate that the burden of carrying inventory be shifted to the supplier from the seller or manufacturer. This has brought on the popularity of just-in-time production, which does away with work-in-process inventories. There is also a greater emphasis on matching production to market requirements, thus greatly reducing finished goods inventory and the costs associated with taking care of it.

12.5 COMPONENTS OF MERCHANDISE INVENTORY MANAGEMENT SYSTEM

This section reviews the various components of the merchandise inventory management system, such as documentation, inputs, files, control procedures, the nature of the database, and reports. Since readers were exposed to most of these elements in Chapters 9 and 10, the survey here will be brief.

(a) Documentation

The key data entry inputs include the purchase requisition (or merchandise reorder report), purchase order, receiving report, shipping report, credit memo, and purchase memo.

(b) Database

The critical file is the merchandise inventory master file. Exhibit 12–2 indicates that the open purchase order and receipts files are involved also. An inventory history file and standard cost reference file can be useful as well.

(c) Controls

Most of the suitable general and transaction controls are listed under the revenue and expenditure cycles. Among those controls especially relevant to the inventory management system are up-to-date and accurate merchandise inventory item records, sound reorder algorithms, and periodic physical inventories followed by reconciliations with inventory records.

(d) Reports and Other Outputs

Exhibit 12–2 portrays several outputs. A fundamental report is the inventory status report. The merchandise reorder report, which is used as an input to the purchasing procedure, is also an output of the inventory management system. The summary of merchandise receipts is, in effect, a transaction listing, as is an open purchase orders report. A report that shows overdue purchase orders can be used for control purposes. A report showing inventory items expected to be out of stock, either in coming days or weeks, can be used for planning purposes.

12.6 RAW MATERIALS MANAGEMENT (PRODUCT CONVERSION) SYSTEM

As noted earlier, in certain industries, such as manufacturing and construction, the inventory resource is varied. In place of just one inventory consisting of merchandise for resale, these firms maintain three distinct inventories: raw materials, work-in-process, and finished goods. These inventories help trace the conversion of raw materials into finished goods.

Raw materials are converted, via a production process, into finished goods. Thus, a system whose purpose is to manage the raw materials resource also can be described as a system whose purpose is to facilitate the conversion of raw materials (and parts) into finished goods (products). Key objectives within this product conversion or raw materials management system are to ensure that: adequate raw materials and other resources are available; production orders are processed and completed in a timely and cost-efficient manner; the products are of specified quality; the finished goods are warehoused or shipped on schedule; and the costs for each order are accumulated and processed.

The functions related to the foregoing objectives are: (1) planning and initiating the production process, (2) moving work-in-process through production operations, (3) costing the work-in-process, (4) transferring completed products into the finished goods inventory, and (5) preparing financial reports that report on the production process and the subsequent sale of finished goods.

Basically, production of goods is performed according to one of these five patterns and their corresponding cost tracking systems:

- Process production, which involves the continuous production of standardized products (e.g., petrochemicals, cement, steel). Costs are usually accumulated in process cost systems in terms of processes or work centers.

- Mass production, which involves the production of discrete and relatively similar products on assembly lines (e.g., automobiles).
- Operations-oriented production, which involves the production of discrete and relatively similar products through a mix of standard operations performed automatically and manually (e.g., suits, shoes).
- Batch production, which involves the production of batches or job lots of distinctly differing products; for example, a metal products firm may manufacture bearings in one batch and gears in another. Costs usually are accumulated by job order cost systems.
- Custom production, which involves the production of uniquely individual products, often of a complex nature (e.g., special machine tools). Costs are accumulated in custom cost systems in terms of individual orders.

Rather than discussing all of the production patterns, the discussions will focus on batch or job lot production, which also subsumes the production of customized products.

12.7 PRODUCTION LOGISTICS

A key element that underscores production function is logistics. All of the units and flows shown within the dashed box in Exhibit 12–3 can be viewed as closely related to the production logistics function. The sales order entry and shipping units, however, may alternatively be grouped under the marketing/distribution function. Since the roles of several of the production logistics units were described in Chapter 10, only the remaining units will be considered in this section.

Engineering design determines the specifications by which the products are to be manufactured. Production planning determines the quantities of products to be manufactured, the production schedule, and the resources to use; production control dispatches an order into the production process, monitors the order, and takes corrective actions when necessary. Materials requirements planning (MRP) assures that the proper quantities of materials, parts, and subassemblies will be available at the proper time to manufacture the scheduled orders.

12.8 EMERGING ORGANIZATIONAL CONTEXT OF PRODUCTION

In recent years manufacturing firms have greatly improved the quality of their production planning processes. The improvements have been made possible through the availability of more powerful computer hardware and software. At the heart of these improvements, broadly called computer-integrated manufacturing (CIM), are several sophisticated planning approaches. Two of the most useful approaches with special significance for inventory management are known as manufacturing resource planning (MRP) and just-in-time (JIT).

12.9 MATERIAL REQUIREMENTS PLANNING

MRP is a planning system concerned with the acquisition of dependent demand goods. Its focus is on knowing the quantity and timing of inventory items needed in accordance with the master production schedule. It seeks to ensure that materials, components, and

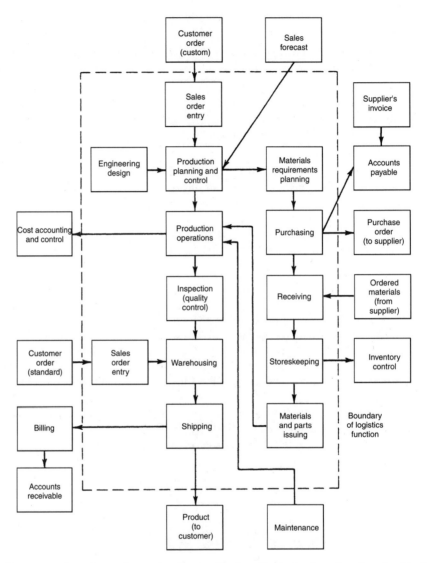

Exhibit 12–3.   Flow chart of organizational units that direct the functions involved in the product conversion system and the filling of customers' orders.

Adapted from J. Wilkinson, *Accounting Information System: Essential Concepts and Applications,* 2nd ed. (New York: John Wiley & Sons, 1993).

subassemblies needed are available in the right quantity. When used effectively, MRP can reduce various inventory costs and improve scheduling effectiveness and response to changing market conditions.

The details pertaining to MRP are highly involved, but at its very basic level, MRP is similar to the kind of planning needed to have all the ingredients for a given recipe on hand before cooking. A cake is a discrete item, and the acquisition of the ingredients (materials requirement planning) to coincide with actual baking is done easily. But it is immensely more complex when dealing with the continuous production of goods that have many models; that require hundreds and often thousands of parts, components, and sub-assemblies; and that have different lead times and vendors. MRP helps to address the logistics of such complexity.

The key factors in an MRP system are: a master production schedule (MPS), a bill of materials (BOM), an inventory profile, and lead times of all inventory items. Using these factors, computer algorithms can help schedule the acquisition of inventory and its subsequent release for production. The same algorithms can respond quickly to unexpected changes in the customers' demands for its products. Closed-loop MRP includes feedback from both internal production sources and vendor reports. Regenerative MRP systems use batch processing to replan the requirements on a regular basis, perhaps monthly or even weekly. In contrast, net-change MRP systems are on-line and can respond continuously to transactions pertaining to production schedule, vendor reports, and inventory status of various items.

The success of MRP is closely tied to making effective use of a firm's production capacity. Capacity requirements planning (CRP) is to personnel and equipment what MRP is to materials. The acquisition of materials on schedule is of no use unless capacity is available to convert them into finished products as planned. Because of this, CRP must be effectively integrated with MRP.

In recent years, it has become clear that requirements planning cannot be limited to material and capacity. A firm does not live by material and capacity alone; other company functions, such as purchasing, marketing, management, and accounting, also must be involved if the firm is to endure. Material requirements do not effectively describe a planning system that involves all the company functions. To describe the system that involves all the resources of a manufacturing firm in requirements planning, a new term was coined: manufacturing resource planning (MRP II). It is a system that allows all the departments of a firm to work according to the same plan. A number of application software packages are available that allow implementation of MRP II, among them IBM's MAPICS, Arthur Andersen's MAC-PAC, Hewlett-Packard's FMS, and Martin Marietta's MAS II.

At present, MRP is limited mostly to manufacturing environments. However, potential exists to use MRP in the service sector. Hospitals and academic institutions can use it to schedule equipment, space, and personnel.

Despite the considerable usefulness of MRP, there have been problems in its implementation. Problems can occur because of an insufficient management commitment or a failure to realize that MRP is only a computerized scheduling tool; it is only a part of the system, not a replacement for the system. In some instances, MRP is taken to mean no more than meeting the schedule. Such a limited perception defeats the spirit of MRP and its potential rewards. MRP's effectiveness ultimately is constrained by the personnel using it and the environments in which it is used.

An alternative to MRP is synchronized manufacturing. It seeks to optimize the use of resources such as production time, inventory, and operating expenses by focusing on the actual and potential bottlenecks in the production process.

In short, the MRP procedure consists of "exploding" the materials requirements by multiplying the quantity of products scheduled by the number of materials and parts required per unit. It then leads to requisitioning of needed materials and parts from the storeroom and requesting that purchasing order any additional materials and parts not in house. On the issuance of materials and parts into production, line production departments actually perform the conversion of raw material into work-in-process and finally to finished goods. In the past, the inspection department sought to provide assurance that the products met established quality standards. The current philosophy is that the production crews do their own inspection and that they actually do the right job so that there is no need for inspection. In the jargon of activity-based costing, inspection is a non–value-adding chore that adds costs to production.

12.10 INVENTORY IN THE JIT ENVIRONMENT

The JIT system is characterized by goals such as minimizing inventory investment, uncovering quality problems, reacting faster to demand changes, and shortening the time needed to process a batch. JIT insists on the production or acquisition of the units when and where they are needed. Under JIT, the production line is run on a demand-pull basis. As a result, the work at each station is authorized by the demand of the station following it. Production is stopped when problems occur, such as absent parts or defective work.

The underlying philosophy of JIT is constant improvement sought by ongoing simplification of the production process and elimination of non–value-adding activities. The elimination of nonessential activity, the underlying basis of what has come to be known as activity management, can extend to the staffing needs of the accounting department. Under JIT, bookkeeping is reduced to two entries: one made at the start of the process and one made when finished goods exit production and are received by the warehouse.

12.11 PRODUCTION-RELATED MANAGERIAL DECISION MAKING

Strategic decisions affecting the inventory management in a manufacturing environment usually are made by a group of higher-level managers, including the production manager and marketing manager. They rely primarily on the logistics and marketing information systems to provide key information, such as available production levels and sales forecasts. Some of the decisions that must be made at the strategic level include:

- Which products and product components should be manufactured?
- How much added production capacity should be acquired in each year for the next several years?
- What method of physical production should be employed?
- What materials should be included in each unit product, and what steps should be followed in the production process?
- From what sources should raw materials and direct labor be obtained?
- Where should the production facilities be located?

Other decisions must follow the resolution of these strategic matters. Some of the decisions primarily concern the accounting department. Among such decisions are:

- What type of costing system should be employed?
- If standard costing is selected, what standard costs should be assigned to units of material, hours of direct labor, and applied manufacturing overhead?
- What budget levels should be established for the production departments?

Similarly, decisions related to production include:

- What quantity of goods should be produced for inventory?
- When should production jobs be scheduled to begin and end?

12.12 DOCUMENTATION FOR PRODUCT CONVERSION

Data used in the product conversion system are based on a variety of inputs from documents generated by customers and departments involved in the logistics of production. Other sources are the various finance and accounting files pertaining to raw materials purchases, receivables, and payables.

Source documents typically used in the product conversion system (other than those already discussed) include:

- Bill of material. A bill of material, also called a product specification, lists the quantities of materials and parts to be used in a particular product.
- Operations list. An operations list specifies the sequence of operations to be performed in fashioning and assembling the materials and parts required for a particular product. In effect, it is a "recipe" or guide for production employees. The list may mention the work centers at which the specified operations are to take place as well as machine requirements and standard time allowances.
- Production (work) order. The document identifying a specific job that is to flow through the production process is known as a production order or work order. It incorporates key data from the initiating customer order (or from a sales forecast, in the case of standard products), from the relevant operations list, and from the production schedule.
- Materials issue slip. A materials issue slip, also known as a materials requisition, directs the storekeeper to issue materials or parts to designated work centers, jobs, or people. It may list the costs of that material or the costs may be entered later by the inventory control department.
- Move ticket. A move ticket, also called a traveler, authorizes the physical transfer of a production order from one work center to the next one listed on the order. It also records the quantities of items received and shows the date received, thereby enabling progress to be tracked.
- Other source documents. Additional source documents used in the logistics activity include the purchase requisitions, purchase orders, receiving reports, and labor job-time tickets. In the case of custom production, the sales orders from customers are also needed.

12.13 ACCOUNTING IN A MANUFACTURING CONTEXT

The objectives and most of the units of the finance/accounting function have been discussed in Chapters 9 and 10. But in production environments, the cost accounting and control unit appears for the first time. It accumulates material, labor, and overhead costs incurred in the production process and prepares cost variance reports. This unit also develops labor and material cost standards and assigns values to work-in-process inventory.

Product costs consist of direct materials costs, direct labor costs, and manufacturing overhead costs. Included as manufacturing overhead are costs of indirect labor, supplies, utilities, small tools, depreciation of machines, and other costs related to the production process. Manufacturing overhead is essentially all production-related costs that are not identified as direct material or labor. These product costs are accumulated to reflect the value of the jobs flowing through production operations. Periodically, the costs are posted to the work-in-process records; the total of the costs for all current jobs is then posted to the general ledger from an entry having the following form, to record costs applicable to current work-in-process:

Dr. Work-in-Process	XXX
Cr. Raw Materials Inventory	XXX
Cr. Labor or Payroll Payable	XXX
Cr. Overhead Applied	XXX

When a production order or job has flowed through all required production operations and thus is completed, the costs for the finished goods are posted from the following entry, to record the completion and transfer of work-in-process to finished goods:

Dr. Finished Goods	XXX
Cr. Work-in-Process Inventory	XXX

12.14 DATABASE FOR PRODUCT CONVERSION

The database for the product conversion system of a manufacturing firm interfaces closely with the revenue and expenditure cycle databases. Its master files pertain to raw materials, work-in-process, and finished goods. The principal transaction file is the open production order file. Other files might contain data concerning the product specifications, production order schedule, work center schedule, machine loadings, standard costs, overhead rates, and production order history.

Since the finished goods master file is similar in content to the merchandise inventory master file, we focus on the raw materials and work-in-process inventory master files. We also look at the production order file.

(a) Raw Materials Master File

Each record in the raw materials master file reflects the receipts, issues, orders, and on-hand balances pertaining to a particular material, part, or subassembly. All the records in this file comprise a subsidiary ledger supporting the raw materials inventory account in the general ledger.

(b) Work-in-Process Master File

Each record in the work-in-process master file (i.e., job cost sheet) summarizes the costs incurred—for raw materials, parts, direct labor, and overhead—with respect to a current (open) production order. All of the job-oriented records in this file comprise a subsidiary ledger supporting the work-in-process inventory account in the general ledger.

Production order number (primary key)
Customer number (if a special order)
Customer name (if a special order)
Customer order number (if a special order)
Date of order
Date started (or to be started) in production
Date to be completed
Product number (or line number)
Product description
Quantity
Weight (if applicable)
Operation number
Operation description
Date scheduled
Time started
Time ended
Machine number
Special instructions (such as tools needed)
Work center numbers
Inspection results

Exhibit 12–4. Table of data elements within a production order.

Adapted from J. Wilkinson, *Accounting Information System: Essential Concepts and Applications,* 2nd ed. (New York: John Wiley & Sons, 1993).

(c) Open Production Order File

Like the work-in-process master file, the focus of this file is the individual production order. Thus, the two files are closely related. For instance, both use the production number as the primary and sorting key. However, the open production order file does not contain costs. Instead, it shows the current status of each production order in the production process. The data contained in a typical production order are listed in Exhibit 12–4.

12.15 DATA FLOWS AND PROCESSING

Exhibit 12–5 presents a document-oriented flow diagram that emphasizes the flows of source and output documents among organizational units. In effect, it connects the pertinent documents to the units portrayed in Exhibit 12–6. Note that the diagram places the product conversion process in perspective. That is, it includes the documents and flows for sales order entry, purchasing of materials, and shipping of finished goods as well as those involved in production. The description of data flows and processing will be in accordance with the listed functions. The focus will be on on-line computer-based information systems, since they offer the following benefits to the product conversion system:

- Better integration of highly interdependent activities
- Improved production efficiency and use of resources resulting from better scheduling of orders
- Immediate editing of data when entered on-line
- Better control over orders due to up-to-date files and timely reports

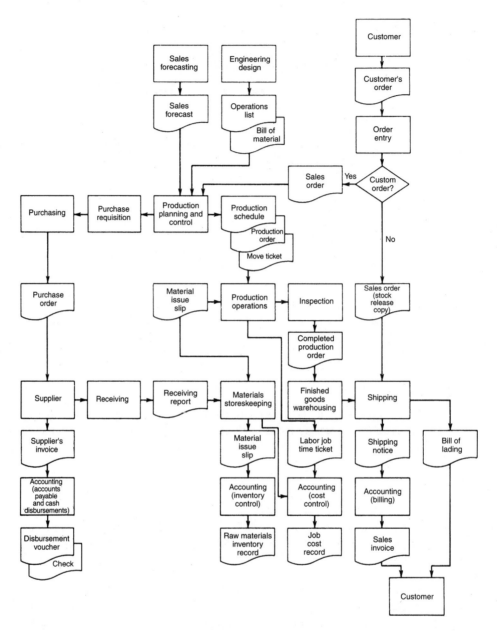

Exhibit 12–5.　Diagram depicting the flow of documents among the organizational units involved in product conversion and logistics.

Adapted from J. Wilkinson, *Accounting Information System: Essential Concepts and Applications,* 2nd ed. (New York: John Wiley & Sons, 1993).

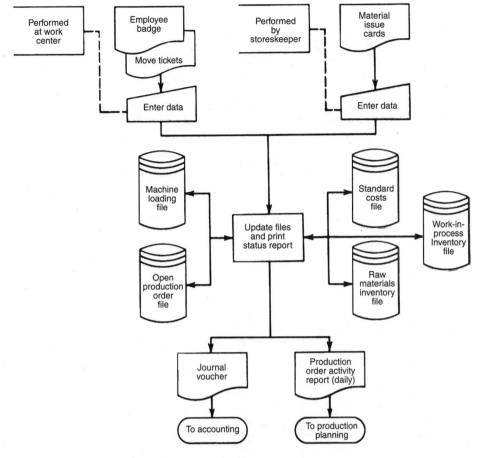

Exhibit 12–6.   Computer system flow chart of processing steps during production operations.

Adapted from J. Wilkinson, *Accounting Information System: Essential Concepts and Applications,* 2nd ed. (New York: John Wiley & Sons, 1993).

(a) Planning and Initiating the Production Process

Exhibit 12–5 shows a computer system flow chart of production planning. One input into the planning process is a set of specifications for special orders, as prepared by engineering design. These specifications are added to the product specifications and operations files. At the end of each day, revised sales forecasts and backorders are also entered into the system.

A production planning program can perform several complex steps. First, it prints prenumbered production orders that are needed to initiate the production of custom ordered and standard products, based on the listed inputs. It also updates the open production orders file. Second, the program prints move tickets and material issues (requisitions) to accompany the new production orders. Third, it prints bills of material and operations lists for each product shown on the production orders, so that they may be reviewed by customers and used by planning personnel. Fourth, the program prints a

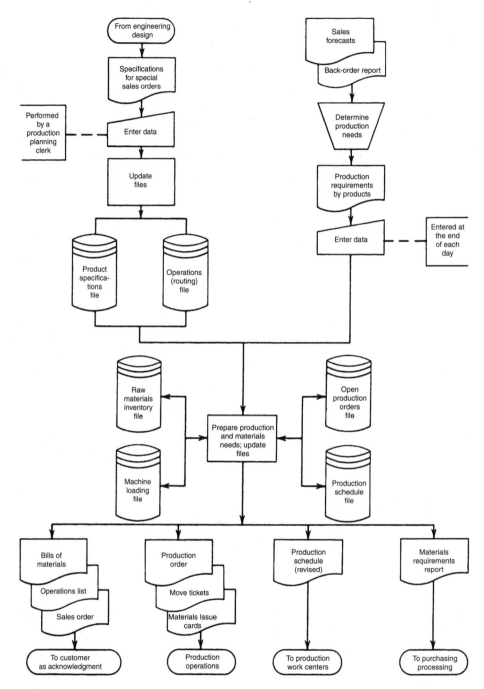

Exhibit 12–7. Computer system flow chart of production planning.

Adapted from J. Wilkinson, *Acccounting Information System: Essential Concepts and Applications,* 2nd ed. (New York: John Wiley & Sons, 1993).

revised production schedule, showing starting dates for the new orders, and updates the schedule in the file. Fifth, it "explodes" materials requirements and prepares a report showing the materials and parts needed to fill the production orders. It then updates the materials file to reserve materials in the current raw materials inventory file for specific production orders. Finally, it updates the machine loading file to assign machines as needed for the new orders.

(b) Moving Work-in-Process Through Production Operations

Exhibit 12–6 shows a computer system flow chart pertaining to production operations. When a new production order is scheduled to start into production, raw materials and parts are issued by the storekeeper. They are delivered to the first work center and accompanied by the first move ticket. Employees and machines are assigned in accordance with data in the production order. As employees begin work on the order, they enter their employee number and the order number. When they finish the operation involving the order, they repeat the entry.

Based on these variously entered inputs, the production operations program performs several steps. First, it updates the materials inventory file to reflect the issued materials and parts. Second, it updates the open production order file to show that the operation at the work center is completed. In addition, the program prints a production order activity report to show the current status of all open production orders. Third, it updates the machine loading file to show that the machine is free for the next scheduled operation. Fourth, the program updates the work-in-process file to show the accumulation of production costs. These costs are computed by reference to the standard unit costs and overhead rates in a standard costs file. Finally, it prints a journal voucher that reflects the costs to be posted to the work-in-process inventory account in the general ledger.

(c) Costing the Work-in-Process Inventory

Accumulating costs related to production orders is a very important step to accountants. Although this cost accounting step was mentioned in the previous paragraph, it deserves special attention. To see the step more clearly, it is helpful to return briefly to a manual processing system. Exhibit 12–8 shows the postings of production costs in a job order cost accounting system. Raw materials costs pertaining to a particular production order are posted to a work-in-process cost record from materials issue slips (requisitions). Direct labor costs are posted to the cost sheet from job-time tickets. Manufacturing overhead is applied on the basis of direct labor hours. Periodically, a department such as cost accounting and control prepares a journal voucher that summarizes these cost accumulations for the current jobs in production.

The journal voucher is transmitted to the general ledger department for posting. The procedure just described can be identified as an actual job order cost accounting system, using normal costing for manufacturing overhead. In contrast, the standard costs file shown in Exhibit 12–3 depicts a system that employs standard costs. In a standard system, the unit prices and quantities for materials, hourly cost rates and hours allowed for direct labor, and manufacturing overhead rate and base level are carefully preestablished. These standards are applied consistently over a reasonable period (e.g., a year). Standard cost systems enable useful manufacturing cost variances to be computed. Thus, they help production managers to monitor and control costs more effectively. Consequently, the efficiency of production operations can be increased while costs are monitored and, it is hoped, controlled. An alternative type of

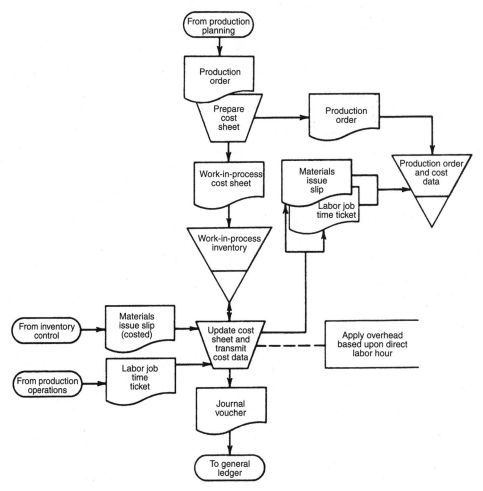

Exhibit 12–8. Document system flow chart showing the posting of production costs by cost accounting and control.

Adapted from J. Wilkinson, *Accounting Information System: Essential Concepts and Applications,* 2nd ed. (New York: John Wiley & Sons, 1993).

cost allocation system is centered on activities and is discussed in Chapter 17, which examines activity-based costing.

(d) Completing the Production Process

Exhibit 12–9 shows a computer system flow chart relating to the completion of production operations. As work is completed on a production order, the finished goods are inspected; the results are entered into a terminal to update the production order. Those orders that pass inspection are transferred either to the warehouse or to the shipping department. At either destination, data are entered from the final move ticket. This notification causes the production order to be closed, transferred to a history file, and listed in a report. It also causes the work-in-process cost record to be totaled and transferred to the

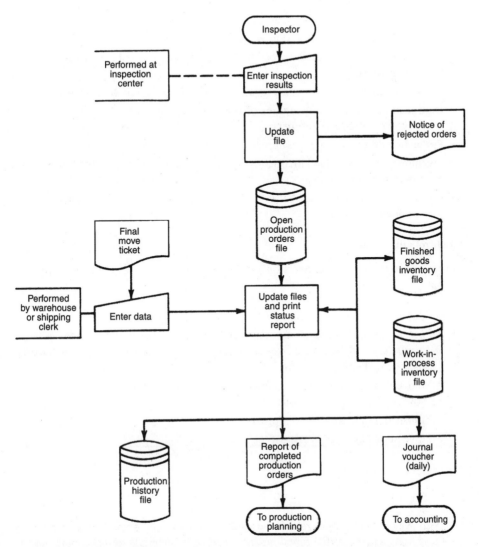

Exhibit 12–9. Computer system flow chart of processing steps after completion of production operations.

Adapted from J. Wilkinson, *Accounting Information System: Essential Concepts and Applications,* 2nd ed. (New York: John Wiley & Sons, 1993).

finished goods inventory. Finally, a journal voucher is printed that transfers incurred costs for the day's completed orders to finished goods inventory.

(e) Controls Needed for Product Conversion System

Product conversion inventory systems are exposed to a variety of risks. In designing the procedures to be implemented, attention must be paid to risks:

- Raw materials, finished goods, or scrap may be lost or stolen.
- Incorrect costs may be charged to work-in-process inventory.
- Quantities of finished goods exceeding the quantities specified by production orders may be produced.
- Recorded quantities of work-in-process or finished goods may be inaccurate.
- Insufficient or excessive quantities of raw materials may be issued into production with respect to production orders.
- Production orders may be lost during production operations.
- Inventories may be valued incorrectly because of improper use of cost flow methods or charges to wrong accounts.
- Inventories may be inflated because obsolete or slow-moving items have not been written down in amount.

(f) Control Objectives

With respect to the product conversion system, several key control objectives are to ensure that:

- All production orders are properly authorized and scheduled.
- All needed raw materials and other resources are assigned to production orders promptly and accurately, and the related costs are accumulated fully in accordance with the established system of cost accounting.
- All movements of production orders through the production process are reflected by acknowledgments at the various work centers.
- All finished goods are valued properly.
- All inventories are adequately safeguarded.

(g) General Controls

The following general controls can serve to counteract the risks due to exposures:

- With respect to the organization, the production operations should be separated from those units with custodial functions (i.e., receiving, materials storeskeeping, finished goods warehousing), and both should be separated from those units having recording functions (i.e., production planning, inventory control, cost accounting and control, data processing, general ledger).
- Complete and up-to-date documentation should be available concerning production planning and operations.
- Security should be maintained (in the case of on-line computer systems) by techniques such as (a) requiring clerks to enter passwords before accessing production-related files; (b) employing terminals with restricted functions; (c) generating audit reports (access logs) that monitor accesses of system files; and (d) dumping the production files onto magnetic tape backup. Physical security measures should include locked enclosures for materials and finished goods.
- Operating practices relating to processing schedules, reports, changes in programs, and other matters should be clearly established.

(h) Transaction (Application) Controls

The following controls and control procedures are applicable to the product conversion system:

- Prenumbered and well-designed materials requisitions and production orders, as well as carefully established production schedules
- Required authorizations to issue materials and place orders into production
- Validation of input data by means of edit programs containing a variety of programmed checks
- Verification and transfer of responsibility at every step through the production process
- Up-to-date work-in-process cost records
- Reconciliations of work-in-process cost records and the balance of the control account in the general ledger
- Periodic physical inventories of materials, parts, and finished goods, with the results being reconciled with the balances in the inventory records
- Prompt preparation of reports relating to work-in-process costs, finished goods transfers, batch controls, errors, and so on

12.16 REPORTS AND OTHER OUTPUTS

Several listings can be provided on a frequent basis, including the materials requirements report, production activity report, completed production orders report, raw materials status report, and finished goods status report. Inquiries may involve individual production orders, costs of individual materials and parts, and activity at individual work centers.

Among the production-oriented reports of interest to managers are the:

- Work-in process cost report, which compares the actual accumulated costs of production orders against the budgeted costs
- Employee efficiency report, which compares the outputs of production employees against established quotas
- Production overdue report, which shows those production orders that are behind schedule and the number of days that each is behind
- Equipment utilization report, which shows the percentage of time that each piece of production equipment is utilized during a work week
- Work center performance report, which shows the utilization and efficiency of each work center
- Production waste report, which shows the percentages of scrap, rework, and rejects that result from production during a week

12.17 CONCLUSION

The inventory management system can be separated into the merchandise inventory management system and the raw materials management system. The merchandise inventory management system integrates the transactions related to merchandise inventory, including ordering, receiving, shipping, and returns. Its main file is the merchandise inventory master file, and the key organizational unit is the inventory control department. Useful outputs include the stock status report, merchandise reorder report, and inventory items expected to be out of stock.

The raw materials management system, also called the product conversion system, includes the functions of planning and initiating the production process, moving orders through production operations, costing the work-in-process inventory, and completing the production process. Key inputs include the production (work) order, materials requisition, job-time ticket, move ticket, bill of materials, and operations list. The database includes the production order file and the work-in-process inventory file. Outputs include the materials requirements report, work-in-process cost report, and raw materials inventory status report.

CHAPTER 13

THE RESOURCES MANAGEMENT CYCLE: FACILITIES AND FUNDS

13.1 INTRODUCTION

This chapter continues the coverage of resources management, focusing on two kinds of resources, facilities and funds, also known as fixed assets and working capital, respectively. First the chapter describes functions, relationships, and components of the system involved in the management of the facilities resource. Then it describes functions and relationships of the system involved in the management of the funds resource.

13.2 FACILITIES MANAGEMENT CYCLE

The facilities resource concerns the plant assets, also known as fixed assets, or property, plant, and equipment. Within the wide range of plant assets are buildings, machines, furniture, fixtures, vehicles, and other items requiring capital expenditures. The useful lives of these assets extends beyond one year, which subjects them to depreciation—the need to spread the costs incurred in acquiring them over their useful lives. The costs of acquiring these assets is relatively high. While these assets represent a relatively large portion of the total asset value of a firm, they also comprise the ultimate source of organizational revenue. Without its investment in property, plant, and equipment, a firm may not be in a position to realize revenue and, by implication, income.

The major purpose of the facilities management system is to facilitate the acquisition of the plant assets, safeguard and maintain them over their economic lives, account for their use over their lives in financial statements, and then see to their disposal. Specifically, the system's objectives are to: (1) ensure that all acquisitions are properly approved and recorded and exchanged for cash or equivalents; (2) safeguard the plant assets in assigned locations; (3) reflect depreciation expense properly and consistently in accordance with an acceptable depreciation method; and (4) ensure that all disposals are properly approved and recorded.

13.3 CAPITAL BUDGETING CONCEPT

To appreciate the working of facilities management cycle, it is best to start by understanding capital budgeting both as a concept and as a process in organizations, both public and private. Accordingly, an overview of the nature and working of capital budgeting follows.

Capital budgeting must be seen as a resource investment, since it involves committing resources in the present in the hope of receiving future rewards. The decision to invest is made in order to purchase new equipment, introduce new product lines, modernize plant equipment, or allow for cost reduction or productivity enhancements. In recent years, investments made in capital assets may well be to help meet regulatory requirements.

Spending for capital needs involves major amounts. Moreover, such spending ties up a major part of organizational resources, especially the monetary assets. Money for one project often is obtained by taking it away from some other use. Rare is the organization that has unlimited resources for undertaking all projects that seem desirable to its managers. These decisions affect the long-term financial health of the organization. The choices are made even more difficult because managers cannot predict the future. Managers in the American automobile industry might not have so wholeheartedly ignored the threat posed by foreign-made, fuel-efficient automobiles in the 1960s if they could have predicted the high price and the fluctuating availability of gasoline in the decades that followed.

Given the high stakes that capital budgeting decisions represent, firms use elaborate processes in order to make them. Such processes are meant to help them make informed decisions. They do so by examining a proposed project to see if it meets preestablished organizational criteria, such as a return of 15 percent on investments involving cost reduction. Or instead of such screening by means of preestablished standards, firms may decide to select a project from among several competing courses of action. Firms may decide to use both screening and selection in order to choose capital projects.

To help make informed decisions, firms seek to use objective means to screen and/or rank projects. The texts used for teaching accounting and finance courses devote considerable space to mathematical models for capital budgeting decisions that use discounted cash flows. The use of discounted cash flows or time value of money better measures the costs and the resulting benefits that will accrue over the life of the project. Since inflation is a constant fact of life, such consideration to the time value of money is highly justified.

The two models that incorporate time value of money in their calculations are the net present value method and the time-adjusted rate of return, otherwise known as the internal rate of return method. Under the present value method, the discounted value of all cash inflows is compared with the present value of all cash outflows that the project will require. The difference between the present values of proposed projects will help determine their relative acceptability. The internal rate of return method seeks to measure the rate of return promised by a project over its useful life. It is the rate of return that will render the net present value of a project to be zero, that is, the discounted outflows and inflows will break even. It is based on forecasting the future cash flows, while the net present value method is based on the selection of a discount rate.

Both techniques are only that, techniques. They must not become a surrogate for strategic planning. All the more so because the predicted cash flows and the chosen discount rate are subject to manipulation. Managers will be better served if they focus on improving their strategic assumptions and operating considerations instead of relying entirely on discounted cash flows for their capital budgeting decisions. Firms will be better served if their screening and/or selection criteria is broad-based and relies on a number of factors.

Strict and sole reliance on rate of return has been shown to be counterproductive as a measure of managerial performance. Projects need time and infusion of money before they reach their profit potential. Such infusion of money, when invested in projects, initially leads to a lowered rate of return for the firm or the division involved. Once the project is operational, rates tend to increase. But this may not be enough or be timely for managers whose performance is measured by the current returns. For them a project that leads to a lowered return in the short term, even while promising future increases, is not rewarding enough and they refuse to undertake it, even when strategic considerations call for its acceptance.

13.4 CAPITAL BUDGETING PROCESS

The capital expenditure process begins when a manager perceives that his or her department, division, or other organizational unit needs an additional plant asset or needs to replace an asset. For instance, a shipping manager may learn from his drivers that certain delivery trucks need replacement. This need should be substantiated through formal capital investment analyses. Such analysis requires that expected benefits and costs be gathered for the economic lives of the new plant assets as well as for factors such as the expected disposal or salvage values of the current assets. Furthermore, these benefits and costs must be discounted to the present time by a factor (i.e., desired rate of return or opportunity cost of capital) that management specifies.

The manager places a formal request for the needed plant asset. Senior-level management then must approve such a request. The larger the amount involved, the higher the request must ascend for approval. On receiving approval, the request follows a procedure similar to the acquisition of merchandise. That is, a copy of the request is sent to the purchasing department or, in the case of highly technical equipment, the engineering department. Bids are requested, a supplier is selected, and a purchase order is prepared. When the plant asset arrives, a receiving report is completed, and the asset is delivered to the requesting organizational unit. On the receipt of the supplier's invoice, a disbursement voucher is prepared (if the voucher system is in effect). On the due date a check is written and mailed.

13.5 MAINTENANCE AND DISPOSAL OF CAPITAL ASSETS

While capital budgeting itself generally is limited to the acquisition of major assets, the facilities management cycle goes beyond the acquisitions to include their subsequent maintenance and disposal. These capital assets usually represent valuable property. In order to safeguard and maintain each acquired plant asset, generally all relevant details are recorded. Included are all acquisition costs, the estimated salvage value, the estimated economic life, and the location. If a plant asset is transferred to a new location, this move is recorded. If costs are incurred during the life of the asset that increase its service potential or extend its economic life, these are added to the asset's cost basis.

A plant asset diminishes in value during use of the passage of time. An allocated portion of the asset's original cost, called a depreciation expense, must be removed at periodic intervals. The amount of the depreciation expense is determined in part by the method of depreciation that is selected for the asset and in part by the estimated economic life of the asset. These depreciation amounts are included in the record of the individual plant asset as well as in adjustments to general ledger accounts.

When their economic lives have come to an end, plant assets are sold, retired, or exchanged for replacement assets. These disposals, like acquisitions, require the approval of management. They also lead to the removal of asset amounts from the general ledger accounts.

13.6 ORGANIZATIONAL CONTEXT OF THE CYCLE

The facilities management system functions are under the direction of the finance/accounting organizational unit of the firm. The key departments involved are budgeting, accounts payable, cash disbursements, property accounting, and general ledger. The budgeting department develops capital expenditures budgets and coordinates these budgets with the short-range and cash budgets. The accounts payable department approves the suppliers' invoices pertaining to plant assets for payment. The cash disbursements department, an arm of the cashier, prepares checks for disbursement to suppliers of plant assets. The property accounting department establishes and maintains the records concerning plant assets. The general ledger department maintains control over all asset, equity, expense, and income accounts.

Other units of the organization are involved to various degrees. Higher-level managers from various organizational functions (e.g., production), in addition to the finance and accounting functions, must approve the acquisition and disposal of plant assets. As might be expected, the process is subject to considerable organizational politics. As in the case of the expenditure cycle, the purchasing and receiving departments are responsible for ordering and receiving the plant assets.

13.7 DOCUMENTATION NEEDED FOR THE CYCLE

The system's documentation is based mainly on inputs from the managers in departments needing new plant assets. Other sources are the plant assets records maintained by accounting departments. Source documents typically used in the management of facilities include the following:

(a) Capital Investment Proposal

The initiating form is the capital investment proposal, also called the property expenditure request. As the form indicates, it is accompanied by a capital investment analysis form. This latter form lists all future cost and benefit flows that are expected to accrue from the asset investment, with the net cash flows being discounted to present values. The proposal package, including both forms, is forwarded to higher-level managers—such as the controller, vice-president, and president—for approval. On approval, a copy of the proposal is sent to the purchasing department, where it serves as a requisition.

(b) Plant Asset Change Form

A plant asset change form is used as the basis for transferring plant assets from one department to another or for retiring, selling, or trading in plant assets. It lists net book values of the assets and the amounts to be received (if disposed of). It also provides spaces for justifying the disposal and for the approval signatures of higher-level managers.

Other Source Documents

Since expenditures are involved, additional documents include the request for quotation, purchase order, bill of lading, receiving report, supplier's invoice, disbursement voucher, check voucher, and journal voucher. These documents were discussed in Chapter 10.

13.8 ACCOUNTING FOR THE FACILITIES MANAGEMENT CYCLE

The acquisition of plant assets, such as a drill press with a useful life of three years, is recorded by an entry such as the following, which records the acquisition of machinery having an estimated life of three years:

| Dr. Capital Asset | XXX |
| Cr. Accounts Payable | XXX |

The depreciation of plant assets is recorded periodically by an entry such as the following (using machinery as the example) to record the depreciation expense for the year:

| Dr. Depreciation Expense | XXX |
| Cr. Accumulated Depreciation—Machinery | XXX |

The disposition of plant assets is recorded by an entry similar to the following, assuming that machinery is sold for its book value, to record the disposal of machines acquired on (date):

Dr. Cash	XXX
Dr. Accumulated Depreciation-Machinery	XXX
Cr. Machinery	XXX

13.9 DATABASE FOR THE FACILITIES MANAGEMENT CYCLE

The distinctive files needed in managing facilities are the plant assets master file and the plant assets transaction file. Other files are those used in all expenditure transactions and described in Chapter 10, such as the supplier master, open purchase order, open voucher, and check disbursement files. An important concern in this cycle, as in the others, is keeping the records and their permanent data up-to-date. When an asset is relocated, for instance, the location code should be changed promptly. When a new plant asset is approved and acquired, a new record should appear in the file.

(a) Plant Assets Master File

A key file needed for the cycle is the plant assets master file, a subsidiary ledger that supports the plant assets control accounts in the general ledger. The contents of a typical record for a single plant asset will include the plant asset number, a unique identifier that generally serves as the primary and sorting key. The asset type code identifies the major classification of plant assets (e.g., land, buildings, equipment) to which the individual asset belongs. The location code refers to the department or physical site to which the asset is assigned.

(b) Plant Assets Transaction File

A plant assets transaction file contains transactions pertaining to new acquisitions, sales of currently held plant assets, retirements, major additions to asset costs or to economic lives, and transfers between locations. It is needed if plant asset transactions are accumulated for a period of time (e.g., a week) and then processed in a batch. If the transactions are posted to the records as they arise, the file will likely not exist in a physical sense. Transactions that allocate depreciation expense for each plant asset are not included in this file. Instead, they are included in the adjusting journal entries at the end of each accounting period.

13.10 DATA FLOWS AND PROCESSING

To help illustrate the data flows and processing for the cycle, two processing procedures are described. The first description emphasizes the logical sequence and the key source documents. The second focuses on the processing of the master file within a computer-based system.

Exhibit 13–1 presents a data flow diagram of the plant assets activity. In essence, it follows the functions discussed earlier, although it shows the installation as a separate process.

1. Acquisition of plant assets. To begin the acquisition, a manager in a user department prepares a request. Together with a capital investment analysis, this form is forwarded to senior-level management. After the request is reviewed and approved, it is distributed to the purchasing and accounts payable departments. Then the regular purchasing, payables, and cash disbursements steps are followed. These steps are not included in the data flow diagram, so that we may focus on the distinctive steps involving plant assets.

2. Receipt and installation of plant assets. On receiving the ordered plant asset from the supplier, the plant asset is sent to the requesting department and installed. The receiving report, which accompanies the plant asset, is signed in the using department to acknowledge receipt. Then a suitable department within the accounting function, such as the property accounting department, assigns a number to the new plant asset and prepares a record that shows the relevant details. A journal voucher is prepared and forwarded for posting to the general ledger accounts.

3. Depreciation of plant assets. At the end of each accounting period, an amount representing the depreciation expense, determined in accordance with the specified depreciation method and economic life, is computed. An adjusting journal entry is prepared and posted to the general ledger accounts.

4. Disposal of plant assets. The disposal procedure likewise begins with a request. After the request is approved, the plant asset is shipped to the person or firm that has agreed to accept the plant asset. Based on a copy of the approved request form, a property accounting clerk posts and removes the appropriate record from the plant assets file. Then the clerk prepares a journal voucher that reflects the final depreciation expense, actual salvage value (if any), and the gain or loss on the disposal.

Exhibit 13–2 shows a system flow chart of a procedure involving plant assets transactions. The on-line method has been selected for discussion because the number of plant asset transactions is relatively small in many firms and the records can easily be kept up-to-date. The flow chart begins at the point when the property accounting department has been notified of an acquisition or disposal. A clerk uses the department terminal to enter data from each transaction document when received. The entered data are

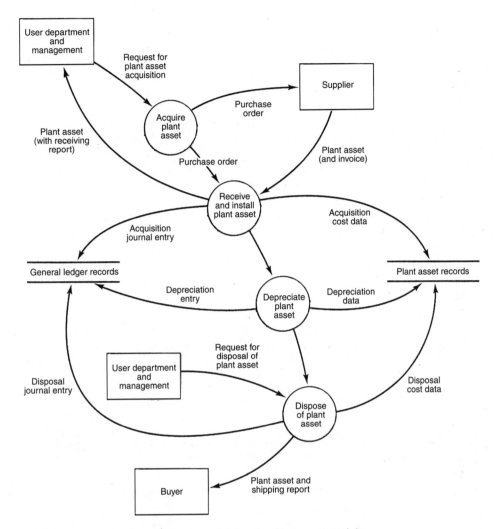

Exhibit 13–1.   Data flow diagram pertaining to plant assets activity.

Adapted from J. Wilkinson, *Accounting Information System: Essential Concepts and Applications,* 2nd ed. (New York: John Wiley & Sons, 1993).

first validated by programmed checks. Then the data are immediately posted by an updating program to the appropriate record in the plant assets master file. If the transaction affects general ledger accounts, the program also prepares a journal voucher and stores it on the general ledger transaction file. At the end of the accounting period (e.g., month) a print program generates useful reports. It also prepares journal vouchers that reflect depreciation entries.

13.11 CONTROLS NEEDED FOR FACILITIES MANAGEMENT

Exhibit 13–3 lists representative risks to which the facilities management system is exposed and the consequent exposures due to these risks.

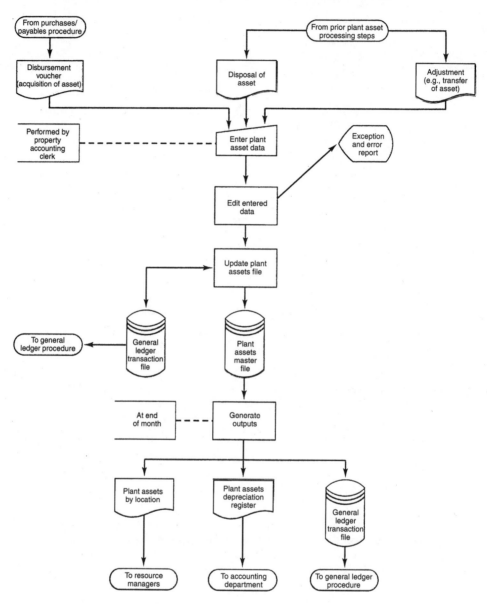

Exhibit 13–2. A system flow chart of an on-line computer-based plant assets transaction processing procedure.

Adapted from J. Wilkinson, *Accounting Information System: Essential Concepts and Applications,* 2nd. ed. (New York: John Wiley & Sons, 1993).

Risk	Exposure(s)
1. Improper acquisition of plant assets	1. Excessive costs for plant assets
2. Improper disposal of plant assets	2. Loss of productive capability; loss of disposal values
3. Theft or loss of plant assets	3. Loss in plant-asset values
4. Errors in billing for ordered plant assets	4. Possibility of excessive costs for plant assets
5. Errors in balances in plant-asset accounts	5. Over- or undervaluation of total assets

Exhibit 13–3. Table of risk exposure within a facilities managed system.

Adapted from J. Wilkinson, *Accounting Information System: Essential Concepts and Applications,* 2nd ed. (New York: John Wiley & Sons, 1993).

(a) General Controls

These general controls help counteract risks due to exposures:

- Within the organization, the managers who approve requests relating to plant assets should be separated from the users of the plant assets and from all units involved in the processing of expenditures and disposal. Otherwise, the organizational segregation described for the expenditure cycle pertains.
- Complete and up-to-date documentation should be available concerning plant assets transactions.
- Security should be maintained (in the case of on-line systems) by techniques such as: (a) requiring that clerks enter assigned passwords before accessing plant assets files; (b) employing terminals with restricted functions for the entry of plant assets transactions; (c) generating audit reports (access logs) that monitor accesses of system files; and (d) dumping the plant assets files onto magnetic tape backups.
- Operating practices relating to processing schedules, reports, changes in programs, and other matters should be clearly established.

(b) Transaction (Application) Controls

The following controls and control procedures are applicable to transactions involving plant assets:

- Documents relating to requests for acquisitions and disposal are prenumbered and well designed. Also, they are approved by responsible higher-level managers before being issued.
- Acquisitions of plant assets are required to follow the same purchasing, receiving, payables, and cash disbursements procedures employed for merchandise, raw materials, and supplies.
- A unique identification number is assigned to each plant asset, and a tag bearing this number is affixed to the asset.

- Detailed and up-to-date records of plant assets are maintained.
- Balances in the plant assets subsidiary ledger (master file) are reconciled at least monthly with the balances of the plant assets control accounts in the general ledger.

13.12 REPORTS AND OTHER OUTPUTS

Managers track the cycle with the help of the following reports.

- The plant assets register is a listing of all plant assets, arranged by plant asset numbers, and showing book and/or tax values of the assets.
- The plant assets acquisition listing shows all assets acquired during an accounting period, including capitalized amounts and estimated salvage values.
- The assets retirement register shows all assets disposed of during the accounting period.
- A plant assets change register for an accounting period is very useful. It allows accountants to review all transactions that affect plant assets and can serve as an audit trail.
- The plant assets depreciation expense report lists depreciation expenses for every plant asset for the current accounting period, plus related costs and accumulated depreciation amounts.
- Certain reports also are needed to fulfill information requirements of the Securities and Exchange Commission, the Internal Revenue Service, and local property tax authorities. An example is a summary of all acquisitions, transfers, and retirements during a year.

In addition to the above reports, the system should be able to provide additional reports of interest to managers, such as those showing plant assets reported by location or by department. Other reports can show maintenance schedules and costs and projected depreciation expenses.

13.13 FUNDS MANAGEMENT SYSTEM

Within a firm, the funds resource consists of the working capital and long-term investment assets. The funds resource, therefore, extends beyond cash to include receivables, prepaid expenses, short-term marketable securities, and investments in the long-term bonds and stocks of corporations. Even payables and current accrued liabilities are encompassed, since they enter the computation of working capital. Moreover, the term "funds" can be viewed broadly as including the net capital of the owners of a firm; in the case of a corporation, the capital consists of bonds, common and preferred stock, contributed capital, and retained earnings. Although the net capital is an equity of the firm, rather than a resource, it does give rise to transactions and does need to be managed.

13.14 OBJECTIVES OF THE SYSTEM

The major purpose of the funds management system, also known as the treasury or the financial or investment cycle, is to facilitate the inflows and outflows of the funds needed to maintain a business. Key objectives within this system are to (1) assure that an adequate quantity of funds is available to meet all legitimate needs, (2) reflect reasonable values for funds at all times, and (3) safeguard funds from theft and loss. Among the functions related to funds are acquisition of needed funds, uses of funds, and maintenance of control over funds.

(a) Acquisition of Funds

Sources of funds include sales to customers, loans from banks, issues of bonds, sales of stock, sales of plant assets, dividends and interest, sales of investments, factoring of accounts receivable, and delays in payments on accounts payable.

Two key procedural concerns when acquiring funds are to (1) require clear authorization for the acquisition by a responsible manager and (2) ascertain that the intermediaries are qualified and responsive to the best interests of the acquiring firm. Sound funds management depends on careful planning. A time-tested tool is the funds-oriented budget, such as a projected sources and uses of funds statement. In addition, projected cash flow statements can be quite useful. By knowing a firm's needs in advance, financial managers are more likely to obtain funds at the lowest feasible rates. Funds management should also consider long-term needs and opportunities. For instance, by means of foresight a number of firms have accrued the funds to reacquire their own stock at advantageous prices when financial markets have become depressed.

(b) Uses of Funds

Funds may be disbursed for purchase of goods and services, conversion into plant assets or investments, repurchase of the firm's own stock (as noted above), retirement of loans and bond issues, payment of dividends and interest, and redemption of stock rights or options. Procedures involved in the use of funds were discussed in Chapters 11 and 12. As in the case of acquiring funds, planning is important to the sound uses of funds.

(c) Maintenance of Controls over Funds

Accounting controls are needed to ensure the reliability of financial statement balances and to safeguard the funds. Although most of the controls have been listed earlier, several of the most desirable controls involve:

- Close supervision of all activities involving funds
- Prompt endorsement and recording of all cash receipts, with the deposit of all received cash intact
- Tight physical security over liquid funds, including the use of locked cash registers, safes, lockboxes, and safe deposit boxes
- Separate imprest bank accounts for payroll expenditures
- Issuance of prenumbered checks for all expenditures (except petty cash items)
- Reconciliation of each bank account monthly by a person not otherwise involved in cash transactions
- Separate ledgers for long-term investments, notes receivable, bonds, stock (or stockholders), and other sizable funds
- Audits, on a surprise basis, of all cash and securities

13.15 CONCLUSION

This chapter brings to completion the subject of resources management by discussing facilities management and funds management cycle. A firm's resources include not only its employees and its inventories, the topics of the previous chapters, but also comprise its property, plant, and equipment as well as its working capital.

The facilities management system includes the functions of acquiring, maintaining, and disposing of plant assets. This system involves such organizational units as budgeting, accounts payable, cash disbursements, property accounting, and general ledger. Key inputs are the capital investment proposal and plant assets change form. The database includes the plant assets master and transaction files. Outputs include the plant assets register, retirement and depreciation expense registers, reports of plant assets by location, and inquiry screens concerning individual plant assets.

The funds management system includes the functions of acquiring funds, using funds, and maintaining control over funds. This system involves such organizational units as finance, credit, budgeting, and cash receipts and disbursements. Many of the system components are those pertaining to cash receipts and disbursements, although other funds such as long-term investments require their own master files.

EVOLUTIONARY COMPETENCE

14.1 INTRODUCTION

This chapter focuses on an organization's ability to evolve while the environment in which it functions is changing. If the documentation of accounting procedures and policies is to be more than an archival exercise meant to perpetuate the status quo, then those in charge of documentation should have the knowledge of techniques and tools that facilitate turning documentation into an occasion for organizational introspection. Such introspection takes an illuminative look at the procedures as well as the system in place. Through such illuminative introspection, organizations can ascertain the adequacy of procedures as well as the system in place to respond effectively and efficiently to the changing environment. Doing this periodically can prevent organizations from following in the wake of dinosaurs, horse buggies, and manual typewriters. Documentation can facilitate organizational learning provided those seeking to do so are able to bring to their job what this chapter refers to as evolutionary competence.

14.2 WHAT IS EVOLUTIONARY COMPETENCE?

Evolutionary competence is the ability of an organism to survive the changing environment by adapting to the changes. In a biological context, we know of species that are no longer around because they were unable to change with the environment. Such failure to adapt, cope, and evolve rendered them extinct. The evolutionary competence that allows species to continue has its counterpart in the organizational context as well. A number of organizations are able to evolve, while many more fail to do so and are found no more. Indeed, there is evidence that proves that the institutional life span tends to be short; a survey taken by Shell Oil showed that about one-third of the firms listed among the Fortune 500 in 1970 no longer existed by 1983.

A considerable body of literature exists that argues that institutional survival need not be a matter of random chance. Such literature highlights organizations that are able to confront changing and, indeed, hostile environments, and still manage to prevail, not just survive. Such documented cases pertaining to firms that display evolutionary competence demonstrate that skills to organizationally evolve can be learned, indeed institutionalized.

This chapter introduces tools and techniques that are actually being practiced and that are helping firms to evolve and prosper. In addition to an overview of these cutting-edge tools is a discussion of the elements that are common to all of these various techniques being used to help institutions grow and become more productive. A brief discussion is also provided on why acquiring such competence may be imperative for firms at this point in time. Following this introductory chapter, we take a more detailed look at several evolutionary competencies.

14.3 A SHORT LIST OF EVOLUTIONARY COMPETENCIES

Over the years a number of approaches aimed at improving organizational performance have evolved. Some examples are:

(a) Quality Circles and Suggestion Systems

The two are attempts dating back to the 1960s to involve employees in improving the efficiency of the institutional processes and thus enhance productivity. Quality circles are groups, usually small, of employees meeting regularly to identify, analyze, and solve problems involving quality, costs, performance measurement, and other problems related to their work and its environment. Suggestion systems are designed to capture, evaluate, implement, and reward ideas generated by individuals or groups seeking to improve work processes. Even though one does not hear much about quality circles and suggestion systems these days, they have been incorporated within more recent approaches aimed at improved institutional efficiencies.

(b) Continuous Improvement

Continuous improvement, variously called total quality management (TQM), total quality environment (TQE), and *kaizen* (in Japan), is the philosophy of work management that owes its fame to Edward Deming. It encompasses much more than simple work techniques; rather it involves attitudes and is properly seen as the philosophy of work itself. It stresses that managers and workers ought to focus on continuous improvement and ongoing elimination of activities that are non–value-adding. Just such a focus was behind the relentless advance of Japanese firms like Sony, Toyota, and Honda. The search for continuous improvement starts with a permanent dissatisfaction with the status quo. Such identification with change leads to relentless, continuous improvement in all areas and all levels of the organizational hierarchy. It is a collective effort and has to be coordinated and supported by all levels of the institutional hierarchy.

(c) Activity-Based Management and Activity-Based Costing

As their names imply, the two focus on activities undertaken by firms to produce and deliver products and service to their customers. Activity-based management focuses on activities such as the measure of efficiency, while activity-based costing assigns costs to products and services by evaluating activities needed to make them. The focus on activities often is tied to improving the time needed to complete the production process. Despite their common focus, the two are technically different: One is concerned primarily with learning the costs incurred to produce and deliver a product, while the other does not involve the allocation of costs. However, the proponents of activity-based costing try to portray it not just as a costing tool but as a comprehensive way to improve management by illuminating and eliminating activities that are wasteful and do not add value to the product or service.

(d) Just-in-Time Inventory Systems (JIT)

JIT refers to an inventory system that has material needed for making products arrive from the vendors as it is needed. Indeed, the supplies are delivered not to a receiving warehouse but to the production centers within the plant. The implementation of such a system can reduce a firm's investment in inventory, often the largest component of the working capital. It will no longer purchase and store inventories needed to produce products, and so cash is no longer tied up in inventories or in the facilities needed to store and look after them. Instead the burden is outsourced to the vendors who supply the firm with the needed raw material.

The process of implementing JIT requires high levels of coordination and cooperation between the company and its vendors. Firms have to devote considerable resources to planning and scheduling work so that raw material needed is available when needed. For JIT to work well, a firm and its suppliers have to be able to communicate about the exact specifications of the material required and about reliable delivery. JIT cannot work if a supplier ships bucket seats when the cars on the assembly line require bench seats. Nor will it work if the truck carrying the steering columns is stranded in traffic.

(e) Process Reengineering

Another approach to institutional evolution is the emerging discipline of process redesign, or reengineering. In contrast to continuous improvement, it seeks more immediate changes. It incorporates and brings forward techniques associated with task analysis, operational auditing, and work simplification. It focuses on organizational processes instead of specific functions, and is based on the premise that by reexamining why and how things are being done and by imaginatively using emergent technology, an organization can achieve major productivity gains and systemically change the way its work is performed. The reengineering process starts by asking why something is done in a given way. Following such an analysis, it focuses on achieving the same goals by more efficient means. Fundamental to such redesign is the desire to eliminate non–value-adding steps from the process and to approach the process from a cross-functional, rather than a departmental, perspective. Use of emergent technologies, particularly information technologies, is likewise crucial to process redesign.

A large number of current work practices exist because of the tradition that they break work into its component tasks and then let different specialists take care of their respective assignments, usually narrow segments of the overall process. Such thinking focuses on individual tasks much more than on the underlying goal, and the result is costly delays as well as an excess of stakeholders in different departments all fighting for their own turf. A major rationale for implementing reengineering within an organization is to get past such a functionally based, narrowly focused orientation and think in terms of broader processes.

(f) Learning Organization Paradigm

Paralleling the development of activity-based cost systems, process redesign, and continuous improvement is the recent emergence of what is being called a learning organization paradigm. It focuses much more on the future rather than on simply improving the status quo. However, all the approaches listed emphasize individual and institutional learning.

Indeed, the term "learning paradigm" can well be seen as the label for the common denominator underlying the various approaches used by institutions to attain evolutionary competence. The term "learning" must not be equated with simply digesting information and taking in details. Learning organizations allow their workers to expand their ability to deal with current problems and visualize future opportunities. A learning organization is concerned with things as they could be and not just as they are; it seeks to anticipate opportunities, not just deal with crises as they occur.

While each of these techniques has its distinctive features, they have much in common: They all seek to help an institution evolve and improve. Furthermore, implementation of one approach does not exclude others from being used at the same firm. An organization may well devise a strategy that combines elements from several of these approaches. The choice of the specific approach to implement depends on the needs of the firm, in the context of its particular resources and strategic orientation. They all have some basic common elements, which are surveyed in the next section.

14.4 BUILDING BLOCKS OF INSTITUTIONAL EVOLUTIONARY COMPETENCE

The most important elements needed to fashion and implement an institution's evolutionary strategy include: customer orientation, an institution-wide sense of shared vision, facilitative leadership, empowerment of the employees, an organizational culture supportive of ongoing participation by all levels of employees, a training program that enables employees to be involved and keep developing their skills, and, finally, an effective reward structure that encourages employee creativity. All of these elements must be part of any efforts to make institutions more efficient. Each of these are necessary building blocks.

(a) Customer Focus

One usually thinks of a customer as one who purchases products. It has long been known that in order to prosper a business must practice strategies aimed at pleasing its customers and providing them with value. But the attitude that the customer is always right need not be limited to externally based sales, because ensuring that external customers receive a good value cannot be accomplished if it is limited only to the final transaction. It is also important to satisfy internal customers, the users of information within the organization. Making external customers happy can only be the result of a chain of customer-supplier relationships that stretches throughout the organization and culminates finally in giving the purchasers of goods or services what they need. Every employee performs work that results in creating or providing services or products that in turn are used by others to repeat the process. Each employee acts to add an incremental value, a building block, in the process that finally ends in giving external customers what they want.

This orientation implies that employees must view the next step in the process, next link in the chain, as their respective customers and work towards keeping these internal clients happy by providing them with products and services that they actually need. The customer for an area accountant is the department in the factory he or she is assigned to cover. It is incumbent on the accountant to keep that department supplied with information it actually needs in a timely fashion and in a form that is understandable to the production area manager. The bottom line for this manager is not the same as the bottom line for an investor in the company's stock.

(b) Fostering a Shared Vision

It is the responsibility of the organizational leader to develop a clear vision of what the company is, what it should be doing, and where it should go. However, simply getting senior managers to have a clear vision of institutional mission is not enough. The vision must be in tune with the institution's unique nature and makeup, and it must be shared throughout the organization. Only when the vision is communicated to all the employees does it become conducive for focused growth. Understanding clearly what a strategy for change is meant to achieve is the responsibility of the top manager, as is selecting the optimum change strategy. But the senior management must share the strategy with others, foster a consensus about what it is meant to accomplish, and ensure that skills and resources are available to implement the changes. Symbols and rituals can effectively communicate the vision of change and growth to all levels of the institution—indeed, Japanese companies have done just that, making symbols and rituals an important component for continuous improvement.

(c) Facilitative Leadership

It is well known that a large ship requires a good deal of time in order to change direction. Institutional leaders, like captains of large ships, cannot just will the change. A firm, like an ocean liner, takes time to change direction. Senior executives invariably realize the limited ability they have to mandate change; however, they can leverage their ability to change the institution's direction by fostering an organizational culture and environment that supports change. In so doing, top managers are exercising a facilitative leadership role. A very important ingredient of facilitative leadership is the communicational climate within the firm and communication of the results of activities undertaken. A good communicational climate will encourage individuals and groups to cooperate with each other, while communicating results openly will ensure the motivation to be proactive and work toward change. Leaders who practice facilitative leadership know key stakeholders and include them in decision making, demonstrate constancy of purpose, and intervene when necessary. Intervention may be required if the employees' dedication to change is uneven, if they do not fully understand the necessity and the nature of change, or if they are lacking in the skills to implement changes.

(d) Employee Empowerment

Employee empowerment refers to the delegation of authority to levels where activity is taking place. It contrasts with wisdom dating back to nineteenth-century gurus such as Adam Smith and Frederick Taylor. Through empowerment, frontline employees are allowed to make adjustments without seeking approval from higher-level supervisors. They can deviate from established procedure if a given situation calls for such deviation without waiting for a clearance from the supervisors. When empowered, employees do not feel a need to cover up problems; instead, they seek to solve the problems in an expeditious manner. Empowerment comes about when an institution is willing to trust its employees to do the right thing. For such trust to develop, the corporate culture must promote shared vision and risk taking. It also requires properly trained employees, who know more than a narrowly defined function and are capable of understanding the whole process. Empowerment is also dependent on properly rewarding employees for taking on a higher level of responsibility and for continuously upgrading their skills.

(e) Employee Involvement

As mentioned earlier, senior management cannot mandate change on their own; they must have help from their employees. Efforts to get employees involved must rely on voluntary, collaborative efforts within a nonthreatening, relaxed environment. All too often employees will resist changes. Such resistance is caused by uncertainty about what lies ahead or what the changes imply for their jobs. In the face of ambiguity, employees understandably become anxious. Related to uncertainty is a perceived threat to employees' self-interest. Both managers and employees may feel that the changes will lead to loss of their jobs, or at least a reduction in their power and perks. Another reason may be the fear that existing relationships and social networks will be disturbed.

Differences in perceptions about the need for changes also can lead to uneasiness. Lower-level employees may not know why the changes have to be made, or they may see change as just another fad. Senior managers may be assessing the situation differently based on information provided only to upper-level managers. Such perceptual differences can lead employees to react negatively to changes being instituted. A reward system that rewards individual instead of team efforts can also be a barrier to participation.

(f) Training the Employees

Institutional evolution requires skill building and employee training. Employees need new competencies to keep up with the changes taking place within an organization. If the work is redesigned but the employees do not learn the new skills, the redesign will be counterproductive. As part of the total quality management implementation, employees need to learn about problem solving, statistics, and data collection techniques. But, in addition to such specific skills needed to implement TQM, employees also need to cultivate a learning attitude, since such a willingness makes optimum learning possible. A learning attitude will entice workers to expand their ability to deal with current problems, visualize future opportunities, and anticipate opportunities rather than just dealing with crises as they occur.

(g) Reward Structure

Employee learning and participation can be facilitated with the help of a proper reward and recognition structure. Traditional forms of reward are meant to reward individuals; however, this can be a disincentive for employees to become team players. Many of the approaches being used to promote organizational development at present are meant to be team based. Given this trend, it is better to create a reward system that recognizes and promotes team efforts and participation.

14.5 PRIMARY FORMS OF EVOLUTIONARY BEHAVIOR

A *primary* form of behavior is one that can be undertaken and sustained with minimal and summary efforts. Even though such organizational behavior can be put in place and/or summarily suspended easily, these efforts, policies, or manifestations of organizational culture must remain in place over the long term for maximum benefit. They should not take the form of ad hoc lip service paid to fads in vogue, adopted today and abandoned tomorrow. They include the following:

- Solicit ideas for improvement from all employee levels.
- Encourage collective or team approaches to identify and solve problems.
- Solicit widespread participation for operational, planning, and strategic efforts.
- Develop and train customer service staff to be entrepreneurial and innovative to find ways to improve.
- Benchmark major organizational activities to ensure that they are done efficiently and effectively.
- Use process management techniques to improve operations, particularly those involving customers.

This list of primary strategies includes the common denominators underscoring the successful strategies employed by organizations in their quest to remain or become more competitive in their respective industries.

(a) Solicit Ideas for Improvement from all Employee Levels

The solicitation of ideas for improvement from employees is not a new practice. During World War II, billboards exhorted individuals to share their insight and ideas to help win the war and defeat the enemy. Eaton Corporation, a maker of components and parts for the automotive and related industries, found that the best way to control costs is by explaining to employees how cost savings and improved productivity benefit them. One employee suggestion about preheating dies before use extended die life considerably, thus generating considerable savings for the corporation.

(b) Encourage Collective or Team Approaches to Identify and Solve Problems

A number of organizations now use teams of experts to identify and solve problems. It has been shown that highly empowered teams are the best vehicle for problem resolution. Organizational problems are many-faceted and have multiple causes. Isolating them is easier when a team of people is brought in to analyze the problems and help solve them. A single individual can easily miss a problem or may not even be aware of it.

(c) Solicit Widespread Participation for Operational, Planning, and Strategic Efforts

Related to the team approach for resolving problems is the strategy of promoting company-wide participative behavior. This too is widely practiced by progressive firms such as British Telecom, New York Life Insurance, Goodyear Tire and Rubber, Pratt and Whitney, and Eaton Corporation. These firms have in place permanent programs that encourage employees to participate on an ongoing basis, without prompting by managers, through the appointment of special committees. Workers focus on quality improvements as part of their regular responsibilities.

(d) Develop and Train Customer Service Staff to Be Entrepreneurial and Innovative to Find Ways to Improve

The next strategy is closely related to widespread employee participation. It involves letting the staff be entrepreneurial and innovative in finding ways to improve customer service. The ability to adapt operations to meet the shifting needs of customers is a prerequisite for survival in the business marketplace. To be competitive, a firm's culture must promote entrepreneurial and innovative behavior among its employees as a habit, not just an occasional occurrence.

(e) Benchmark Major Organizational Activities to Ensure That They Are Done Efficiently and Effectively

The practice of benchmarking every major organizational activity, to ensure that it is done in the most efficient and effective way, is gaining tremendous popularity. It is being practiced by such firms as Ford Motor Company, Xerox, AT&T, Motorola, DuPont, and General Motors, to mention just a few. The first act of John F. Smith, after being appointed president of General Motors, was to mandate benchmarking in the organization before each major investment. The Ford Taurus is an example of product benchmarking. Prior to making Taurus, Ford compiled a list of 400 features its customers found important. Using these 400 features, it found the existing car with the best of each one, and used those as models for features in the Taurus. Ford also used Mazda as a benchmark when it decided to restructure its accounts payable. IBM maintains a separate office to keep track of benchmarking activities. AT&T maintains fourteen consultants in its benchmarking office to advise divisional managers on how and what to benchmark; its consultants have conducted more than 120 studies during the past few years. Xerox is the leader in benchmarking. Its first study was done in 1979, and many more have followed since. In one critical study, Xerox discovered that it was spending from $80 to $95 to process an order, whereas the company against which it benchmarked was spending only $25 to $35. Benchmarking is a critical activity, and not using that method may cause a firm to become noncompetitive.

(f) Use Process Management Techniques to Improve Operations, Particularly Those Involving Customers

The use of process management techniques to improve customer service and reduce cycle time is yet another practice widely used by cutting-edge firms. Process management looks not at the individual steps involved in a process but rather at the entire process. It follows all the steps required from customer initiation until customer order delivery and eliminates steps that are ineffective, inefficient, or inflexible from the customer's perspective. In effect, it moves away from narrow specialization and a departmental focus, and instead looks at the whole process. Checking on the creditworthiness of a customer is examined in the context of a larger process involving many departments, such as sale of goods or services to customers and receipt of payment, rather than being considered a distinct bureaucratic fiefdom.

The approaches described in this section are basic things a well-managed business ought to be doing as a matter of course. They make good common sense, and their implementation within an organization can help to prevent that company from losing touch with its environment and becoming obsolete. The remainder of the chapter examines the various ways in which these primary approaches can be put into practice.

14.6 IMPLEMENTING EVOLUTIONARY STRATEGIES

Implementation of the basic improvement strategies can take many forms. To promote organizational evolution, companies employ a variety of secondary strategies aimed at improving operations and profitability, especially over the long term.

To facilitate a survey of approaches used by firms for organizational improvement, it is best to group them. We have chosen to group them as follows:

- Maintaining continuous contact with customers to understand and anticipate their needs
- Providing value, thereby developing loyal customers
- Working closely and developing harmonious relationships with vendors to make sure they do not work at cross-purposes
- Utilizing information and communication technology to improve operations
- Developing a process awareness within the organization by making sure that the process is organized into manageable and focused units, to improve performance
- Utilizing concurrent or simultaneous engineering
- Encouraging, supporting, and rewarding ongoing employee training and education
- Improving operation cycles and working on removing constraints (minimizing all cycle times)
- Focusing on quality, productivity, profitability, timeliness, and flexibility

In the rest of this section, we amplify and illustrate these approaches to implementing organizational evolution.

(a) Getting to Know the Customers

It is a truism to claim that the customer is to be treated like royalty—like the king or queen whose whims rule the domain. But putting the rhetoric of such a slogan into practice requires maintaining continuous contact with customers to understand and anticipate their needs. To do so, ask customers to specify their expectations in terms of improvement goals for the company's products and services, including better delivery and quality responsiveness. Then make it the goal to deliver what the customers asked for.

To have satisfied customers, a strong customer focus must become a part of organizational culture. Customer focus must include not only the external customers who receive the end products but the internal customers as well. The warehouse must consider production the same way as the organization would its customers who buy the finished products.

(b) Working on Customer Satisfaction and Loyalty

Businesses must earn their customers' confidence and loyalty with quality performance and continual attention. Xerox reorganized itself so that the operational management level is closest to the customers. Through such responsiveness to its customers, quality improved and continues to do so. Extensive and ongoing research is almost always needed to identify the drivers of customer satisfaction, and researching these drivers is easier when firms like Xerox get closer to their customers. Such customer awareness gained through research must then become the basis for training customer service representatives so that they know how to respond to customer needs. This is the practice at Xerox.

Johnson Controls' circles of excellence program represents another firm's approach to customer satisfaction. Customer satisfaction was the strategic focus as far back as 1985 and the subject of company-wide training. Similarly, the Forum Corporation found that quality improvement efforts work best when top managers spend significant time with customers, listening to their needs and concerns, and then use the information gained to focus on the internal improvement process.

Besides closeness, by providing value a firm can develop loyalty among its customers, not only pleasing them but exceeding their expectations. Exceeding customer expectations means doing more for the customer than is expected under normal circumstances. Do not stop after ringing up a sale. Do more, through research and development, innovation, and searching for ways to expand the products or services to enhance the customer's business. Providing value to customers is not solely an altruistic act. Procter & Gamble knows that when it pleases customers with product innovation and consistent value, it earns loyalty to its brands. New York Life believes that customer confidence and customer loyalty are built by searching for ways to enhance the services it provides to its customers. Some firms that set exceeding the customer's expectations as the corporate goal make money in the process. These companies exemplify the strategy of not limiting themselves to the immediate sale and not resting after meeting customer expectations. They go beyond merely selling to focus on providing value by exceeding the customer's expectations.

(c) Cooperating with Vendors

The poet John Donne wrote that no man is an island. That maxim is applicable to businesses operating in the twenty-first century as well. A firm has to depend on its vendors to carry out its mission, as very few firms can be self-sufficient and free of suppliers. If the services and products provided by its vendors are at cross-purposes, then no business is likely to attain its goals. It is imperative to work closely with suppliers to improve their product/service quality and productivity. Instead of a confrontational relationship with many vendors, what is needed is a close working relationship with a few good, dependable suppliers. Such an approach requires a firm to work very closely with its suppliers to ensure that their quality and delivery are satisfactory.

(d) Using Technology

Providing value to customers and working closely with vendors can be facilitated by utilizing information and communication technology. Ignoring emergent technology is a peril no business can afford. Appropriate use of technology can improve customer service, enhance product value, and develop closer ties with vendors. Technology has allowed VF Corporation to develop a sense of partnership with large retailers such as Wal-Mart through its market response system (MRS), which controls more than 30 percent of VF's business. MRS allows VF to maintain a 97 percent in-stock (in retail stores) rate versus 70 percent for the industry as a whole. Using technology allows store inventory to be replenished much faster, thus providing improved customer service and profitability. A technology-based Holiday Inn Reservation Optimization (HIRO) system allows that firm more flexibility and wider access in making reservations. The HIRO system allows the firm to provide more options to its customers and to make sure reservations are not lost. Fidelity also uses information technology to improve quality and customer service. Use of a high-speed fiber-optic communications network has given Fidelity a competitive edge because it allows the firm to provide information in high-quality format at a reasonable cost in a timely fashion.

(e) Modifying Organizational Structures

A number of organizations are learning that structuring organizations into manageable and focused units aids improved performance. Chrysler found more focus by reorganizing itself into platform teams consisting of large car, small car, minivan, and jeep/truck. Such platform teams are composed of product and manufacturing engineers, planners and buyers, marketers, designers, financial analysts, and outside suppliers. Each team is responsible for getting its vehicles to the market and ensuring better quality, lower cost, and faster development of the product to market. Essentially, Chrysler is breaking itself up into smaller, semi-independent corporations.

The more focused organizational structure works well when firms also use concurrent or simultaneous engineering as part of their strategy. One of Pratt and Whitney's vital quality initiatives is integrated product development. The concurrent engineering process pulls together employee experts in engineering, manufacturing, purchasing, and customer support at the beginning of each product life cycle. This group then works together and closely coordinates its activities until completion of the project.

(f) Educating Employees

Beside working with customers, technology, and organizational structure, a firm seeking to be on the cutting edge must encourage, support, and develop employee training and education programs. British Telecom launched a massive new education program for its managers, which focused on participative leadership centered on the company's key values. Its main key value is a clear focus on the customer. Johnson Controls utilizes training and implementation methodologies to make its employees thoroughly familiar with total quality control, ISO 9000 standards, and other customer focus criteria. Corning's goal is to have its employees devote up to 5 percent of their time to education and training programs. That much time devoted to education and training demonstrates a major commitment by the organization to improving the quality of its workforce and the resultant services to its customers.

(g) Reducing Cycle Time

Improving timeliness of all operation cycles (also referred to as minimizing cycle times) is yet another goal sought by many firms. It has been documented that cutting down on slack time (much of it nonproductive) can improve quality, productivity, and profit. Motorola has set reduction of cycle times as one of its main foci. Such reduction even extended to the mail arrival rate at one of its plants. Instead of waiting for the usual mail delivery, it asked an employee to pick up the plant's mail at the local post office. As a result, recipients got their mail as much as thirty six hours earlier. The speedup in mail delivery was important in improving customer service, because a good deal of the mail was from customers. Time is equated with money, so important benefits can be obtained by reducing cycle times of activities that are notorious for unnecessary delays. Delays in activities add costs and frequently displease customers, both internal and external.

(h) Organizational Flexibility

Finally, improvements in cycle time can be supplemented through flexibility. VF Corporation, through its market response system, is able to obtain almost immediate information on the sales rates of its products, including which style, fabric, color, and size of each garment sells well or poorly. Aided by such detailed and immediate market information, it can restock retailers quickly so as not to lose sales for itself or its intermediary customer, the retailer. Chrysler and General Motors were able to trim their new vehicle design and development time significantly. Through a logistics management program, AMP was able to improve its on-time shipments from 65 percent to 95 percent. It is able to deliver nationwide AMP products within three days or less in more than half of its U.S. sales.

Clearly an organization should not be content with maintaining the status quo. There are any number of ways in which a firm can set about its evolutionary climb—our survey of organizational practices amply demonstrates this. In the rest of this chapter, we discuss tools and techniques that can aid organizations in attaining evolutionary competence.

14.7 ELEMENTS OF TOOLS AND TECHNIQUES

To better appreciate brainstorming's role in organizational development as well as the role of various other techniques, recall that any tool or technique used for organizational improvement or problem solving consists of four basic elements:

1. Problem identification
2. Problem selection
3. Problem analysis
4. Recommendation to management

Human beings require language to identify, organize, express, and communicate their thoughts. Similarly, each of these four operational elements involved in organizational attempts to improve requires the use of one or more of the following techniques in order to be better analyzed, organized, understood, and communicated. They are useful for understanding the causes of and solutions to the problems that organizations encounter. The following tools help in organizational problem solving by systematically gathering data and making sense of it. Such techniques require involvement on the part of more than just those seeking to document the procedures. They are, in other words, communal efforts to understand the environment within which they work and meant to make use of the collective intelligence of the entire organization. The techniques include:

- Brainstorming
- Affinity charting
- Benchmarking

These techniques can be applied at each of the four operational steps, depending on the problem under analysis. For example, brainstorming may be necessary to verify the existence of the problem as well as to discover and analyze its cause. These techniques help to identify and solve problems and find opportunities for evolution.

14.8 BRAINSTORMING

Brainstorming can be applied to problems, causes, or solutions. It can identify opportunities and isolate obstacles that keep an organization from being effective. It is an organized, focused attempt to get a group of individuals to think out loud. Doing so can produce better ideas than those contributed by the individual members of the group acting alone. By thinking aloud and collectively, group members stimulate each others' creative processes, which leads to synergistic benefits.

To keep brainstorming from becoming the proverbial Tower of Babel, adherence to several rules is advisable. A verbal free-for-all does not optimize brainstorming—it only creates logjams.

(a) Do Not Be Critical

First, criticism of others' ideas should not be permitted; it generates ill-will and curbs creativity. The purpose of brainstorming is to generate ideas, with one idea leading to another. In fact, what one individual sees as a crazy, impossible idea may very well be very practical. It also could stimulate the group to generate a more pragmatic solution during exploration by the group. Looking at things from a different perspective may well be just the right approach. Criticism inhibits this kind of creative thinking and interrupts the flow of ideas.

(b) Seek Out the Unfamiliar

Preventing familiarity from blocking one's creativity is very important. Group members should be encouraged to forget their current perceptions about how a certain job or task is done or should be done. They must feel unencumbered by preconceptions if they are to generate new ideas. It is helpful to know how things are; such knowledge anchors us to reality and keeps us from going off on tangents. The fear of being out in the far left field could easily have prevented not only the invention of the wheel itself but also the subsequent variations. Stereotypes can be straitjackets for creative thinking.

(c) Facilitate Group Interaction

It is best not to put any form of organizational limitations on brainstorming, because they can inhibit the group from being truly creative. The purpose of the group is, in large measure, to help generate more ideas. Barriers to communication must be eliminated as far as possible. Employees and supervisors should meet on equal terms. In bringing the group together, it is imperative that all members have equal opportunity to participate. Certain individuals can dominate brainstorming if they are left free to do so. Such domination of the group, be it rank-based or the result of personality traits, must be prevented from taking hold. To avoid domination by one person, have each member give one idea in turn; those who do not have any can be silent and "pass" for that particular round.

(d) Keep a Record

Although generating the ideas is important, it is imperative to keep a record of them. The team leader or an assigned member should arrange to record every idea that is suggested, regardless of the initial perception of its value. The recording should be public and visible to the entire group. Such devices as flip charts, chalkboards, or overhead projectors can help. Tape recorders and camcorders also can be used, but they have some limitations. The members should be able to constantly review the ideas that have been suggested, and those ideas then can become stimuli for yet other thoughts.

Following completion of the brainstorming session, the complete record of all ideas contributed should be made available to the team members. Then they can refer to it as they work on the next phase, preferably in a meeting following the original session. Once the ideas have been brainstormed, they must be evaluated and examined to see how well they fit the organizational needs and circumstances. After the initial session, members can meet to examine and prioritize the ideas and select one or more for implementation. Selection preferably takes the form of group consensus, but at times majority rule may be the optimum way to proceed. While selecting and prioritizing organizational options, group members should supplement their decisions with information from other organizational sources.

Brainstorming is an important activity because it identifies problems as well as solutions. Businesses involved with continuous improvement activities have learned that the problem-finding phase of brainstorming is very important because it identifies and articulates the problems to be solved. Knowing what the problem is often reveals the beginning of the road to its solution. No cure without a diagnosis, doctors tell us. The problem-solving phase is meant to help implement new, useful, and imaginative solutions, but it can only follow in the wake of the problem's discovery. Problem-finding must come before problem solving, but brainstorming can help in both phases.

Brainstorming can turn into a Tower of Babel very easily. A wrong turn can cause the group to lose its focus. Another problem with brainstorming is that it does produce lots of ideas, expose many problems, raise a lot of questions, and suggest various solutions—but processing such disorganized abundance can be time and resource consuming. The outpouring of creativity unleashed through brainstorming can itself raise questions, such as:

- How is the generated material to be organized?
- Who will do the organizing?
- When will it be done?
- Will the circumstantial exigencies allow an allocation of resources to further explore such organizational creativity?

To avoid such problems, a variation of traditional brainstorming, based on the use of affinity charts, can bring more focus to the process. When affinity charts are used, the participants also brainstorm, generating questions, problems, and solutions, but they do so silently and in written form. Such brainstorming is usually done on large self-stick notes, which are then stuck on a wall for everyone to see. To focus the process, prior to the start of written brainstorming, participants usually agree on a question, problem, or idea as the topic for exploration. They then make their ideas available to the rest of the group by simply posting them.

After participants have posted their respective notes on the wall, they all help organize them in an orderly fashion. In other words, common responses, ideas, and suggestions are clustered together. All of this takes place in silence. (It is best to stick to the silent mode until all group members have posted their responses.) In somewhat larger groups, it may be desirable for each participant to announce his or her response before sticking it on the wall. In smaller groups, total silence may be more desirable. Exhibit 14–1 shows the steps used during the exercise.

At some point the group must, of course, terminate the silent process. At this point another question is addressed or the posted responses to the original issue are discussed. The stage during which the written responses contributed by the group are discussed and scrutinized is often treated as an independent process dedicated to exploration of the interrelationships among the ideas contributed; this is described in Exhibit 14–2.

I.   Agree on a topic.
   A.   Come to an agreement on the question, problem, or idea to be addressed.
   B.   Do not discuss or clarify the chosen topic, to avoid biasing participants.
II. Appoint or select a group facilitator to keep things moving.
III. Brainstorm in silence.
   A.   Each participant writes responses on large self-stick notes and sticks them on a wall.
   B.   Responses should take the form of sentences or even clauses, consisting of a noun, verb, and a few other words, rather than paragraphs. Be as brief as possible. Limit responses to a selected number of words.
IV. Explore other responses. Participants can, will, and should respond to their fellow participants' responses. These reactions should then be grouped with the original response.
V.   Organize responses in groups.
   A.   Based on relationships between responses, group them together.
   B.   Everyone should participate in this without obstruction.
   C.   Try to attain consensus.
   D.   Add other responses if deemed necessary.
VI. Summarize responses.
   A.   Head up each group of responses with a concise topic title.
   B.   Organize the responses under each title in a logical, useful order.
VII. Before dispersing, decide what is to be done with the output. Agree on follow-up.

Exhibit 14–1.   Guidelines for the affinity charting process.

Objective: To draw logical connections among the responses generated by an affinity chart process exercise.
I.   Brainstorm.
   A.   Take output of affinity chart process and verbally discuss each group of responses.
   B.   Expand ideas to strengthen the original input.
II. Classify.
   A.   Sort the responses into groups.
   B.   Label each topic title card with a number or an alphabetic character to facilitate identification.
III. Group the responses.
   A.   Identify relationships among topics.
   B.   Determine which topic titles are related, including the direction of the relationships.
IV. Diagram the responses.
   A.   Develop a diagram with topic identifiers and arrows to show how topics are related.
   B.   Continue to diagram until all topic titles appear on the diagram.
V.   May need subdiagram.
   A.   Not all responses may be related or fit within a completely connected diagram.
   B.   However, too many subdiagrams may be an indication of fuzzy thinking.
VI. May require repetition of the process if responses do not fit within a coherent, logical diagram. If this happens, return to step 1 and repeat the process.

Exhibit 14–2.   Guidelines for interrelationship diagramming process.

The affinity charting process can produce results superior to traditional brainstorming by being more focused. Ordinarily the affinity chart process takes more time, but because the responses are written, they are easier and quicker to organize. Such better-organized results facilitate subsequent planning and implementation. The affinity chart does, however, have limitations. For example, it does not work well when the group is too large. It may be desirable to break up larger groups into smaller subgroups. The simple physical space used for such a session must allow all group participants to view the notes posted by other participants. Brainstorming, in contrast, can be used with larger groups of participants.

The new information technology allows brainstorming to occur with the help of client-servers. On-line services facilitate individual brainstorming that is not under the same roof or even in the same city. E-mail and local area network (LAN) technology can offset the limitation of distance and let individuals in different locales brainstorm electronically.

14.9 BENCHMARKING

Benchmarking is a new word, but the underlying concept may be as old as humanity. The adage, "imitation is the sincerest form of flattery" is testament to the ancient origin of the practice of learning from others. In a more contemporary vein, one could equate benchmarking with searching for a better way of doing something by observing how others are doing the same thing. The benchmarking process can apply to a search for new ideas, methods, practices, and procedures. If ideas, methods, practices, and procedures of others are superior to the ones you are using now, they become benchmarks; they can then be adapted to your needs and be implemented. Benchmarking is a continuing process. The implementation of an improved process does not end the need to keep seeing if others have found something better and forged ahead by their adaptation of those improvements. The search for the best, the most efficient, and the most effective must never stop. It should be continuous.

Despite the ancient origin of the practice, benchmarking is not universally followed, largely because what is easy for one firm to do may not be very practical for others. According to an Urdu saying, when a crow tries to be a peacock, it ends up being neither. Similarly, strict imitation of others may not be entirely appropriate to one's specific circumstances. Going out in the noonday sun of the United Kingdom is one thing; doing so in the equatorial heat is quite another. Finding appropriate role models for benchmarking is not easy.

Another difficulty involves identification of the best-in-class performers. Even after such an identification, determining why those best-in-class firms are both more efficient and more effective than others continues to be difficult. Difficulties also crop up due to human egos and cultural habits. By all accounts, the task of convincing employees and managers to change what they have been doing—that is, to implement an improved method that was identified through benchmarking—is bound to be very difficult and is sure to run up against the human tendency to stick with the comfort of the familiar.

A survey reported that, out of a sample of 580 firms operating globally in four industries (computers, automobiles, hospitals, and banks), 31 percent of U.S. enterprises regularly benchmarked their products and services. The number of those that never did benchmarking was 7 percent. The survey showed that U.S. firms are more heavily engaged in benchmarking than either German or Japanese firms.[1]

One of the earlier incarnations of benchmarking is the practice of reverse engineering, which has been around for some time. Reverse engineering, which is actually product benchmarking, consists of breaking down a competitor's product to learn its technical and design details. Such a product dissection lets one compare a product with that of the competition and permits one to evaluate whether the product design is as effective and as efficient as the competitor's.

Automobile firms use product benchmarking extensively to identify features in competitors' products that are or may be more desirable than the firm's own products. Automobiles are taken apart piece by piece, and each component is analyzed to determine how it compares with similar components in the firm's own products.

In contrast to such product analysis and comparison, current benchmarking activities tend to be mostly process-oriented. Firms are interested in learning not only about who has the most effective and efficient process for a given activity but also about what makes them better. Besides finding out who is doing things efficiently and effectively, people also want to determine if what is good for others also fits their own needs, and if they can adopt and implement those methods within their specific firm.

The current literature differentiates among various forms of benchmarking. In *internal benchmarking,* operations are compared against other similar or identical operations within one organization—if not at one location, probably at a different division, location, plant, or other facility. Alternatively, benchmarking can involve comparing operations with those of direct competitors. Such imitation of the competition is, not surprisingly, called *competitive benchmarking.* Yet another type of comparison deals with specific functions. Ford's learning from Mazda how to handle accounts payable is a form of *functional benchmarking;* it could be internal or external. Yet another form of benchmarking occurs when someone borrows the underlying concept. A maker of copying machines seeks to learn customer service and order processing from L.L. Bean, the catalog retailer, or tries to learn about product delivery from a pizza maker known for its on-time delivery. Such conceptual imitation, sometimes called *generic benchmarking,* is probably the most difficult approach to benchmarking. The underlying assumption requires a firm to change its way of looking at its business as well as its organizational culture. It extends beyond the specifics about a given process or a product.

Even though benchmarking is not easily implemented, numerous companies have done so all over the world. A number of companies have successfully improved their status by benchmarking studies. Examples of companies engaged in benchmarking include Xerox, NCR, Motorola, Digital Equipment, Kodak, Hewlett-Packard, General Motors, and Ford Motor. Efforts by these firms have been widely reported. The information released by and for Xerox is among the most comprehensive testimonials to the effectiveness of benchmarking. It has been reported that, through benchmarking, Xerox was able to reduce its suppliers with whom it did business; increase the ratio of common parts used by its various products; reduce the number of quality problems; and reduce the cost of manufacturing its products by 50 percent. It also reduced the time needed for new product development and the amount of direct labor consumed for manufacturing. Not only was it able to reduce its corporate staff, Xerox further introduced concurrent engineering and reduced layers of its management hierarchy.

Motorola is another well-known example of benchmarking implementation. It consistently seeks to be considered best in its class. Such a corporate goal was made possible by benchmarking what the Japanese were doing in product lines in which Motorola was active. Being best in its class has allowed Motorola to reduce its defect rate in manufacturing by 99 percent, to generate cost savings of about $900 million in 1992 alone and billions in cumulative terms.

The accomplishments of these two multinational companies clearly show that benchmarking can produce substantial savings and improve overall competitiveness.

14.10 THE PROCESS OF BENCHMARKING

The five-step benchmarking process can be described as follows:

1. Decide on what is to be benchmarked. At any given point, various functions, activities, and processes being used by a firm may need improvement. Given this, the firm may need to rank them in terms of priority and/or feasibility. The decision to implement benchmarking should be part of an ongoing process, not an occasional occurrence. If firms are in the habit of periodic self-examination, benchmarking will become the rule rather than the exception.

2. An important element of the benchmarking process is the ability to measure progress. To do so, identify the key cost, time, and quality performance indicators. It is a good idea to focus on performance indicators related to customer needs and customer satisfaction. They are the most important because they determine the difference between success and failure.

3. Focus on items that rank high in importance and follow them by developing a formal search for benchmarks, either internal or external to the organization. This requires identification of organizations that have good reputations, especially in the area one is seeking to benchmark. The most useful benchmarks will be related to the performance indicators chosen to measure success, namely, those related to customers.

4. Measure the performance of the indicators identified in step 2 and compare them with similar indicators of the benchmarked firms. A comparison of how one is doing with how others do it is more easily carried out with tangible measurements.

5. Decide, using the comparison in step 4, if the company needs to change its own process, activity, or function. If performance indicators lag behind those of the benchmarked source, investigate how the firm can improve its own performance. The goal may be simply to close the gap, or it could be to surpass the performance of the benchmarked firm to become the model for that particular activity, process, or function.

The steps involved in the benchmarking process can be related to the well-known Deming cycle of plan, do, check, and act. In effect, the benchmarking process is an extension of the Deming cycle. (See Chapter 16.)

If we examine the literature dealing with the benchmarking process, two alternative methods seem to emerge. The difference has to do with the scope of change being sought through benchmarking. One could attempt to make a major change to a current process through detailed, comprehensive, time-consuming use of resources. The other alternative is an incremental approach that seeks more modest, incremental improvements to the current operations process over a shorter period.

Xerox's effort exemplifies the major form of benchmarking. Xerox discovered that its midsize copiers were no longer price-competitive with similar Japanese copiers; that is, the Japanese were selling comparable machines for less. Matching that price would have required Xerox to sell its machines at cost, without any profit margin. This shook up and led Xerox to benchmark its manufacturing process against that of the Japanese competition. It undertook a comprehensive study, including site visits by its manufacturing managers at all levels to the Japanese locations, to convince them that change was crucial to achieve the product cost reductions required to compete with the Japanese in the midsize copier market.

Another comprehensive benchmarking study carried out and implemented by Xerox was of its order-processing operations. After observing the customer order-processing activity at fourteen other firms, Xerox found that they spent only a fraction of what Xerox was incurring to process its orders. One particularly effective order-processing system was discovered by Xerox at L.L. Bean. Since the study by Xerox, numerous other companies have visited L.L. Bean's order-processing complex to study how it processes customer orders.

In contrast to these comprehensive benchmarking projects, others may prefer to focus on small, incremental improvements. These improvements usually can be achieved through brief, low-cost benchmarking projects. Such changes may simply require a change in the design of a form, or purchase of a more up-to-date software package after learning about others who made a similar change.

14.11 BENCHMARKING ACCOUNTING FUNCTIONS

Of special interest are the cases pertaining to benchmarking projects in the administrative sector. One such effort was undertaken in 1991 when Mellon Bank of Pittsburgh became involved in benchmarking. Its first project sought to speed up the resolution of credit card billing disputes. To find ways to resolve the problem, it assembled a team of eight staff members from different departments that played a role in the process. The internal team benchmarked seven companies, including a bank, an airline, and credit card companies. The team relied mostly on telephone interviews, supplemented by a few site visits to investigate how others were dealing with the issue. The approach that eventually reduced the customer dispute problem for Mellon involved a computerized database that allowed the customer service clerks to find out all the facts pertaining to the issue and to communicate with the customer about all aspects of the dispute. One individual had the ability to access all the relevant facts and deal with the customer.

14.12 POTENTIAL BENCHMARKING PITFALL

A major problem consultants have discovered about benchmarking is the tendency to stick with the familiar while trying to compare oneself with others. Businesses limit their search for models to be imitated to their own industries. This prevents the attainment of optimum improvements. It is helpful to look outside the familiar (i.e., outside one's own industry) to see what is being done and how that way of operating can be implemented within one's firm. For example, customer service is done by every business; it may be instructive for a university to look not just to other academic institutions, but also to other organizations. Casting a wider net in search of models may hold more promise than those emanating from your own industry. The classic case is Xerox's adoption of L.L. Bean's order-fulfillment method.

14.13 BENCHMARKING NETWORKS

Given the growing popularity of benchmarking, it made sense for companies to cooperate with other companies in studying each other's operations. Most companies do share with others, but some are reluctant to cooperate. To get around such reluctance, organizations have developed. Among them is the American Productivity and Quality Center, which has established the nonprofit International Benchmarking Clearinghouse and is supported by a large number of company members that pay an annual fee to support the activities of the information exchange. Another organization is the Strategic Planning Institute Council on Benchmarking, which is not as large as the American Productivity and Quality Center but seeks to perform a similar role. The Institute of Management Accountants, located in Montvale, New Jersey, provides benchmarking information to accountants. The benefits of these organizations include their ability to provide communications, statistics, and data banks of benchmarking information to their memberships.

Beside various benchmarking information clearinghouses, firms can learn from each other through informed networking. Major consulting firms, such as Towers Perrin and A.T. Kearney, as well as major international accounting firms, provide channels for exchanging information about benchmarking to their clients, which may be competing firms. Because direct collaboration between competing firms can be seen as a violation of regulatory and legal requirements, it is best to avoid it. The appearance of collaboration is avoided by using consultants as a channel to obtain information; still, benchmarking comparison can be undertaken through intermediaries.

14.14 FUTURE OF BENCHMARKING

Benchmarking is one of the many activities that firms engage in both to become more competitive and to merely survive. It has become popular recently because of the globalization of product markets and raw material sources. Products purchased in stores in Asia, Europe, or North America may have been manufactured in a wide variety of countries. Even before international trade agreements such as the North American Free Trade Agreement (NAFTA) were fully implemented, trade in finished products and components of finished products was widely practiced. The emerging information technology has made access to information easier, and it has made communication and contact across the national boundaries easier. Benchmarking has been around under other names for some time; it will evolve over time and may even be called by a new name in the future. What will not change, however, is the need, born of environmental and market necessity, to have a process in place that is as good or nearly as good as the best-in-class process. Worldwide competition means survival of the fittest. Firms that are not best-in-class, yet seek to compete in world markets, will not be able to remain in business if what they do is not comparable to the others in that league.

NOTES

1. Jeremy, Main. "How to Steal the Best Ideas Around," *Fortune,* October 19, 1992: 102–106.

CHAPTER 15

ORGANIZATIONAL FLEXIBILITY

15.1 INTRODUCTION

An essential requirement for organizational evolution is structural flexibility. Lack of flexibility destroys tall trees during stormy weather. Shrubs, given their flexibility, are much more likely to survive stresses. Organizations are less likely to change and adapt to their environments if they are too rigid—structurally and culturally. Organizations are changing their structures not only to become more responsive to the current and future needs of their customers but also to improve their competitive preparedness. In addition, organizations are seeking to become more adaptable through strategic alliances with others. The search for organizational flexibility requires negotiating hazardous roadblocks that can frustrate the process.

15.2 WHAT IS A FLEXIBLE ORGANIZATION?

Dictionaries define *flexibility* as the ability to be bent; susceptibility to adaptation; willing or disposed to yield; pliant; elastic; supple; nimble; limber. *Chameleon* and *metamorphosis* also bring to mind the attributes one seeks when talking about organizational flexibility.

In a more technical sense, *organizational flexibility* refers to a firm's ability to respond to changing markets and consumer demands. It can refer to the ability to make many different products in sequential runs, or it could refer to the ability to make more than one product at the same location. It also may be construed as the ability to trim setup costs involved in production runs themselves or in switching from one setup to another. The ability to change production volume to suit customer demand can be a manifestation of organizational adaptiveness as well. Alternatively, increasing the range of products that can be supplied in response to customers' demand may be a reflection of organizational adaptability. One also could equate flexibility with a workforce capable of doing many things or able to learn new skills. In short, organizational flexibility can refer to product diversity, production volumes, and/or processing variety as well as to the skills, knowledge, adaptability, and willingness to continue learning on the part of the organizational workforce. It boils down to the ability of an organization to adapt itself to do all or any of these things as well as to its ability to quickly market new or redesigned products in response to changes in customer tastes and needs.

The U.S. automotive industry's ability to shorten vehicle design and development times is an example of improvement in the industry's flexibility, at least as far as product development is concerned. The ability of vendors to restock department stores' inventory almost as fast as it is sold can be seen as a form of organizational flexibility.

Being a flexible organization is not simply a matter of installing the latest technology and employing an army of technocratic nerds. It is not limited to the ability to rapidly mobilize cross-functional employee teams. Being flexible is also not limited to dealing with current market demands and emerging tastes, or even in generating speedier response to customers' orders. The flexible corporation of today and tomorrow must be responsive to customers' existing, emerging, and future needs and wants. Being responsive to customers and having access to cutting-edge technology and highly trained technocrats is necessary but not sufficient to make an organization flexible. The ability and the creativity to develop products to meet needs that the customers themselves are not quite familiar with are important requisites for the flexible corporation to incorporate into its culture.

Corporate flexibility extends to more than product design, design modification, and product variety; it also must encompass organizational structures. In addition, a flexible organization seeks to change from traditional, functional-based departmental structure to an activity- or project-based structure. In a flexibly structured organization, activities and projects are undertaken by multifunctional teams working together rather than departments devoting themselves to projects or tasks in a linearly sequenced process. Membership in these cross-department, multifunctional employee teams changes over time as requirements change. The team approach can help organizations to be flexible and adaptive at all times.

15.3 HOW IS ORGANIZATIONAL FLEXIBILITY ACHIEVED?

Organizational flexibility is achieved in a variety of ways. Product flexibility, an important manifestation of organizational flexibility, is achieved by two important determinants, or factors. The first factor allows a company to produce many different models of a product with the same machinery, and usually on the same assembly line, at low cost and with little disruption in the production process when models are changed. That is, small production runs can be made of any component or any final assembly, and the production process can be switched quickly, with little or no disruption, to another model or product.

The second flexibility factor is the ability to switch production operations with only minimum disruption when introducing an entirely new model to the production process. This is extremely important; in the past, lack of flexibility as to this second factor created considerable lost production and resulted in plants being idle for weeks, if not months.

The Japanese have focused their attention on both flexibility factors and have made considerable progress. They have achieved this progress at a price: Massive capital investment in advanced technology had to be added to production operations to achieve these abilities in flexible production. Between 1986 and 1991, Japan's industry reportedly spent $3 trillion on domestic plants and equipment. Japan's industry spending, on a per-capita basis, was more than two and a half times as much as equivalent spending on new plants and equipment by the U.S. industry in 1991.

Such investment has allowed Toshiba to assemble nine different word processors simultaneously on just one assembly line while, at the same location, its factory is also putting together twenty different laptop computers on an adjacent assembly line. The different models are made in batch sizes averaging twenty units. Such diversity of product manufacture is attainable with a heavy dose of computer technology, which even extends to the manner in which instructions are provided for those who work on these assembly lines. Loose sheets of job orders have been replaced with computer screens at the work station on the assembly line.

An example of the ability to add new models to the production process at low cost with minimum delays (the second flexibility factor listed earlier) is the speed with which Nissan is able to prepare an automobile plant to produce a new model car. It can do so without stopping its current work; its assembly line keeps assembling automobiles even while the change is being made. The change that allows the line to handle a different model is now made in three months; it used to take twelve months. Like Nissan, Toyota is able to do its model changeover amazingly fast. Through several months of advance planning and logistical preparation, only one shift of downtime is needed to add a new model to the assembly line. Before 1982, model changes required lengthy shutdowns of the entire automobile assembly line. Toyota has been able to increase its capacity utilization of its assembly lines through this ability to change the line within one shift.

In the past, Japanese firms were known for their efforts in improving product quality and low-inventory production and operations. Judging from the examples just cited, Japan's industry is now turning its attention to operational flexibility and product variety. The latter can be seen as an outgrowth of the former. The Japanese are positioning themselves strategically to be formidable competitors, not only in high-volume but also in low-volume product markets by developing operations that are flexible enough to provide a wide variety of product models at a low cost.

15.4 PRODUCT MODULARIZATION AND FLEXIBILITY

Manufacturers of goods are finding that product modularization, using interchangeable parts and subassemblies in different models, can make them much more flexible and responsive to customers. This approach to manufacturing is called *modularization* because several modules, or subassemblies, are identical for each product or configuration. The concept of modularization is not new. What is new is the extent to which the concept is taking hold despite the fact that doing so requires investment to build newer factories and resources devoted to helping both supervisors and employees adapt to the new environment. The degree to which firms are able to implement modularization will determine the extent to which they attain manufacturing flexibility. There should be no doubt that the ability to cultivate manufacturing flexibility will determine how well manufacturers will be able to compete in the future.

Product modularization is being extensively used in the making of automobile components, including car engines. It is also used in the household appliance industry, in electronics and computer products, in farm equipment, and in a host of others. Indeed, it need not be limited to a factory; the accounting department of Seton Hall University, located in New Jersey, is using the concept for its graduate study program.

An example of how modularization can provide flexibility and give a firm the ability to switch from making one product model to another is the making of automobile engines. Traditionally, automobile engines were assembled in engine plants designed for one specific model. Because the plants limited their production to just one model, they were able to attain high product volumes. Producing half a million engines in one plant, all basically of the same design, was fairly common in the recent past. Such one-model plants were quite economical and efficient so long as the demand for that particular engine remained unchanged. However, because of keen competition in catering to customers' changing tastes, as well as the need to incorporate technological improvements in the car engines, the high-volume but limited production mode is losing its dominance.

Plants that produce one model in very high volume tend to be disadvantageous in today's global market. Unfortunately, American automakers have far too many such limited-diversity plants. However, automobile manufacturers are in the process of building new engine plants that will enable them to produce a variety of different types and sizes in one location. As demand for a given engine type changes, they can quickly vary the production mix of engines.

Ford is constructing a type of engine-making plant that will allow it to build both V8 and V6 engines around a basic unit, the combustion chamber, designed for maximum fuel efficiency. Ford's new engine plants, using this flexible manufacturing approach, will be able to produce more than a dozen engine sizes and configurations on a single production and assembly line. The key to achieving this product flexibility lies in the sharing of about 350 common parts for each engine size or configuration.

Ford is by no means the only American firm to utilize modularization to produce engines. Caterpillar utilized modular design to produce VI2, V10, and V8 engines on the same production and assembly line. American automakers are seeking to catch up with Toyota, which uses the same flexible manufacturing approach to produce several basic engines on the same production and assembly line. The main reason U.S. manufacturers are lagging behind in adoption of the modular production of engines is the enormous investment they have in engine plants that specialize in only one type of engine.

15.5 ADMINISTRATIVE FLEXIBILITY

Organizational flexibility is an important element in an organization's effort to attain evolutionary competence. Responsive management, continuous improvements, being in touch with one's customers, and benchmarking of both products and organizational processes are among the important attributes of a flexible management organization.

Achieving organizational flexibility requires ongoing work on organizational structures and systems. Large organizations are in special danger because of their lack of organizational, operational, and managerial flexibility. Large organizations tend to maintain the status quo. Their bureaucratic bulk tends to discourage systemic change and prevent improvements in procedures because of their hierarchical or established management style. Unfortunately, the lack of structural flexibility in large organizations constrains them like patients in a straitjacket.

The tendency to manage by the book and to insist that employees live up to the standards set contributes to a lack of adaptability. If the rules and the standards emphasize the wrong goals, they can hinder rather than assist effective and timely decision making. They could even work at cross-purposes. What may be needed is a faster response, but standards may reward plant utilization. Adherence to rules can be overdone while experimentation is ostracized. Workers may not learn new skills if what the standards promote is conformity.

In industries experiencing product, technological, structural, and environmental changes, large organizations are particularly prone to competitive dangers. Large organizations, and especially very large organizations, are like large oil tankers, which cannot turn or stop without a considerable investment of time and effort. The larger the organization, the more difficult it is to change the organizational structure, operations, and overall direction.

A number of large American corporations failed to respond quickly enough to rapid technological, structural, and competitive changes in their respective industries. In the computer hardware industry, both IBM and Digital Equipment Corporation (DEC) were victims of such organizational inertia. They stumbled badly and were forced to pay for their inertia. In the retailing field, the inventor of retailing and mail-order sales, Sears, Roebuck & Co., had to undergo radical, emergency, and costly structural and organizational treatment because of its slow response. The closing of Sears' mail order business was a direct result of its inertia.

Another example of an organization that got victimized by not changing its management style in a timely manner is Hewlett-Packard (HP)—an unlikely candidate, given its reputation as a cutting-edge organization. HP is traditionally given to a highly participatory management style that uses the committee structure widely and extensively. Its culture and structure originally engendered wide participation by its employees, engineers, and middle-level managers, but the committee format turned into a straitjacket as HP grew larger. What was appropriate at one time mutated into an unmanageable format that was responsible for costly problems. Those problems led HP to radically change its management structure to speed up the decision-making process. Such responsive decision making allowed new products to reach the market much sooner. The change meant a major modification of HP's organizational culture, and it drastically reduced the number of committees without entirely eliminating them.

The slow decision-making process and lethargic response to market was not present throughout the HP organization. HP's own laser printer subsidiary, located in Boise, Idaho, was not infected with the same malaise. Its geographic location, some distance from Palo Alto headquarters, and the product it made kept it free from the organizational problems that affected the rest of the organization. The Boise operation was able to bring an economically priced, highly profitable laser printer to market in record time, beating its competition. Even after the market got crowded with other competitors, HP's division was able to maintain its market share.

The HP example illustrates the importance of organizational, structural, and operational flexibility. It is not the only large firm to have been damaged by the inertia inherent in large organizations; over time, many firms have fallen victim to it, all across the globe. Despite its widespread nature, inertia becomes harmful only when organizations allow it to do so. Organizations can minimize the danger from operational inertia, but if they ignore it, they do so at their peril. They must restructure, reorganize, and be more responsive—or they can go out of business entirely.

15.6 FLEXIBILITY THROUGH OPTIMUM CAPACITY UTILIZATION

In addition to investment in new machines and plants, organizational flexibility can be achieved through optimum utilization of capacity. Using the capacity to the fullest extent possible allows a firm to do more with respect to its production volume or product diversity. A company may not need new plants; it just needs to learn to use its existing plant(s) more efficiently.

In the United States, plant underutilization is widespread and is not limited to industry. Throughout the nation, school buildings are empty more often than they are used. The idea of working on weekends is strongly resisted by labor unions and by the majority of nonunion employees. It is a strongly embedded part of the national culture. If weekend work is done at all, it usually requires time-and-a-half or double-time pay. Yet factories, like school buildings, sit idle on weekends, even though they represent enormous invest-ments in building, plants, and equipment. Such underutilization of the infrastructure puts Americans at a distinct disadvantage and makes them less flexible in matching today's global competition.

To improve its capacity utilization, General Motors instituted a third shift at its Lord-stown, Ohio, plant in 1991. This change in work practices was an exception, which took place only after extensive labor-management negotiations and only after concessions were made by both management and unions. With three shifts per week, the plant turned out automobiles for 120 hours out of a total of 168 hours. The 48 idle hours per week were utilized for plant and equipment maintenance, replenishment of supplies, and gen-eral get-ready activities for each work shift. Being able to work 120 hours is quite an achievement for an automobile assembly operation in the United States.

15.7 MAKING AGILE MANUFACTURING AMERICAN

Given the ingrained American culture, the movement toward flexible corporations has led to organized efforts such as those undertaken by Lehigh University's Iacocca Institute. The institute is actively seeking to introduce agility to the American business scene, and it has even coined its own term, "agile manufacturing," to describe a conceptual system of designing, manufacturing, and marketing products to help match and even surpass Japan's current lead in flexible, high-quality, lean, low-cost manufacturing. Agile manufacturing has developed into a movement called the Agile Manufacturing Forum (AMF). It is a col-laborative movement supported by more than one hundred of the largest U.S. companies plus the National Center for Manufacturing Sciences (NCMS), the Microelectronics and Computer Technology Corporation (MCC), Sandia National Laboratories (SNL), Massa-chusetts Institute of Technology (MIT), the U.S. Department of Defense, the U.S. Depart-ment of Commerce, and numerous other organizations. Through a twenty-five-year plan, the forum is seeking to set in place a high-technology infrastructure that can develop, de-sign, manufacture, and market high-quality, innovative, low-cost products quicker than competing industries in the rest of the world.

The necessary ingredients to help attain AMF's objectives are emergent information communication technologies and corporate strategic alliances. The means of accomplish-ing AMF's objectives are concurrent engineering, electronic data interchange, benchmark-ing, design and product flexibility, cycle-time compression, and modular manufacturing. The concept of concurrent engineering would be extended, with the help of strategic al-liances, to a group of firms, not just one company. Two or more companies would work to-gether on design and development of new products. In the process, they would pool resources and avoid unnecessary duplication for their common good, such as developing equipment that will control pollution. Emergent information technology will be able to provide rapid communication among members of the concurrent engineering teams. This approach will permit the alliances to compress time significantly and bring new products to market faster than their competition.

The objective of all of AMF's approaches is to bring down developmental and opera-tional costs, to create greater awareness of innovation among its members, to teach its members how to go about responding rapidly to new demands, to raise quality and relia-bility, and to improve overall competitiveness. There is, however, a potential problem with the AMF approach: Antitrust legislation works against close cooperation between competing firms in the United States. Trying to promote competition while at the same time encouraging cooperation is difficult because of legal constraints, but the issue has to be dealt with if the efforts of AMF are to make any significant impact.

15.8 STRATEGIC ALLIANCES

Organizational flexibility also can be achieved with the help of other organizations—for instance, through a firm's vendors. Although antitrust laws limit alliances among competing firms within the United States, that is not an issue for getting ahead in other countries. Joint ventures or strategic alliances are an important vehicle for a company entering a market in a foreign country, especially if the economic activity in the foreign country is tightly controlled by the government (as in mainland China) or if the economic structure of the country is difficult to penetrate (as in Japan).

In recent years, strategic alliances have become more popular between corporations within a developed country or economy as well as between corporations from different developed countries with the purpose of serving multiple countries. A consortium may be formed to undertake projects in one particular country or to develop trade across many international borders.

Strategic alliances are seldom undertaken strictly for economic reasons or even for economies of scale; more likely, they are to benefit from others' technological, engineering, financial, or marketing strengths. Often the purpose is to gain access to a new market, to stimulate faster product development, to help develop new market(s), and to attain operational flexibility.

An example of a successful strategic alliance is the one between Ford and Mazda. Their cooperation has extended to both engineering and manufacturing. In the engineering area, Mazda designs the small cars and Ford designs the four-wheel-drive vehicles. Both types of vehicles are then marketed and sold under both Ford and Mazda brand names. In the manufacturing area, the two firms also share resources and produce vehicles that are sold under both the Ford and Mazda brand names. By sharing engineering and manufacturing, both firms can offer a broader range of models than either one could alone. Both firms also share each other's expertise in other areas such as marketing and accounting.

Violation of antitrust laws is a constant concern in the Ford-Mazda strategic alliance. But because Mazda is a Japanese firm and Ford is a U.S. firm, and joint marketing does not occur, the antitrust laws are not violated. The Ford-Mazda strategic alliance can be viewed as a strategic alliance that has as its main purpose economies of scope through each firm's ability to offer a wider array of vehicles.

15.9 WHAT ALLOWS ALLIANCES TO WORK

If a joint venture is to work, it must be appropriately structured. When the two partners bring equal strengths to the venture, it has a high chance of success. Management of the joint venture usually works best when one of the partners takes control and responsibility (a condition to be agreed on prior to formation of the venture). If both sides share in the management of a joint venture, it is almost certainly doomed to failure. It becomes a case of too many cooks working on the same broth.

Often large joint ventures by two partners are set up as separate corporations with their own boards of directors and organization. For example, Dow Corning Inc. is a joint venture between Dow Chemical and Corning. Dow Corning has grown into a large corporation and is a member of the Fortune 500. Other joint venture partners include Merck and Johnson & Johnson; Merck and DuPont; Merck and A.B. Astra of Sweden; IBM, Siemens of Germany, and Toshiba of Japan; and Corning and Vitro of Mexico. The most important benefit of strategic alliances is the ability to use the strengths unique to each of the partners. Such alliances provide management with the means to take advantage of opportunities, share risks, and compete while relying on existing expertise, instead of creating it anew.

15.10 FUTURE PROSPECTS

In the coming years, to be adaptive and flexible, corporations will use teamwork and demand close cooperation among members of functional areas (if those functional areas still exist in their traditional formats). Teams will be flexible and changeable. They will be organized around tasks, activities, and projects. In many cases activity or project management will replace the traditional functional area framework. Functional areas, where they still exist, will become service activities providing support and services to the team activities and projects.

To make such organizational structure possible, human resources departments must develop new means of knowing the employees and inventorying their skill portfolios. They also must be ready to retrain and further educate the employees, because the skills needed to work in a changing environment will change as well.

The new adaptive, flexible corporation will have to develop and maintain efficiencies of scope, that is, the ability to deliver a wide variety of products or services to a constantly changing marketplace. Cost alone will not matter. Economies of scale will still be important in many high-volume markets, but economies of scale alone will not be sufficient to be competitive in the global marketplace of the future. In fact, companies that had located production plants overseas, due to lower costs, are now coming back to North America because of other competitive efficiencies.

In the product development area, the focus will be on global customers. Indeed, global markets will be the drivers for product development. This does not imply that products will be standardized for all global markets. Diversity will remain a key requirement to remain competitive across the diversity and barrier of cultures, languages, and national tastes. In the future, firms will be required to practice a mode of behavior very different from the one that made Henry Ford say that his customers could have any color car they wanted, as long as it was black. Because of the need for a wide variety of products for each national or regional market, a central focus on product development, design, and production through project teams will ensure that response to global market changes will not be hampered by the borders between nations and regions.

For many decades, the successful corporation was one with a hierarchical management organization, focused on efficiency and economies of scale and with a vast marketing division to promote and sell its products. The organization was organized along functional lines, with each functional area operating somewhat independently and focused on its own interests. Control was exercised through strong financial controls but relatively weak controls in the critical areas that add value, such as quality, manufacturing, inventory, engineering, and product development.

Nowadays, the new adaptive and flexible environment within which organizations function makes it imperative for them to be flexible and able to respond to changes in the market, the industry structure, the customer base, the technology, and other critical areas, including the social, cultural, and political. The organizational focus must be on customers and on satisfying their present and future needs. The organization must anticipate customer needs and respond to them by developing products and/or services to meet those new needs and wants.

15.11 REALIZING THE MAXIMUM CUSTOMER POTENTIAL

The organization will have to be faster, more agile, and capable of responding to the changing needs and wants of its customers. The successful corporation of the future will focus on customer needs and wants. In fact, corporations are and will continue to devote major efforts to understanding customer behavior.

Grocery stores, airlines, and financial service companies are devoting considerable resources to learn more about their customers, because doing so allows them to offer what is being called *value exchange*. AT&T, Taco Time, and FedEx go to considerable lengths to determine their customers' needs because they have learned that today's customers no longer pay for "value" they do not need or desire. First USA, based in Texas, has experienced enormous growth by tailoring its credit card offers to the specific needs of its customers. The card offerings are differentiated by annual interest rates, the fees charged, the credit limit, and other add-ons, such as insurance coverage on rental cars.

Such attempts to tailor one's products and services to the specific combination of customers needs and tastes will not be possible without the benefit of the current information technology. This technology allows organizations to keep track of their customers and to analyze and anticipate their behavior. In addition to the technology, firms need to be certain of whom they want to serve and with what. They need to select the customers they want to have.

They cannot and need not be everything to everyone; instead, they must target customers and demographic segments. They must analyze consumer behavior and invest in predictive behavior models that tell them what segment of the customer base is likely to provide the best contribution margins. They also must invest in revising their operational processes to provide better customer service. Be it insurance or air travel, customers like better and faster service. Cross-functionally trained employees who can better serve customers are crucial, as is differentiating the customers at the outset and directing them to the right person who can answer the customers' concerns.

In the traditional hierarchical command and control structure inherent in many companies, managers become responsible to each other instead of to their customers. In the customer-driven company, the focus on the customer affects how management and employees think about their work, their responsibilities, and how they fit into the organization. The customer focus has provided a new orientation that provides motivation to employees and gives them incentives to get to better know and serve their customers and satisfy their needs.

15.12 IMPEDIMENTS TO ATTAINING ADAPTIBILITY

Tomorrow's corporations must be flexible and adaptive to respond to changes in the environment, and they must be proactive in seeking ways in which they can gain advantage over their competitors. To become organizationally flexible, agile, and adaptive requires teamwork; awareness of employee skills and competencies; in-depth knowledge of customer behavior; continual focus on reducing response time; and continuous improvement in the quality and durability of products, services, and value provided.

Becoming organizationally flexible, agile, and adaptive costs a great deal. These costs must, of course, be borne by the corporation that is becoming competitive; not all of them can be borne by the customers. Customers will not cease to be price-conscious; cost and the ability to be cost-competitive will always be important. Some expenses should not be construed as costs but rather as necessary investments that can set in motion returns that get compounded over time. Investments in flexibility, if managed properly, can lead to a snowballing of benefits in time, even as costs incurred are reduced.

One cannot invest one's way to organizational flexibility. A number of hazardous potholes exist on the road to acquiring adaptive competence, and none is more potentially dangerous than failure of the change managers to fully appreciate human factors. Equally dangerous can be a confusion with respect to the goal of organizational ability to adapt.

Managers must decide what they really want: making different products in sequential runs; making many products at the same time in a given location; trimming the setup cost of different production runs; changing production volume to suit customer demands; increasing the range of products available; employees who are able to do many things and are also eager to learn what they need to in response to changing needs. Flexibility can deal with number of products, production volumes, and processes as well as the skills, knowledge, and adaptability of employees. It boils down to the ability to adapt oneself to do all or any of these things.

Such ability can best be cultivated when there is a congruence in all the factors involved and their interaction: technology; organizational structure; training opportunities available to workers; reward and compensation schemes; awareness of customer demands and market conditions; the willingness of managers to encourage change, experimentation, and risk-taking on the part of the organization; and, perhaps most important, knowing exactly what kind of flexibility is desired. Without a managerial cultivation, such congruence cannot be attained.

Yet another requirement is knowing the role technology can play. Investments in technology do not always produce results—they can, in fact, turn into straitjackets. Both software and hardware can be culpable. Technology does not by itself reduce setup or product changeover time—they depend on operators who are nimble and adaptive thinkers. Technology is still useful, even if huge investments in computer-integrated manufacture is problematic. Technology helps information processing; it can improve or redesign operational processes, and is indispensable if one is seeking organizational adaptive competence in a global context. The human factor is the most crucial factor in an organization's ability to respond like a shrub and not be uprooted like a tree in a windstorm.

15.13 IMPLEMENTING A STRATEGY FOR CHANGE

If proposed changes are meeting resistance among employees, it could be because they are drastic in nature and were imposed without any warning. Given such imposition from above, resistance on the part of employees is to be expected. Resistance can be minimized through participation, education, communication, and facilitation. Sharing with employees the rationale behind the changes is a good first step in fostering cooperation among all levels of employees. Dissatisfaction within the organization can be a great motivator for implementing evolutionary changes.

Changes become more acceptable to employees if they are involved in the planning and implementation of change. Their participation allows them to better understand the change itself and the reasons for making the change.

Open communication between various administrative layers should also help reduce employees' fears and uncertainty. Communication is essential for employees' participation in the planning and implementation of the changes. Furthermore, changes ought to be made gradually. Abrupt imposition of major changes can cause resistance among the employees. Management should also take care to ensure it is not promoting change as a magic, instantaneous cure without any discomfort or side effects. The changes must not be seen by employees as change for the sake of change or, even worse, as being faddish.

At the same time, managers should not wait indefinitely for the resistance to subside. There is always going to be fear, anger, and uncertainty in the wake of change; if the choice is entirely up to employees, they will opt for the path of least uncertainty. While educating the employees and establishing open communication, managers may sometimes find it necessary to mandate the change, even if employees are unenthusiastic. Acceptance of the changes will grow as employees recognize the benefits.

Implementation must be well planned and evaluated strategically prior to being put into effect. Changes can be less than optimal if plans are the result of oversimplification or if the difficulties involved are underestimated. They also will be counterproductive if they rely entirely on technology while ignoring human factors.

Care should be taken to ensure that implementation takes place as planned. Once the change has been implemented, efforts should be made to measure its impact.

15.14 WHY THE IMPERATIVE TO EVOLVE?

The operating environment changed in the 1990s. International competition, the end of the Cold War, new technologies, and worldwide demographic changes are all making the world a different place from what it was in the quarter century following World War II. Back then, the increases in demands allowed American firms to ignore quality issues and even customers' concerns. They usually could rely on marketing to pull the sales through for them. But to their chagrin, foreign competition began delivering products and services that far exceeded customer expectations.

There is a tendency to retreat into a buy-American isolationism and to erect artificial barriers to counter the shrinking of the globe. But neither such ostrich-like behavior nor the short-term remedies of "trimming the fat" and emphasizing "lean and mean" management is likely to develop viable institutional evolutionary competence.

Management experts, such as Peter Drucker, seem to be calling for institutional organization that incorporates built-in structures to respond to change, indeed make the ability to change faster than the competition a cardinal virtue and a strategic advantage. According to current theory, knowledge is power and knowledge is always evolving. The experts are calling for organizations to force change, to examine periodically what they do, and to justify to themselves and their stakeholders the adequacy or viability of what they do and what they know. In making their arguments, the experts cite cutting-edge organizations that are able to bail out before the markets reach maturity or saturation, and can do so because of their willingness to cultivate organizational learning, the essence of any evolutionary strategy.

Throughout the ages and all over the world, educational institutions have fostered learning and continue to do so globally. Their nearly universal presence argues that the structure educational institutions provide and the environment they create makes for improved learning. Giving individuals books and letting them read if and when they so desire is not seen as the optimum way to promote learning. Similarly, organizations must also provide structures, occasions, and incentives to foster institutional learning. The role being argued in this book for the procedures documentation process does just that; it structures organizational learning and institutionalizes evolution.

Institutional survival and organizational evolution need not be a matter of random chance. An ability to prevail over changing and even hostile environments can be learned and institutionalized, provided the organization makes available to all its employees opportunities to learn and then uses the experience and knowledge acquired as a result of such opportunities. These opportunities can be as ordinary as simply changing the prevailing perception of the documentation process as being merely archival. Opportunities for organizational learning have been provided by cutting-edge organizations in recent years as part of their organizational strategic design.

At the outset, a variety of approaches and practices are utilized, depending on the views of individual managers and on the perceived needs of their companies. The provision of such opportunities becomes a part of the organization's strategy. By and large, the learning opportunities made available by institutions must not be seen as reactive, ad hoc attempts to fight daily crises; instead, they must become part of a long-term design and culture.

15.15 TIME-BASED COMPETENCE

Organizational ability to be flexible is not the only approach to organizational evolution. Organizations are using time-based strategies to improve their operational and strategic competencies. The adage that time is money now has a new meaning, given the manner in which firms are seeking to reduce the time it takes them to respond to their customers or to changes in the markets they serve.

Specifically, *time-based competence* refers to the ability to respond to demands made by customers. The following illustration involving Wausau Paper Mills Company defines the concept. Wausau found that its plant was not set up to compete with larger competitors. It calculated that it would need to invest $600 million in new high-volume equipment to bring its technology up to the level of its larger competitors. Instead of investing capital in its plant machinery, it decided to differentiate itself from others in the industry by how fast it responded to its customers. It specifically decided to concentrate on lowering the time it needed to deliver orders to its customers. The time to deliver is now no longer weeks or even days; the firm delivers 95 percent of orders within twenty-four hours after receipt.

Wausau's rapid response enabled its customers to reduce their inventories substantially. Its customers were willing to pay higher prices in exchange for the reduction in their inventory holding costs. Through faster delivery, Wausau improved its competitive advantage. It elected to invest not in additional equipment to help lower its production cost but in improving its ability to respond to its customers faster and more efficiently. This strategy allowed it to compete despite its higher operating cost.

15.16 VARIOUS TIME-BASED COMPETENCIES

Time-based advantage can help an organization evolve. Activity-based management, cycle-time reduction, and just-in-time operations as well as concurrent engineering are approaches that allow an organization to achieve time-based evolution. All these approaches seek to reduce the time needed to undertake operational activities. All of them also rely on emergent technology. However, if the technology is to be of optimum help, the firms must first get rid of activities that consume resources without adding any value to processes, products, or services being provided. Such companies thus also rely on process analysis to differentiate between value-adding and non–value-added activities.

Reducing the cycle time of every task, activity, or project in an organization is now considered by many firms to be the best means of lowering cost, improving quality, reducing excess inventory, becoming more flexible, motivating employees, and improving customer satisfaction. There is no question that consumer satisfaction and cycle-time reduction are closely related.

The success achieved by firms that provide quick or instant service is clear and well documented in the professional literature. Instant banking, twenty-four-hour restaurants and supermarkets, frequent flight schedules, and airline shuttle service with on-board ticketing are all examples of time-based competition allowing quick turnaround times or reduced cycle times. The various time-based competencies are indeed useful tools that help firms evolve, no matter what they are engaged in: manufacturing, retailing, wholesaling, transportation, or any other form of activity.

15.17 WHAT DOES IT TAKE TO REDUCE CYCLE TIME?

Obviously there are many benefits from reducing cycle time in day-to-day operations. Cycle-time reduction provides considerable value especially to an organization's customers. For instance, reducing sizes of orders and shipping orders out more frequently not only helps lower finished goods inventory levels, it leads to greater customer satisfaction. Similarly, ordering smaller batches of products from suppliers lowers inventory levels and in the process reduces inventory holding costs, pilferage costs, and obsolescence costs. The reduction in inventory levels on hand or the frequency of orders placed do not by themselves lead to organizational improvement or enhanced customer service. Instead, the lower inventory levels lead to improved planning and scheduling, which in turn leads to organizational evolution.

Along with organizational planning, cycle-time reduction requires not only the internal cooperation of employees but extensive retraining of the workers as well. In addition, suppliers' cooperation is needed. More often than not, such cooperation can be attained only when suppliers are not treated as adversaries to be played off against each other. Knowing what customers want is also important to ensure that cycle-time reduction does not become counterproductive. Success as a time-based competitor requires cooperation from all parties that interface in day-to-day operations.

The meaning of cycle-time reduction is best broadly defined. It should not mean only the cycle time of a specific manufacturing or administrative operation; rather, it should be seen in the context of the entire process, not its individual steps. It is not sufficient to focus on a faster response to questions asked by customers. Responding to a customer's inquiry, request, or complaint can take varying amounts of time, depending on the nature of the response itself and the availability of resources. Clearly, both internal and external customers like their needs to be responded to instantaneously, but in most cases they have to wait because the resources are not there. Response time can be improved by differentiating between questions and directing them to those who can provide answers.

Responding to the customer may not be simply a matter of coming through with an answer to a question. Selling an insurance policy is an example where more than a simple inquiry is involved. College admissions also could be considered as being more than just a question requiring a simple answer. An adequate response could involve performing a project that requires many people and involves many activities, interactions, or consultations. A sale involves marketing, the credit department, production scheduling, production itself, packing, the warehouse, and shipping. Any or all departments could introduce delay. Making sure that a project spanning many departments can be completed in the shortest possible time requires effective coordination, rapid responses, swift communication, and continual interaction among all participants in the project. Such interaction is what time-based competencies, grounded in reducing cycle time and getting rid of non–value-added activities, are all about.

Considerable assistance in achieving time-based competition is derived from electronic and computer-based technology. Electronic data interchange systems now connect many suppliers with the central or hub firm, and many customers are similarly connected with the central or hub firm. This communications technology provides considerable potential improvement through its ability to compress activities such as ordering supplies, receiving orders from customers, and sending modifications of orders or specifications to suppliers. Similarly, customers can revise their orders, modify specifications, lodge complaints, and otherwise communicate with the hub or central firm instantaneously. Electronic data interchange thus provides rapid communications between customers and suppliers. However, cycle-time reduction can be achieved fully only if the receivers of the information react immediately, or at least promptly, to the information transmitted by electronic data interchange messages. Furthermore, information must *aid* decision making, not replace it. Doing so leads to rule-based management, and management-by-the-book does not rival human creativity.

Cycle-time reduction or time-based competition is beginning to be actively practiced by many firms. It has proven to be a focused way to improve operations, reduce waste, enhance product design and development, and improve quality and customer satisfaction. Cycle-time improvements allow changes to be incorporated in products more quickly, allow faster response to customers' complaints, and lead to a reduction in inventory obsolescence. Customers are more satisfied because their requests, orders, and specification changes are responded to quickly.

The reduction of waste extends not only to reduction of material waste but also to valuable time spent by employees in nonproductive activities. In addition, resources and time may be wasted not just from non–value-added activities, but also from the way in which products are designed. The more complex their design, the more time-consuming production will become. Expense vouchers with five copies will require more processing time; so will a printer whose design calls for a large number of separate parts. There is a growing trend toward reengineering products through redesign and away from redesigning processes.

15.18 USING CYCLE TIME TO GAIN COMPETITIVE ADVANTAGE

The success of the Japanese in world markets for manufactured goods, and especially for traditional goods, is often traced to their ability to produce a higher-quality, more dependable product for the same or a lower price than the traditional competition. There is yet another reason for their rise to higher levels. It is their ability to do things faster. The successful Japanese firms are able to respond much quicker than their rivals, be they Japanese, European, or American.

An example of such response can be seen by comparing Honda's Acura division to General Motors' Saturn division. The formation of both divisions was announced at about the same time, but Honda's Acura division had already completed three major Acura model changes before Saturn reached the marketplace.

Another example of competitive advantage acquired through mastery of cycle-time reduction is the expertise Mitsubishi brings to the making and marketing of its heat pumps. Between 1979 and 1988, Mitsubishi was able to introduce either a major design change or a new feature to its three-horsepower heat pump, including the introduction of integrated circuits to control the heat pump cycle in 1980. The American firms that were competing against Mitsubishi could not match those rapid technological changes. They even started buying their critical components from Mitsubishi! As a result, Mitsubishi increased not only its market share but also the value provided to customers by heat pumps it sold.

Yet another example of how cycle time can be used to gain advantage over one's competition relates to the rivalry between Honda and Yamaha, two major manufacturers of motorcycles. Honda was able to introduce new product features or new product models at a faster pace than Yamaha, its major competitor, and this allowed it to outsell Yamaha. Both firms marketed about the same number of models. However, Honda was able, within a period of eighteen months, to turn its product line over twice, by introducing new models or rapidly replacing its existing models. It introduced new features, such as four-cycle engines, and started using components made from composite materials that strengthened and lightened the motorcycles. In contrast, Honda's rival could turn over only about half its product line in the same time frame. The impact on Yamaha, because of its failure to move its inventory of motorcycles, was significant. The Honda-Yamaha rivalry illustrates how one firm, by being able to change product designs quickly, can gain a significant competitive advantage over a major competitor.

Americans are starting to catch up. Time-based improvements were utilized effectively in the design and development of the Ford Taurus. Ford abandoned its rigidly hierarchical, top-down pyramid approach to product design and replaced it with a hub-rim approach. Under this approach, the overall design and development program management remains at the center (the hub), while all other design and development activities (such as automobile styling, product engineering, manufacturing engineering, manufacturing itself, purchasing, logistics, and suppliers) are on the rim, connected by spokes to the center of the wheel—the overall design and development team.

Ford sought time-based design improvement with the help of structural changes to its organization. Concurrent engineering and the theory of constraint are approaches that help an organization attain cycle-time reduction.

15.19 CONCURRENT ENGINEERING

The traditional approach to organizational management was based on departmentalization. An organization typically consisted of many functional departments that served as quasi-autonomous entities. Often these functionally organized departments got into each other's bad graces. Anecdotes about conflicts between accounting and computer departments are numerous, as are reports of conflicts between production and marketing. One could argue that organizational structures in place in American firms exemplified functional specialization gone overboard.

In recent years, businesses have realized that when individual departments act as independent fiefdoms, they take something away from the organization as a whole, making it less than the sum of its departmental parts. Such realization was brought home to Americans in large part from observing the faster response on the part of Japanese businesses to market forces and customers' needs. The Japanese could bring out new product models much faster than could their American counterparts. Even though the Americans had better technology to work with in their factories, the synergy seemed to be lacking. The culprit, in many instances, was departmental division taken to extremes.

Since the 1980s, there have been attempts to break down the barriers that exist among the different organizational departments of a business. Such efforts have been given different names, among them *integrated functional approach* and *concurrent engineering*. Some experts have called the approach *overlapping* and have differentiated it from the traditional sequential approach. Whatever the label, the approach is grounded in improving communication and interaction among departments. No longer do various departments in the organization take turns doing their bit for the project; instead, their roles overlap, and there is a considerable degree of interaction among them. Instead of being like autonomous states not on speaking terms with each other, departments are urged to cooperate, coordinate, and integrate their respective roles.

Traditionally, product styling came before design, which preceded engineering. This sequential progress was slow and cumbersome. Under concurrent engineering, all three of them can work together, or at least have considerable interaction among them as the product evolves. Even though concurrent engineering is mostly associated with product manufacturing, it does not have to be limited thereto. Its underlying philosophy of not allowing artificial barriers to delay communication, hamper coordination, or preclude cooperation between functional areas can apply equally well to academia, merchandising, and governmental units.

The philosophy permeating concurrent engineering is very pertinent to effective performance of various accounting functions. For instance, paying bills can be much less of an ordeal if ordering, receiving, and actual use of the goods ordered was coordinated with paying for them.

Attempts to do away with departmental structure entirely can be counterproductive, however. Specialization came about because it served a function, and doing away entirely with functional specializations will lead one to reinvent them out of sheer necessity. It is far better not to throw away the good, even while one prunes away the overgrowth that is responsible for delays and that gets in the way of functional integration. Emergent information technology, with its local area networks, wide area networks, and client servers, makes integration more feasible than in the past. Technology is here, and organizational culture must change to use it most appropriately.

15.20 THEORY OF CONSTRAINTS

Another technique to help improve time-based organizational competencies is the theory of constraints (TOC). This theory is grounded in the belief that the output of systems and organizations is limited by the constraints. Were it not for constraints, organizations or even individuals would be able to accomplish whatever they desire to do. Individuals are well aware that what we desire and what we actually can perform are not congruent.

The TOC views businesses as a linked sequence of processes and subprocesses that seek to convert inputs into outputs that can be sold. Not all processes (links in the chain) are equally efficient, and some actually retard the entire sequence by causing logjams. Those implementing TOC seek to identify such constraints and to remedy the situation by removing those constraints. The TOC does not have to be limited to just manufacturing, as constraints can occur in every context—there are weak links in all chains.

The TOC approach seeks to identify the constraint that is most retarding and delaying the production. Once the worst constraint is identified, the immediate reaction ought to be not to overload the system; rather, work within the limitations imposed by the constraint. Nevertheless, one need not accept the status quo implicit in the work centers causing the logjams. Management, once the constraint is identified, must concentrate on remediation of the causes that create the logjams. Once a given constraint is corrected, other constraints are focused on.

In contrast to some other approaches, the TOC is appealing because it is incremental and works within current systems. It does not seek to replace everything, just to fix the problems, especially those whose impact seems to be widespread. It will even tolerate a considerable amount of slack in the process to not overload the constraint.

Certainly accounting department and functions suffer from a variety of constraints. As we have argued, such weak links in the process must be recognized while documenting various functions. If the documentation process is to become an occasion to foster evolutionary competence, it must be used to analyze and identify the causes leading to delays. Identifying the non–value-added activities and getting rid of them is one approach; getting rid of what causes logjams or constrains the system is another. Both can coexist and complement the other.

Effective use of managerial time is equally important. The constraints on the effective management of time cannot be ignored, because they also can hamper performance. The manner in which managers manage their time and their priorities can itself turn into an organizational constraint.

Time-based evolution is important and very useful to organizations seeking to excel and sometimes just to survive. As stated earlier, the growing attention being paid to improving response time is in effect a recognition that time is money. Being more responsive to market forces and customer needs can ensure that time turns into profit.

CHAPTER 16

REPERTOIRE OF THE DEMING APPROACH

16.1 INTRODUCTION

This chapter seeks to advance the techniques that help organizations attain the evolutionary competence. The focus in this chapter is on providing an overview of total quality environment (TQE), which will allow readers to incorporate elements of it into the process governing the documentation of accounting procedures manual. Naming this chapter after Edward Deming is a recognition of the fact that the contemporary concern of managers around the world for implementing TQE—also referred to as *kaizen,* continuous improvement, and total quality management—within their respective organizations is largely owing to his efforts.

TQE has spawned other approaches to improve work, such as process redesign, activity-based costing, and the learning organization paradigm. Ample literature describes success stories stemming from the use of these techniques. This evidence helps to substantiate the value and practicality of using TQE, process redesign, activity-based costing, and the learning organization paradigm to enhance organizational performance and processes.

16.2 WHAT IS TOTAL QUALITY ENVIRONMENT?

The focus of TQE is quality, but it must not be taken to mean simply a freedom from defects. Instead, organizational TQE should be seen as being concerned with an ongoing self-examination on the part of an organization directed to improve all aspects of its performance. TQE is concerned on a continuous basis with doing things better, not just in a factory but in offices, schools, and even our homes. The starting point for such continuous efforts is self-knowledge: that is, an understanding of what organizational components do, why they do it, who does it, where they do it, and the resources it requires to get done. The organizational, departmental, and individual self-knowledge sought by TQE is not couched in abstract terms. In other words, statistics and quantitative performance measures serve as surrogates to facilitate an understanding of what, why, who, where, and how. To make organizational understanding tangible, performance measures drawn from statistics are brought into the picture. Using statistics, it is possible to portray and forecast how a given system operates and see to it that the system continues to operate in an efficient manner.

In effect, statistics help to isolate variances in managerial and production processes. They help to identify exceptions that are random and not subject to control, as well as variances that are due to a given source or a malfunction in the production or managerial process. This permits supervisors to practice management by exception and allocate their attention to problems that can be controlled, if not solved. In contrast to accounting standard cost variances, the TQE variances are not expressed in monetary amounts. Instead of translating production measures into the relatively unfamiliar jargon of accounting terminology, production is described through terms such as labor time, time needed to complete a batch, material usage, number of units produced, and number of units rejected. Using the language of the production department makes the production-related exceptions more familiar to those responsible and thus allows easier solutions for those exceptions. Converting various production factors into monetary amounts does not provide any greater insight to those interested in those factors. The number of hours a process took is easier to represent than the number of hours times price per hour, because price is subject to a greater degree of fluctuation than are the hours needed to complete a process. For airlines, graphing a distribution consisting of fuel consumed for each mile flown is more predictable than a distribution of fuel cost per mile flown.

16.3 NOT BEING CONTENT WITH THE STATUS QUO

In addition to the concern with self-awareness, TQE also is based on a belief that an organization and its various components cannot remain still. Instead of being content with the status quo, TQE seeks ongoing evolution, continuous improvement. Like self-knowledge, self-improvement is also meant to be tangible and measurable. To become tangible, improvements are described in statistical measures. Improvement in the safety record can be measured by the reduction in the number of actual accidents that occur.

The Deming-inspired gospel of TQE does not subscribe to the notion of maintaining the status quo; instead, it urges that the system should be improved continuously. Maintaining the status quo can lead only to obsolescence. Continuous improvement of the system is facilitated through a constancy of focus and an understanding of the mission.

In acquiring and constantly renewing the understanding of their mission, individuals and organizations must be able to go beyond the obvious. Universities may see their role as teaching accounting, when in fact they are teaching the means to measure and report about an organization's present performance and its future prospects in monetary terms. Those involved in the business of making horse buggies may have thought they were making buggies, when in fact they were providing people with means of transportation. Those who could not see beyond horses and buggies became obsolete, but those who saw themselves as being involved in the transportation business moved on to the horseless carriages of the twentieth century. Fiber optics may well be the horseless carriage of the twenty-first century, accomplishing business interaction without requiring the hassles and hazards of travel. By transporting work to the employees, instead of the employees to work, technology can and is redefining the focus of transportation.

16.4 CHANGE IS INEXORABLE

A major part of being focused in a continuously changing environment is keeping up with customers, knowing not just their current needs but also being in tune with their potential future wants. Customers' preferences are subject to redefinition with the changing of environment. A critical factor for TQE is the realization that nothing can or ought to remain unchanged. Instead, those responsible for doing the work should strive for constant improvement in the way things are done. To improve processes, it is important to first understand them. Second, within an organization there must be uniformity regarding how specific processes are performed. It is the function of management to see that all workers are following standard operating procedures. Through policies, rules, directives, training, and, if need be, disciplinary action, employees must be made to follow the standard procedures.

After such uniformity is achieved, managers and employees ought to focus on improving the process by doing things better. Improving means setting higher standards and then making sure they are met. Meeting the standards involves solving problems and overcoming obstacles. Furthermore, the attainment of set standards is not judged entirely on the basis of end results achieved. Managers seeking to implement TQE must not limit themselves to judging by the results; instead they should measure the efforts that go into improving the process. A sales manager may not limit himself just to evaluating the units sold; instead, he must analyze the time spent on cultivating rapport with customers, developing new customers, and examining the sales approach of the individual salespeople. TQE does not limit itself to the summary reports, the proverbial bottom line; instead, it is also oriented to the underlying efforts.

Following the establishment and attainment of higher standards, it is necessary to ensure that the improvements are monitored on an ongoing basis. Such maintenance of the improved performance level is akin to catching one's breath before starting the upward spiral movement again. The ongoing climb up the spiral is done through what is known as the Deming cycle, which consists of the following steps:

Plan: Decide what needs to be done: define the problem, analyze it, identify its causes, and develop solutions
Do: Implement the plan agreed upon and decide on measures that will help judge and evaluate the implementation
Check: See that the implementation of the plan is having the desired impact
Act: Explore to see what could be improved upon next

In business parlance, the Deming cycle's four steps correspond to designing a product, producing the product, selling it, and then researching possible improvements in the product itself or in the way it is made.

Self-awareness and the perpetual search for improvement is the goal sought by the Deming cycle, calling for a Plan-Do-Check-Action approach on a continuous basis. Self-examination and the desire to improve leads to a plan that can be implemented. Such implementation then must be checked and measured to see if it follows the intended course of action. Once the desired improvement is firmly in place, an organization or its various components must once again subject itself to self-examination and a further search for improvement, which also will be implemented, checked, and measured to be followed by further self-examinations and quests for improvement.

16.5 SYSTEM AS A PROCESS

The quest for TQE is facilitated by seeing the organization as a system involved in interlinked processes, with beginnings and endings. Manufacturing or office systems are made up of several such interlinked and interdependent processes. Each process transforms input it receives from suppliers or an earlier process into something different by adding value to the input before sending it forth as an output. The problem in one process may have its origin somewhere upstream, and this origin may not be discovered, unless the interdependency of the processes is understood.

TQE's concern for organizational improvement is manifested in a realization that problems exist, but can be resolved by the cooperation of all those involved in the entire process, not just those directly responsible for problems. Problem resolution can be facilitated by addressing not just the symptoms but the underlying causes that are responsible for the existence of the problem. For example, 20 percent of the production may be unacceptable during a typical week. Following such diagnosis, steps can be taken to ensure that not only the symptoms but the underlying factors responsible for the unacceptable production are eliminated. Ideally, there should be no defects, but if they do occur, then the defective production must be eliminated as close to the source as possible. The farther downstream a problem is caught, the more expensive it is to the business. Additionally, an organization wastes money and resources when it is forced to have a significant amount of the workforce devoted to inspecting and catching mistakes made upstream. Quality should be the concern of everyone in the system, not just the quality inspectors.

TQE proceeds under the assumption that the unacceptable production is merely a symptom of underlying problems that exist within the system. Problems occurring at one stage of production can have roots in another part of the system. If accounting clerks are making too many mistakes entering data in the journals, then it may well be due to faulty design of the source documents and not the carelessness or the incompetence of the clerks.

Addressing the underlying causes may seem like a course of action calling for additional expenses and a major commitment of resources. However, such a course of action directed at improvement in quality actually can lead to lower costs. Quality should be the focus throughout the system, but quality cannot be assured by just inspecting the finished product or spending more money doing things the same old way.

16.6 CROSS-FUNCTIONAL COOPERATION, NOT DEPARTMENTAL COMPETITION

TQE thinking does not promote the isolating of a department. Instead of niche obsessions and turf protections, it calls for cross-functional approaches to quality assurance, cost reduction, safety, product innovation, and vendor relations as well as in meeting production quotas and delivery schedules. If the system is to work well and if it is to improve, the individual functions that comprise a process must cooperate and not compete. The cogs must move in unison if the wheel is to continue its movements. Activities such as individual performance evaluation or performance rating can direct attention away from the system. They can make workers compete with each other, instead of working for the good of the system. Management must lead, but should do so by getting all the components of the system to work together instead of competing with each other.

Such cross-functional cooperation is made easier when workers understand what they are doing and why they do it. They must not be simply trained but educated—make everyone smarter, so that they will work smarter. Being educated means acquiring an expertise that allows employees to see not just the symptoms of a problem but also gives them the motivation to learn the underlying causes responsible for the problematic exceptions and variances. Workers must be educated to see not just the twigs and the leaves on an individual branch but to reflect upon the entire tree (of which the branch, with its twigs and leaves, is only a small part) and even the forest, together with its environment.

Cooperation applies not only to internal processes, such as different departments and responsibility centers within the systems, but also to the external processes linked with a given system, such as the vendors, who supply the raw material for a factory or consumer goods for a department store. Customers can be those buying the finished product, or they can be the employees working on the product-in-process at the next stage of its manufacture. The customers, be they internal or external, should not be treated as adversaries but as an integral extension of the system. The vendors upstream, as well as the customers downstream, must be seen as part of the system, as partners, whose satisfaction should be the motivating force as well as the "weather vane" for the firm.

Customers' satisfaction is the most important factor a business must consider, notwithstanding its quirkiness and irritating unpredictability. A business's reason for being is making sure that its customers are satisfied enough to keep coming back for more. If anything can be described as representing the core of TQE, it would be the desire to satisfy the customers and to remove whatever inconveniences them.

16.7 WHO DOES WHAT IN TOTAL QUALITY ENVIRONMENTS

Typically, organizations are made up of layers of top managers, middle managers, supervisors, and employees. The numbers in each organizational layer follow an increasing order—one queen bee, presumably a few supervisor bees, and many workers. In bringing about continuous improvement and keeping the organizational hive functional, all of them have roles to play. In the context of TQE, the functions of each layer are as follows:

Top managers:	Must decide a strategy for improvement and then let their plans be known throughout the firm. They must provide support and direction as well as conduct ongoing audits to see that the policy as established and plans as drafted are being implemented. Without their total commitment to its implementation, the structure of organizational TQE could never get off the ground. It is their responsibility to make sure that the middle management and supervisors are also dedicated to implementing TQE.
Middle managers:	Help to bring about a cross-functional perspective. They also establish, maintain, and ensure the upgrading of standards. This may require them to conduct skill audits to see that workers have the skills needed to implement plans. When TQE is getting off its foundation, the middle managers must learn that there is a culture change underway that empowers the employees to use their initiative, downplays organizational chain of authority, and fosters team efforts. The efforts directed at culture change, so crucial to the success of TQE, can be sabotaged if the middle managers insist on maintaining rigid organizational structures.
Supervisors:	They serve as the link between managers and workers. They may be called upon to maintain discipline, suggest improvements, and explain to workers what needs to be done. The supervisors, like the middle managers, must promote team spirit rather than insisting on playing the role of authoritarian taskmasters.
Workers:	They carry out established procedures, but at the same time are empowered and encouraged to use their work experience to suggest ways to improve the process. They also engage in self-improvement through education and training.

16.8 IMPLEMENTATION LEVELS FOR TOTAL QUALITY ENVIRONMENT

Improvements cannot be implemented only at the management level, since they must filter down throughout the organization to be effective. The implementation of TQE requires tailoring the implementation to suit the organizational layer where it is being implemented. Some experts argue that TQE's implementation at the management level, segment/process level, and individual level will require different perspectives. Implementation at the three levels will use similar tools and will be interdependent; however, the three respective implementations differ in their scope and duration. Management-level TQE implementation lasts for the entire duration of a project, which may be spread over several years, while the segment-level project may last only a few months and is limited within the segment. The action at the individual level may be instantaneous and is limited to a specific employee. At the management level, managers and professionals are integrally involved in the TQE approach; at the segment level, it is likely to be a group of people, such as those working in a quality circle; at the individual level, each employee works for TQE individually, albeit in a supportive environment, accompanied by others who are also working for TQE.

The costs of improvements at the individual level are relatively low but are higher at the group and the management level. Changing the factory layout can only be authorized at the management level; decreasing the level of inventory maintained or adopting the just-in-time approach are also management-level decisions. Improving processes through quality circles is an example of segment-level TQE, while a suggestion system exemplifies individual-level TQE.

16.9 SETTING THE STAGE FOR TOTAL QUALITY ENVIRONMENT

Introducing TQE into an organization almost always involves a culture change. Such a change requires profound efforts. A survey of the literature describing implementation of TQE around the world suggests that the following factors should be considered prior to implementing TQE:

(a) Concern for the Customers

TQE starts with the willingness to place customers' satisfaction as the motivation, the raison d'être, for all organizational efforts. Customer satisfaction must be measured in terms that reflect quality, price, and delivery. Efforts must be made to monitor customers' perceptions and to measure them on an ongoing basis.

(b) Recognizing the Links

A fundamental tenet of TQE has been the knowledge that product or service quality downstream is best attained by helping to inspire it upstream. If the high schools do a poor job, then the colleges will have a much harder time ensuring that their graduates are properly educated. The concept holds not only for processes within the firm but also applies to the relationships between the firm and its suppliers and customers. The efforts to implement TQE must include every link in the chain. To ensure that, a firm must not think of the vendors who supply the raw materials or those who actually sell its products as adversaries.

(c) Getting Everyone Involved

Recently the College of Business of a midsized, privately owned American university sought to implement TQE. The dean, prodded by his associates, agreed that the initial step needed was to hold a faculty retreat to come up with ideas and to set the stage. For economic reasons, only 40 percent of the faculty were invited to the weekend retreat held at a resort off-campus. Unfortunately, this favoritism was seen negatively by those who were not invited. Many of the uninvited saw their exclusion as akin to setting up a caste system, in which some were "in" and others were "out." As a result, those particular efforts at implementing TQE at the College of Business were doomed. In addition to universal inclusion, getting everyone to subscribe to the tenets of TQE requires open communication throughout the organization. It also calls for a relationship based on trust, loyalty, and cooperation between managers and employees. In committees that bring together supervisors and workers, it is imperative that supervisors stop supervising and deal with their employees in an egalitarian spirit. Otherwise, they will inhibit trust and communication.

(d) Process Orientation

Hitherto, the preferred organizational structure has been a departmental arrangement, but the focus of TQE is on processes that cross departmental lines. Accounting took care of the numbers that were reported in financial statements, while management information systems (MISs) tackled the machinery that processed the data into financial statements. The medium and the message went their separate ways, given the way accounting and systems guarded their respective areas under the prevailing departmental focus. However, a process focus can change the procedures and processes that comprise the accounting systems as well as the relationship between accounting and MIS. Getting managers, who were trained as relatively narrow specialists, to adopt a cross-functional process orientation is a demanding task, and calls for changes in an organization's planning and control systems as well as alternative means to measure and reward managerial performance.

(e) Longer Planning Horizons

American managers have become notorious for their short-term focus. But reaping the potential of TQE does not occur overnight, it requires extended cultivation and care. To benefit from TQE, managers must extend their horizons beyond improvement in the bottom line for the next quarter, and they must be allowed and encouraged to do so by the directors and the investors.

(f) Willingness to Seek Out Problems

Upon confronting problems, the typical manager's tendency is to ignore their existence. Managers and employees fear that they will be blamed for the problems they uncover. In addition to pretending that problems do not even exist, procrastination as to their solution seems the preferred choice of many supervisors and workers. Under TQE, problems are seen as opportunities for improvement rather than as skeletons that must be locked up in closets. The organization must encourage, and even train, its workers to find problems and then help find solutions in order to make TQE become a reality.

(g) Taking Time Out to Think through the Work

In addition to being willing to confront problems and exploit opportunities for improvement continuously, managers have to provide occasions to do so. While employees are consumed with everyday routines, they don't have time to seek out exceptions. TQE can be achieved only by stepping back and looking at routines and standard operating procedures with a new perspective. This requires provision for reflective occasions, retraining, continuing education, and intermingling of specializations and diversity of cultures. Learning is facilitated by institutionalized occasions and structures for it.

(h) Top Management's Commitment

All the factors listed require substantial and sustained efforts throughout the organization. They require a focus away from adversarial relationships and short-term focus. But what they require more than anything else is the dedication and wholehearted subscription of the senior management to the idea and culture of TQE. Some questions that must be raised, and which require positive answers, before implementing TQE are:

- Is top management dedicated to TQE as a corporate strategy?
- Is it committed to spending enough resources to really understand the implication of TQE for itself and the firm?
- Is it committed to introducing cross-functional focus in place of a niche approach?
- Is it willing to adopt the controls and corporate structures that will support cross-functional process emphasis?
- Is top management dedicated to making TQE an ongoing, intrinsic part of the organizational culture rather than a one-shot, seasonal fad?

16.10   IMPLEMENTING TOTAL QUALITY ENVIRONMENT

No matter how well intentioned the members of an organization are, they cannot just will TQE into being. Sustained efforts are needed to implement TQE. In this section we discuss what is required to implement quality management.

The improvement must start somewhere, and suggestions originating at any implementation level can set in motion the improvement process. Through suggestions provided by individuals, working on their own or in teams, almost every phase of work can be improved, among them:

- Ideas for new products
- Improvement in the use of tools
- Faster completion of processes
- Improvement in customer services
- More efficient use of resources
- Higher productivity and better safety records
- A more pleasant and less monotonous environment

While it is best to start with the problems, it is very common for workers to fail to see the problems. First, managers must educate workers to look for problems in their work routines.

The discovery of problems and/or opportunities can be made easier if daily routines are viewed with different perspectives. Putting groups of employees together makes it possible to look at old habits under a new light. Groups that are drawn from across the departments are even more likely to see old routines with new vision and think through the replacement of out-dated ways of doing things. Cross-functional teams can not only unearth problems but they can also help discover cutting-edge solutions.

Cross-functional management is central to the organizational implementation of a total quality program. Traditionally, companies are organized along functional lines such as design, production, marketing, and accounting. Each department works on a given, assigned function, and is, for all practical purposes, a separate entity unto itself. Such traditional hierarchies can be suboptimal when it concerns implementation of TQE. As a result, cross-functional management teams have evolved to help expedite policy implementation throughout the organization.

Goals having to do with quality assurance, cost reduction, and production scheduling cannot be limited to a given department; most, if not all, functional departments must get involved in order to attain them. This involvement can be accomplished through cross-functional teams. Functional departments can be assigned the responsibility of implementing tasks by the cross-functional teams. Cross-functional teams also help to minimize the impact of turf fighting among the functional departments.

Yet another reason for the use of cross-functional teams is to minimize the disruption that can occur if an organization is trying to continue with business while seeking to implement changes associated with TQE. Functional departments can maintain the current operations while the cross-functional teams seek out ways to improve and to implement them in an optimum manner. The cross-functional team members can serve as the liaison for their respective departments, keeping others informed about the team's progress.

The following points also need to be mentioned in connection with cross-functional (CF) teams:

- Cross-functional teams are organized at the top-management level. They may be assigned specific tasks, such as new product development, product design, raw material acquisition, sales inspection, profit management, and quality assurance.
- Cross-functional goals should be established before the determination of department goals. Using the organization-wide CF goals, each level develops its own goals that will help reach the overall goals drawn up by the CF teams.
- Cross-functional policy should be formulated in terms of goals before it is deployed. The same applies to the goals developed at each level within the organization.
- The progress made in the implementation of the CF goals should be audited periodically to ensure that the goals are indeed being implemented. Such audits may start with the top management auditing the divisions, divisions auditing their segments, and so on until all levels are touched.
- Cross-functional teams also decide among various options. They are the ones who set priorities.

16.11 POLICY IMPLEMENTATION

The cross-functional teams develop the overall policies, which are then assigned to the respective departments for implementation. Prior years' performance serves as the yardstick for deciding new goals and before settling on new goals, potential obstacles to their implementation at each level are considered.

The policy and mission statements may begin in abstract terms at the top but become more concrete as they move downward. Policy statements are formulated differently at various levels:

Top management:	Issues general statement of direction for change, expressed qualitatively; sets priorities; allocates resources between divisions
Divisional management:	Elaborates the top management's statement in quantitative terms
Middle management:	Sets specific goals in quantitative terms
Supervisors:	See to it that specific actions are undertaken by the employees working for them

It is not sufficient just to verbalize policy and plans; they will remain empty rhetoric unless properly implemented. Managers and supervisors must work with their employees to make sure that the planned goals are being implemented. Implementation must also be seen as a collective act that involves the entire organization. It is critical that managers discuss plans with their supervisors as well as their employees; they must not do the planning in isolation from the levels above and below them.

Policy development can be facilitated by using set formats that help document the policy and the measures. Managers can use forms to standardize the work that goes into developing the plans envisaged by the policy. Such forms may include the following fields of information:

- Top managers' long-range strategy
- Top managers' short-range objectives
- Last year's departmental goals and objectives
- Last year's actual results for the department
- This year's goals and measures
- Schedule
- Task assignments

Management can facilitate policy implementation in two ways: First, it can make sure that goals are accompanied by specific control measures, actions that need to be taken at each level of the organization. Second, management must conduct periodic audits to see if the implementation of the policy is proceeding as planned. For example, top management may decide that delays in paying vendors ought to be eliminated. This would represent the policy. To implement it, managers must decide on measures that will indicate that the policy is being implemented. One such measure could be the number of bills that were paid after their payment date. The successful implementation of the agreed policy will mean that there were no late payments of invoices.

Audits to investigate that implementation is proceeding as planned are not meant to find scapegoats, rather they must be seen as diagnostic sessions. They are meant to help workers recognize where the process may be experiencing problems. They are meant to expose what is wrong, not to assign blame.

16.12 CONTROL POINTS AND CHECKPOINTS

The control measures that are selected to monitor implementation of plans rely on the use of what are described as control points and checkpoints. These points have their origin in statistical quality control (SQC) charts and the concept of manageable margin. In everyday language they may be translated as given effects and their probable causes. The SQC charts indicate the acceptable and unacceptable ranges. In a service station, management may set up fifteen to twenty minutes as the time allowed to change the oil in customers' cars. Somewhere in the shop, a chart will display the time it actually takes to change oil on customers' vehicles. As long as the time taken to perform the task remains between fifteen and twenty minutes, no action is called for by the manager. If the time taken exceeds the acceptable range, it suggests that an abnormal situation has arisen and corrective action is called for by the supervisor. Exceeding the acceptable range is an effect, and it prompts the manager to look for the causes of delay.

The likely causes for the delay in oil change may be due to any or all of the following:

- Availability of oil at the workstation
- Delay in getting the paperwork processed
- Poor performance of the workers

In the jargon of SQC, checking the time it took to get the job done will be a control point, while the factors listed above will be checkpoints. At times the control points are called result (R) criteria and checkpoints are called process (P) criteria. The control points are handled with the help of data, while the checkpoints are attended to with the help of a process or the workers involved in the process.

It is important to remember that the control point at one level may be the checkpoint for the level above. For the shop foreman, the time taken is the control point and the three possible causes are the checkpoints. For the worker who does the paperwork, the control point may be the time it takes to do the paperwork and the checkpoint may be knowing who will do the oil change itself.

16.13 TOOLS USED FOR TOTAL QUALITY ENVIRONMENT

Even though TQE can help an organization be at the cutting edge, the tools used for implementing TQE are by no means high tech. Beyond the right attitudes and shared perceptions, the tools and techniques of TQE consist of checklists and charts aimed at inducing desired employee behavior and improving organizational communication. Getting employees and managers to do the right thing requires educating them to notice dysfunctional factors in their work. Following are some commonly used TQE tools and techniques.

(a) Three-Mu Checklists

One popular technique used by Japanese companies to help expose dysfunctional aspects pertaining to their work is known as the Three-Mu checklist. The checklist has employees look for *Muda, Muri,* and *Mura* in the work they do. *Muda* means waste or unproductive use of resources; *Muri* refers to strain or extraordinary exertion of efforts; and *Mura* refers to variances or discrepancies. The Three-Mu exhort workers to look for unproductive use of resources, extraordinary exertion of efforts, and variances between expectation and outcomes. They are to look for *Muda, Muri,* and *Mura* in the environment around them. Specifically, they are to look for such symptoms in the specified control points. Below are eleven typical control points used, along with an example of waste, strain, or variance common to each particular control point:

1. Workers employed → Excess number of workers
2. Techniques used → Time allowed for production seems inadequate
3. Methods applied → Methods used seem too complicated
4. Time expended → Excess of idle time between setups
5. Facilities employed → Takes too long to get material delivered to production centers
6. Tools used → Inventory movements in and out of warehouse are tracked manually
7. Materials → Using material in excess of that allowed by specification
8. Output generated → High rejection rates
9. Inventory → Too much diversity in parts specification
10. Environment → Toxic substances are not controlled
11. Way of thinking → Discrimination based on gender or ethnic origin

(b) Questionnaires

Journalism students are instructed to get the who, what, where, when, why, and how of their news stories in the opening sentences of the stories they write for their newspaper. Japanese companies use the same questions to analyze processes and to discover problems and/or opportunities for improvement. Often the questionnaires are used in conjunction with the Three-Mu checklist. Questions may pertain to the entire process or to a small task involved in a larger process. Alternatively, they may refer to the operators, facilities, machines, and materials used; to operating techniques; or even to performance measures employed. They may be formulated as follows:

- Who is doing it? Who should be doing it? Who else can do it?
- What is being done? What should be done? What else can be done?
- Where is it being done? Where should it be done? Where else can it be done?
- When is it done? When should it be done? Can it be done at some other time?
- Why is it done? Why is it done a given way or at a given time? Can it be done in another way or at another time?
- How is it done? How should it be done? Can it be done in some other way?

Clearly, the questions asked of a control point, be it a task or the entire process, are meant to increase workers' knowledge of it and to change their perceptions and perspectives.

(c) Visual Aids: Charts, Graphs, and Diagrams

Earlier we briefly discussed the role of statistics in a TQE environment. Here we describe some of the ways in which statistics is brought to production and operating processes.

Note that most of these are visual tools, which are invaluable in making statistics under-standable for all employees. By using visual tools such as those described below, Deming's gospel becomes easier to implement in production and other organizational environments.

(i) Pareto Diagrams.   These diagrams classify problems according to cause and phenomenon. The problems are diagrammed according to priority, using a bar-graph format, with 100 percent indicating the total value lost. Value lost represents the phenomenon that is plotted against different factors that are responsible for the value lost. A number of factors may be causing the units to be rejected at a particular process. By plotting them on a graph, one can learn which factors cause the most rejects. It may be that of a total of ten possible factors, three are responsible for up to 80 percent of the rejected units. Such graphic representations help isolate factors/problems responsible for most of the value lost.

(ii) Cause-and-Effect Diagrams.   These diagrams are used to analyze the characteristics of a process or situation and the factors that contribute to them. Cause-and-effect diagrams may be accompanied with a Pareto diagram to help isolate and rank causes for most of the damage. Flow charts describing the steps involved in managerial processes are a variation of cause-and-effect diagrams that can aid employees' understanding of their work.

(iii) Graphs.   Many kinds of graphs are employed, depending on the shape desired and the purpose of analysis. Bar graphs compare values via parallel bars, while line graphs are used to illustrate variations over a period of time. Circle graphs indicate the categorical breakdown of values, and radar charts assist in the analysis of previously evaluated items. Frequency distributions, histograms, and scatter diagrams are used to describe organizational processes, in addition to ordinary graphs.

(iv) Control Charts.   Perhaps the most important of the visual aids in use are control charts. Control charts serve to detect abnormal trends with the help of line graphs. These graphs differ from standard line graphs in that they have control limit lines at the center, top, and bottom levels. Sample data are plotted in dots on the graph to evaluate process situations and trends. These charts seek to differentiate between two types of variations: the inevitable variations that occur under normal conditions and those that can be traced to a cause. The latter variations, often called "abnormal," are the ones that set off remedial actions. Control charts also help in pointing out developing trends, which could become the reason for countermeasures by employees. These visual tools are widely used by quality circles and other small groups as well as by staff engineers and managers, for identifying and solving problems. Since most of them use statistical analysis, employees have to be trained to use these tools in their routine activities. The firm must provide such training to its employees; indeed, it should be a part of the efforts to help employees develop themselves.

(d) Slogans, Signs, and Ceremonies

Human beings like to be reminded about things that need doing. The commercials blaring forth from radios are proof that timely reminders help in getting human beings to act in a given way. Similarly, slogans, signs, and ceremonies are used extensively by Japanese firms employing TQE to reinforce employees' willingness to improve the work they do. Slogans may be used to urge workers to organize their workstation, the tools they use, and even their work habits. Awards and recognition ceremonies are also very much a part of TQE implementation.

All these tools and others yet to be discovered do not help if they are not used. It is imperative to provide workers with time out from the daily grind to let them think through the work they do. Without these reflective intervals, whether they are in the form of informal meetings, in quality circles, or in focus groups, TQE cannot be attained. It is also best to initiate the search for TQE in good times, because once the bad times take over a company, its employees may be too immersed in putting out the brushfires to be distracted by the promises of TQE.

Terms like quality circles and continuous improvement and acronyms like TQE and TQM are very much a part of the current managerial landscape. Their spread attests to their efficacy. Quality improvement is not mere hype; it is useful. Indeed, what keeps it from becoming just another fad is the fact that TQE does work. It works well enough to put at risk of oblivion those firms that do not value continuous improvement in what they do and how they do it.

TQE is concerned on a continuous basis with organizational improvements brought about by a commitment on the part of individuals, acting alone and in groups, to seek a better understanding of their work and to do it better. The starting point for such continuous efforts directed toward evolution is self-knowledge—an understanding of the organizational/departmental goals and objectives in terms of what, why, who, where, when, and how. Such awareness culminates in an unceasing search to evolve, not by means of expensive technology or through adoption of fads, and certainly not by mere wishful thinking, but through dedication, by the application of good sense, and by taking on the self-imposed obligation to provide quality service and value to customers, whether they are in another country or in the department located down the hall.

16.14 BUSINESS PROCESS REDESIGN

This section surveys business process redesign (BPR), more popularly known as reengineering or process innovation. Business process redesign has much in common with the Deming approach, although it requires the use of information technology in addition to the tools of TQE. It has a different impact and requires a somewhat different sort of implementation.

Business process redesign is based on the premise that by exploring the what, when, where, why, who, and how of processes, an organization can achieve exponential productivity gains. In other words, the reengineering process starts by asking questions about the organization's activities. Following such inquiries into the nature of processes and procedures, BPR focuses on attaining the same goals by alternative, streamlined, more efficient, and presumably more technologically advanced means. Fundamental to such redesign is the desire to eliminate the non–value-adding steps from the process and to approach it from a cross-functional, rather than a departmental, perspective. Through focused reexamination and by using emergent information technology (IT), an organization can systemically change the way its work is performed and enhance its evolutionary competence.

A large number of current work practices exists because of the tradition that breaks work into its component tasks and then lets different specialists take care of their respective assignments, usually narrow segments of the overall process. Such thinking focuses on individual tasks much more than on the underlying goals or the entire process; the results of this approach are costly delays, lengthy paper trails, and an excess number of clerical employees whose function is to tend to clogged paper trails. The traditional philosophy also promotes departments to fight suboptimally for their own pieces of the procedural turf. Instead of focusing on the entire process, such as getting merchandise into the hands of the customer and collecting payment in the most efficient, cost-effective way, the current organizational philosophy focuses on smaller segments of the process, such as ordering, credit analysis, shipment, billing, collecting, and depositing. The various tasks are assigned to different individuals dispersed throughout the organization. By the time all the tasks get accomplished, customers may well be on their way elsewhere.

A similar compartmentalization governs purchasing and other organizational processes. Under the present setup, a decision to purchase an item is broken into its six component tasks:

1. A department makes a formal request to the purchasing department for a specific item, after getting due authorization for the request (a complete, paper-laden process in its own right, often distinct from the purchasing process).

2. The purchasing department then selects the vendor. Such selections can involve solicitation of bids and other such measures.

3. Following vendor selection, the purchasing department orders the goods, with the help of a purchase order—a document that has as many as five copies to be distributed among not just the vendors and those making the requests but also the receiving, payable, and cash disbursement departments. Because of such voucher outpouring, each of these different-colored siblings of the original document engenders the need for one or more employees to handle the respective copies.

4. When the shipment is received, yet another specialist verifies its accuracy with the help of a copy of the purchase order, which, no doubt, has to be hunted down in the paper thicket.

5. Accounting waits to receive the pertinent pieces of paper from internal departments such as purchasing and receiving as well as from the external vendor. After all the matching copies are in the hands of accounts payable personnel, the accountants then issue a voucher, also in multiple copies, authorizing payment to the vendor.

6. This voucher and its technicolor multiples have to travel all over the organization to get approved and be finally paid.

Clearly, a lot of paper shuffling goes on in the paper-clogged trails, but what is worse, and much more costly to the firm, is the waiting between the various steps involved in the entire process. That waiting takes up most of the time spent by vouchers in the paper trail.

One of the most talked-about instances of reengineering of the accounts payable process originally occurred at the Ford Motor Company, and has since been duplicated by others. Ford reengineered its process so that the delays were eliminated and cut 375 of the 500 employees who worked in accounts payable. What Ford did was this: First, it developed close relationships with a few vendors so that time was not wasted selecting the right vendor to supply a given item. Second, it stopped authorizing payments for purchases after the invoice was received; instead, payments are made when the goods are received. Paperwork is eliminated by creating the purchase orders on computer. These electronic purchase vouchers are available to those in receiving, so that when the order is received, it can be read directly into the voucher within the system. Gone is the waiting for, and matching of, all the copies. The same voucher is available to those in charge of disbursements, so that upon receipt of the order, payments can be processed electronically. Vendors agree to, and enter into, such relationships because they have a much greater assurance of getting the business and also of getting paid sooner.

Wal-Mart, the retailing behemoth, went the same route as Ford, perhaps traveling even further when it did away with those involved with placement of orders. This way, the replenishment of inventory does not wait for a decision on the part of a narrow specialist who must rely on a paper trail. Instead, suppliers are beeped from Wal-Mart's point-of-sale information system, which is tied directly into their own information process. Inventory replenishment is triggered by the actual sales in real time and is delivered by the manufacturer to the store where it is needed. Intermediaries such as buyers, distributors, and wholesalers are becoming extinct. The manufacturers themselves can plan production based on sales being reported in real time, not through guesswork.

16.15 THE INFORMATION TECHNOLOGY CONNECTION

The agent of change for Ford, Wal-Mart, and others who have implemented similar systems happens to be the emergent IT. Using such technology, purchasing can do away with its multiple-copy purchase vouchers that require availability of different individuals in various departments to take care of their respective copies. Instead, while placing an order, purchasing agents can enter it into the on-line system, also called the client-server system. In some cases, as we have seen with Wal-Mart, it does not even have to be entered by purchasing agents but can be put into the system by the requesting department. When the ordered goods are received, the receiving agent checks for the order on the system. (He or she may actually scan the packing slip with the help of imaging technology.) If the order is found, then with the push of a button, the receiving agent lets the system know that the order was delivered. At this point, the system takes over and coordinates the processing as well as the issuing of payments.

BPR is for real, and what is allowing this reality is a revolution in software. Four key technologies are helping to make BPR a reality. They are graphical user interfaces (GUI), networking software, flexible databases, and imaging technology (IT).

(a) Graphical User Interface

GUI allows an image, a picture on the screen, to represent the object in the real world. The image of a file folder serves the same functions file folders do in the world that surrounds the desktop client-server. GUIs such as Windows software or the system used by Apple Computer Inc.'s Macintosh makes computers easier to use.

(b) Networking Software

This software allows for geographically separated workers, even groups of workers, to work on a project jointly. Networking makes for easier and faster communication. It represents the information highway, which links schedules, permits electronic conferences, allows instant feedback, and facilitates distribution of reports.

(c) Flexible Databases

Flexible databases (or relational databases) assemble in one place all the data in an organization in a form that can be shared by many, if not all, departments and individuals working on their respective jobs. The information system permits the entry of data by anyone in the system and instantly adjusts to the new information. Each time a sales clerk enters a transaction, the system updates its files. Relational databases make the system of tracking inventory truly perpetual.

(d) Imaging Technology

IT allows information to be entered and processed by means of electronic scanners. A photocopier can now be turned into a source of input into systems: Words, numbers, and bar codes are scanned at cash registers, in controllers' departments, and at the suppliers' warehouses. Insurance claims are available to the adjusters and to their supervisors in the blink of an electronic eye. Tax returns can now be faxed to the Internal Revenue Service.

The IT software delivers information directly to those who need it when they need it. IT's advancements permit access to information across geographic distances. This permits coordination to a degree that was hitherto difficult, if not impossible, to achieve. BPR should be implemented with IT's capabilities in mind. This does not mean buy first and think later. It is still important to think through, and to justify strategically, the context within which IT will be used, but the possibilities made available through technology can now be considered in the early stages of BPR.

To illustrate the potential made available by IT for BPR, here is a brief list of some of the possibilities:

- It is possible to dispense with intermediaries by connecting buyers and sellers of goods as well as suppliers and the users of information.
- Tracking the status of a product, a document, a payment, or even the entire process can be done in real time.
- Knowledge and expertise can be disseminated at the speed of light: The books in the Library of Congress or the British Museum will soon become available to someone waiting for a plane in Timbuktu.
- Vast numbers of details can be processed, analyzed, and portrayed in formats that are understandable and convenient. The preparation of budgets does not rely on filling out the bulky twelve-columns ledger paper with handwritten data received from various parts of the organization. As a result, what-if situations can be made tangible and studied. Activity-based costing, the subject of the next chapter, is possible because of the IT now available.
- The process does not have to progress in a step-by-step sequence. Steps can be worked on jointly or even simultaneously.
- Geography is no longer a barrier, thanks to IT. Distance does not keep information from moving rapidly and being accessible as soon as it is available.
- Transactions are handled in forms that were unimaginable a few years ago: Cash withdrawals, test taking, and mortgage applications are commonly subject to such IT-inspired intermediation and structures.

Until recently, the information systems in use were set in place to meet departmental needs. It was not uncommon to find several systems being used by the different subunits of the same department, and it was very common to find different systems in different departments. The sales, credit check, and accounts receivable departments could all be using different systems. Such manifestations of the Tower of Babel syndrome were not conducive to process-oriented thinking. The emergent IT makes communicating across departments possible and makes it more effective and efficient.

16.16 BUSINESS PROCESS REDESIGN VERSUS TOTAL QUALITY ENVIRONMENT

BPR has much in common with TQE. Both seek to furnish organizations with evolutionary competence, and both are made possible with the help of frequent communication, deployment of sufficient resources, commitment of the leadership, and the cooperation of the employees. Both prefer a cross-functional perspective and have been shown to be quite practical, yet the two must be seen as contrasting, though not mutually exclusive, approaches.

TQE requires a long-term perspective and delivers long-lasting impact in return for undramatic but steady commitment. It is slow-paced but continuous. Adjectives that describe it are "gradual," "constant," and "incremental." To be implemented, it requires universal involvement and collective effort. It judges the efforts invested as much as the result obtained. It seeks to rebuild on the existing foundations and does not require breakthrough technology or major investments.

In contrast to TQE, BPR seeks its impact in short-term, dramatic steps. The adjectives to be associated with it are "abrupt," "intermittent," and "volatile." It does not seek maintenance but instead opts for rebuilding. It depends on technological innovations and major financial commitments, and is implemented by a few with a trickle-down approach.

The literature on BPR has at times made it seem more desirable than TQE. Indeed, some have wrapped BPR in patriotic colors, seeing it as more attuned to the American myth of rugged individualism. But setting up the two approaches as polar extremes is not at all necessary. The two can coexist. TQE can and will facilitate BPR. TQE can easily lead to reengineering if and when the need is felt, technology is available, and money is available to make the needed investments. Once the process is reengineered, its true potential benefit can best be realized with the help of a consciousness and work attitude borrowed from TQE. There is a case to be made for practicing TQE while waiting for BPR, and even after it has been put in place. In denying the organization the advantages of TQE while waiting for the dramatic dawn of reengineering, the company can subject itself to stagnation and a loss of business. While waiting for heart bypass surgery, the patient is urged to foreswear fat and cholesterol. Similarly, it is best for an organization not to entirely depend on the surgical solutions of BPR.

16.17 PREDECESSORS OF BUSINESS PROCESS REDESIGN

It is worth noting that even though the word is new, the concept of reengineering is not. The history of the rise of systems in American management at the turn of the twentieth century shows that such developments were really attempts in corporate reengineering using the emergent technology of the time. Frederick Taylor's philosophy of scientific management also anticipated today's reengineering, as did Henry Ford's assembly line.

BPR brings forward the earlier practices of disciplines such as task analysis, operational auditing, and work simplification in order to redesign the way work is undertaken. More recently, a relationship between improved, redesigned procedures and greater productivity was demonstrated by Intel Corporation. This correlation was documented in 1981 in an article in *Fortune* magazine several years before the word "reengineering" took on its mythic aura. By carefully reviewing its operating procedures, the firm was able to reduce the number of steps needed to hire an employee from 364 to 250. Its engineers no longer needed twelve pieces of paper and ninety-five administrative steps to order a mechanical pencil. The review of operating procedures cut the steps involved to eight and the forms used to only one. The cost savings were in the millions of dollars and were accomplished by using techniques that were not dependent on cutting-edge technology. By methodically analyzing administrative procedures, they were able to distinguish value-adding steps from those that were not. A breakdown of a process into its components permitted differentiation between those that were necessary activities and those that caused delays, were redundant, or were useless yet added to costs. Following the analysis, the activities that were necessary parts of the process were retained, while the non–value-adding tasks were eliminated. Even though the 1981 article described the technique used as work simplification, it is quite similar to BPR.

16.18 BENEFITS OF BUSINESS PROCESS REDESIGN

Clearly, the question of BPR's historical origin is interesting, but it is immaterial for organizational well-being. What is of significance is the realization that reengineering can be helpful in ensuring organizational evolution. The advent of BPR and its increasing use is, in large part, a result of the growing need to improve the productivity of white-collar workers. This imperative is becoming increasingly desirable in banks, thrifts, insurance companies, accounting firms, airlines, and major retailers. Another factor that is causing the increasing use of BPR is the imperative to focus on a flexible, team-oriented approach that promotes interdependent activities throughout the organization. This leads to cross-functional problem solving rather than narrow specialization.

The improvement of white-collar productivity cannot be induced by firing the low-paid employees or by opening the corporate checkbook for high-tech automation. Often the billions spent on IT has led only to employees and managers doing the same work but doing it somewhat faster. Computers were no more than expensive calculators, and they failed to revolutionize the process, though they expedited productivity. Productivity can be increased more effectively by removing bottlenecks, avoiding mistakes, and focusing on customer service. Resorting to new technology should follow, not precede, removal of non–value-adding activities. Often mistakes are made and procedural gridlocks are created not because of careless, indolent employees but because of the way workers have been told to do their work. Outdated, complex, and redundant standard operating procedures also contribute to low productivity.

Bell Atlantic, concerned about the time it took to fill orders for telephone lines from a long-distance carrier, undertook an analysis of its process. It found the delays were the result of its functional structure. Different tasks were handled in different locales and, given that the order passed through twenty-five different tasks, the average time it took to complete the process was measured in days and weeks. By means of a BPR, Bell Atlantic dispensed with less useful, non–value-adding tasks and assigned teams to follow through with an entire order instead of having different individuals performing different tasks. As a result, the time needed to fill an order by Bell Atlantic has been reduced to a matter of hours.

16.19 WHAT DOES BUSINESS PROCESS REDESIGN INVOLVE?

The *Random House Dictionary* defines "process" as a systematic series of action directed to some predefined end. This definition is a good starting point for understanding a business process. Here the word "business" is used broadly by not limiting it to organizations involved in making money. While talking about a business process, it is best to include some additional attributes to the dictionary definition. A process is undertaken in order to meet some needs within an organization, and those needs are felt by and associated with those who work for or with the organization. These processes have outcomes that affect both those within and those outside of the organization. Those affected by the process have a vested interest in the outcomes, and those with such interests can be customers, owners, or stakeholders in the process. For the sake of convenience, we will use the term "customers" to refer to all those who have a vested interest in the outcome of a process.

In addition to having customers, a process usually involves more than one organizational department. Most organizational structures do not reflect the processes undertaken by the organization. This is largely because the emphasis on process orientation is of relatively recent origin. The organizational structure usually was composed of functions such as accounting, finance, development, distribution, purchasing production, personnel, security, and quality. Such a structure downplayed the fact that within each function, processes being performed require inputs from throughout the organization. There are, however, processes that are unique to each function. Downplaying the cross-functionality of processes and its pervasiveness within organizations of all sorts and sizes ignores a basic truth of business. New product development, creation of a strategic marketing plan, the processing of an insurance claim, and the hiring of an employee, all cross-functional processes, are what organizations do all the time.

Most of the processes performed by the accounting department are cross-functional. Among them are ledger control, payroll, tax planning, accounts receivable, accounts payable, cash control, fixed assets control, cost accounting, labor distribution, budget preparation, pensions, benefits, and employee expense accounts. These processes affect others, and such impact often helps to shape the organization's behavior. At the same time, the processes performed by the accounting department are affected by others within and outside the organization. This is one reason that accounting cannot be seen as being solely the concern of accountants, just as an information system does not belong only to the systems department.

16.20 PROCESS MANAGEMENT

Good management can help make processes more effective by allowing them to be performed in an optimum, streamlined manner. Management can help see to it that a process is efficient and makes effective use of resources. Additionally, management will allow a process to have flexibility built into it. Customers change, and so do environments. The processes in place can best respond to changes if they are flexible.

If processes are managed well, they will display the following traits:

- Ownership of the process is well defined. Someone is designated to manage the process, and that person can be held accountable for it.
- The scope of the process can be identified.
- There exist measures that help evaluate the effectiveness and efficiency of the process.
- The process is flexible enough to deal with changes and exceptions.
- The process has built-in provision for feedback.
- Written procedures documentation exist, indicating effective process management. Such documentation should help new employees understand tasks and how to perform them.
- There is effective communication between those in different departments who perform the various tasks that comprise the process. There also should be an absence of turf battles between those who work on the different tasks of the same process.

Managed processes are geared to eliminate errors, are not subject to non–value-adding delays, make optimum use of resources, are adaptable, rely on cutting-edge technology, are documented, and are easy to understand. Well-managed processes can provide an organization with a competitive advantage, while poorly managed processes can be costly to an organization. But such mismanagement can be recognized and, given the importance of processes to an organization, must be eliminated. If the process is out of control, then it is time for process redesign.

16.21 HOW TO REDESIGN?

Process redesign is itself a process, and it can be more effective if it is implemented in a well-planned manner. A discussion of a nine-step, well-planned implementation of BPR follows.

1. Identify the process to be redesigned. Process redesign is a major undertaking, and it ties up a considerable amount of resources. Given this, it is best to select processes that merit such a commitment of resources. Most managers have some perception of what processes are most crucial to their success, and this can help the selection. Alternatively or additionally, the selection may be based on how poorly an important process is performing. An additional impetus to redesign or select a process for redesign may be through benchmarking the process against industry standards. It may be advisable to measure the performance against firms that are rated high and are recognized as the industry pacesetters.

   Such identification of a process for redesign will be facilitated if the goals of the redesign have been defined. Reduction of cost, elimination of production delays, faster and improved customer service, and improved quality are objectives typically sought through reengineering of processes. The objectives should be specific. It is better if they are measurable. Above all, they should be an outgrowth of the firm's strategic vision, goals, and objectives.
2. Analyze the effectiveness and the efficiency of the process. Before any attempt is made to redesign a process, its current performance must be analyzed. Such analysis can use the attributes of well-managed processes discussed earlier to judge the

current performance of the process in question. Or specific outputs of the process can be measured. Additionally, benchmarking comparisons can be used to measure the effectiveness and the efficiency of the process and its outputs. Such comparative measures will not only reveal how much the process needs to be improved, they also will help to judge the subsequent success of the redesign. But such measures may not be of much help if radical change is desired. Redesign seeks to change things, not to improve them incrementally. Using old performance measures to judge the merits of the new process may be like comparing the speed of a mule with that of a four-wheel-drive truck.

3. Analyze the relationship between BPR and the firm's strategic plans. Conventional wisdom requires that an organization consider its overriding strategic objectives before it makes a major investment of its resources. Since process redesign commitment calls for just such investments of resources, it is best to consider how the objectives sought through redesign fit with the firm's strategic plans.

4. Identify how the BPR can support strategic goals of the firm. This, in effect, continues the examination of the relationship between redesign and the firm's strategic plans. However, it should include an analysis to show that goals being sought from the redesigned process do not negatively affect other processes in use by the firm.

5. Explore IT that may be useful. IT is constantly changing, and it will certainly be worthwhile to explore how emergent technology can help realize the objectives sought by process redesign. Since knowing the technology available can have an impact on the objectives being sought through BPR, consideration of IT should occur early in the redesign process.

6. Design a prototype. It is best to test the new before giving up the old. Testing is necessary to reveal the redesign in action, and may help catch and correct unforeseen flaws. The new may not turn out to be as good as had been hoped, and it could cause unexpected problems. It may have an adverse impact on other processes within the firm. Plans on paper often seem more attractive than they actually are in practice. Testing of a prototype will save costs and resources. Furthermore, such testing will ensure that the final results are satisfying. Implementation on a pilot basis can allow time to make changes in the plan to better achieve the objectives desired before the plan is implemented organization-wide.

7. Measure the prototype for its effectiveness and efficiency. Once a prototype is operational, it should be tested against the original process for its effectiveness and increased efficiency. Such measurements may reveal a need for modifying the changes. The testing should rely not on anecdotal impressions but on tangible measures.

8. Carry out full implementation. After testing the plan on a pilot basis and making any changes that may be called for, the project is ready to be implemented. Special efforts may be needed to manage the changeover smoothly. Employees and supervisors may be resistant to performing their work in a new way.

9. Measure how well the redesigned process performs. Like all plans, BPR should be tested periodically to see if it needs improvement. In theory, after the major change, the redesigned process should satisfy the owners" needs for some time. However, the changing environment within which business operates today will not permit such "resting." Holding on to the status quo may not be in the best interests of a firm. Indeed, it is best to follow up a BPR with a TQE to realize maximum benefits.

At its most basic, BPR means starting with a clean sheet of paper and a clean organizational slate, and drawing new sets of tasks to be carried out with new technology to fulfill organizational vision and goals. Reengineering is much in the news these days. But the benefits of BPR are likely to be greater if it is not touted as the only way; there is no such thing as the one and only way in the world of processes. Indeed, BPR in combination with other techniques may be more effective than BPR used as a make-or-break intervention.

Firms of all stripes are scrambling to let reengineering duplicate for them what it did for Motorola, Ford, Xerox, and Bell Atlantic, namely, exponential productivity gains. However, reengineering is not for everyone. It is a costly and extreme remedy, which should be used only when absolutely needed. A surgical remedy may not be the only solution. Furthermore, some experts advise that BPR be accompanied by a restructuring of the networks and environments within which the firm operates. Fast-moving cars are of little use if the roads and highways do not support their optimum performance. Similarly, IT-inspired streamlining of the processes may be only the first step, which must be followed by a search for environments that allow the potential of such changes to be realized.

Despite the caveat about prescribing reengineering indiscriminately, the fact remains that it is a useful managerial tool. It is one more tool to help organizations acquire evolutionary competence. It can coexist with TQE.

16.22 ORGANIZATIONAL LEARNING

This book began by comparing traditional and current views of procedures documentation, a business communication genre. Seen as archival afterthoughts, procedures manuals have turned into neglected tools that are rarely used even though well-written, current documentation can play many useful roles. Given the lack of respect accorded procedures manuals, it is not enough merely to advocate a greater respect for them; instead, it is better to change the very perception of the procedures documentation process. The documentation process must involve not only the end product, namely, the finished procedures manual, but also the steps that create it. When a valuable process is created, the product that results is inevitably worthy of respect.

16.23 RETHINKING THE DOCUMENTATION PROCESS

It is time to change the role currently assigned to procedures documentation. The justification for such a shift lies in the changes taking place in the global environment, in the introduction of more effective management practices, and in the emergent information technology. But an even greater imperative to change the perception of the documentation process is the current redefinition of authority and managerial leadership.

Today, leaders need not be omniscient managers at the top of the organizational pyramid. Instead, managers are being urged to exercise their leadership by acting as designers, teachers, and stewards who seek to build shared visions, challenge prevailing work patterns, and foster systemic patterns of intellectual exploration. This type of leadership encourages employees to expand their contributions for shaping the organization's future and allows them to learn. Such learning is crucial to developing an evolutionary competence—the ability of an organism to survive in a rapidly changing environment.

Changing the perception of how the documentation process is viewed can help make it an occasion for institutional learning. Managers should see to it that the process governing procedures documentation serves as an occasion for sharing mental maps, for challenging work habits, and for exploring and improving. That such a shift in perception is practical is evidenced by the success of techniques that help organizations attain evolutionary competence. Techniques such as TQE and BPR have shown themselves capable of changing the way organizations perform. If it is possible, practical, and profitable to redesign and continuously improve procedures and activities, why not do the same for the process involved in their documentation? Indeed, why not redesign the documentation process so that it will serve as an occasion for institutional learning and not be seen as a neglected afterthought?

16.24 WHAT PREVENTS ORGANIZATIONAL LEARNING?

As we stressed earlier, organizations need evolutionary competence if they are to survive, let alone flourish and prosper. To acquire it, they must provide their employees with occasions where institutional learning may occur, and where personnel can step back from daily chores and reflect on their work.

One of the most common obstacles that prevents personnel from attending to organizational evolution is their workload. The cause for such absorption in work may not be the slowness of the employees, or even the workload itself, but rather the work design. When daily "firefighting" overwhelms personnel to the extent that they can no longer maintain normal operations, let alone keep up with the changing environment or technology, organizational and accounting standard operating procedures have passed the point of being useful. Such organizations must rethink what work they do, why they do it, when they do it, who does it, and where it is done. Indeed, knowing when organizational routines and standard operating procedures are about to lose their effectiveness may well be the key to preventing obsolescence.

16.25 RETHINKING THE PERCEPTION OF WORK

To facilitate organizational learning, we need to rethink how work is viewed. In the closing decades of the nineteenth century, Frederick Taylor observed that the emphasis in the industrial environment needed to shift from the end product to the processes that help create the product. He also realized the importance of employee motivation, even though he saw employees as playing a passive role. But Taylor's ideas emphasized reductionism: breaking things down into isolated parts in order to better control them. Scientific management emphasized finding the one best way to perform and then enforcing it. The enforced standardization that was gospel for Taylor promoted efficiency in the first half of the twentieth century. But in a shrinking, unpredictable world dominated by volatility and ever-accelerating change, reductionism and enforced standardization may become a one-way ticket to oblivion. Today the call is for self-management, learning through feedback, and for systems that are able to redesign themselves.

Some management experts also are calling for institutional structures that incorporate built-in mechanisms to respond to change. Indeed, these experts see the ability to change faster than the competition as a cardinal virtue and a strategic advantage.

It is becoming the norm for organizations to force change, to periodically examine the work they do and justify to themselves and their stakeholders the viability of what they do and what they know. Journals are busily writing about cutting-edge organizations that are able to "bail out" before the markets for their products reach maturity or saturation. These companies keep reinventing their products and services. Such organizations prosper because of their willingness to cultivate organizational learning.

16.26 LEARNING PARADIGM

Notwithstanding the current resurgence of the term "learning organization," the concept has been around for some time. The paradigm also underlies Edward Deming's crusade for improved productivity. The term "learning" should not be equated with simply digesting information and taking in details. Instead, learning organizations allow workers to expand their ability to deal with current problems and visualize future opportunities. A learning organization is concerned with things as they could be, not just as they are; it seeks to anticipate opportunities, not simply deal with crises when they occur. As noted by management expert David Garvin, a learning organization has skills that not only allow it to create, acquire, and transfer emergent knowledge, it also is able to modify itself in keeping with its newly acquired knowledge and experiential insights. Employees in learning organizations are skilled at the following activities, according to Garvin: systematic problem solving, experimentation with new approaches, learning from their own experiences and best practices of others, and transferring knowledge quickly and efficiently throughout the organization.

(a) Promoting the Learning Attitude

To foster learning in an organization, leaders of organizations must ensure that their employees are able to question currently held stereotypes and abandon them if they are unable to meet changing needs. Left to itself, organizational learning is likely to be very slow. Personnel are likely to find learning difficult when they are harried or rushed. Organizational learning, however, can be expedited by fostering an environment conducive to learning. A learning environment allows employees freedom for reflection, analysis, and creativity, and permits them to invent better ways of working and to ask questions about customer needs and current work processes.

A number of techniques are available to promote an environment suitable for learning within an organization. Garvin lists the following as the catalyst for learning: frequent strategic reviews of a firm's competitive environment, product portfolio, technology, and market positioning; periodic audits of various systems, in particular those involving cross-functional processes and delivery systems; internal and external benchmarking; and study missions and symposiums to share and learn from each other. In a similar vein, management expert Daniel Kim has proposed a model for promoting organizational learning, which he calls the OADI-SAMM model. The acronym means "*o*bserve, *a*ssess, *d*esign, *i*mplement— *s*hared *m*ental *m*odels." Kim argues that by creating systems and processes that support these activities and integrate them into the fabric of daily operations, companies can enhance institutional learning.

It is worth noting that the advice given by Garvin and Kim echoes the tools used by those implementing TQE as well as the ideas of Deming. Indeed, TQE and organizational learning are sometimes seen as identical; however, we believe the latter represents the attitudes that ensure that an organization will not only seek out and foster learning opportunities for its employees but will see to it that the lessons learned and the knowledge acquired are put to use. TQE is the set of techniques that allow learning. It is the implementation of the learning paradigm. Both are needed—the willingness and motivation on one hand, the tools and the knowledge on the other—for learning to occur.

This book seeks to add the procedures documentation process to the techniques suggested to enhance learning. The role being argued here for the procedures documentation process presupposes that it will incorporate elements from the various evolutionary competencies being surveyed. By incorporating these techniques within the documentation process, organizational learning can be instituted in the accounting department as well as the firm.

In the rest of this chapter we talk about frame breaking, a technique used to promote organizational learning. Organizational learning can be enhanced if those seeking to promote it are familiar with techniques that facilitate group efforts. Such behavioral expertise is as important as knowledge of emergent technologies in inculcating evolutionary competence in an organization.

16.27 FRAME BREAKING

Another variation of organizational learning is frame breaking, an exercise that helps managers think about scenarios that are unlikely and yet could somehow come to pass—like the price of oil falling to ten dollars a barrel at a time when the rate was more than thirty. Such a scenario was far from the minds of oil barons. Yet the managers at Shell were planning strategies for dealing with just such an event, were it to come about. When it actually did happen, they were ready, having planned for it as a learning exercise.

Thinking through and planning such scenarios can help disrupt the familiar mental models, which can lead to enhanced creativity. Being in a rut is not the route to becoming imaginative. The key that turns frame breaking into learning is being able to visualize the unusual and develop plans for strategic response in the face of the unlikely. Such planning, even without deployment of the plans, expedites learning, according to its practitioners. One of the more famous practitioners of scenario planning is Shell. Another firm that goes to considerable lengths in planning scenarios, according to Peter Senge, is the insurance firm Hanover. The approach is also used in Japan. Given all this, it is fair to assume that frame breaking is not mere science fiction; instead, it is an effective tool in training managers as creative planners. Such exercises in creative learning translate to enhanced evolutionary competence as well as the all-important profits.

Certainly a role for frame breaking exists within accounting contexts. Some years ago the thought that a firm could operate without working capital would have ranked as managerial heresy, if not outright lunacy. Yet today there are Fortune 100 firms that are doing just that. Twenty years ago a few accountants could have enriched themselves considerably if they had planned for a world without working capital and convinced their top managers of the benefits of traveling down such a strategic highway.

CHAPTER 17

ACTIVITY-BASED COSTING AND ACTIVITY-BASED MANAGEMENT

17.1 INTRODUCTION

Like total quality environment and business process redesign, activity-based costing (ABC) and activity-based management (ABM) are techniques that help organizations attain evolutionary competence. Like the former tools, activity-based techniques require organizational introspection. Such self-awareness is the starting point for organizational evolution. Armed with a thorough understanding of what they do, organizations are better able to create value for their customers. The various techniques used for organizational evolution all help managers better understand their organizations. ABC seeks to enhance such understanding in monetary terms. Both ABC and ABM can coexist and complement other approaches, such as total quality environment (TQE) and BPR. But unlike TQE and BPR, ABC is accounting-oriented. The focus of ABC, in particular, is on cost tracking. In the process of revealing the what, who, where, when, why, and how of cost occurrences, those charged with ABC analysis also can reveal task inefficiencies and suboptimal processes that drain away resources. Managers must know where the inefficiencies are before they can take steps to correct them. Since they help cost the inefficiencies, ABC and ABM give such knowledge to managers. ABC also satisfies the call for tangible measurements made by those implementing TQE.

17.2 COST TRACKING TO HELP MANAGERIAL DECISIONS

Tracking costs helps managers assess use of the resources needed to manufacture products or provide services for both internal and external customers. Effective use of resources is dependent on making production cost-effective. As part of their cost-tracking function, accountants prepare financial statements and other reports for management, which is then better able to make informed decisions pertaining to functions such as:

- Pricing products and bidding on projects
- Planning and control
- Performing strategic analyses, both short term and long term
- Evaluating performance

Cost tracking always has been critical to effective managerial performance, but the need for more accurate cost measurements is being driven by the growing global competition

353

as well as the technological, regulatory, demographic, and behavioral changes in the business environment.

17.3 FOCUS ON ACTIVITIES

The need for greater accuracy through less aggregation and less distortion in accounting reports has led to the increasing adoption of ABC. It focuses on assigning the costs incurred by each of the various activities performed to manufacture products or provide services rather than simply pricing aggregate production resources. Such a focus stems from the realization that costs occur because activities are undertaken.

Activities drive up costs, yet not all activities are equally capable of adding value to the outputs. Furthermore, the cost-benefit criteria applied to activities actually can enhance the quality of managerial decisions concerning the replacement of obsolete or suboptimal activities that drive up costs. Such decisions are the necessary ingredients for attaining evolutionary competence, and they can be facilitated by ABC.

17.4 ACCURATE REFLECTION OF RESOURCE USAGE

An incentive to management for actually using information provided through ABC is the presumption that it is a more accurate reflection of how resources are being used. In the 1980s, widely accused academicians and practitioners alike widely accused the cost systems in place in the United States, Canada, and Britain since World War II of being too aggregated and too distorted to be relevant in managerial decision making. The increase in the popularity of ABC owes a considerable debt to such disenchantment with outdated cost-tracking techniques. Cost accounting textbooks have since added chapters on activity-based costing, while retaining the traditional techniques of cost tracking.

17.5 DEFINITION OF ACTIVITY-BASED COSTING AND ACTIVITY-BASED MANAGEMENT

Seeing activities as a product's building blocks allows accountants to track costs by tracking activities. Recognizing such cause-and-effect relationships between activities and costs incurred can help to minimize aggregation and distortion and leads to more accurate costing.

ABC has been defined as an activity-focused costing technique that seeks to calculate costs of products and services by assigning them costs in keeping with their use of resources. Such assignment of costs is tantamount to an assignment of resource usage among the various outputs. It is based on using activities as the vehicle for cost accumulation, instead of departments or even the plant itself, a more traditional means of collecting cost pools.

ABM is the approach management can use to ensure that activities necessary to produce goods and services are value-adding. Such an assessment of the value provided is done by means of activity-based costing techniques as well as information pertaining to revenue, customer demographics, quality measures, and market factors.

The relationship between ABC and ABM is explained by realizing that the initial step is activity analysis devoted to charting the relationship between inputs and outputs. The inputs are measured as activities. These activities are then costed, which gives rise to ABC. In the process of costing activities, the extent to which they add or do not add value to outputs is assessed. A number of activities may be found to not add any value at all. Such measurements of costs incurred and benefits realized are among the many factors that permit the management of activities for optimum results.

17.6 DIRECT VERSUS INDIRECT COSTS

To explain activity-based costing, it is best to start by explaining the meaning of such terms as activity, cost center, and cost-driver and by differentiating between direct and indirect costs. When accounts talk about an activity, they have in mind those activities that result in costs being accrued. Obtaining a college education is an activity that is responsible for costs occurring for students or their parents. The son or daughter attending college can be seen as a cost center or cost objective, which is another way of describing any activity for which a separate measurement of costs is desired by those who foot the bill. Parents like to know the costs involved in the undertaking. Attending college is not only an activity, it should also be seen as a cost driver, which, by definition, is the reason costs are being incurred.

All the costs involved in obtaining a college education are not alike. Money paid as tuition and to purchase textbooks are the direct costs of obtaining an education. The expenses involved in commuting to and from college, assuming the student lives at home, will be an indirect cost, because the car is very likely also used for other activities, or cost objectives. Hence, the expense of getting to college must be calculated by first obtaining the total costs associated with the car and then allocating the portion of such costs that pertains to obtaining a college education by our cost center. If the car is used only to commute to college, then the expenses involved in its purchase and upkeep would be a direct cost of attending college. In other words, an indirect cost is shared among more than one cost objective. Such sharing is what accountants call cost allocation or, more recently, cost assignment.

A direct cost also can be conveniently traced to the product or the output. If it cannot be traced easily or if it is not cost-effective to be so tracked, then it is classified as an indirect cost, making it a part of the overhead. For the sake of convenience, the wood used in making furniture is classified as a direct cost, while the glue used for the same sofa is seen as indirect. Even though both can be physically traced to the product, the reason for not treating glue used as a direct cost is because it is inconvenient to do so. Tracking the actual cost of the drops of glue that went into the sofa is not a job easily justified, since the amount is not material. Hence its classification as a part of the overhead, which will in turn be allocated to the final products.

Items such as the glue used on sofas are lumped together as overhead. Anything used in the production that was not specifically identified as direct labor or material is considered overhead. This includes the depreciation of the long-term assets as well as the expenses of having staff members who work for all the cost centers—for example, maintenance workers in a factory. Even the salaries paid to supervisors are classified as indirect costs, since their time is spent between different jobs, in contrast to the wages of assembly-line workers, whose labor is more easily traced to specific jobs. Inventory-related costs such as those associated with receiving the raw material, getting it to the cost centers on the production floor, and keeping it secure are also seen as overhead items. Salaries of accountants and timekeepers are also overhead because their services usually are shared among all the cost centers.

At one time, overhead was not seen as a major item, judging from the use of the word "prime cost" to describe direct labor and direct material. However, overhead now tends to be much higher than direct labor costs. Moreover, today support activities make up a higher share of the total costs. For some firms, overhead can represent 90 percent or more of the costs incurred in getting their outputs into the hands of their customers. Consequently, management of overhead is of prime importance. The upward creep in overhead must not be seen as being a phenomenon of the 1990s. Accountants have traced the upward trend back to the 1920s. Allocation almost always involves estimating. When overhead management was not given prime importance, the accuracy of the estimated overhead allocations was not critical. But with overhead representing an ever-higher share of the total costs, it is imperative to allocate it more accurately. Allocating common costs more correctly is what ABC is all about.

17.7 COST BEHAVIOR

It is generally known that different kinds of costs behave differently when the production volume changes. In the past, cost behavior emphasized the following differentiation of costs:

- Committed fixed costs. Changes in production volume do not result in changing committed fixed costs, as long as the changes in volume fall within a certain range. A factory built to produce ten thousand units presumably will not show changes in fixed costs, as long as volume produced was ten thousand units or less.
- Discretionary fixed costs. These remain fixed for a designated period. The salary of the controller remains the same for the year, at the end of which there may be a change in it. The budgets for training or advertising similarly can remain fixed until the new budget, when, at the discretion of managers, they may change.
- Variable costs. These vary directly in proportion to the volume. One battery per car and the hourly pay rate of direct labor are examples of variable costs.
- Step-variable costs. These vary in steps, hence their name. The costs for an automobile oil change every three thousand miles and the salaries of a mechanic and other maintenance workers are examples of costs that change in discrete blocks.
- Mixed costs. These have a fixed component as well as a portion that varies with the activity volume. A phone bill can have a fixed portion, such as the monthly fee for having a connection. It also can have variable charges based on the long-distance calls made.

17.8 COST BEHAVIOR UNDER ACTIVITY-BASED COSTING

Costs classification under ABC is on the basis of their association with activities at the following levels: unit level, batch level, facility level, and product level. None of these except the unit-level costs can be traced directly to the units of production, and from the perspective of units produced, they are fixed costs. But when linked to activity drivers, they become variable. These costs are first collected in a cost pool and then assigned/ allocated using an appropriate basis. The allocation bases under ABC are labeled *cost drivers*. If an activity is to be considered a cost driver, there must be some relationship between it and the accrual of costs. A larger number of cost drivers are employed under ABC, compared with the traditional costing methods. Even now, firms using just one driver to allocate all the indirect costs are easy to find.

Costing activities reveal the extent to which they add or do not add value to outputs. Some activities may not add any value at all. A firm may be providing more product options than can be justified given its sales or resources. Such measurements of the costs incurred and the benefits realized permit management of activities for optimum benefits. Such assistance to management is the real value of ABM.

17.9 ACTIVITY LEVELS FOR ACTIVITY-BASED COSTING

The four levels of activities and the costs associated with each are described next.

Unit-Level Costs

Unit-level costs are the variable costs, and they correspond with the level of production. Direct labor or machine hours vary with the number of units produced.

An example of an activity that creates unit-level costs is assembly-line production. This activity results in the consumption of resources, such as hourly wages of workers, and direct material used, such as tires and batteries for automobiles.

The cost drivers typically used to assign unit-level costs are the number of units produced as well as labor hours and quantity of material.

Batch-Level Costs

Batch-level costs are those that correspond to the number of batches produced. A batch-level cost will accrue whenever a batch of units is made.

Examples of such costs are those associated with activities such as machine setup, order processing, and material handling. The resources used for these activities are labor costs of setting up machinery, processing job orders, and writing up purchase vouchers.

Typical cost drivers used at this level are the number of purchase orders issued, the number of times machines were set up, and the number of batches produced.

Facility-Level Costs

Facility-level costs are incurred to maintain the plant where the product is manufactured. These are the most difficult to assign.

The resources used at this level are for plant depreciation, payment of taxes, salaries of plant managers, and expenses incurred for the general training of employees.

The typical cost drivers used for facility-level costs are the number of employees in the activity centers, the volume of units produced, and the allocation percentages arrived at by management.

Product-Level Costs

Product-level costs are those that pertain to activities such as product design, special handling, storage, and parts and product testing. Maintaining bills of materials and routing information are also seen as product-level activities.

Resources this level requires include the specialized equipment needed for a given product as well as the costs incurred to design and test it.

The cost drivers used at this level are the number of products developed or manufactured as well as the number of parts used by a given product.

17.10 SEARCH FOR MORE ACCURATE ALLOCATION

The search for more accurate allocation has been around for some time, even before the advent of ABC. Indeed, ABC itself was known at the end of the nineteenth century. Its failure to gain greater acceptance was due largely to a lack of computers that could perform the large number of calculations needed by an ABC system. Below are the various methods used to allocate indirect costs—they range from least to most accurate with respect to the cost assignments made.

- The basic method involves all indirect costs incurred being added up and then assigned to units manufactured by means of a single basis such as direct labor hours incurred in the production. Such a method obviously is most subject to aggregation and distortion of costs.
- A greater degree of accuracy is produced when, instead of using just one basis for all the production departments, different bases are used for each of them. These drivers could be the cost of direct materials used in one department, direct labor hours in the next, and machine hours in yet another.
- Even more accurate are systems that isolate from the total overhead the service departments' costs and assign them first to production departments and, through them, to units produced. Service departments are those that are not directly involved in the manufacturing process but facilitate the work of those departments that are so involved. These could be human resources, maintenance, cafeteria, and inventory warehouse. At times, the service departments will use different bases for assigning fixed and variable costs incurred by the service departments; for instance, budgeted machine hours for variable costs, but machine hours based on total capacity available for fixed costs.

All of these methods described seek allocations of common costs. The allocation is mandated by the generally accepted accounting principles (GAAP) for external reporting. However, such a mandate is self-defeating because it is willing to accept allocation methods that are questionable. An example of such questionable method is discussed in the following section.

17.11 ACCEPTANCE OF IRRATIONAL ALLOCATIONS BY GENERALLY ACCEPTED ACCOUNTING PRINCIPLE

One example where questionable methods are acceptable for allocating common costs is through examining the so-called joint product costing. Joint products are separate products that are obtained from a common source but then split into distinct products, which can in turn be further processed into yet more products. From an oil well, natural gas and crude oil are obtained. Both of them are joint products and both are further processed into yet more joint products.

In the meat products industry, the common source, such as a cow, turns into a number of different products, like steaks, ground beef, and bones. The costs that pertain to the purchase of the common source and getting it ready to be split into different products are called joint costs. GAAP requires that such joint costs be allocated among all the products that result after the common source is split into its components.

A number of methods are acceptable for allocating joint costs. One uses the net realizable value of each product as a basis for allocating; another uses the quantities by weight of separate products obtained at the split-off as the basis. Under the latter, steaks, ground beef, soup bones, and hide and entrails will all be allocated a share of common costs based on their respective weights at the split-off. The values assigned to bones, hides, and chitterlings will be higher, because by weight they represent considerably more than they do in terms of final profits realized. Such cost allocations will make them appear to be the losers in financial reporting because the revenue they provide is less than their allocated costs. But dropping them from the portfolio of products sold will lower the total profits. Dropping them causes the loss of whatever revenue they realized, but the common costs will not change in the total. The share that was being allocated to these less fashionable products must now be split among those that remain—the ones remaining will be allocated a higher share of the common costs. Notwithstanding the problem described, this method can be used for financial reporting.

Under each method used for joint cost allocation, the cost of goods sold and the inventory values for each joint product is different, often vastly different. However, such distortions are offset when they are aggregated for the final accounting statements. So, for the external reporting using cost and revenue aggregates, it does not matter if the costs and the profits reported for individual joint products are inaccurate, since the bottom line will take care of the inaccuracies. But in decisions concerning individual products, for instance, those that involve product pricing, such distorted costs are not to be believed. Pricing decisions for joint products are best made by treating joint costs as common costs that need not be allocated.

17.12 TRYING TO DO WITHOUT ALLOCATIONS

Not allocating common costs is against GAAP, but for decisions that are of concern only to internal decision makers, such a departure from GAAP is acceptable and is indeed quite widespread. Pricing decisions for joint products are not the only ones to treat indirect costs in this way by ignoring allocations of the common costs. The contribution approach to costing is applicable and useful for a wide variety of policy decisions, and it will not allocate common fixed costs to respective products or even divisions. Instead of cumbersome allocation, common costs are treated as a corporate period expense. But the danger in such a treatment is that product managers will ignore the common costs, since they are not being charged for them. It is acceptable to ignore common fixed costs for some short-term policy decisions, but the same does not hold for strategic policy decisions.

Unfortunately, a firm will not survive long if its strategic policies do not seek to recover its common costs. In recent years, the airlines in the United States have shown just such an obliviousness toward common costs, judging from the frequent price wars that occur between them. The bankruptcy of Pan American and others can be attributed partly to their failure to recover the common fixed costs of operating an airline through their pricing policies. Their pricing policies incorrectly relied on the application of a short-term remedy for long-term structural problems, such as too many airlines competing in the same markets.

17.13 TRACKING ACTIVITY-BASED COSTING

Tracking cost under an ABC system will occur through the following five steps:

1. Assemble related actions into activity groups.
2. Track and pool costs by activities.
3. Select cost drivers that link cost pools for activities with outputs (cost objectives), such as units produced.
4. Calculate rates to help assign the cost of activities to outputs in keeping with their activity usage.
5. Assign common costs, or rather the cost of activities, to units produced or other cost objectives.

These steps are briefly explained below.

(a) Assemble Activity Groups

A large number of activities are performed in any organization. The cost accounting ideal is to cost each activity on an à la carte basis. However, doing this outside of a restaurant menu is very likely not cost effective. Hence, actions are arranged in activity groups to help make cost-effective tracking more manageable. These groupings often are done in terms of their relationship to different activity levels.

Care must be taken to arrange the costs in a given pool only if they are driven by the same or at least correlated activities. Setup costs are actually a mixture of labor and supplies, and the two of them are not necessarily correlated. But if they are pooled together and then assigned using just one driver, such as the setup time in a combined pool, distortion will result. Similarly, if costs arranged in the pool do not have the same degree of proportionality with the driver used, there will be distortion. An example of such distortion is seen when the variable and fixed portions of utility costs are combined and a single rate is used to assign the combination to the output. As previously mentioned, the activity levels of use in ABC are unit, batch, facility, and product. Some activity groups may be contained within one department, while others can be spread across several departments.

(b) Track Cost by Activities

Following the development of activity groups, costs must be grouped by the activities. In order for costs to be so tracked and pooled, changes in the typical charts of accounts may be necessary.

(c) Select Cost Drivers

Cost drivers are the connecting link among costs, activities, and outputs. A cost driver can link a cost pool associated with an activity to units produced, or it can link costs in one activity center to activities in another center. One way to help classify cost drivers is in terms of first-stage and second-stage cost drivers. First-stage drivers link the cost of resources consumed in an individual activity to other activity centers. Such assignments are similar to the way a service department allocates its costs to other departments. The second-stage drivers link costs from the activity center to actual units of production.

(d) Calculate Rates to Assign Cost

Once costs are tracked to the pools of activities and cost drivers have been agreed upon, then the rates per cost driver unit can be calculated. This rate could be based on either the planned or the actual activity level.

(e) Assign Costs of Activities to Outputs

Using the rates calculated above, the final step can be undertaken. This consists of distributing costs to units of output or rather the cost objectives. Eventually all costs involved in the manufacturing process are assigned to products.

17.14 ACTIVITY-BASED COSTING MINUS THE HYPE

H. Thomas Johnson's, It's Time to Stop Overselling Activity-Based Concepts (*Management Accounting,* Sept. 1992, p. 40), argues that by itself ABC does not help bring a firm long-term financial health or the ability to compete effectively in the global economy. The approach will indeed provide managers better information to do the following:

- Help evaluate and plan pricing strategy.
- Help decide upon product and customer mix policies.
- Help make choices among different alternatives.
- Help calculate profit margins.
- Help calculate cost of services provided.
- Help cost production more accurately.

Johnson by no means denies the benefits of ABC in helping to overcome the distortions that can result if cost accounting relies on allocating methods that prevailed in the 1960s and 1970s. While upholding the usefulness of ABC for better cost allocation, he cautions against using it as a substitute for effective management in tune with customers' needs.

By itself, Johnson warns, ABC will not help firms attain ongoing evolution. To do that, companies must change their perceptions about customers, employees, and the traditional ideas about how the organizational structures ought to function. Activity-based costing and the information it provides do not ensure evolution, especially if management insists on keeping the traditional ways of doing things, such as top managers commanding those who work for them to do certain tasks and hoping that such top-down strategy will ensure continued and ongoing profitability. He subscribes to the view that ABC-based information would not have prevented by themselves the kind of difficulties that confronted U.S. manufacturers in the 1970s.

Johnson does not want the American firms to get bogged down in activity analysis. He wants organizations to think beyond the activities, analyze customers' needs, and find ways to best satisfy them. The ABC analysis fails to communicate the needs of the customers or the weaknesses in the processes in place to managers. Merely by allocating the cost of resources used more effectively will not make one a leader in the marketplace of the present-day global village. Instead of relying excessively on cost allocation, those seeking organizational evolution will do well to create conditions allowing everyone working for the firm to be committed to serving the customers (both internal and external) as well as to improving the processes in place. Long-term improvement occurs when the firms are able to take timely actions that will lead to improved outcomes and eliminate variations in production and service. In seeking to improve outcomes, one must pay attention to the processes and not on rating the performance of the people who work them. These views, espoused by W. Edwards Deming, are accepted by Johnson, who makes them the basis for his advocacy of caution in thinking about the usefulness of ABC analysis.

What Johnson is suggesting is that while ABC does represents an improvement over the costing methods that were the rules in the 1960s and 1970s, it is not the ticket to profitability nirvana. Getting the costs matched with their alleged cost drivers by itself will not serve customers any better. Cost control does not lead to evolutionary competence; what does work is the willingness of a firm to permit its workers, its most valued assets, to find ways to better anticipate and satisfy the needs of their customers. Instead of forcing workers to see everything in terms of its costs, managers will do well to train them to find and eliminate wasteful deployment of resources. Activities are to the processes as are trees to a forest. Firms are better advised to keep their focus on the intertwined processes they are involved with, and not limit themselves to computing the dollar value of activities that are undertaken. Non–value-adding activities can be eliminated without putting a dollar value on them.

Johnson has raised a flag that warns accountants and managers not to see ABC as the solution to all problems, while not denying its value as a cost allocation tool. What is important for Johnson is the knowledge that one does not live by more effective cost-allocation techniques alone. Much more is needed to prevail rather than just subsist in the marketplace.

Anyone who is seeking to be informed about ABC would do well to start by reading Johnson's article and his book; *Relevance Regained: From Top-Down Control to Bottom-Up Empowerment* (1992). These keep ABC in the proper perspective.

CHAPTER 18

INFORMATION TECHNOLOGY AS AN AGENT OF CHANGE

18.1 INTRODUCTION

This chapter sheds light on a perplexing problem today's corporate controllers confront: How does one determine whether to apply information technology (IT) to help solve departmental problems and to improve operating procedures? If IT is to be used, then which technology? Such a choice would not be difficult were it not for IT's mixed record. It is this mixed record that can lead a controller to see the promise of IT as either marketing hype or an enabler.

18.2 PROMISE AND PERFORMANCE

Since computers were first introduced in the 1950s, their potential for changing procedures and processes has been loudly proclaimed. Unfortunately, this prediction has not always been fulfilled. Incidents of complete failure of IT systems or significant variances between promised and attained benefits are not uncommon. The much-touted advantages of IT failed to appear in manufacturing as well as in white-collar jobs, such as those in a controller's department. Indeed, instances have been recorded when large investments in IT actually lowered productivity and thus profitability.

18.3 TECHNOLOGY IS NOT AT FAULT

Instances of the disappointing performance of IT notwithstanding, the emergent technology has indeed compiled an impressive record. In the manufacturing sector, it has helped evolve newer tools such as robots, sensors, and automatic, self-correcting testing. It has helped enhance material handling with automatic storage and retrieval systems in warehouses around the world. In addition, the impact of IT is visible through computer-aided design and manufacture, material requirement planning, production scheduling, and a variety of decision-support systems. In the world of white-collar work, IT also is changing how things get done through word processing, spreadsheets, databases, automated filing, transaction systems, computer conferencing, electronic mail, computer bulletin boards, and expert systems.

There should be no doubt that in the future, the price-to-performance ratio of IT hardware and software will continue to improve—computers will keep getting better, faster, and, most important, cheaper to own and operate. They can facilitate an increase in the productivity of many business functions. But as a consequence of implementing an IT solution, new and unexpected problems may well occur. In some cases, these new problems are either not severe or can be remedied over time. For example, on-line systems provide a mechanism that could allow anyone with computer know-how access to secret information. To fix this problem, software security can be incorporated into the system. In other cases the new problems prove to be sizable and reduce the productivity gains that were anticipated. Customized systems that provide needed functionality but require programming support staffs to keep them operational represent one such problem. Estimates of the maintenance cost of existing software systems run from 60 to 80 percent of the entire data processing budget!

It can be argued that the unrealized promise of IT is not due to the failure of technology but to the failure to integrate it with the existing work environment. If the new technology is introduced in a well-planned manner, the chances of its failure or a suboptimal performance can be minimized. More important, IT will be much more helpful if it is not seen as an electronic tool to do the same old things. Even today, many companies require vouchers with five and more copies to take care of purchases and related payments. When there are five or more copies of a document, five or more employees will be needed to handle the tasks. If a computer is being brought in to keep turning out the same vouchers with the same number of copies, the productivity gains will not be all that impressive. The work may get done faster, but it will remain the same work with the same paper glut.

In other words, controllers need not view IT as "snake oil," but if IT is to truly revolutionize work, its introduction must be well planned. It will be even better if the work IT is meant to perform is redesigned.

18.4 DEMONSTRATING THE USEFULNESS OF INFORMATION TECHNOLOGY

The usefulness of IT as a tool to help solve the recurrent and common problems faced by accounting departments was examined in 1982 in an article by Vincent Giovinazzo.[1] In this article, Giovinazzo discussed a number of everyday problems that plague accounting departments in all sorts of organizations. The list includes problems having to do with the use of IT to help perform accounting functions as well as problems that predated the advent of IT. While past performance is no guarantee of future success, the progress made in addressing old problems would seem to be an appropriate reference point to show the effectiveness of IT in helping to provide solutions to operating problems.

Despite their universality, the problems listed by Giovinazzo lacked the chic or the glamour that might have allowed them to be discussed systematically in the professional literature. Such persistent, universally occurring but rarely discussed problems, according to Giovinazzo, are:

- Source data vulnerability
- Involvement of nonaccounting personnel
- Nonintegrated accounting systems
- Processing and reporting lags
- Uneven workload
- Underestimation of time requirements
- Human relations problems

For each of these issues, we examine the problem in the IT climate of 1982, Giovinazzo's proposed solution(s), and the extent to which IT solutions exist today. In order to avoid reliance on untested technology, we will limit the solutions to commercially available products. Finally, we will compare solutions available now with the 1982 proposals.

(a) Source Data Vulnerability

Problem.   The smooth working of accounting systems depends on accurate data entry. Incorrect data input tends to be the result of human error manifested in the form of miscalculations, typing errors, misreading of forms, sloppy handwriting, and the failure to follow directions. With early versions of IT, yet another source of potential errors was introduced as a result of the coding of data to make it computer-readable.

Proposed Solution.   Giovinazzo proposed to minimize the source errors by the use of well-designed forms, effective training, well-understood procedures, a clearly defined chart of accounts, better coding, manual reviews, establishing and meeting deadlines, and prompt feedback on errors. His technological recommendation was the use of intelligent terminals that code and input data at the point of entry. He alluded to such point-of-sale terminals (POS) being already at work in selected industries, such as retailing. He also argued the importance of on-line technology and saw it as becoming a part of the solution but did not see it as becoming universal.

Current Solution.   IT today offers technological solutions that can minimize the impact of human errors and carelessness. Today, on-line systems are much more prevalent and allow for better (more accurate) data entry. Application software can instantaneously detect erroneous input of data; modern programming environments facilitate error detection capabilities. For example, modern database management systems provide for referential and range testing of data. Additionally, on-line systems allow entry of data at the source point by someone closer to the transactions, rather than a generic data-entry clerk who simply keypunches without knowing what was being entered into the system. Finally, much more is now known about human factors that were conducive to erroneous data inputs. As a result of such awareness, screen design techniques have been developed that minimize the errors attributable to data input.

An even greater impact on the reduction of source errors is due to the explosion of alternative input devices. POS, bar code scanners, optical character recognizers, and custom-built input devices permit direct input of data with minimal (and often complete) elimination of human involvement.

These devices not only improve the customer-service function; they also store and transmit transactions to various accounting subsystems. Previously these functions were accomplished primarily by clerks. The inexpensive nature of such alternative input devices makes them cost-effective for small and medium-size businesses.

During recent years, efforts have been made to facilitate the transfer of information between organizations. Electronic data interchange (EDI) allows data generated from the business process of one organization to be entered directly into the information system of another organization. With EDI, a customer can enter a purchase order in a system and have it transmitted to the appropriate vendor's information system. Once there, it is converted into a sales order on the vendor's information system. This technology increases data accuracy as it reduces the number of people who are responsible for creating and/or processing documents. In addition, accuracy is increased as data from the document are mechanically entered into the accounting system rather than keyed in by a clerk.

(b) Involvement of Nonaccounting Personnel

Problem.   Data enters accounting systems from within the firm and outside the firm. Almost all departments and operational areas constantly must provide source data to the accounting department. It is not uncommon for departments to resent this role. Besides such resentment, given the external origin of source data, the accounting department cannot control the clarity, accuracy, and timeliness of data entering the system. Thus, there are really two problems: resentment and the opportunity for data entry error (a potential cause of problem source data vulnerability, previously discussed).

Proposed Solution.   As with source data errors, Giovinazzo saw better forms as helping to minimize the errors in the data received from external sources. In addition, he argued the need for better communication between accountants and others within the organization to reduce resentment. The relationship between accountants and the rest of the organization could be improved if the reports provided by accountants were timely, error-free, and relevant to internal users. Such reports should have a managerial (rather than financial) accounting orientation.

Current Solution.   Increasingly, the direct entry of data from the "process" into the accounting system is being facilitated by input devices described previously. Since these devices increase the rate at which data is entered and the accuracy of the data, they reduce the data error problem. In addition, the devices generate the accounting data as a by-product of the action performed by the nonaccounting worker. For example, clerks at supermarkets use bar code scanners to compute the customers' bill and print a receipt. As a by-product of this function, the accounting system will receive inventory and sales data that can be used to update appropriate ledgers. The generation of this (accurate) data requires no additional effort by the employee computing the customers' purchases, so data accuracy is improved and resentment is reduced or eliminated.

(c) Nonintegrated Accounting Systems

Problem.   The typical accounting system is comprised of a series of subsystems that are interdependent but not fully integrated. Not all software subsystems integrate with all other applicable subsystems. That is, many firms have payroll, billing, and inventory subsystems that do not automatically integrate with the general ledger. It is common to find the various subsystems physically dispersed, with no communications mechanism to transmit and integrate the data between the subsystems. Not all subsystems are computerized; often when they are, the software package is unable to handle many of the exceptional transactions. In addition, the application packages are so detail oriented that no single person could use the entire package. Each individual knows different parts but not the entire package.

Proposed Solution.   Giovinazzo argued that systems should be designed so that relevant data would be transmitted automatically among related systems. Accountants should insist that there be greater integration between the accounting subsystems. In general, he stressed that management accountants should have a larger role in defining specifications for accounting systems.

Current Solution.   Today, IT solutions address these problems. The problem of subsystem integration has been addressed. Firms obtain accounting software by developing it or purchasing packaged systems. For the custom approach, it is now a standard requirement that all subsystems be integrated. If the software cannot achieve the requirement, it will not be installed. For package systems, complete integration is a requirement.

The ability to communicate data generated by systems of this sort is standard within any hardware platform. In the past, the cost of such communications over long distances or to many locations was prohibitive. Competition and technological innovations have dramatically reduced this cost.

Finally, most package systems provide functions that address the problems of all departments. In the packaged solution area, much effort has been made to understand the entire processing of the subsystem so that a clear and streamlined process is programmed. Current tools such as help screens and graphical user interfaces (GUI) also help to make the software easier to use.

If a business is operating today without an integrated accounting system, it is not because of the unavailability of IT. Integrated accounting packages are now available to fit a variety of needs.

(d) Processing and Reporting Lags

Problem. The time lag between when transactions actually occur and when they are reported in the form of accounting statements is a long-standing accounting problem. This delay is caused both by procedural and mechanical deficiencies. The large amount of data to be entered, examined, verified, and processed takes time. Since most systems are batch oriented, delays occur as a consequence of gathering the data, ensuring its accuracy, coding it, and then entering it into the system. Additional delays are encountered in processing the data as a result of limited machine processing speed.

Proposed Solution. This problem is seen as being primarily one of scheduling. Hence, the proposed solution is to improve the scheduling of work and then ensure that those assigned to various tasks met established deadlines.

Current Solution. Faster machines have allowed the information systems to keep up with the increased transaction rates, even though the on-line systems require additional processing power. Notwithstanding the advances in technology, up-to-date reporting of transactions and their impact on accounting reports is not universally available. This is a consequence of continued difficulty in getting all relevant accounting data assembled and entered. As discussed, input device technology has progressed significantly towards the goal of complete on-line entry of data at the source. Unfortunately, it has not solved this problem for the myriad of sources that the general ledger requires in order to generate its standard periodic reports.

(e) Uneven Workload

Problem. Traditionally, accounting departments have had uneven workloads. During events such as the closing of the books, physical inventory, and/or audits, the department suffers from an overload; the rest of the time the workload tends to be relatively slow. In large part, problems of the reporting lags and the uneven workloads are a direct result of the fact that the accounting department is not where transactions actually occur. The purchasing department orders the merchandise, and it is received by the inventory department. Accounting gets the paperwork from both departments and must further process it (1) so that payment can be made for the goods ordered and (2) to update the accounting records. In organizations that do not have fully integrated systems, the occurrence of a transaction, the transmittal of paperwork relating to that transaction, and the updating of accounting records do not occur simultaneously. Prior to monthly closings, accounting records must be brought up to date. This requires accounting clerks to go hunting for the documentation elsewhere in the organization, process it, and then enter it so that accounting records are ready for the monthly closing. Sources of the accounting department logjams are often external to the department. Consequently, when the deadline of monthly closing approaches and/or when auditors arrive, the workloads of the accounting department increase considerably; this can lead to errors in the reports generated.

Proposed Solution.   Giovinazzo noted that possible causes of the buildup could be late arrival of data from outside the accounting department or inappropriate processing procedures within the accounting department. As a solution to the problem, he suggested analyzing how the work is done over a period of time and determining what factors cause the logjams. Measuring the quantity of work as well as measuring the error rates could help isolate and eliminate the logjams. Such work measurements also could support the argument for additional staffing, at least during peak work periods. In addition to analyzing how accounting work is done, he suggested that the problem may be abated by convincing the operating departments to adhere to transmittal deadlines and data accuracy.

Current Solution.   With the computerized systems now available, there is no reason for lags between transactions and the updating of the accounting records. Since the system automatically updates the accounting records, there should not be a need to manually update the books before the monthly closings. Given the availability of such technology and the improved means of communication now available, work flow within the accounting department can be more evenly paced.

(f) Underestimation of Time Requirements

Problem.   The problem of not estimating time requirements correctly occurs because accountants have to pay attention to many details, which can be time consuming and require close scrutiny. Additionally, verification and follow-up can take time because they involve personnel outside the accounting department, who may not cooperate. Finally, changes in plans are always being made.

Proposed Solution.   Giovinazzo did not suggest a specific solution for this problem; however, the work measurement he recommended to even the work flow within the accounting department can lead to better estimates of the time required for various assignments.

Current Solution.   These are not IT-related problems; however, even here e-mail, voice mail, and other IT-related means of communicating can reduce the time required to get discrepancies resolved and/or questions answered. In addition, robust systems should provide for much higher levels of accuracy, thus reducing the need for close review of the data.

(g) Human Relations Problems

Problem.   Reference already has been made to the tensions between the accounting department and the operating departments. In addition, resentment between accounting and information systems (IS) personnel is common. Friction between accountants and IS personnel is the result of factors such as:

- The perception by accounting personnel that their needs were not accorded the proper priority by the IS department.
- The failure of either group to remain on schedule.
- Accountants' perception that IS keeps changing the systems.
- Too much technical jargon in both departments makes communication difficult.
- Accountants lack IS expertise, so they fail to understand the technological constraints.
- IS is seen as taking over some of the functions previously done by accountants; this leads to "tuff battles" between accountants and IS personnel.

Proposed Solution.   Giovinazzo suggested that accountants acquire better communication skills and show greater understanding toward the operating personnel and their work constraints. Efforts should be made to have accounting reports serve the needs of the operating managers. Relevant reports would improve the attitude of the operating managers toward accounting and make them more willing to work with accounting. Accountants also should be more involved in the design of the IS system(s).

Current Solution.   This particular problem has abated for a variety of reasons. Some of the accounting IS needs have been reduced because of software available to accountants. Principally through advanced use of spreadsheets, accountants have been able to fend for themselves in terms of data processing needs. In addition, database management system query languages provide a means for nonprogrammers to retrieve information from the database in an ad hoc manner. These two features are part of a general trend, called end-user computing; this approach encourages the user to retrieve, compute, and display information in any manner they choose without the need of the IS staff.

In addition, accounting personnel, by training and experience, have become more computer literate. This means they are able to use IT more readily, and they are more familiar with the jargon. To a lesser extent, IS personnel are becoming more accounting literate. IS departments have become more concerned with having personnel who not only understand technology but also the business problems that they are being asked to address.

18.5 ASSESSING THE PROMISE OF INFORMATION TECHNOLOGY

In general, it is difficult to assess the success achieved by using IT. Part of the problem results from the fact that many benefits associated with IT are intangible. We sought to get around the difficulties by using a 1982 article referring to commonly occurring accounting problems as our point of departure. The extent to which these problems can be resolved using the IT available now is convincing evidence that IT's promises are not just marketing hype.

At the time Giovinazzo wrote his article, the technology was less advanced. Using the IT then available, Giovinazzo recognized the need for the use of integrated systems, the importance of on-line capabilities, and a greater involvement of the accountants in the design and operation of the IS systems. As one looks at today's environment and technology, it is clear that the IT currently available has reduced the problem of accuracy and speed. Today it is feasible to have on-line, integrated accounting systems with built-in controls available to ensure accurate data input. The price/performance ratios are improving, and the systems are easier to use. In addition, accountants are becoming more knowledgeable about IT. The predictions made about technology have been greatly exceeded, and today it is entirely possible to find IT solutions for problems dealing with data acquisition, manipulation, speed of processing, and analysis. Using IT, source data vulnerability, nonintegrated accounting systems, and uneven workloads can be virtually eliminated.

The remaining four of the seven problems mentioned cannot be resolved completely through IT because they are people problems; nevertheless, here too, IT has helped. This was also perceived by Giovinazzo. He expected the main thrust for solving the problems to come from nontechnical steps such as:

- Better forms to reduce data entry errors
- Cooperation between information producers and information users to ensure that the information being reported is relevant
- Better relationships between accountants and operating departments so that data concerning operations could be communicated expeditiously
- Need to analyze and measure work done by accounting workers with a view toward the elimination of logjams

Given this analysis, it is clear that technical problems have been greatly reduced, but the same is not true of other, nontechnical problems. In other words, problems that involve routine, repetitive work have been virtually eliminated. But problems that involve the system itself or deal with human behavior remain unsolved. If the procedures required by the system are cumbersome, they are not likely to become less so just by giving workers computers instead of hand-held calculators and spreadsheets in place of twelve-column ledger sheets. Many operating departments also remain unconvinced of the importance of the accounting reports. Loud voices are being raised to complain about the relevance of accounting reports to the needs of many of today's users.

These problems are not likely to disappear as long as the current structures remain, and they cannot be made to disappear by IT alone. As long as an organization is structured in terms of departments, and performance is judged on a departmental basis, there are likely to be turf battles and struggles over getting the maximum share of the resources for one's own department. Furthermore, such departmentalization promotes partial answers rather than innovative, comprehensive solutions.

Techniques such as total quality management, activity-based costing, and, most notably, reengineering have been shown to have considerable success with the systemic problems encountered by accounting departments when they are used in conjunction with the IT now available. Using these proven tools, managers can help reevaluate the accounting procedures currently being used in the hope of eliminating procedural gridlocks and redefine the procedures documentation process.

18.6 EMERGING INFORMATION TECHNOLOGY

This part of the chapter introduces readers to the current state of information technology, particularly as it impacts the accounting function. Given the very large body of material, it seemed best to leverage such coverage by focusing on key topics: Data warehouse, wide area networks (WANs), extranets and intranets, electronic data interchange (EDI), client/server technology, and enterprise resource planning (ERP). These topics seem very relevant to the emerging accounting information systems.

18.7 DATA WAREHOUSES AND DATAMARTS

Pooling the data from separate applications into a large, common body of information is called a *data warehouse*. It is in effect a repository of enterprise-wide data. One advantage of a data warehouse is to make organizational information available throughout the enterprise. For example, with such an approach, a company's marketing representatives might gain access to the company's production data and thereby be better able to inform customers about the future availability of desired but as-yet unmanufactured products. This idea is also central to the concept of an enterprise-wide database—a large repository of organizational data that comes from, and is available to, a wide range of employees. Another advantage is that the data warehouse may facilitate data mining and enable its users to better identify target markets or its most desirable customers.

Data warehouses are an attempt to get clean, unified data that has been optimized for query-intensive activities into a single database. The data may come from internal or external systems and it may be deployed at various levels within a distributed enterprise. Then the warehouse can be surrounded with specialized query and reporting tools that can extract data stored in the warehouse.

An alternative approach for the storage of a large amount of data is the datamart. Unlike data warehouse, a datamart is a smaller-scale information-delivery initiative that is designed to service a specific functional need, such as sales and marketing analysis, or a specific user group, such as executive management. These datamarts may be set up as separately managed databases fed from one or more source transaction systems, or they may be fed from the main data warehouse. Datamarts also may be used as a stepping-stone to the main corporate data warehouse.

18.8 WIDE AREA NETWORKS

WANs are rather complex, multifaceted information systems that can serve the needs of a variety of users. They are dedicated to specific tasks: Most shopping mall ATM cash-vending machines are connected in WANs to help centralize account information pertaining to thousands, possibly hundreds of thousands, of their clients. Regional and national supermarket chains also rely on WANs to gather inventory data, cash receipts data, and sales information from the many stores in their chains. Even very large information distribution systems such as America Online (AOL) and CompuServe maintain WANs that permit their customers to access centralized databases through local phone numbers. Many other Internet-access providers also operate their own WANs.

WANs have been used for performing the following kinds of communication:

- Gathering financial information from geographically remote sites
- Distributing information to and from headquarters
- Facilitating communications among users with e-mail
- Enabling organizations to create intranets
- Supporting electronic data exchange such as electronic transmission of documents
- Providing users access to the Internet
- Enabling groups, such as students, employees, or organizations, to teleconference

One need not belabor the all too obvious point that the tasks of installing, evaluating, controlling, and auditing such networks can be challenging but worthwhile, given how WANs support organizational communication.

Many WANs are organized in a hierarchy, in which the individual microcomputers of a specific branch office are connected to a file server on a local area network (LAN). The file servers of several LANs then can be connected to a regional computer, and several regional computers are, in turn, linked to a corporate mainframe. This hierarchical network facilitates a large organization to collect, archive, and distribute financial and nonfinancial information at the appropriate geographic level of the company.

18.9 EXTRANETS AND INTRANETS

Distinct from the Internet are intranets, private networks employed by organizations to use web browser software that businesses create for such internal purposes as distributing e-mail. Extranets are similar to intranets, but they allow external parties to access internal network files and databases. Extranets allow vendors to link up with purchasers and to share information. Extranets may rely on GroupWare (software that supports e-mail on business networks and also permits users to share computer files, schedule appointments, and develop custom applications).

18.10 ELECTRONIC DATA INTERCHANGE

Electronic data interchange allows organizations to transmit standard business data over high-speed data communications channels. Examples of business documents that can be communicated using EDI include:

- Requests for quotes (Rfqs)
- Materials requirement planning (MRP) documents
- Purchase orders
- Bills of lading
- Freight bills
- Sales invoices
- Customs documents
- Payment remittance forms
- Credit memos

All of these documents can be transmitted electronically at the speed of light to the intended recipients, who could number in the hundreds or thousands. EDI automates the exchange of business information and permits organizations to conduct many forms of commerce electronically.

For many firms, EDI is a superior way of doing business. Perhaps the most important advantage is that EDI users no longer are required to transcribe manually the data from a trading partner's hard-copy forms (such as purchase order information) into their own systems; the data are already in computer-readable formats. This saves businesses time and labor and significantly reduces the number of errors introduced into job streams when manual data transcription is required. EDI also streamlines processing tasks because:

- Business partners exchange documents quickly and easily.
- There are no postal delays.
- EDI eliminates most of the paperwork.

Some firms find the advantages of EDI so compelling that they refuse to do business with those companies that do not use it. This helps explain what makes EDI the fastest-growing segment of electronic commerce, with an annual growth rate of 29 percent. A 1997 survey found that approximately 95 percent of the Fortune 1000 companies use EDI in some form. Experts predict that, in the near future, such time-honored functions as processing accounts receivable will disappear as higher-level linkages between cash management and billing become available. There are problems associated with EDI: while it helps improve the communication of data, it can create other problems. For one thing, it makes auditing a greater burden because electronic transactions are more difficult to verify, authenticate, and therefore audit.

18.11 VALUE-ADDED NETWORKS VERSUS THE INTERNET AS A BASIS FOR ELECTRONIC DATA INTERCHANGE

To implement EDI applications, most businesses currently use private, point-to-point communication channels called value-added networks (VANs). These VANs, like extranets mentioned earlier, are proprietary networks that large IT organizations such as General Electric (GE) design and maintain for facilitating communications with their customers and vendors. An alternative to VAN-based EDI is to use the Internet, which, like VAN-based EDI, is also growing rapidly. One advantage of Internet-based EDI over VAN-based EDI is the ability to use well-understood Internet technology and a preexisting, cost-free channel to transmit business data. This allows companies to avoid acquiring or building a private VAN. Another advantage is convenience. For example, several familiar accounting packages now support Internet modules that enable users to transmit basic accounting data electronically.

But these advantages come at a cost. By far the largest concern is safety. Over 80 percent of business managers cite "security" as the leading barrier to expanding electronic links to customers and business partners over the Internet. Another problem is the lack of consulting expertise to assist a business in the conversion to EDI from its manual system. A third problem is a current lack of formatting standards for Internet documents.

18.12 ILLUSTRATING THE USES OF ELECTRONIC DATA INTERCHANGE

GE, which spends about $30 billion on supplies annually, relies on its proprietary network, "Trading Process Network," for communicating with over 1,400 of its vendors on-line. Through its network GE can distribute bids to its vendors, provide information on how to bid, and receive bids from suppliers. In 1997 GE bought about $1 billion worth of supplies this way. GE estimates that it will save $500 million in three years from using its extranet for EDI. Although most EDI applications are found in private businesses, like GE, they also can be used effectively by the public sector including government agencies

(a) Pratt and Whitney

A large-engine manufacturer, Pratt and Whitney buys over 26,000 parts from more than 700 suppliers. This company now transmits over 50,000 EDI documents per month, including purchase orders, procurement schedules, and sales invoices. The company estimates that it saves between $10 and $20 on every purchase order, which adds up to over $6 million per year.

(b) U.S. Customs Service

Another example is furnished by the U.S. Customs Service, which is using EDI to process all but 5 percent of customs declarations in Los Angeles. Before it started using EDI, imported goods waited on docks for weeks, since it took that long to process the paper documentation. In many cases, information about some orders arrives weeks before the merchandise itself reaches the docks. The use of EDI has brought the error rates from 17 percent before to about 1.7 percent after. The error rate decrease and other improvements have meant annual savings of $500 million in processing costs. The productivity gains realized by the Customs Service amounted to about 10 percent. Those importing goods reap additional savings.

(c) Los Angeles County

Yet another example of EDI use is at Los Angeles County's procurement services, which bought up to $650 million in goods and services yearly using paper forms. The county had no unified purchasing system, and buyers responsible for stocking the county's offices, hospitals, and jails had to deal with more than 25,000 suppliers. The process was chaotic to the degree that one office could order supplies, not knowing that large quantities of the same item were already available in a county warehouse. They selected a high-tech approach to solving the procurement problems. In tandem with the county's overhaul of its mainframe-based finance system, the service implemented a $2 million Internet-based procurement program. Now buyers with browser-equipped desktop PCs use a network and can do comparison shopping among approved suppliers linked to the county's network. Routine purchases are approved using rules built into the software, while special purchases are automatically routed to managers for approval. Orders and payments are all electronic. Comparison shopping alone may shave as much as 5 percent off prices, which will result in estimated savings in excess of $10 million. Even better, improved inventory management and the savings from closing the county's central warehouse are expected to return $38 million over the next five years.

18.13 CLIENT/SERVER COMPUTING

Client/server computing has emerged as an alternate to mainframe technology and/or hierarchical networks. When an organization uses a client/server network, it connects desktop workstations at its regional, national, and international offices with each other and with others external to the organization, such as vendors. Depending on the type of client/server system, data processing can be performed by any computer on the network. The software application, such as a spreadsheet program, resides on the client computer—typically, a microcomputer. However, the database and related software that the individual needs to work with are stored on the server computers—typically networked minicomputers. In contrast to the mainframe systems that typically centralize everything (including control of the system), client/server applications distribute data and software among the servers and client computers of the system. This allows the client/server network to play a major communicational role by linking the entire enterprise in an information network. Any transaction taking place anywhere in the organization gets processed by the system, and the results are available instantly throughout the enterprise. Such an enterprise network allows the desktop to have more computing power, even though the database it needs to work with remains with the server part of the network.

A client/server system may be viewed as a set of three interacting components:

1. A presentation component
2. An application logic component
3. A data management component

The presentation component of a client/server system is the user's view of the system—what the user has on the workstation and what links up with the system. Simple client/server systems that focus on this presentation task are called distributed presentation systems. Most Internet uses are example of such a category.

The application logic component of a client/server system refers to the processing logic of a specific application, such as the logic involved in preparing payroll checks. Unlike a connection that allows users to surf the Internet web as a simple "host/terminal" computing, the application logic component of a client/server network gives users the ability to question or manipulate the data stored on the server. Users can ask what-if questions of the server's database and can process a transaction that may involve data stored on both client and server computers, or alter data stored elsewhere on the network. Some systems enable users to write their own data queries (that ask for specific information from the server database) and also to store such queries on local files for later reuse. This customized-query capability allowed a bank to reduce the turnaround time for data requests from an average of one week to a few minutes.

The client computer and the server share the processing tasks involved in each application, sometimes unequally between them. The division of processing labor depends on the particular application involved. In a payroll application, the client's contribution may be limited to validating the data entered into the system, in contrast to a word processing application, where the client computer might perform nearly all the processing tasks required. Those client/server systems that enable this distributed processing are called distributed applications systems or distributed logic systems.

The data management component of a client/server system refers to the databases and the ways they are stored on the system. Typically these databases are copied onto several file servers, thereby speeding user access to the data they contain. They commonly called distributed database systems. These systems are also the most complex, which makes them a major challenge to accountants on account of control and audit considerations.

Despite their high cost and complex technology, client/server systems do offer advantages, including the flexibility of distributing hardware, software, data, and processing capabilities throughout a computer network. A further advantage can be reduced telecommunications costs—an advantage, for example, that enabled Avis Rent-a-Car to save 30 seconds on each of its 23 million annual customer calls and therefore $1 million. A third advantage is the ability to install inexpensive desktop units—sometimes without disk drives—instead of more expensive models, which allows an enterprise to save money on system acquisition and maintenance costs.

There are also significant negatives with respect to client/server forms of computing systems. They require developers to create multiple copies of the same file, which they then store on the system's various servers. Backup and recovery procedures become more difficult because multiple copies of the same file (or several parts of a single file) exist on several different computers. This multiple-copy problem also causes difficulties in data synchronization—that is, the need to update all copies of the same file when a change is made to any one copy. Other client/server problems include the cost and resources involved in changing from one system to another or even from one version of the package to another. Changing from one version of an application program to another is also more difficult in client/server systems because the system usually requires consistency in these programs across servers. Yet another problem has to do with security and deciding who should have access to what parts of the system. User access can vary widely among employees due to security concerns. Security is more of a problem since there are more files and application programs to access. Finally, the need for user training is often greater in client/server systems because employees must not only know how to use the data and application programs required by their jobs but also understand the system software that enables them to access these databases and programs. The problem is made worse because employees have to do their jobs even as they are being called upon to learn a new system.

18.14 AUDITING CLIENT/SERVER SYSTEMS

While client/server systems offer users many computing advantages, they pose a number of problems from the perspective of audit and control. The problem relating to access has been mentioned already. Auditors can control physical access to a mainframe computer easily by placing the equipment in a designated room with door locks. In client/server systems, users have computing power on their desktop computers. But it is not feasible to lock up desktop computers, many of which may be located on desks in cubicles rather than in separate offices.

Client/server systems also pose problems with respect to electronic access to data files and programs. In a mainframe environment, a librarian may control access to programs and data files. In contrast, a client/server computing system generally relies on passwords to control logical access. Unfortunately, there are many ways in which one can obtain or guess passwords and use them for gaining access to the system. Organizations using such systems must install a number of controls, such as limits on the number of unauthorized access attempts and minimum password lengths, to restrict logical access to programs and data files in client/server systems.

Organizations must make sure that there are a sufficient number of controls in place to ensure the security of information systems. However, by making the system too cumbersome and costly to use, control procedures can undo the benefits of distributed processing. On the other hand, a control procedure, such as required use of virus scanning software, can save a company both dollars and headaches.

18.15 HANDLING EXPENSE ACCOUNTS

The example of reimbursement of travel and entertainment (T&E) expenses to a company's employees is a good illustration of what could happen to other forms of corporate expenditures given the technology that is now available. According to experts, it is the third largest controllable corporate expense; only those for payroll and information systems are said to exceed it. Not only does it represent a fairly large expense, it is also a category where differences between expenditures reported at the departmental levels and the total T&E as reported in the general ledger are quite common. Given the materiality of this expense, it is important to find ways of cutting costs. Doing so would require accurate details about the way those traveling on company business actually spend company money. Without accurate accounting data, one may not know which travel agents to negotiate with for possible price breaks. Such negotiations can lead to considerable savings. However, reliable information is the key to all these initiatives.

(a) Automated Reimbursement

Automated expense reimbursement systems could be used to obtain an accurate picture of this significant corporate expense. These electronic tools can help with the collection, submission, approval, evaluation, and distribution of T&E expense data. Through such accounting, they can capture actual spending dollars and allow for its analysis. By automating expense entry and simplifying expense categorization, these products not only report on actual spending but also help reduce employees' frustration. They also allow managers to review only those line items that do not comply with corporate travel policy, and they provide the information needed to evaluate total travel program costs and negotiate better deals.

(b) Availability of Automated Systems

Expense reimbursement systems are available widely today. They can be obtained from travel agencies, payment system vendors, third-party software developers, and travel service bureaus. The features and functionality of the products themselves do not vary greatly across vendor type, but a product's ability to integrate with a company's particular mix of software and hardware systems does vary considerably. In their ideal configuration, these products interface with the payment system vendor, the general ledger, the accounts payable and payroll systems, the human resources database, and the Internet for up-to-date foreign currency exchange rates. They also use either the e-mail system or network to transport data files.

18.16 HANDLING INFORMATION TECHNOLOGY WITH CARE

Even though IT can be a strategic tool that can help reinvent a business and its profit margins, it remains a double-edged sword. Success in its use is not automatically assured. Organizations should not jump into the Information Age blindly. A number of organizations across the country are seeing their cutting-edge computer systems fail to live up to expectations. In some situations, a company's current system, with possible minor revisions, may be more cost-effective than trying to keep up with information technology.

Extremely few companies today do not have some form of computerized system in place. Companies have encountered many real-world problems associated with IT. In general, the Information Age has caused a number of companies to upgrade both their hardware and software on a regular basis, whether these upgrades were really needed or not. Such changes tend not to improve productivity enough to justify their costs. Companies should develop a wait-and-see attitude before they commit organizational resources to keep up with the latest IT change. We cite some cases where the hopes associated with the investment in IT proved unrealistic and costly.

In 1996 Pacific Gas & Electric (PG&E) Company began spending many millions on a system developed by IBM that allegedly was capable of handling customer billing and many other tasks. When deregulation hit the California utility industry at the beginning of 1998, customers were permitted to choose their energy suppliers. As a consequence of deregulation, PG&E had the vastly more complicated responsibility of keeping track of fast-changing prices and multiple suppliers of energy. Although massive, the new IBM-based system could not handle the additional burden quickly enough. As a result, PG&E scrapped the fancy IBM system and went back to the drawing board. Today there is a new four-year project under way, but this time PG&E has kept its thirty-year-old first-generation computer system, which it is upgrading and replacing only gradually. Furthermore, the new system under construction at PG&E will not include the latest in point-and-click features for the utility's 1,000 customer-service representatives. Rather, the company will keep old-fashioned keyboard strokes and menus—1970s-era technology that is reliable and surprisingly swift.

Chrysler Financial recently tossed out a highly sophisticated NeXT Software Inc. system that had been purchased for use of the company's finance managers. However, Chrysler's auto sales force was still using Windows. The different divisions could not even send e-mail to each other. Chrysler Financial therefore abandoned the NeXT System and moved entirely to Windows. Instead of trying to monitor dealer activity with a fully computerized system, the company allowed clerks to obtain information from dealers over the phone. The information obtained was timely enough for financial managers wanting to know how dealers were moving large numbers of cars or the kind of loans they were making to customers. By hiring some additional employees, they got most of the information they needed in a timely manner, and setting up the operation took only ninety days. Had they gone for a full computerized system, it would have cost many millions of dollars more and taken years to install.

In yet another example, Blue Cross and Blue Shield of Massachusetts had to abandon a planned new information system after six years and $120 million. The project was canceled and Blue Cross turned its computer operations over to Electronic Data Systems, an outsourcing organization. One major reason for the problems at Blue Cross was the failure to properly supervise the information system project. Blue Cross hired an independent vendor to develop the software and then appointed someone to coordinate and manage the project. But top management did not establish a firm set of priorities stating which features of the information system were essential and which applications should be developed first. When the independent vendor presented the claims processing software to Blue Cross, the vendor thought the software was a finished product. However, managers and users at Blue Cross had other ideas. They were not happy with the product and asked for numerous changes. As a result, the whole information system project was delayed. This led to ever-increasing cost overruns. By the time System 21 was implemented, Blue Cross had fallen way behind its competitors in its ability to process an ever-swelling load of paperwork. In fact, between 1985 and 1991 Blue Cross lost a million subscribers and came close to bankruptcy. It also had to work with a poorly integrated system composed of nine different claims processing systems running on hardware dating back to the early 1970s. After spending six years and a lot of money, it turned its hardware over to Electronic Data Systems.

While information system failures of this magnitude are rare, they happen more often than would be expected. According to a KPMG Peat Marwick survey, 35 percent of all major information system projects become runaways (projects that are millions of dollars over budget and months or years behind schedule). Such cases are not rare.

18.17 CHANGING SYSTEMS

Even though a majority of projects involving IT run into problems, that still is not a sufficient reason to not evolve. Users simply must invest the time before undertaking the change of systems. Many different activities are involved when installing a new computer system into an organization. It starts with getting a physical site prepared for delivery of the computer system. At the same time, consultants must determine what functional changes are necessary. After completing this activity, the selection, assignment, and training of personnel must be undertaken. This may well be the most crucial aspect of the entire project, since human factors can make or break the new system.

Other implementation activities include obtaining and installing the computer equipment, establishing controls, converting the data files to computer storage media, acquiring and testing the computer programs, and, finally, testing the new system's operational capabilities. Regarding the acquisition of computer programs, the initial decision required is whether to obtain software from an independent vendor or to develop it in-house. If the former is selected, a determination must be made regarding which vendor's software should be acquired.

Once the new system is operational, follow-up work should take place to evaluate whether the newly implemented system has solved a company's previous systems problems and is therefore making a positive contribution toward the company's goals. After the new system has been functioning for a period of time, consultants will evaluate the system's effectiveness in accomplishing its intended purpose(s). If the revised system has failed to solve previous systems problems or possibly caused new problems, further changes are required. Typically, after consultants finish their follow-up work, the responsibility for operating a company's information system is given to systems experts within the company's information processing subsystem.

It is not uncommon for a company to decide to outsource its data processing functions rather than maintain them in-house. This means hiring an outside organization to handle all or some of the company's data processing services. Such an arrangement, commonly known as outsourcing, is discussed next.

18.18 OUTSOURCING

Many companies decide to outsource their information system rather than designing and implementing their own computerized data processing systems. Many companies that elected this option have been very pleased with the results. But before any company commits to outsourcing, its management must thoroughly analyze the advantages and disadvantages associated with this approach to data processing. In using an outsourcing organization to process most, if not all, of a company's data, there is the possibility over the long run that the company will lose a basic understanding of its own IS needs and how the system can provide it with competitive advantages. A company's information system must continue to evolve and improve, thereby adding value to the company that helps attain its strategic goals. It is not likely that goals will be realized when an outsourcing organization takes over a company's IS operations. Obviously, outsourcing is not a systems development approach suitable for every company.

18.19 ENTERPRISE-WIDE ACCOUNTING

While letting someone else manage a company's information system is one extreme approach, investing in enterprise resource planning (ERP) software for a company's information system could be seen as the other end of the IT spectrum available in the market today. Some organizations are finding that they need to integrate their functions into one large, seamless database or data warehouse, discussed earlier in this chapter. This integration allows the manager and, to some extent, external parties to obtain the information needed for planning, decision making, and control, whether that information is for marketing, accounting, or another functional area in the organization. Software vendors are developing *software programs* that link all of an organization's information subsystems into one application and that allow instant updating of its information. Because of such software, users need not wait for the monthly closing to find out the impact of any given transaction on income or balance sheet, since the systems can provide reports as soon as the transaction has occurred. Enterprise-wide accounting software does much more than process financial data. Examples of software in this category include J. D. Edwards, PeopleSoft, Oracle, and SAP. SAP R/3, sold by SAP AG, is the largest-selling accounting software program that is truly an enterprise-wide software solution. SAP R/3 is a software program that automates an organization's financial, human resources, and manufacturing business processes. Since it can cost millions of dollars to implement, it is appropriate today only for the world's largest business organizations.

Despite its high cost, however, many organizations find that the savings enterprise-wide accounting brings make it a good investment. It forces companies to reengineer or redesign their business processes for maximum efficiency. Such multinational corporations as Eastman Kodak Company, Owens-Corning Fiberglass Corporation, and Procter & Gamble have spent millions of dollars implementing SAP R/3 for its potential cost savings.

18.20 CONCLUSION

Clearly, IT is useful and can be even more so. Indeed, the technology has almost always worked. Applications of IT fail because of a misunderstanding of the problems, improper application/implementation of the technology, or the embryonic nature of the IT itself.

What are the chances of a "misfit" between IT purchased today and the problems to be addressed? It is best first to identify the needs that IT is expected to satisfy. The likelihood of an IT failure can be greatly reduced by a clear understanding of the needs to be met, careful planning of the changeover, and proper training of the employees. Merely purchasing computers will not make a business operate like clockwork. When we buy clothes, we try them on for size; when doctors prescribe medication, they make it specific to the symptoms. The same holds true for IT and IT applications.

IT cannot help accounting information become more relevant or make the controller's department become more productive if the same old way of doing business survives. If this happens, then IT will only have replaced the calculators with a more expensive alternative that may not pay back the investment made to acquire it.

To make optimum use of the emergent technology, accounting procedures must be redesigned keeping in mind the IT currently available. If IT is being bought to solve systemic problems, it is better first to address the systemic problem itself and, while investigating the problem, explore the potential use of IT to solve the problem or to design a way around it. To better address systemic problems, changes in accounting functions are needed. Such changes can be made by applying cross-functional approaches to many accounting functions.

Indeed, to facilitate changes in accounting functions, it may be better to think of accounting as a part of the information resource management function rather than as a distinct entity. Audit and internal control constraints may dictate the separation of accounting and IS; however, there ought to be greater coordination between the two departments in order to ensure effective management of information resources. The accounting department will never be trouble-free, but it can become a more optimally used resource for decision makers in the Information Age if its functions are redesigned with the help of emerging IT.

NOTES

1. "Accounting Problems Nobody Talks About," *Management Accounting* (October 1982).

CHAPTER 19

ELECTRONIC COMMERCE AND COMPUTER SECURITY

19.1 INTRODUCTION

In this chapter we resume the discussion of control and the impediments to it. Here our focus is on electronic impediments to the safety and credibility of information systems. Clearly, protecting the safety of an information system is on par with the safety of other important assets. Information systems are like other assets; they, too, must be guarded from threats and misuse. We start this chapter by a discussion of business being transacted with the help of the Internet, better known as e-commerce. Such an introduction is necessary for the topic that follows, that of computer crimes, including threats to e-commerce. Following the general discussion of computer crimes, we discuss investment securities frauds that are being carried out with the help of the Internet. We conclude the chapter by discussing disaster readiness planning.

19.2 OVERVIEW OF E-COMMERCE

The Internet is a collection of local, wide-area, and even global information technology-based networks that is increasingly used for communication, research, and business. The World Wide Web, the graphics portion of the Internet, is also used for similar purposes. In fact, it has become synonymous with the Internet. The most common use of the Internet is as a vehicle for e-mail transmitting text messages and perhaps graphics attachments. In many ways e-mail is replacing phone conversations and letters sent by postal mail. Besides facilitating correspondence, the Internet and its graphical counterpart are ushering the world into electronic commerce (EC). Retail sales are booming on the Internet, as are applications of electronic data interchange (EDI), which was discussed in Chapter 18.

The term "electronic commerce" refers to conducting business with computers and data communications. A great deal of EC is carried out with the help of the Internet, but a number of businesses are using other means to conduct a considerable amount of it. For example, increasingly EC is done over proprietary transmission lines—which includes extranets set up between vendors and the manufacturers. Many types of electronic commerce use proprietary systems in remarkably profitable enterprises. Wal-Mart, for example, which is currently the largest retailer in the world, controls its entire retailing system through a proprietary global network of computers and private satellites from its home base in Bentonville, Arkansas. American Airlines does much the same thing from Dallas, Texas, as does FedEx, located in Memphis, Tennessee. The Federal Bureau of Investigation estimates that the banking industry worldwide transfers over $1 trillion each week using electronic means.

(a) Retail Sales

The World Wide Web has enabled businesses to open virtual stores that sell merchandise directly to customers. Virtual stores in the form of web pages offer the following benefits:

- Creating web pages is usually much cheaper than creating and mailing catalogs.
- Buyers can be anywhere in the world.
- Selling can occur continuously; it never stops.
- Product descriptions, sales prices, and information on merchandise availability can be updated immediately as they become known or change.
- Customers create their own sales orders on-line.
- The staffing required for these virtual stores is minimal.

Testimony to the success of electronic commerce abounds. The Dell Computer Company is selling $5 million worth of computer equipment daily on the Web and its sales are growing. The figure for Cisco Systems is $11 million in daily sales. Then there is Amazon.com, the on-line bookseller with over 2.5 million books listed as its inventory. Others are joining the virtual market, including airlines, Sears, the United States Postal Service, universities, and pharmacies.

(b) E-Cash

Individuals who do their shopping over the Web can use credit cards to pay for their purchases. Buyers supply a credit card number to pay for their merchandise, but this method presents a problem to vendors. Acceptable credit card numbers indicate only that a card is valid; they do not indicate that the person using it as an on-line customer is actually authorized to use it. Identity fraud, in which individuals' identities are stolen and their good credit is used by others to buy merchandise, is on the rise. Hundreds of unsuspecting people are learning that their credit identity has been stolen by criminals, who charge thousands of dollars worth of merchandise after getting hold of social security numbers and credits cards of others. Given such problems, some merchants are hoping that a more desirable payment method will be electronic cash (e-cash), which is touted as a faster, easier, and safer means of exchange for both buyers and sellers. To use e-cash, Internet customers must first establish an account at a bank, which could be a virtual bank existing within the confines of the Internet. They then can access their bank account electronically and download electronic cash in various denominations to their hard drive. Finally, using software from such companies as Digicash or Cybercash, they can use their e-cash to pay for their purchases on-line. Merchants later redeem the e-cash much the same way the customers deposited it. They can exchange it for real money. The e-cash has many attributes of chips gamblers use in casinos.

The most important advantage of e-cash is the ability to identify those who are using it. It cannot be used to steal identities. Unlike real cash, which is anonymous, e-cash contains encrypted information that identifies the bank that issued it as well as the person to whom it was issued. This makes theft more difficult and provides an audit trail for the transactions that use it. It also does away with the need to transmit credit card numbers over the Internet. It makes customers confine their purchasing to the e-cash available to them, since as yet their credit is not available for e-cash.

19.3 SECURITY ON THE INTERNET

The most important advantage of the World Wide Web is the ability to dispense with constraints of space and time, physical borders, and scheduling clocks through its round-the-clock, global accessibility. But that same ease of access is also the source of its greatest weakness, its vulnerability. Any and all e-mails, web pages, and computer files can be accessed by authorized users as well as by counterfeits. Someone has only to pose as that authorized user in order to commit unauthorized acts. Steps are being taken to keep such fraudulent activity from nipping the e-commerce bloom. They are discussed below.

(a) Firewalls

In order to gain access to a company's files, a computer hacker must gain access to its information systems. Firewalls are one way to prevent such unwarranted intrusions from external parties into the information systems. Firewalls (see Exhibit 19–1 for an example) help guard sensitive filed information against unauthorized access by external Internet users or even the computer hackers.

Firewalls represent security software that a company installs on computers that are a part of its information system; these firewalls can limit system and file access to the authorized users only. The firewalls examine incoming messages and check to see that they are from authorized users, using a list of authorized users. If the firewall software does not recognize would-be users, it refuses them the access. Such firewalls are used for commercial applications and others: Universities commonly use the same technique to limit access to their library and research resources to authorized parties; faculty may use them to check the identity of those attending their virtual classrooms. Even though firewalls are

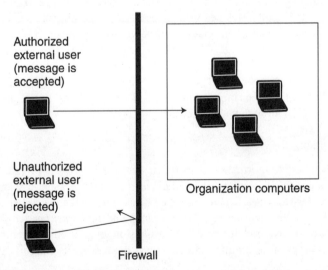

A firewall acts as a barrier between unauthorized external users and an organization's computers.

Exhibit 19–1.   A simple representation of a firewall.

Adapted from Stephen A. Moscove, Mark G. Simkin, and Nancy A Bagranoff, *Core Concepts of Accounting Information Systems,* 6th ed. (New York: John Wiley & Sons, 1999).

useful for Internet security control, they are not perfect. One obvious problem is called spoofing, that is, masquerading as authorized users. Another problem is the ability of a determined hacker to copy the contents of the access control list itself. Such a security breach would be especially difficult to detect, let alone overcome.

(b) Proxy Servers

Given the large amount of information now available on the web, organizations like to limit the number of sites that employees can visit in order to ensure that they do not use access privileges for frivolous or counterproductive purposes. A proxy server creates a transparent gateway to and from the Internet that can be used to control web access. In a typical application, a user logs onto the computer—file server—but when the user attempts to access a page on the World Wide Web, the initial network server contacts the proxy server to perform the requested Internet access. A proxy server enables an organization to channel all incoming and outgoing Internet requests through a single server. This can make web access more efficient because the proxy server is specifically designed to handle requests for Internet information. A second advantage is the server's ability to examine all incoming requests for information and test them for authenticity; in other words, it serves as a firewall. Yet another benefit is the ability to limit employee Internet access to approved web sites. This is, in effect, a form of censorship, which allows an organization to deny employees access to, say, pornographic web sites that are unlikely to have any business work-related benefits. Courts seem to have upheld the right of an employer to check e-mails sent and received by its employees. Another advantage is the ability to limit the information that is stored on the proxy server to information that the company can afford to lose. If hackers compromise the information being made available through the proxy server, the organization's information system is not sabotaged. To recover, the company can simply restart the system and reinitialize the server with backup data. A final advantage of proxy servers is the ability to store frequently accessed web pages in cache memory (i.e., in computer files on the server's own hard disk). This enables the server to respond quickly to user requests for information because the data are already available locally. The time savings can be considerable. The human resources department can use this feature to answer questions from employees about various policies. This caching feature also enables managers to obtain some idea of what information employees most need—and perhaps to take steps to provide it internally rather than through web sources.

(c) Data Encryption

Because so much of the information transmitted over the Internet is private or sensitive, businesses often use the data encryption techniques to transform plain-text messages into unintelligible cipher-text ones. The transformed messages are then decoded at the receiving station back into plain text for use. The advantage of this system is that the encrypted message cannot be understood during data transmission, even if unauthorized users intercept it. Many encryption techniques and standards are available. Exhibit 19–2 shows a simple method.

The exhibit uses a cyclic substitution of the alphabet with a displacement value of "5" to transform the letters of a plain-text message into alternate letters of the alphabet. To decode the message, the recipient's computer performs the encryption process in reverse, decrypting the coded message back into readable text. To make things more secure, the sender can use a different displacement value for each coded message.

Encryption Scheme:

Letters of the alphabet:	A	B	C	D	E	F	G	H	I	J...
Numerical equivalent:	1	2	3	4	5	6	7	8	9	10...
Plus displacement key:	5	5	5	5	5	5	5	5	5	5
New values:	6	7	8	9	10	11	12	13	14	15
Letters to use in code:	F	G	H	I	J	K	L	M	N	O

Example:

Plaintext Message:	HI, ABE!
Cyphertext Message:	MN, FGJ!

Exhibit 19–2.   A simple representation of encryption techniques.

Adapted from Stephen A. Moscove, Mark G. Simkin, and Nancy A Bagranoff, *Core Concepts of Accounting Information Systems,* 6th ed. (New York: John Wiley & Sons, 1999).

(d) Digital Signatures

For legal as well as other reasons, businesses require proof that the accounting documents they transmit or receive over the Internet are authentic and accurate. Documentation such as purchase order, bids for contracts, and acceptance letters must be in writing for greater credibility, and they should be authentic. To provide such assurance about the authenticity of documents transmitted, a company may send a complete document in plain text, while a portion of that same text may be in an encrypted format. The encrypted portion serves as a digital signature, which provides the proof that the document transmitted is authentic. In 1994 the National Institute of Standards and Technology adopted Federal Information Processing Standard 186—the digital signature standard (DSS). The presence of such a digital signature authenticates a document. Some individuals believe that digital signatures are even more secure than written signatures, which can be forged by unauthorized people. Furthermore, for greater assurance, complete messages could be sent in both plain text and cipher text. The encrypted messages can provide assurance that no one has altered them, if they are identical to the copy in plain text. If someone has forged or altered the plain text, the two copies will not be identical.

(e) Digital Time Stamping

Many important business documents are time sensitive; the date and the time of submission can make a difference to those submitting them. Among such time-sensitive documentation are: bidding documents that must be submitted by preestablished deadlines; deposit slips that must be presented to banks before the close of business; buy orders for stock purchases that depend on the date and time of issue; and legal documents that must be filed in a timely fashion. In addition, businesses also want to have records of when particular purchases were ordered, when funds were disbursed for required expenditures, or when specific data items were entered or modified in important databases. What all these documents have in common is the need for a time stamp that unambiguously indicates the time of transmission, filing, or data entry. This certification is provided by digital time-stamping services (DTSSs) that attach digital time stamps to documents either for a small fee or for free. In a typical application, the user sends the document to the service's e-mail address along with the Internet address of the final recipient. When the service receives the document, it performs its time-stamping task and then forwards the document as required. Digital time stamping is the electronic variation of the function official seals and other time stamps perform manually. Both provide certification about the time and perhaps the place of a business transaction. Such details are important even when the Internet is the channel used for communicating documents. Although most documents are transmitted almost instantaneously, time delays can occur—for example, when file servers temporarily falter or when power failures disrupt wide area networks. Time stamps enable businesses to overcome these problems.

19.4 OVERVIEW OF COMPUTER CRIME

Decision makers of all kinds, managers, accountants, and investors use computerized information to control valuable resources, help sell products, authenticate accounting transactions, and make investment decisions. Given the growing role information systems play in the life of an organization, they must be treated like other assets of a firm. Information systems and their contents must be guarded, because the usefulness of the system's content can be compromised or even destroyed if the information it contains is incorrect or has been altered.

Protection of an information system mandates that those in charge of the systems as well as those in charge of the organization be informed about computer crimes and ways to keep them from harming the system. Knowing how computers can be used to commit criminal activities may be as important as understanding the information system itself. Understanding how computer abuses are committed can help organizations identify what control and audit procedures can prevent them or at least minimize their impact. Articles in such professional publications as *Fortune, Business Week,* various accounting journals, and newspapers like the *Wall Street Journal* testify to the high level of public interest in computer abuse. Experts believe that a relatively small proportion of computer crime is detected and of that, even a smaller proportion ultimately gets reported in sufficient detail to permit accurate classification and evaluation.

19.5 UNDERSTANDING COMPUTER CRIME

The term "computer crime" is rather ambiguous. Actually, what is meant is using computers to carry out criminal activities. The term "computer-assisted crime" probably better describes what is meant. By whichever name is used, it is a difficult concept to define. Consider, for example, this definition: Computer crime is the use of a computer to deceive for personal gain. Based on this definition, a clerk in the police office caught altering his own driving record through an on-line computer terminal could be considered to have committed a computer crime. But the definition does not fit all possible situations, in part because computers are being used to carry out acts that involve no financial or personal rewards yet cause a great deal of tangible and intangible losses. A woman used a virus to disrupt a computer network; however, she was not seeking to realize any personal gain from such an act. In another case, a group of individuals used e-mail to convince investors to buy overpriced investment assets. In the third case, an individual deliberately broke the computer terminal and its screen at his place of work. In the fourth case, an individual stole computer software. Last, an individual programmed the system to deliver to him a shipment of computers, which he then sold to a retail shop and kept the money. All these acts were done using computers, but calling all of them computer crimes does not seem quite accurate.

Given such ambiguity, we cannot treat all computer-assisted crimes in the same way. For that matter, we cannot treat them as something totally different from other kinds of criminal activities. Crimes involving some form of information technology (IT) have a lot in common with crimes committed without the use of computers. Perhaps the more important lesson to remember is that computers do not commit crimes; people do. Organizational assets must be protected from human beings likely to steal or misuse them. Complacency results from assuming that internal control is adequate.

19.6 INADEQUATE COMPUTER-CRIME STATISTICS

It is difficult to give the costs of computer abuse; credible statistics on computer crimes are mostly lacking. One likely reason for this lack of data is that private business organizations, where most computer abuse takes place, handle it as an internal matter and do not report it to law enforcement agencies. In addition, surveys of computer abuse are often ambiguous, making the results difficult to interpret. Recently a survey of several thousand employees of a federal agency asked them to list all the computer crimes that had been detected during the previous year; only one person stated that a computer crime had occurred. When the survey was redistributed to the same employees and they were asked about deceptions in data that eventually would be processed by a computer, there were thousands of affirmative responses. The absence of a precise definition of computer crime is partly responsible for the lack of information about the incidence of crimes committed using computers.

Most of the crimes involving IT remain undiscovered; in all likelihood this fact contributes to the lack of the knowledge about the true extent of abuses committed with the help of computers. Most such crimes are brought to light through luck, chance, or accident, according to experts. Many experts believe that the computer crimes that are exposed are only the tip of the iceberg. Despite the lack of adequate statistical data, there are several reasons to think such activity is growing. Computers are being used to a much greater extent. Given the exponential growth in the use of IT—microcomputers, computer networks, and the Internet—it seems likely that there must be a corresponding increase in abuse involving various forms of information technology. The growth in computer usage increases the potential for abuses. In addition, as more people learn about computers and the related IT, it seems likely that there will be a corresponding increase in the number of people who can compromise computer systems and who will use information technology as a tool with which to commit fraud.

What compounds the problem is the apathy on the part of the millions of business microcomputer users in the world. Most of them are not aware of or seem even to care about computer security. Such apathy makes it easier for dishonest employees or malicious individuals to abuse information systems. Yet another reason for the likely increase in the growth of computer crimes may well be the growing gap between what is spent on computer equipment compared with what is spent on trying to improve computer system safety. A lot more is spent buying computers, and this disparity in spending suggests that the potential for computer abuse is being ignored. This lack of concern as shown by the amount spent for securing the system could well be a reason for an increase in computer-related crimes.

Despite the relative lack of credible information, it is still safe to argue that computer abuse has impacted a large proportion of firms. A 1998 study by the Computer Security Institute (CSI), for example, suggests that about two-thirds of all U.S. organizations suffer at least one serious computer abuse each year. The figure over time (rather than for any given year) probably exceeds 90 percent for all U.S. organizations. The FBI and other government agencies estimate that the annual business losses caused by computer abuse are as much as $5 billion. The impact on the firms that suffer computer abuse varies widely. Losses from one-time hits can be as little as a few thousand dollars. The average loss estimated in the 1998 CSI study was close to $57,000. Experts say that the cost of the actual loss due to computer abuse is dwarfed by the auditing and investigative costs incurred after the problem is discovered.

19.7 UNDERSTANDING THE NATURE OF COMPUTER ABUSE

The absence of good computer-crime statistics should not detract readers from recognizing the seriousness of the threat posed by such abuse. It is necessary to understand the nature of a problem in order to help prevent it. Accountants and others involved with the control of financial assets, the most favored target of the computer felons, should be particularly concerned with the potential problem and its prevention. Cash, as a liquid asset, is a more likely target, but information systems themselves also rank high as a potential target of abuse among unhappy employees bearing grudges against the employers.

An understanding of computer crime is perhaps best gained by studying selected abuses that have occurred in the past. Despite the problems involving the definition of computer crimes and the lack of credible data concerning them and their financial impact, a pattern has started to emerge. There are at least two basic kinds of crimes involving information technology: One involves the falsification of input data while the other seeks unauthorized access to computerized files. In certain crimes the two merge or overlap—for example, virus infection seeks to corrupt the content of the databases through unauthorized access. Exhibit 19–3 provides an estimate of various forms of computer crimes.

---

1. A graduate student infected a computer network with a virus that eventually disrupted over 10,000 separate systems.
2. A company accused a computer-equipment vendor of fraudulently representing the capabilities of a computer system, charging that the full system was never delivered and that the software was inadequate.
3. In a fit of resentment, a keyboard operator shattered a CRT screen with her high-heeled shoe.
4. Some employees of a credit bureau sent notices to some of the individuals listed as bad risks in the files. For a fee, the employees would withhold the damaging information, thereby enhancing the creditworthiness of the applicants.
5. A computer dating service was sued because referrals for dates were few and inappropriate.
6. A programmer changed a dividends-payment program to reduce the dividends of selected stockholders, and to issue a check to himself for the sum of the reductions—$56,000.

Exhibit 19–3.   Some examples of computer abuse.

Adapted from Stephen A. Moscove, Mark G. Simkin, and Nancy A Bagranoff, *Core Concepts of Accounting Information Systems,* 6th ed. (New York: John Wiley & Sons, 1999).

Programmers and Systems Analysts	27%
Clerical, Data Entry, and Machine Operators	23%
Managers and Top Executives	15%
Other System Users	14%
Students	12%
Consultants	3%
Other Information Processing Staff	3%
All others	3%
Total	100%

Exhibit 19–4.   Occupational profiles of computer abusers.
Adapted from Stephen A. Moscove, Mark G. Simkin, and Nancy A Bagranoff, *Core Concepts of Accounting Information Systems,* 6th ed. (New York: John Wiley & Sons, 1999).

19.8 IDENTIFYING COMPUTER CRIMINALS

To prevent given types of crimes, criminologists often look for some common character traits that can be used to screen potential culprits. Despite the potential misuse of such profiling, it can be useful when due regard is paid to individuals' legal rights. Knowing the personality traits of individuals who abuse computers can indeed help prevent such a problem. Careful and adequate investigation can be done before employing people who display such profiles. Exhibit 19–4 gives some information about those who commit crimes involving computers.

It is estimated that most computer abuse is performed by a company's own employees, not external hackers. Such individuals are not always technically competent. Although people with strong technical backgrounds do commit computer abuse, clerical personnel, data-entry clerks, and similar individuals with limited technical skills commit a lot more. They have greater opportunity for do so: It is usually easier and safer to alter data before it enters a computer than midway through automated processing cycles. Input data often can be changed anonymously, whereas most computerized data cannot be altered. This can explain why many computer criminals are not even computer literate—and also why computer security cannot be limited to IT personnel. Surprisingly, most computer criminals tend to view themselves as relatively honest. They rationalize their actions as not being the same as stealing from another individual. Computer felons tend to be bright, motivated, talented, and qualified individuals with good intellects and superior educational background. In a study performed by the National Center for Computer Crime Data, over 70 percent of computer crime defendants were men under thirty years old. Because a number of computer-crime cases in this study involved students, there is probably some age bias here.

19.9 RECOGNIZING THE SYMPTOMS OF EMPLOYEE FRAUD

The clues that signal some computer abuses can be subtle and ambiguous and, for this reason, difficult to detect and prevent. But many more are relatively self-evident albeit ignored. For example, a study conducted by KPMG Peat Marwick concluded that nearly half of the employee fraud would have been detected more quickly had obvious symptoms not been ignored. Although recognizing the symptoms of computer abuse will not completely stop or totally eliminate the problem, knowing the symptoms may help early detection and minimize damage.

This can be illustrated by taking a look at the case of the Elgin Corporation, a manufacturing company that had created its own health care plan for its employees. The plan was self-insured for medical claims under $50,000, which it handled internally; claims for larger amounts were forwarded to an independent insurance company. Elgin management believed that the company had excellent control procedures for its system. The company's controls included both internal and external audits. Yet over four years, the manager of the medical claims department was able to embezzle more than $12 million.

What follows is a description of five symptoms of computer abuses typically found in computer crime environment. Each of these symptoms occurred at the Elgin Corporation and was ignored.

(a) Accounting Irregularities

To embezzle funds successfully, employees must alter, forge, or destroy input documents, or perform suspicious accounting adjustments. An unusually high number of such irregularities ought to be a cause for concern. At the Elgin Corporation, no one noticed that payments to twenty-two of the physicians submitting claims to the company were sent to the same two addresses. In addition, no one investigated any of these payments, even though they totaled over $12 million in four years.

(b) Internal Control Weakness

When control procedures are absent, weak, or ignored, computer abuse can occur. At the Elgin Corporation, the medical claims manager had not taken a vacation for years; employees submitting claims ware never sent confirmation notices of medical payments made on their behalf; and physicians receiving these payments were never first investigated or approved.

(c) Suspicious Details

A very important sign of computer abuse being carried out over a long period is the presence of many odd or unusual anomalies that somehow go unchallenged. Such occurrences can be unreasonable and must be critically investigated. Unusual actions cannot be dismissed as harmless coincidence, especially if they require observers to suspend common sense. At the Elgin Corporation, 100 percent of the medical payments to a group of twenty-two physicians came from the self-insured portion of the company program, and no one investigated the anomaly. The checks to those twenty-two physicians were always endorsed by hand and deposited in the same two checking accounts; this too was ignored. Some of the medical claims included hysterectomies for male employees; even that miracle was not investigated.

(d) Drastic Lifestyle Changes

If employees suddenly solve pressing financial problems or start living extravagant lifestyles, sometimes fraud is the source of sudden wealth. At the Elgin Corporation, the medical claims manager's announcement that she had inherited a lot of money was never questioned; nor did anyone become suspicious that she never took a vacation from her job and had a habit of taking her employees to lunches in chauffeured limousines.

(e) Behavioral Changes

Employees who experience guilt or remorse from their crimes, or who fear discovery, often express these feelings in unusual behavior. At the Elgin Corporation, employees joked that the medical claims manager had recently developed a "Jekyll and Hyde personality." Yet her intense mood swings, which seemed unusual and out of character, were ignored.

Clearly, there was a lot that could have led to an earlier detection of the problem. However, very clear symptoms that violated the basic internal control principles were ignored. One can never be complacent.

19.10 PREVENTING COMPUTER ABUSE

The best thing organizations can do to protect themselves against computer abuse is stop being complacent about it. No company is ever immune from computer abuse; it can occur in each and every organization. Despite their presumed complexity, information systems can be protected from abuses with the help of internal control and information technology. For example, computers can be programmed to search for anomalies automatically and to print exception conditions on control reports. The New York Stock Exchange now uses an Integrated Computer-Assisted Surveillance System (ICASS) to search for insider trading activities. These technology-based monitoring systems can be better than old-fashioned manual surveillance methods because they are automatic and can screen the entire population, instead of merely a sample, of the target data. Phone companies take repeated and out-of-pattern calls being charged to a credit card as a sign of a stolen credit card being used. The phone company stopped long-distance calls from being charged to the author's phone credit card after three quick phone calls were made to South American countries from pay phones in Newark, New Jersey.

Many methods for thwarting crimes rely on IT. Most organizations try to use a combination of methods to protect themselves from computer-assisted crimes. Among them, one can list the following:

(a) Involve Top Management

Given their relative lack of computer knowledge, many top managers are not fully aware of the dangers computer abuse can cause. Their lack of awareness makes them unconcerned about it, an attitude that filters down throughout the organization. This sense of complacency even extends to many technically competent IT managers, according to experts. Computer safeguards can be effective only if management takes computer abuse seriously and insists on adherence to the safeguards. Controls must be enforced in order to be effective, and they must be reassessed constantly for their adequacy. Most experts agree about the critical importance of top management support to have effective computer-crime safeguards in place. This awareness can spread through management ranks and can be enhanced further through general training of employees with respect to computer security and internal control.

(b) Increase Employee Awareness and Education

Focusing on increasing awareness among employees can enhance the control of computer crime. People are likely to commit such abuse; hence they must be made aware and educated about controls. As stated earlier, *people* commit computer crimes, not computers.

Although external hackers exist, most computer abusers are employees of the very companies where the crimes take place. Many retail firms have clear prosecution policies regarding shoplifting, however most organizations do not have clear prosecution policies regarding other types of employee fraud. Yet the evidence suggests that prosecuting computer abuses may be one of the most effective restraints on computer crime.

In fairness, employees cannot be expected to understand the problems or ramifications of computer crime automatically. Thus an important ingredient of computer abuse prevention is employee education. Informing employees of the significance of computer abuse, the amount it costs, and the work disruption it creates, helps them understand why computer abuse is a serious matter. Studies suggest that informal discussions, periodic departmental memos, and formal guidelines are among the most popular educational tools for informing employees about computer abuse. Even though there is disagreement about their effectiveness, establishing corporate codes of conduct can help raise employee awareness about the computer-crime problem.

(c) Implement Controls

Computer-crime studies done over the years mostly reach the same conclusion: The number of organizations without proper computer security is high by almost any standard. Most computer abuse succeeds because of the absence of controls rather than the failure of controls. In other words, computer abuse happens mostly because no attempts are being made to stop it. There must be control procedures to help expose fraud and abuse, and such procedures must be implemented. Their implementation should be subject to frequent managerial scrutiny.

There are many reasons why businesses fail to implement control procedures that are already in place to deter computer crime. Those managers who have not detected a computer crime before often feel they have nothing to fear. Then, too, those businesses that do not have a specific computer security officer have no one to articulate this fear or argue for control procedures. Finally, at least some businesses do not feel that security measures are cost-effective—until they incur a problem and actually experience the headaches and costs.

The solution to most of the organizational computer-security problems is straightforward: Design and implement effective and efficient controls. This means that organizations should install control procedures to deter computer crime, managers should enforce them, and both internal and external auditors should test them. Experts also suggest that employee awareness of computer controls and of the certainty of punishment and prosecution also may act as deterrents to computer crime.

When an organization suspects an ongoing computer abuse, often it turns to one or more forensic accountants to investigate problems and make recommendations. Such individuals are professional accountants who have passed the two-day certified fraud examiner (CFE) examination administered by the Association of Certified Fraud Examiners. Thus, forensic accountants have necessary technical and legal experience to research a given concern, follow leads, establish audit trails of questionable transactions, document their findings, organize evidence for external review and law enforcement bodies, and (if necessary) testify in court. Forensic accounting is one of the fastest-growing areas of accounting, and there are now over 15,000 CFEs working in law firms, certified public accountant firms, private practices, and staff positions at larger organizations.

19.11 COMPUTER VIRUS PROBLEMS

A major form of computer abuse is due to infections from computer viruses. Two approaches to prevent such infections are through (1) antiviral software and (2) antiviral procedures. Antiviral software includes computer programs that can scan computer disks for viruslike coding, identify active viruses already lodged in computer systems, cleanse computer systems already infected, or perform some combination of these activities. Recent versions of Microsoft's Windows operating system incorporate software of this type. Generally speaking, however, antiviral programs provide less than complete protection because misguided individuals continuously write new, more powerful viruses that can avoid current detection schemes. Even worse, some antiviral programs have themselves contained virus routines.

For many microcomputer users, better safeguards are often antivirus procedural controls. These include: (1) buying shrink-wrapped software from reputable sources; (2) avoiding illegal software copying; (3) not downloading suspicious Internet files; (4) deleting e-mail messages from unknown sources before opening them; and (5) maintaining complete backup files in the event the system must be rebuilt from scratch. Additional procedural controls include loading operating systems only from one's own disks and being wary of public domain software available on an Internet bulletin.

The best organizational safeguards against computer viruses involve educating employees about viruses and encouraging employees to follow the virus prevention and detection techniques discussed above. Like other crimes carried out over a prolonged period, even computer hackers can provide signs to suggest that security has been compromised. Exhibit 19–5 lists some symptoms that indicate an information system has been sabotaged by unauthorized entries by computer hackers.

Some desirable control procedures to enhance security include: (1) policies that discourage employees from exchanging computer disks or installing privately acquired computer programs on their workstations; (2) requiring the use of computer passwords to make it difficult for unauthorized users to access company operating systems and files; and (3) using antiviral filters on local and wide area networks. Finally, it is critical to have an approved and tested disaster recovery plan (that enables a business to replace its critical computer systems in a timely fashion) in the event a disabling virus does strike. A disaster recovery plan is discussed later in this chapter.

19.12 COMPUTERS AND ETHICAL BEHAVIOR

The operations of an accounting information system frequently raise ethical issues that are unique to information technology. Such problems were not common when paper and ledger were the brick and mortar of accounting. An example of such problems is the practice of unauthorized software copying. Even though software makers are taking steps to prevent this, it remains a fairly common problem. To minimize such crimes, a firm ought not to rely on people's ethical considerations. The vast majority of people stop for red lights and obey traffic rules out of personal choice, even when no one is watching them do so. It stands to reason that many people would refrain from abuse if they are made aware of the impropriety.

Ethical concerns often become important when computer abuse is not performed for financial gain. In cases involving hacking, for example, ignorance or mischief may be the motives. To some, the challenge of breaching the security of a computer system and

Excessive log-on failures: Hackers can break into a system simply by testing a large number of passwords—for example, using a dictionary to test possibilities. But such attempts generate an excessive number of log-on failures. This is one reason why passwords should not be recognizable terms.

New, unknown accounts: The presence of unrecognizable accounts in your system may be evidence that hackers have visited. External hackers as well as internal, dishonest employees typically use these accounts to order merchandise (which they never pay for) or submit invoices (which your company pays before the fiction is discovered).

Duplicate transactions: Computer abusers are especially fond of duplicating bona fide transactions such as invoices or payroll time cards, which your computer system will usually recognize as authentic—and pay. Automated auditing tools can be used to test for this.

Unexpected crashes: Some hackers add new log-on or password codes to a computer system, which they must then reboot to be recognized. If you didn't reboot your system, who did?

Missing logs or gaps in record sequences: Erasing an invoice is as good as paying one, so some hackers find deleting records a good scam. Gaps in sequential files of business transactions are the telltale footprints for this.

Large-than-normal system logs: In smaller companies, only a few people will usually have access to critical files. If a hacker is impersonating one of these people—or a systems administrator ("sys-op")—you'll see it in the system logs for these files.

Heavy traffic after midnight: If your midnight-to-sunrise traffic suddenly exceeds your daylight loads, it could be that someone from overseas is helping himself to your data.

Exhibit 19–5.   Signs that reveal attacks by hackers.

Adapted from Stephen A. Moscove, Mark G. Simkin, and Nancy A Bagranoff, *Core Concepts of Accounting Information Systems,* 6th ed. (New York: John Wiley & Sons, 1999).

avoiding detection is a source of irresistible adventure. Success, even if limited to one's circle of confidants, can bring recognition, notoriety, and even admiration. In these cases, ethical issues are overlooked and the costs of recovering from the abuse are ignored. The acceptability of these motives comes down to issues of morality. But "morality" in corporate cultures is typically a relative value. Other considerations may allow its suppression. Spying may be undertaken, despite its ethical impropriety and questions of legality, in the hope of improving one's competitive posture. We discuss some other considerations next.

(a) Honesty

Organizations expect employees to perform their own work, to refrain from accessing unauthorized information, and to provide authentic results of program outputs. Conversely, submitting false or outdated computerized information may not be illegal, but it is almost certainly classified as less than ethical, yet it may be done for various reasons, including top management pressure to perform.

(b) Denying Access

Computer users can deny others access to system resources without damaging those resources. Examples include tying up network access ports with multiple logins, sending voluminous (but useless) e-mails and computer files to others, and complaining to system administrators about fictitious hardware or software failures. Such behavior can extend to introducing computer viruses into networks. It is also unethical to give unauthorized users access to private computer systems, or to allow such individuals to view the information available from such systems.

(c) Privacy and Confidentiality

Those working with confidential information sometimes make this information available to those without an immediate right to see it. People must disclose financial data on a mortgage loan application or the results of diagnostic medical tests. If such information is disclosed to unauthorized individuals it can be damaging to the individuals. Banks and businesses frequently make information about their customers available to others for a fee. Organizations may not be legally bound to protect this information, although most professionals would argue that employees are morally bound to do so.

(d) Social Responsibility

Individuals should act responsibly and not disclose secret information about their work or the products of their employers. But sometimes social responsibility conflicts with other organizational goals. For example, suppose a programmer discovers that a drug being sold to the public has harmful qualities. His superior tells him to ignore it, since it is none of his business. It is no secret now that employees of tobacco firms knew of the addictive nature of their products and almost all of them did nothing.

(e) Rights of Privacy

Computers can be used to monitor the activities of others. But do organizations have the right to do so if they violate individual privacy? For example, do organizations have the right to read their employees' personal e-mail? For that matter, do employees have the right to use their business e-mail accounts for personal correspondence? The current thinking seems to be that employers should tell employees if they are monitoring e-mail and web surfing.

(f) Conflict of Interest

Accountants are obligated to distinguish between personal preferences and ethical consideration. Conflicts of interest between these two are common, often pitting organizational goals against personal goals. An example is when a manager is so desperate to get rid of an incompetent employee that she is tempted to lie about that person's abilities to another employer.

(g) Acceptable Use

Employees do not automatically have unrestricted uses of the information technology made available to them by the employers. At universities, for example, ethical conduct forbids downloading computer software for personal applications or using free mainframe time for personal gain. While doing this is possible, it is certainly not ethical for a professor to use university resources for private consulting and pocket the income.

The response to such ethical issues is determined not so much by laws or organizational rules as by our own sense of ethics. Many factors, including social expectations, culture, and societal norms, can influence ethical standards of behavior. Human behavior can be a product of the times in which we live. More than anything else, however, ethical behavior requires personal discipline and a commitment to "do the right thing." It is nonetheless possible for organizations to encourage ethical behavior on the part of their employees. It helps if the employers:

- Inform employees about the importance of ethics.
- Educate employees about how to act ethically.
- Teach by example—that is, by managers acting responsibly.
- Use job promotions and other benefits to reward responsible acts.

Encouraging employees to join professional organizations with codes of conduct also may help. Most computer and accounting organizations now have rules defining professional behavior; these rules can reinforce organizational emphasis on employees' ethical behavior.

In conclusion, very little is known about the who, what, why, when, where, and how of computer crime. Often those who are its victims do not, for a variety of reasons, report it. Most of the abuse and crimes are now caught by accident, sheer luck, or the perpetrator's mistakes. Nevertheless, three tentative conclusions about computer abuse can be made:

1. It is difficult to define exactly.
2. Computer crime is very likely increasing in magnitude.
3. It can be very expensive to deal with and even more expensive to recover from.

19.13 PROTECTION FROM COMPUTER ABUSE

Organizations can protect themselves against computer abuse in a variety of ways. These include:

- Educating employees about computer abuse
- Adopting and implementing well-advertised prosecution policies
- Designing and implementing control procedures as well as continuously reassessing them
- Recognizing the symptoms of employee fraud
- Using forensic accountants and fraud auditors to investigate the system periodically
- Obtaining the support of top management in ensuring the security of the AIS accounting information system.

The systems are vulnerable to computer abuse because they directly or indirectly control valuable assets. According to users at a recent security conference, being specific about the threats that face an organization is the best way to get the attention of managers who can approve spending on security. One security manager compiled a long list of potential network vulnerabilities with an itemized list of each network component. He was able to show that even a simple network outage would require two or three network administrators at least two hours to fix and cost us about $10,000. A severe network security breach that would result in loss of data could cost millions. Providing management with information about the cost of recovering from such breaches have helped firms obtain the resources to ensure security of the system.

19.14 FEDERAL LEGISLATION AFFECTING THE USE OF COMPUTERS

Employers seeking to protect their information systems can rely in part on laws that seek to regulate computer abuse. In this section we list some important federal legislation governing activities involving computers. Of these, the most important is probably the Computer Fraud and Abuse Act of 1986. But this act is more than ten years old, and there are doubts over whether it is sufficiently powerful to deal with the computer abuses in the twenty-first century. The Internet was not a big presence when that law was put into practice, and systems were less complex then they are now. Efforts are underway at the federal level to enact laws to address the problems.

In addition to federal laws, state legislation is seeking to regulate computer abuse. Every state now also has at least one computer crime law. Most of these laws seek to define computer crimes, classifying what constitutes misdemeanors and what are felonies. The laws differ from state to state, not only in how they deal with issues but in terminology as well. However, almost all of these laws also require "willful intent" for convictions. Thus, words like "maliciously," "intentionally," or "recklessly" often appear in these laws, and for successful prosecutions, prosecutors must establish willful intent. The National Center for Computer Crime Data (NCCCD), a collection of computer crime statistics, reports that 77 percent of computer cases brought to state courts end in guilty pleas and that another 8 percent of the defendants are found guilty at trial.

(a) Fair Credit Reporting Act of 1970

This act requires that an individual be informed why he or she is denied credit. The act also entities the individual to challenge information maintained by the credit-rating company and to add information if desired. Seven years after this law was put into effect, the annual number of complaints filed under it exceeded 200,000.

(b) Freedom of Information Act of 1970

This federal "sunshine law" guarantees individuals the right to see any information gathered about them by federal agencies.

(c) Federal Privacy Act of 1974

This act goes further than the Freedom of Information Act of 1970 by requiring that individuals can correct information about themselves. It also demands that agency information not be used for alternate purposes without the individual's consent and makes the collecting agency responsible for the accuracy and use of the information. Under this act, an individual may ask a federal judge to order the correction of errors if the federal agency does not do so.

(d) Small Business Computer Security and Education Act of 1984

This act created an educational council that meets annually to advise the Small Business Administration on a variety of computer crime and security issues affecting small businesses.

(e) Computer Fraud and Abuse Act of 1986

This act makes it a federal crime to intentionally access a computer to: (1) obtain top-secret military information, personal financial, or credit information; (2) commit a fraud; or (3) alter or destroy federal information.

(f) Computer Security Act of 1997

This act requires more than 550 federal agencies to develop computer security plans for each computer system that processes sensitive information. The National Institute of Standards and Technology (NIST) reviews the plans. In October 1999 President Clinton issued guidelines about the information contained about individuals in the computerized databases. Such guidelines are to ensure that information contained in the files, such as medical history and credit information, will not be misused.

19.15 FRAUD ON THE INTERNET

The Internet has become an increasingly powerful way to conduct business. But many participants in electronic commerce have concerns about the potential for fraud on the Internet. Some of the concerns that participants in electronic commerce have include:

- Does the company in fact exist beyond the web page?
- Can the company be seen as being trustworthy?
- Is there any chance that a credit card number or bank information provided will be misused?
- If I provide information to a company on its web site, where will the information end up?
- Will one actually receive what the order specified?
- Will delivery of the order be as promised?
- How will any potential problems be resolved?
- Are guarantees going to be honored?
- How soon will one get credit for returned items?
- How quickly will the company perform service as promised in warranty?
- Will the company be around to send necessary replacement parts when needed?

These concerns can exist with all transactions, whether conducted face to face, over the telephone, through the mail, or over the Internet. Customer-oriented firms will take care of such concerns whether they are on the Main Street or on the information highway. Fraud-minded people will try to make a fast buck regardless of the medium through which the transaction is conducted. Some common sense combined with investigation before dealing with a given vendor can take care of such concerns.

Most transactions involving electronic commerce are consummated with credit cards or bank charges. The use of credit cards in electronic commerce provides a certain measure of confidence to consumers because there are legal limits on liability for unauthorized use of credit card information by others. Nevertheless, perpetrators of fraud look for opportunities to obtain credit card information as well as other private information, such as e-mail addresses, personal addresses, phone numbers, birth dates, and social security numbers, which can be sold to e-mail spam lists or misused in various ways. Consequently, this area is ripe for fraud, and individuals and businesses are well advised to be extra vigilant. People should make sure they know to whom they are giving such information.

19.16 PROVIDING ASSURANCES FOR E-COMMERCE

A number of steps are being tried to provide assurance to those using the Internet to conduct business. One of them is through electronic logos by means of which a firm can reassure customers. We survey them.

(a) Electronic Logos

The idea behind an electronic logo is that if an Internet seller meets certain specified criteria, the seller is allowed to place a logo on its web site. It is cyberversion of what has been called "the Good Housekeeping Seal of Approval." An assurance provider, such as a public accounting firm, or another entity organized for this purpose, provides the logo. The logo provides a certain level of assurance that the seller has complied with standards established by the assurance provider. Usually the logo is linked to the assurance provider's web site. The Internet user can link to the assurance provider's web site to read about the degree of assurance provided by the logo. Logo assurance services are becoming quite common. For example, MasterCard and Visa created Secure Electronic Transactions (SET). Companies selling products or services through the web that meet SET standards for sending credit card information can display the SET logo. Another seal of approval/assurance is provided by AICPA and is called WebTrust. It is another logo assurance service that was developed jointly between the American Institute of CPAs (AICPA) and the Canadian Institute of Chartered Accountants (CICA). Accounting associations in the United Kingdom, Australia, and New Zealand are also interested in participating in the accountants' logo assurance program. WebTrust operates under the assumption that consumers seek assurance in the following areas:

- They are dealing with a real company rather than a fraudulent company seeking to obtain and sell credit card numbers, addresses, and other private information.
- They will receive the goods and services ordered, when promised, at the agreed-upon price.
- They have the option to request that the Internet seller not give or sell any private information provided in an on-line transaction so that private information will not be intercepted while being transmitted.

Before issuing a logo, the assurance provider verifies that disclosed practices are being followed by the seller.

To obtain a WebTrust logo, an Internet seller must meet criteria in three areas: (1) business practices disclosure, (2) transaction integrity, and (3) privacy and information protection.

(i) Business Practices Disclosure. The web site must include the seller's postal address and telephone number. The purpose of the disclosures in this area is to provide assurance

to consumers that they are dealing with a real business that abides by its promises. The disclosures relate to several business practices, such as delivery times, product return policies, and warranty information.

(ii) Transaction Integrity.   In this area, assurance is provided that internal controls are in place so that customer orders are recorded and billed properly. The assurance provider is concerned primarily with customer-oriented controls rather than those related to financial statements.

(iii) Privacy and Information Protection.   In this area, assurance is provided that company insiders do not misuse private customer information and that controls are in place to keep information secure from unauthorized parties during and after transmission. Web-Trust also requires that sellers be recertified every ninety days.

Although the WebTrust program has potential to combat fraud on the Internet, the start-up of the WebTrust logo has been slow. As of May 1998, only 1,500 CPAs had been trained by the AICPA, and 65 firms were licensed to issue the WebTrust logo. It is unclear whether this slow start is due to a reluctance on the part of accounting firms to offer the service or whether there is a lack of demand for the WebTrust product. Some researchers believe that the primary market for WebTrust services will be new, Internet-based sellers without well-established reputations. Consumers are reluctant to enter into Internet transactions with sellers with whom they are not familiar. Consequently, an assurance logo located on the web site of the Internet seller can be a marketing tool.

19.17 EXAMPLE OF A WEBTRUST APPLICATION

In October 1998 the AICPA issued a press release indicating that Bennett Gold, a Canadian chartered accounting firm, had provided a WebTrust logo to Competitor Communications, Inc., an Internet service provider for the RocketRoger.com web site. RocketRoger.com (www.RocketRoger.co) is a web site established for fans of Roger Clemens, a well-known baseball player. In addition to information about Clemens's career, the web site offers visitors the opportunity to purchase Clemens memorabilia using credit cards. The RocketRoger.com web site was the first Canadian site to receive the WebTrust logo. Bennett Gold, which is based in Toronto, Canada, issued the logo for the RocketRoger.com web site after performing a WebTrust audit. In a WebTrust audit, an accounting firm examines an Internet company to determine if the business is legitimate, its transactions are secure, the information it collects from consumers is kept private, and its business practices are fully disclosed. This WebTrust audit report is similar to a standard audit report issued for an audit of financial statements; however, it carries an explicit disclaimer of responsibility for fraud. Such a disclaimer means that very little real assurance is being provided even though the logo assurance program may help to reduce consumers' fears about fraud.

The use of logo assurance services and other forms of encryption techniques may help to reduce the level of fraud in electronic commerce. Accountants should urge their clients who are buyers of products or services through the Internet to be aware of the presence or absence of logos on the web sites of the companies with whom they deal, and they should encourage their clients to deal with sellers who have logos from reputable assurance providers. In addition, both accountants and their clients should be familiar with the limits on the level of assurance provided by these logos. It is important to recognize that providers of WebTrust logos disclaim responsibility if the Internet company violates the criteria of the logo or if fraud has been committed.

19.18 SECURITIES FRAUD ON THE INTERNET

The Internet has evolved rapidly into a worldwide network of electronic information and data interchange, serving many different functions, purposes, and activities. Fraud has been an unfortunate by-product of the Internet's rapid growth. The frauds aimed at would-be investors on the net have been extensive enough to call the Securities Exchange Commission (SEC) into action. Activities prohibited under U.S. laws are being conducted over the Internet, and the SEC is taking action to stop such behavior. The SEC's involvement has led to citations against a number of businesses for having used the Internet for fraudulent activities. The threat of such punishment can, at the very least, make the would-be cheater pause in trying to exploit others.

The Internet can be a very useful tool for gathering investment information speedily and with ease. At the same time the Internet can be used to commit securities fraud. In October 1998 the SEC issued a press release citing forty-four companies and individuals for committing securities fraud using the Internet. This 1998 publication is available on the SEC web page, and it underscores the concern of the SEC with respect to the illegal acts being performed with the help of the Internet. Those cited in the press release had failed to inform investors that they were paid for recommending stocks on the Internet. Some of them not only hid their lack of independence, they also circulated false or misleading information about the investments they were recommending. To make matters worse, they took advantage of price increases to sell their own shares at a profit; however, price increases were in large part due to their manipulations.

The ability of the Internet to transmit information at the speed of light allows it to be communicated, speedily, cheaply, and easily to a wide audience. This makes it relatively easier for would-be cheats, seeking to commit security frauds, to find potential victims. By disguising their deceptions into credible-looking messages, they are able to tempt many potential investors, who, due to their unwillingness to investigate the difference between legitimate and false claims, are victimized. Some of the ways that securities frauds have been perpetuated on the Internet include on-line investment newsletters, bulletin boards, and e-mail spam.

(a) On-line Investment Newsletters

Many investment newsletters have appeared recently on the Internet. These cybernewsletters offer investment information and recommend stocks to would-be investors. There is no question that such advice, if legitimate, can help investors in their search for information. Indeed, legitimate newsletters can be effective research tools; however, many are fraudulent. Companies are known to have paid the publishers of such newsletters to recommend their stocks. This practice is not illegal, but the U.S. securities laws require the newsletters to disclose who paid them, the amount, and the type of payment. If the newsletter fails to disclose such a relationship and the payments exchanged with the company being recommended, it has committed securities fraud. Some electronic newsletters provide false information in order to promote worthless stocks. The goal is to drive up the price of the stock and then sell it at a higher price. The play succeeds because there are investors who are willing to spend their money without verifying the "claims" made by the cybernewsletters.

(b) Bulletin Boards

On-line bulletin boards exist in several different forms, and they have become a popular way for investors to share information with others. Bulletin boards often include messages concerning investment opportunities. While some messages may be true, many are fraudulent. People post messages pretending to reveal inside information about upcoming announcements, new products, or lucrative contracts, but in fact they are committing fraud by spreading lies. People claiming to be unbiased observers actually may be company insiders, large shareholders, or paid promoters. A single person can create the illusion of widespread interest in a small, thinly traded stock by posting a series of messages under aliases. It is difficult to ascertain the reliability of such information because bulletin boards allow users to hide their identity; nevertheless, some investors are willing to part with their cash on the basis of such information.

(c) Spam

What junk mail is to your mailbox, e-mail spam is to your e-mail. Because it is very inexpensive and all too easy to distribute to millions, people intent on committing fraud use e-mail spam to locate potential investors for investment schemes or to spread false information about a company. Through it, perpetuators of fraud can target more potential investors and actually reach them. This kind of access is certainly easier than cold calling or even mass mailing. Through the use of bulk e-mail programs, personalized messages can be sent to thousands of Internet users simultaneously; among them are those who are willing to invest on the basis of information contained in such cybermutations of junk mail.

19.19 INTERNET MUTATION OF INVESTMENT FRAUDS

Whatever the vehicle used on the Internet—on-line investment newsletters, bulletin boards, and e-mail spam—many of the frauds carried out are nothing more than classic investment frauds long familiar to law enforcement authorities, such as: the pump and dump; the pyramid; the risk-free fraud; and off-shore frauds. In the past such frauds were carried out using the phone or through the mail.

(a) The Pump and Dump

This type of fraud involves on-line messages that urge investors to buy a stock quickly or recommend selling before the price goes down. The sender of the message usually claims to have inside information about a company or the ability to unerringly pick stocks that will increase in price. The perpetuators of the fraud may be insiders or paid promoters who stand to gain by selling their shares after the stock price is pumped up. Once the fraud perpetrators sell their shares and stop hyping the stock, the price usually falls and investors lose their money. This scheme is usually employed with small, thinly traded companies because it is easier to manipulate a stock when there is relatively little information available about the company.

(b) The Pyramid

This type of fraud involves a message such as: "How to Make Big Money from Your Home Computer!!" An example might be the message claiming that investors could turn

$5 into $60,000 in just three to six weeks. Sound too good to be true? Not to those willing to part with their money without tempering greed by credible investigation of the message. The promotion is an electronic version of the classic pyramid scheme where participants make money only by recruiting new participants into the program.

(c) The Risk-Free Fraud

This type of fraud involves message like "Exciting, Low-Risk Investment Opportunities" inviting participation in wireless cable projects, prime bank securities, or even fish farming. The investment products typically do not exist, but there are always some who get taken by the sting. People have sold the Brooklyn Bridge and gardens in Arizona to willing buyers.

(d) Offshore Frauds

Offshore frauds targeting U.S. investors are quite common. The Internet has removed barriers imposed by different time zones, different currencies, and the high costs of international telephone calls and mailings. When an investment opportunity originates in another country, it is difficult for U.S. law enforcement agencies to investigate and prosecute the frauds.

All these scams can succeed only when individuals are so blinded by their greed that they throw caution aside and chase the mirage of the quick windfall. The old adage, "If something sounds too good to be true, it likely is not true," still holds, but greed can make one lose sight of it.

19.20 ILLUSTRATING CYBERHIGHWAY ROBBERIES

Some of the citations issued by the SEC will help to illustrate the kind of fraud being carried out on the information highway. The SEC cited a firm for sending more than 6 million unsolicited e-mails, building false web sites, and distributing an on-line newsletter in order to promote the stock of two small, thinly traded companies. Because these solicitations failed to tell investors that the companies being recommended had agreed to reimburse the soliciting firm, the SEC sued and imposed a $15,000 penalty. The massive amount of spam distributed by the firm resulted in hundreds of complaints being received by the SEC's on-line Enforcement Complaint Center.

The SEC also cited an Internet newsletter called *The Future Superstock* (*FSS*), written by Jeffrey C. Bruss of West Chicago, Illinois, who recommended to the more than 100,000 subscribers and visitors to the newsletter's web site the purchase of stocks predicted to double or triple in months. In making these recommendations, *FSS* failed to disclose more than $1.6 million of compensation, in cash and stock, from profiled issuers. It also failed to disclose that it had sold stock in many of the issuers shortly after dissemination of recommendations caused the prices of those stocks to rise. Furthermore, it falsely claimed to have performed independent research and analysis in evaluating the issuers profiled by the newsletter when it had conducted little, if any, research. It also falsely claimed its past success in having picked securities that had appreciated in value.

In yet another citation, the SEC said that an investment advisory firm touted the stocks of seven different companies while receiving 276,500 shares and 75,000 options from those companies. It also lied about the financial condition of two of the issuers. Simultaneous with the filing of the complaint by the SEC, the firm consented, without admitting or denying the SEC's allegations, to the entry of a permanent injunction and payment of a civil penalty. Yet another citation involved a group of individuals for secretly distributing to friends and family nearly 42 million shares of Systems of Excellence Inc., known by its ticker symbol SEXI. In a pump-and-dump scheme, this group drove up the price of SEXI shares through false press releases claiming large sales that did not exist, an acquisition that had not occurred, and revenue projections that had no basis in reality. The ringleader of the group also bribed his codefendant to promote the stock to subscribers to his on-line newsletter called *Whisper Stocks*. The SEC fined the individual $12.5 million; two of the defendants, including the author of the on-line newsletter, were sentenced to federal prison. In addition, four others pled guilty to criminal charges.

In other cases cited by the SEC, a firm recruited investors through a direct public offering done entirely over the Internet, which raised $190,000 from 150 investors. Instead of using the money to build the company, the individual involved pocketed the proceeds. The SEC sued him in a civil case, and the Santa Cruz, California, District Attorney's Office prosecuted him criminally. He was convicted of fifty-four felony counts and sentenced to jail. Yet another firm solicited investments to finance the construction of an ethanol plant in the Dominican Republic. The Internet solicitations promised a return of 50 percent or more with no reasonable basis for the prediction. The solicitations included false information about contracts with well-known companies and omitted other important information about the company. After the SEC filed a complaint, the firm agreed to stop breaking the law. The SEC found two people to be offering prime bank securities through the Internet—a type of security that does not exist. They had collected over $3.5 million by promising to double investors' money in four months. The SEC has frozen their assets and prevented them from continuing their fraud. And lastly, a shyster was found to be soliciting investors for a proposed eel farm by promising investors a 20 percent return while claiming that the investment was low risk. When the SEC caught him, he consented to the court order stopping him from breaking the securities laws.

19.21 DEALING WITH SECURITIES FRAUD ON THE INTERNET

Securities frauds on the Internet are similar to frauds that accountants are already familiar with. The perpetrators of fraud often engage accountants for advice concerning accounting, tax, information systems, and other matters. It is important that accountants be aware of the full range of their clients' activities. If those activities include securities fraud using the Internet, accountants should advise clients to avoid such activities. If clients do not respond appropriately, accountants should cease further contact with them. Obviously, if accountants are facilitating such activities, they will be subject to SEC enforcement actions or even criminal prosecution. Accountants are increasingly providing advice and counsel to their clients about investments. Accountants can be of great assistance to their clients in avoiding fraudulent schemes. In order to invest wisely, it is important to obtain accurate and reliable information. Investments should not be made based solely on information appearing in an on-line newsletter or bulletin board, especially if the investment involves a small, thinly traded company that is not well known. People should avoid investing in small companies that do not file regular reports with the SEC, unless they are willing to investigate the company thoroughly and to check the truth of its claims.

Individuals themselves could curb their greed by not falling for get-rich-quick schemes. In addition, they should take the following steps before parting with their money:

- Obtain certified and audited financial statements directly from the company and analyze them thoroughly.
- Verify the claims about new product developments or lucrative contracts.
- Call suppliers and customers of the company and ask if they really do business with the company.
- Check out the people running the company and find out their track record.

The U.S. federal securities laws require most public companies to register with the SEC and file annual and quarterly reports containing audited financial statements. All U.S. companies with more than 500 investors and $10 million in net assets and all companies that list their securities must file reports with the SEC. Anyone can access and download these reports from the SEC's EDGAR database through the Internet. It is important to check whether the company is registered with the SEC and read the reports that are filed with SEC.

19.22 DISASTER READINESS

To say that organizations of all stripes have embraced information technology is admittedly a truism, yet it is not to be treated as just a cliché, because the organizational dependence on IT is indeed subject to Murphy's Law. What can go wrong has a distinct likelihood of actually going wrong. The technology has allowed organizations and individuals to do a lot more than they could otherwise. Organizations have automated an ever-increasing number of internal processes: correspondence, both internal and external; records involving human resources; information about accounts payable; tax records; as well as the recording of sales through to point-of-sale inventory and stock-ordering systems. Through such automation, organizations have become increasingly dependent on IT for carrying out business functions. Such dependence allows them to continue operating, indeed to stay in business. Such dependence requires that computer security be given a high priority.

Security once meant safe storage of materials, equipment, and money. At one time, a few knowledgeable professionals in a centralized batch-processing mode controlled the computing environment. For these people, physical security was of paramount importance. Today the primary threat is to corporate data. Almost unlimited access by a large, knowledgeable community of end users from desktop, dial-in, and network facilities creates a new and extremely vulnerable environment. The threats to data and system security include natural and man-made disasters, errors by loyal employees, and the overt acts of competitors, hackers, and creators of computer viruses.

Hurricane Hugo destroyed power and telecommunications lines, equipment, homes, and businesses. In Hinsdale, Illinois, a fire left the city without telephone service for an extended period. Floods and earthquakes in various parts of the United States have damaged buildings, bridges, and power transmission facilities and have reminded us that computer rooms are much too important to be located in unprotected basements of buildings that were not built with disasters in mind. Individuals such as Robert Morris can plant a computer worm in the Internet's bowels and paralyze networks. Others would like to get in the system for the sheer mischief of it; still others maliciously attempt destruction of all of the data on hundreds of thousands of computers.

The ultimate aim of computer security policy has been the protection of the data contained in the systems. The integrity, availability, and confidentiality of the information contained within the system must be ensured. Systems and the data they contain must be protected from being altered or sabotaged.

Modern organizations increasingly rely on telecommunications to extend their traditional systems' boundaries to share information and other resources. Placing systems and data in remote locations and accessing them via telecommunications is becoming the norm. Organizations are so dependent on computer-based and telecommunications-intensive information systems that they may not survive a significant disruption of either capability. Yet such dependency must not allow us to forget that natural disasters remain a potential disruptive force; employees, organizational culture, and internal organizational procedures can be an even greater danger than the threats from the external competition; and the modems that link the computer to the global village can become the gateway for cyberinfections. IT is less secure than the accounting ledgers of the past.

Naïveté or complacency can compound the problem. Some managers may be lured into complacency by the existence of security groups within their organizations. But the mere creation of a security group does not solve the problems; nor should it allow the rest of the organization to be lulled into risky complacency. The growth of connectivity and dispersion of technology within or between organizations will continue. Management must become more informed of the potential for security breaches via employees' and competitors' actions and not underestimate the potential risk that exists in the highly connected environment in which they operate. They need to increase their awareness of penalties and laws pertaining to computer security. Most important, they must treat internal control seriously.

19.23 ORGANIZATIONAL COMPLACENCY

According to a recent article of a study of businesses operating in the United States, more than 40 percent of the businesses studied had to stop operations after suffering system disasters that caused data losses. Nearly half of them continued operating for about two years but only 6 percent of the businesses survived. The same article surveys showed that:

- Over two-third of companies surveyed were not adequately prepared for disaster recovery.
- Four out of five companies do not have a tested disaster recovery plan in place.
- Three out of four companies do not understand the financial cost that would occur following a system failure.

Documentation is often the overlooked part of internal control. The same is true of disaster recovery plans and their documentation. Even though contingency plans on how to deal with system failures and other disasters are crucial, most companies do not recognize that fact. Perhaps they fail to realize the costs of systems failure. Such failures may be grounded in managers' technophobia. Or perhaps managers believe that such plans are too costly and that they do nothing to immediately increase income or efficiency. Last, managers are also likely to be more devoted to problems that seem pressing rather than worrying about potential disasters.

The absence of disaster readiness plans involving information systems also can be the result of the IT departments' workloads and the performance reward systems that may be in place. The extra work required to prepare, document, test, and continuously update such plans is time-consuming. When employees feel overworked, the rewards associated with readying a viable contingency plan that allows for system backups through storage of data off-site, for example, and periodically testing the plans and changing them if so needed are not appealing.

19.24 HOW TO GET A DISASTER PLAN IN PLACE

The documentation of the plans pertaining to systems failure is the responsibility of IT, even though it is a key part of the internal controls in place. Internal control and its documentation are usually assigned to accountants. Hence accountants ought to convince IT managers first and then get them to help convince top executives to take the need for system disaster recovery planning seriously. Accountants could facilitate this by pointing out the potential costs of a catastrophic failure, showing how much potential business may be lost due to such disasters, and estimating what replacing that which may be lost due to a system failure and other disasters may cost. Another effective approach to raise top managers' awareness about the impact of potential disasters could be something as basic as getting them to answer a series of questions about disaster preparedness and the likely impacts of system failures. It is hoped that asking them if they have a have a plan in place and if they are aware of the liabilities their businesses could incur would not be a total waste of energy.

A case study that may help get their attention: Fiduciary Trust Co. International, a 600-employee private banking and money management company, has offices located in the World Trade Center in New York. Despite the February 26, 1993, bomb explosion, which interrupted operations for most of the building's tenants, Fiduciary Trust had no such problem. Why? It had a thoroughly tested business continuity plan in place, which allowed the company to continue business despite the bombing.

19.25 CONTENT OF A DISASTER RECOVERY PLAN

The effectiveness of a disaster recovery plan rests in how well it provides instructions for dealing with various disasters, both natural and man-made. Disasters can impact an entire region or the whole city, the factory or just a given building. They could impact the IT network only, or they may simply be a matter of building access. An effective disaster recovery pays attention to how best to deal with such contingencies. Having a plan in place is not enough. Employees must know about those plans and their location. Fire drills provide a model for exercises that ought to be carried out to make the organization better prepared for dealing with disasters. Making such information available in hard copy to all employees can forestall a deluge of phone calls when a disaster does occur. Doing so can improve the quality of decision making in the midst of a disastrous event and ensure the safety of employees and customers. In developing a response to a natural disaster or a system failure, it is best to reduce reliance on a small number of key individuals—problems can occur when they may not be around.

The plan must include a phone list with both primary and alternate telephone numbers for each key employee. The list should include emergency company contacts and data on fire and utility companies, the local police department, vendors, customers, service providers, insurance agents, and off-site storage locations. Companies also may want to set up a frequently updated phone message with instructions and system information. Information provided ought to let employees know when to return to work.

More important, the plan ought to provide inventories and location of computer manuals and warranties, communication equipment, insurance policies, computer hardware and software, everything located at the off-site storage location, data files and backup schedules, and a list of keys and where to find them. In drawing up the plan, one is making sure those items do indeed exist, since without them the system can be paralyzed.

In dealing with system failure, it may be helpful to have plans in place for a backup in case of disaster. This could mean deciding whether the company itself needs backup equipment or if an off-site backup system provided by a recovery company is sufficient. Perhaps only part of the system needs backup; is home-site computing an option for a short time? Can an on-site backup server and a system of laptops run the company for a few days? If a service provider is chosen, consider the range of recovery options offered and what level of protection the business needs. Some vendors specialize in off-site periodic backups. Such backups are performed at intervals that can vary depending on organizational needs. Other vendors are able to build custom modular sites containing complete systems that mirror the firm's own. A useful web site for information pertaining to disaster recovery is www.dlttape.com/proveit.

Clearly planning to deal with disasters can be expensive; however, such costs can minimize losses when disasters such as system failures do occur. They can save in the long run by allowing an orderly and faster recovery after the failure. In doing so they can minimize insurance premiums and help protect the assets of the organization. They also can minimize legal liabilities. They can help raise awareness about the potential costs of disruption that can result from disaster of various kinds. In summary, an effective plan should consist of understandable documentation of a step-by-step response to various forms of disaster. Such a plan is not locked away in folders but is known to all concerned, and employees are trained to implement the plan. The plan deals not only with employees but also with the system hardware because needed backup equipment is planned for.

INDEX

A.B. Astra, 316
ABC, *see* Activity-based costing
ABM, *see* Activity-based management
ACCA, *see* Association of Chartered
    Certified Accountants
Accessibility of documentation, 1
Accounting information systems (AISs), 97,
    102–146
  batch processing approach to, 134–138
  computer-based on-line transaction
    processing, 138–141
  computer-based systems, 124–128
  computer transaction processing
    approaches to, 133–134
  and control, 56, 60
  data classification/coding in, 142–145
  data flow diagrams in, 115–120
  decision tables in, 120, 121
  documentation tools/techniques for,
    104–105
  entries in, 130–131
  external/internal users of, 102–104
  file processing/management in, 141
  file storage in, 141–142
  flow-charting in, 105–115
  HIPO charts in, 120–121, 123
  impact of complexity on, 131–132
  manual systems, 124
  narrative documentation in, 121–122
  objectives of, 129–130
  structured English in, 120, 122
  subsystems of, 104
  and transaction processing cycles,
    132–133
Accounting management, role of, 234–236
Accounting manual(s), 19–31. *See also*
    Procedures manuals
  benefits of well-developed, 19–20
  core of, 24
  directives in, 25
  organization of, 22
  physical attributes of, 24
  planning process for, 20

  policing of, 24
  policy/procedure statements in, 25–27
  preparation of, 27–30
  program for starting, 20–22
  review/maintenance of, 22–23
Accounting profession, 7–17
  assurance services provided by, 10
  core competencies required for, 11–13
  expanding role of, 8–15
  and financial planning, 11
  future of, 8, 15–16
  international services provided by, 11
  and management consulting, 11
  and role of management accountant,
    13–15
  studies of, 15–17
  and technological competence, 10–11
Accounting Terminology, 57
Accounts payable:
  computer-based processing of, 220, 222
  manually processed, 213, 218
Accounts payable master file, 210
Accounts receivable detail file, 179
Accounts receivable maintenance procedure
    (revenue cycle), 185–188
Accounts receivable master file, 177
Accruals, 150
Acknowledgment procedures, 73
Activity-based costing (ABC), 290,
    353–362
  activity levels for, 357
  allocations under, 358–359
  cost behavior under, 356–357
  cost tracking in, 353–354, 360–361
  definition of, 354
  direct vs. indirect costs in, 355–356
  focus on activities in, 354
  and GAAP, 358–359
  goal of, 353
  and resource usage, 354
Activity-based management (ABM), 353,
    354
Activity groups, 360

Adjusting entries, 130–131
Administrative flexibility, 312–313
Affinity charting, 302–304
Agile Manufacturing Forum (AMF),
    314–315
AICPA, *see* American Institute of Certified
    Public Accountants
AISs, *see* Accounting information systems
American Accounting Association, 7, 58
American Institute of Certified Public
    Accountants (AICPA), 7, 8, 11, 56–58,
    62, 74, 91, 401
American Productivity and Quality Center,
    308
AMF, *see* Agile Manufacturing Forum
AMP, 300
Archival documentation, 34
Arthur Andersen, 263
Assets:
    accountability controls, 71–73
    theft of, 85
    unintentional loss of, 85
Assistant controller, 26
Association of Chartered Certified
    Accountants (ACCA), 7, 16–17
Assurance services, 10
AT&T, 296, 317
Attendance form, 237
Audits:
    and accounting manual, 24
    of client/server systems, 376–377
    communication, 75–81
    and computer systems, 89
    controls for, 74–75
Audit trails, undermining of, 88
Automotive industry, 309, 311–312. *See
    also specific companies*
Average cost, 256

Backorders, 174
Batch-level costs, 357
Batch processing, 134–138
    advantages/disadvantages of, 137–138
    computer-based vs. manual, 136–137
    sequential, 134–136
Bell Atlantic, 345–346
Benchmarking, 296, 304–308
Big Five accounting firms, 7

Bill of materials (BOM), 263
Bills of lading, 173
Block coding systems, 143–144
Blue Cross and Blue Shield of
    Massachusetts, 378–379
BOM (bill of materials), 263
BPR, *see* Business process redesign
Brainstorming, 300–304
Breaches of security, 85
British Telecom, 299
Budget manuals, 30–31
Budget master file, 153–154
Bulletin boards, computer, 404
Business partners, 76
Business planners, 76
Business process redesign (BPR), 340–342,
    344–349
    benefits of, 345–346
    predecessors of, 344–345
    total quality environment vs., 344

Canon, 5
Capacity requirements planning (CRP), 263
Capacity utilization, optimum, 313–314
Capital budgeting, 277–279
Capital investment proposal, 280
Cash disbursements (computer-based
    processing), 223
Cash flow statements, 199
Cashier, head, 26
Cash planning, 60
Cash receipts:
    internal control of, 61–62
    in revenue cycle, 182–185, 192–194
Cash receipts transaction file, 178
Caterpillar, 312
Central processing unit (CPU), 68, 101
Ceremonies, 340
Certified public accountants (CPAs), 7–11
Charts of accounts, 164–165
Check disbursements transaction file, 211
Checks, endorsement of, 192
Check voucher, 207
Chrysler, 299, 300
Chrysler Financial, 378
Classification, data, 142–143
Client, focus on, 13
Client/server computing, 375–377

Clinton, Bill, 400
Coca-Cola Company, 3, 27–28
Coding system(s), 143–145. *See also*
   Transaction coding
  attributes in, 145
  block, 143–144
  and computers, 144–145
  in general ledger and financial reporting
    cycle, 163–164, 166–169
  group, 144
  mnemonic, 143
  sequence, 143
Collective approach to problem solving,
  295
Collusion, internal, 86
Committee of Sponsoring Organization
  (COSO), 58
Communication, 58
  and organizational flexibility, 318–319
  with other departments, 15–16
  skills, communication, 12
Communication audits, 75–81
  data information provided by, 76–77
  reasons for undertaking, 75–76
  techniques for conducting, 79–81
  when to conduct, 77–78
Compensation reference file, 240
Competitive benchmarking, 305
Computer-based systems, 66–70
  change procedures, 69–70
  control of, 68–69
  data processing function, segregation of
    responsibilities within, 67–68
  departments, segregation of
    responsibilities between, 66
  documentation systems, 124–128, 208,
    218–223
  employee services management cycle,
    244
  fraud/control problems related to, 86–91
  IS function, segregation of
    responsibilities within, 66–67
  new systems development, 70
  on-line transaction processing, 138–141
  processing systems, 175, 188–194
Computer crime/abuse, 388–399
  employee fraud, 391–393
  and identification of criminals, 391
  nature of, 388–391

prevention of, 393–399
  statistics on, 389–390
  viruses, 395
Computer Fraud and Abuse Act of 1986,
  58, 400
Computers/computing. *See also* Electronic
  commerce; Information technology
  client/server computing, 375–377
  and ethical behavior, 395–398
  federal legislation affecting use of,
    399–400
Computer Security Act of 1997, 400
Computer Security Institute, 390
Computer viruses, 395
Concurrent engineering, 323–324
Consulting, management, 11
Continuous improvement, 290
Control activities, 58
Control charts, 339
Control environment, 58
Controller, assistant, 26
Control(s), 55–81
  administrative vs. accounting, 57
  of asset accountability, 71–73
  of audit practices, 74–75
  classifications of, 63–64
  communication audits, use of, 75–81
  computer-based systems, use of, 66–70
  computer control problems, 86–91
  computer crime, 394
  of documentation, 70
  in employee services management cycle,
    244–248
  in expenditure cycle, 223–229
  for facilities management system, 283,
    285–286
  forces for improvement of, 91
  and forensic accounting, 93–95
  in general ledger and financial reporting
    cycle, 158–161
  historical development of, 57–58
  impediments to effective, 83–95
  in inventory management system cycle,
    273–275
  management control system, 62–63
  of management practices, 70–71
  manual systems, use of, 65–66
  meanings of, 55, 56
  nature of, 56–57

Control(s) (*Continued*)
  operational control system, 63
  and organizational structure, 64–65
  of personnel practices, 73–74
  of planning practices, 73
  process of, 58–62
  and responsibilities of auditors, 91–93
  in revenue cycle, 194–198
  and risk exposure, 84–86
  in total quality environment, 337
Converging information, interpretation of, 13
Cooperation, cross-functional, 330–331
Coopers & Lybrand, 58
Core competencies for accounting
  profession, 11–13
Corporate investigations, 95
COSO (Committee of Sponsoring
  Organization), 58
Cost tracking, 353–354, 360–361
CPAs, *see* Certified public accountants
CPA Vision Process, 8
CPU, *see* Central processing unit
Credit checks, 63
Credit memos, 174
Credit sales procedures (revenue cycle),
  179–183, 188–192
Criticism, avoiding, 301
Cross-functional cooperation, 330–331
Cross-functional teams, 16
CRP (capacity requirements planning), 263
Cultural controls, 55
Current journal voucher file, 153
Customer loyalty, 297–298
Customer master file, 177
Customer orders, 173
Customer(s):
  focus on, 13, 292
  getting to know, 297
  and total quality management, 332
Customer satisfaction, 297–298
Customer service, 172, 295–296
Cybercash, 384
Cycle-time reduction, 321–323

Data:
  classification/coding of, 142–145
  fraudulent modification/use of, 87

  information vs., 97
  storage of, 88
Database(s):
  for employee services management cycle,
   239–240
  for expenditure cycle, 210–211
  for facilities management system,
   281–282
  flexible, 343
  for general ledger and financial reporting
   cycle, 153–154
  for inventory management system cycle,
   266–267
  for revenue cycle, 177–179
Data encryption, 386–387
Data files, *see* Files
Data flow diagrams (DFDs), 115–120
  example using, 115–119
  flow charts vs., 115
  guidelines for preparation of, 119–120
  symbols used in, 115
Data flows/processing:
  in employee services management cycle,
   240–243
  in expenditure cycle, 212–218
  in facilities management system,
   282–284
  in general ledger and financial reporting
   cycle, 155–158
  in inventory management system cycle,
   267–275
Datamarts, 371
Data processing function, segregation of
  responsibilities within, 67–68
Data warehouses, 371
Date flow symbols (flow charts), 107
Debit memorandum, 207
DEC, *see* Digital Equipment Corporation
Decision-making process, role of
  management accountants in, 14, 15
Decision support systems (DSS), 102
Decision tables, 120, 121
Deferrals, 151
Deliberate errors, 84–85
Dell Computer Company, 384
Deming, W. Edwards, 351, 362
Departments, segregation of responsibilities
  between, 66
Deposit slips, 174

Desktop publishing, 19
Detective control, 59
DFDs, *see* Data flow diagrams
Digicash, 384
Digital Equipment Corporation (DEC), 305, 313
Digital signatures, 387
Digital time stamping, 387–388
Direct costs, 355–356
Directives (in accounting manual), 25
Disaster recovery plan, 407–410
Disbursement voucher, 207
Documentation. *See also* Illuminative approach to documentation
  accessibility of, 1
  in accounting information system, 104–105
  archival, 34
  and business process reengineering, 349–350
  controls for, 70
  for employee services management cycle, 237
  for expenditure cycle, 206, 208
  for facilities management system, 280
  low priority given to, 2–3
  narrative, 121–122
  of revenue cycle, 172–175
  value of effective, 19–20
Dow Chemical Company, 3, 28–30
Dow Corning Inc., 315–316
Dress codes, 55
Drucker, Peter, 319
DSS, *see* Decision support systems
DuPont, 296, 316

E-cash, 384
E-commerce, *see* Electronic commerce
EDI, *see* Electronic data interchange
EISs (executive information systems), 102
Electronic commerce (e-commerce), 383–384, 401–410
  definition of, 383
  and e-cash, 384
  retail sales, 384
  security issues with, 401–410
Electronic data interchange (EDI), 365, 372–374

Electronic logos, 401–402
Employee payroll master file, 239
Employees:
  educating, 299, 393–394
  empowerment of, 293
  fraud involving, 391–393
  involvement of, 294
  training, 294
Employee services management (resources management cycle), 233–249
  accounting entries in, 238–239
  computer-based systems, 244
  controls needed for, 244–248
  database needed for, 239–240
  data flows/processing for, 240–243
  documentation needed for, 237
  manual systems, 240–243
  objectives of, 233–234
  organizational context of, 234–237
  reports for, 248
  risk exposures in, 244–246
  transaction coding in, 239
Empowerment, employee, 293
Encryption, data, 386–387
End-of-day processing (revenue cycle), 192, 194
End-user systems (EUSs), 102
Enforcement, lack of, 86
Enterprise resource planning (ERP), 76–77, 380
Entries, 130–131
Equity Funding Corporation, 87
ERP, *see* Enterprise resource planning
Errors:
  deliberate, 84–85
  unintentional, 84
ESs (expert systems), 102
Ethical standards (and control), 90–91
EUSs (end-user systems), 102
Evolutionary competence, 289–308
  and activity-based management/costing, 290
  behaviors encouraging, 294–296
  and benchmarking, 304–308
  and brainstorming, 300–304
  building blocks of, 292–294
  and continuous improvement, 290
  definition of, 289
  and JIT inventory systems, 291

Evolutionary competence (*Continued*)
  and learning organization, 291–292
  and process reengineering, 291
  and quality circles, 290
  strategy implementation, 296–300
  and suggestion systems, 290
Executive information systems (EISs), 102
Executives, 75–76
Expenditure cycle, 133, 201–231
  accounting entries in, 208–209
  computer-based documentation systems,
    208, 218–223
  controls needed for, 223–229
  database for, 210–211
  data flows/processing for, 212–218
  documentation needed for, 206, 208
  functions of, 201–203
  and managerial decision making,
    205–206
  manual documentation systems, 206–207,
    212–218
  organizational context of, 202, 204–205
  purpose of, 201
  reports generated by, 229–230
  risk exposures within, 223–226
  transaction coding in, 209–210
Expense accounts, 377
Expert systems (ESs), 102
Extranets, 372

Facilitative leadership, 293
Facilities management system, 277–286
  accounting in, 281
  and capital budgeting, 277–279
  controls needed for, 283, 285–286
  database for, 281–282
  data flows/processing in, 282–284
  documentation needed for, 280
  maintenance/disposal of capital assets in,
    279
  organizational context of, 280
  purpose of, 277
  reports generated by, 286
Facility-level costs, 357
Fair Credit Reporting Act of 1970, 399
FCPA, *see* Foreign Corrupt Practices Act
Federal Privacy Act of 1974, 399
FedEx, 317

Feedback systems, 59–60
FIFO, *see* First In First Out
Files:
  processing/management of, 141
  storage of, 141–142
Financial Executives Institute, 58
Financial management, role of, 234–236
Financial planning services, 11
Financial reports format file, 154
Financial statements, 162
Firewalls, 385–386
First In First Out (FIFO), 151, 256–257
First-order feedback systems, 59
First USA, 317
Flexibility, organizational, *see*
    Organizational flexibility
Flexible databases, 343
Flow charts, 105–115
  data flow diagrams vs., 115
  guidelines for preparation of, 112–115
  inventory records, updating of, 112
  as process, 108
  purchase order, preparation of, 109–112
  purchase requisition, preparation of,
    108–109
  symbols used in, 105–107
Ford, Henry, 344
Ford Motor Company, 296, 305, 312, 315,
    323, 341–342
Foreign Corrupt Practices Act (FCPA),
    57–58
Forensic accounting, 93–95
Forum Corporation, 297–298
Frame breaking, 352
Fraud, 65, 86–95
  and auditors' responsibilities, 91–93
  computer-related, 86–91
  employee, 391–393
  and forensic accounting, 93–95
Freedom of Information Act of 1970, 399
Functional benchmarking, 305
Funds management system, 286–287

GAAP, *see* Generally accepted accounting
    principles
Garvin, David, 351
General Electric (GE), 373–374
General ledger analysis, 162

General ledger and financial reporting cycle (general ledger system), 147–169
 accounting controls in, 158–161
 charts of accounts in, 164–165
 coding of accounts in, 163–164, 166–169
 database used for, 153–154
 data flows/processing in, 155–158
 inputs to, 150–153
 objectives/functions of, 147–150
 reports generated by, 162–163
General ledger history file, 153
General ledger master file, 153
Generally accepted accounting principles (GAAP), 93, 358–359
General Motors, 296, 300, 305
Generic benchmarking, 305
Giovinazzo, Vincent, 364–370
Goods, 201
Graphical user interface (GUI), 342, 367
Graphs, 339
Gross-margin method (of inventory pricing), 257
Group coding systems, 144
Group interactions, 301
GUI, see Graphical user interface

Head cashier, 26
Hewlett-Packard (HP), 263, 305, 313
HIPO charts, 120–121, 123
Holiday Inn, 298
Honda, 5, 290, 323
HP, see Hewlett-Packard

IBM, 263, 313, 316, 378
Ideas, solicitation of, 295
IIA, see Institute of Internal Auditors
Illuminative approach to documentation, 33–53
 elements of, 37
 example of, 38–53
 implications of, 37
 and procedures, 37–38
 questions about, 34–35
 tracking components of, 35–36
IMA, see Institute of Management Accountants
Imaging technology, 343–344

Independence, organizational, 65–66
Indirect costs, 355–356
Informal controls, 55
Information, 58
 characteristics of, 97–98
 from communication audits, 76–77
 data vs., 97
 definition of, 97
 interpretation of converging, 13
 managers' need for, 101
Information analysts, 76
Information flow symbols (flow charts), 107
Information integrity services, 10
Information interfaces, 102
Information systems (IS), 98–102, 369
 accounting, see Accounting information systems
 classification of, 98
 components of, 100–102
 limitations of, 99–100
 narrative documentation of, 121–122
 outsourcing of, 380
 roles performed by, 98–99
 segregation of responsibilities within, 66–67
 types of, 102
Information technology (IT), 17, 363–381
 assessing promise of, 369–372
 and changing systems, 379
 client/server computing, 375–377
 and customer value, 298
 datamarts, 371
 data warehouses, 371
 development and future of, 363–364
 electronic data interchange, 372–374
 and enterprise-wide accounting, 380
 extranets, 372
 and human relations, 369
 intranets, 372
 and nonaccounting personnel, 366
 with nonintegrated accounting systems, 366–367
 and outsourcing, 380
 and processing/reporting lags, 367
 and source data vulnerability, 365
 success with, 378–379
 and time requirements, 368
 and total quality environment, 342–344
 and uneven workloads, 367–368

Information technology (*Continued*)
  usefulness of, 364–369
  wide area networks, 371–372
Input—output symbols (flow charts), 107
Inputs:
  to general ledger and financial reporting
    cycle, 150–153
  information system, 100
Inquiry screens, 230
Institute of Internal Auditors (IIA), 58, 91
Institute of Management Accountants
    (IMA), 7, 13–16, 58, 308
Insurance claims, 95
Intel Corporation, 345
Internal benchmarking, 305
Internal collusion, 86
Internal control, 55, 60–62
International Benchmarking Clearinghouse,
    308
International services, 11
Internet security, 385–388, 400–401
Interpretation of converging information, 13
Intranets, 372
Inventory management system (resources
    management cycle), 251–276
  components of, 259–260
  controls needed for, 273–275
  database for, 266–267
  data flows/processing in, 267–275
  and JIT system, 264
  manufacturing context, accounting in,
    265–266
  material requirements planning in,
    261–264
  merchandise, 251–260
  organizational context of, 258–259
  product conversion, 265–267
  and production logistics, 261–265
  purpose/functions of, 251–255
  raw materials, 260–261
  reports generated by, 275
  valuation methods, 255–258
Inventory record updates, flow-charting of,
    112
Investigations, corporate, 95
Investment newsletters, on-line, 403
Invoice, supplier's, 207
IS, *see* Information systems
IT, *see* Information technology

Japan, 5, 290, 310, 323, 324, 337–338
JIT, *see* Just-in-time inventory systems
Job-time ticket, 237
Johnson Controls, 297
Johnson & Johnson, 316
Journal entries, 130, 175–176
Journals, special, 131–132
Just-in-time (JIT) inventory systems, 264,
    291

Kaizen, *see* Total quality environment
Kim, Daniel, 351
"Knowledge-creating" companies, 5
Kodak, 305

Last In First Out (LIFO), 151, 257
Leadership, facilitative, 293
Leadership skills, 12
Learning organization, 291–292
LIFO, *see* Last In First Out
Line managers, 76
Litigation support, 95
L.L. Bean, 307
Logos, electronic, 401–402
Logs, 72–73
Los Angeles County, 374

Management:
  controls and needs of, 91
  role of accounting, 234–236
Management accountant, expanding role of,
    13–15
Management consulting, 11
Management control system, 62–63
Management information systems (MISs),
    97, 102, 333
Management practice controls, 70–71
Management techniques, 2
Managerial reports, 162–163, 230, 248
Manual control systems, 65–66
Manual documentation systems, 124
  employee services management cycle,
    240–243
  expenditure cycle, 206–207,
    212–218
  revenue cycle, 179–188

Manuals, budget, 30–31. *See also*
    Accounting manual(s); Procedures
    manuals
Market, focus on, 13
Martin Marietta, 263
Master production schedule (MPS),
    263
Material requirements planning (MRP),
    261–264
Mellon Bank, 307
Merchandise inventory management
    system, 251–260
  acquisition in, 253
  components of, 259–260
  functions of, 251–252
  organizational context of, 258–259
  receiving/storage in, 253
  shipping of sold merchandise, 253,
    255
  valuation methods, 255–258
Merchandise inventory master file, 177,
    210
Merck, 316
MISs, *see* Management information
    systems
Mitsubishi, 323
Mnemonic coding systems, 143
Monitoring, 58
Morris, Robert, 407
Motorola, 296, 305–306
MPS (master production schedule), 263
MRP, *see* Material requirements planning

NAFTA (North American Free Trade
    Agreement), 308
Narrative documentation, 121–122
Natural disasters, 85
NCR, 305
Negative perceptions of accounting
    profession, 15
Nepotism, 65
Networking software, 342
New perspective, need for, 5–6
New York Life, 298
NeXT Software Inc., 378
Nissan, 311
Nonaccounting personnel, involvement of,
    366

Non-value-adding elements (in illuminative
    approach to documentation), 35–36
North American Free Trade Agreement
    (NAFTA), 308

OADI-SAMM model, 351
OASs (office automation systems), 102
Objectives classification (of controls),
    63–64
Office automation systems (OASs), 102
Office technology, 1
Offshore frauds, 405
On-line transaction processing, 138–141
  advantages/disadvantages of, 140–141
  computer-based batch processing vs., 140
Open document files, 178
Open production order file, 267
Operational control system, 63
Operational reports, 230, 248
Order acknowledgments, 173
Organizational controls, *see* Control(s)
Organizational flexibility, 299–300,
    309–325
  achievement of, 310–311
  and administrative flexibility, 312–313
  and Agile Manufacturing Forum,
    314–315
  and concurrent engineering, 323–324
  and customer potential, 317
  definition of, 309
  enabling, 315–316
  future prospects for, 316–317
  impediments to, 317–318
  imperatives for, 319–320
  and implementation of change strategy,
    318–319
  and optimum capacity utilization,
    313–314
  and product modularization, 311–312
  scope of, 309–310
  strategic alliances encouraging,
    315–316
  and theory of constraints, 324–325
  and time-based competence, 320–323
Organizational independence, 65–66
Organizational learning, 349–352
Organizational memory, 3
Organizational structure(s), 64–65, 299

Outputs, information system, 100
Outsourcing of information systems, 380

Pacific Gase & Electric, 378
Packing lists/slips, 173
Pareto diagrams, 339
Partners, business, 76
Paychecks, 237
Paycheck transaction file, 240
Payroll, internal control of, 60–61
Payroll reference and history file, 239–240
Performance reports, 199
Personnel action form, 237
Personnel management, role of, 234
Personnel planning file, 240
Personnel practices, controls for, 73–74
Picking lists, 173
Planning practices, controls for, 73
Plant asset change form, 280
Plant assets master file, 281
Plant assets transaction file, 281–282
Policy and procedures system, 19
Policy and procedure statements (P/PSs),
   26–27
Policy statements (in accounting manual),
   25
P/PSs, *see* Policy and procedure statements
Pratt and Whitney, 299, 374
Privacy, computer, 397
Procedure bulletins, 25–26
Procedures manuals. *See also* Accounting
   manual(s)
   lack of respect for, 2–3
   origins of, 1
   review/updating of, 4–5
   uses of, 3–4
Processing, computer, 87–88
Processing symbols (flow charts), 107
Process management, 296
Process reengineering, 291
Product conversion (inventory management
   system cycle), 265–267
Production logistics (inventory
   management system cycle), 261–265
Product-level costs, 357
Product modularization, 311–312
Profession, accounting, *see* Accounting
   profession

Property expenditure request, 280
Proxy servers, 386
Pump and dump, 404
Purchase order file, 211
Purchase orders, 109–112, 206
Purchase requisitions, 108–109, 206
Purchases:
   computer-based processing, 218–220
   manually processed, 212–213
Pyramid, 404–405

Quality circles, 290
Questionnaires, 338

Raw materials (inventory management
   system cycle), 260–261
Raw materials management system,
   260–261
Raw materials master file, 266
Reassessments, 73
Receiving, 220, 221
Receiving report, 206
Reconciliations, 72
Records, keeping, 301–302
Reengineering, 291. *See also* Business
   process redesign
Reference source, procedures manuals as, 3
Registers, 72–73
Regulatory compliance, 3
Remittance advice, 174
Reports:
   from batch processing, 136
   communication audit, 79
   for employee services management cycle,
      248
   expenditure cycle, 229–230
   facilities management system, 286
   general ledger and financial reporting
      cycle, 162–163
   inventory management system cycle, 275
   managerial, 162–163, 230, 248
   operational, 230, 248
   receiving, 206
   revenue cycle, 198–199
Resources management cycle, 133. *See also*
   Employee services management;
   Inventory management system

Responsibility center master file, 153
Revaluations, 151
Revenue cycle, 133, 171–199
  accounts receivable maintenance
    procedure, 185–188
  cash receipts procedure, 182–185,
    192–194
  components of, 171
  computer-based processing systems,
    188–194
  with computer-based systems, 175
  controls for, 194–198
  credit sales procedures, 179–183,
    188–192
  database files in, 177–179
  documentation of, 172–175
  journal entries used for, 175–176
  manual processing systems, 179–188
  objectives of, 171
  organizational context of, 171–172
  reports generated by, 198–199
  risk exposures within, 194–196
  steps in, 179
  transaction coding in, 176–177
Reviewers, 65
Reviews, 4–5, 73
Rewards, 294
Risk assessment, 58
Risk aversion classification (of controls), 64
Risk exposure(s). *See also* Control(s)
  degree of, 85–86
  in employee services management cycle,
    244–246
  in expenditure cycle, 223–226
  in revenue cycle, 194–196
  types of, 84–85
Risk-free fraud, 405

Sales analyses, 199
Sales history file, 178–179
Sales invoice transaction file, 178
Sales order file, 178
Sales orders, 173
Sales personnel, 172
"Sandwich" rule (flow charts), 114
SAP R/3, 380
SAS, *see* Statements on Auditing Standards
Sears, Roebuck & Co., 5, 313

SEC, *see* Securities and Exchange
  Commission
Second-order feedback systems, 59
Securities and Exchange Commission
  (SEC), 57, 403, 405–407
Securities fraud, 403–407
Security:
  breaches of, 85
  e-commerce, 401–410
  and information system, 101
  on Internet, 385–388, 400–401
  in revenue cycle, 197
Segregation of responsibilities, 66–68
Self-awareness, 329
Senior executives, 75–76
Sequence coding systems, 143
Sequential batch processing, 134–136
Services, 201
Settings classification (of controls), 64
SFAS No. 95, 29
Shared vision, 293
Shipping notices, 173–174
Siemens, 316
Signs, 340
Slogans, 339–340
Small Business Computer Security and
  Education Act of 1984, 399
Smith, John F., 296
Sony, 290
Source data, vulnerability of, 365
Spam, 404
Special journals, 131–132
SQC (statistical quality control), 337
Standard costs, 256
Statements on Auditing Standards (SAS):
  No. 1, 62, 91
  No. 48, 64
  No. 55, 64
  No. 78, 56, 74, 75
  No. 82, 83, 91–93
Statistical quality control (SQC), 337
Storage symbols (flow charts), 107
Strategic alliances, 315–316
Strategic and critical thinking skills, 12
Strategic Finance, 7
Strategic Planning Institute Council, 308
Structured English, 120, 122
Subsidiary ledgers, 72, 131
Subsystems, accounting information, 104

Suggestion systems, 290
Supplier master file, 210
Supplier's invoice, 207
Suppliers invoice transaction file, 211
System architectures classification (of controls), 64

Taco Time, 317
Taylor, Frederick, 344
Team approach to problem solving, 295
Teams, cross-functional, 16
Technological competence of accountants, 13
Technology. *See also* Information technology
    and changing role of accounting profession, 10–11
    and organizational flexibility, 318
Technology, office, 1
Theft. *See also* Fraud
    of assets, 85
    of computer hardware/software, 87
Theory of constraints (TOC), 324–325
Thermostatic mechanisms, 58–59
Third-order feedback systems, 59–60
Three-Mu checklists, 337–338
Time-based competence, 320–321
Time cards, 244
Time form, 237
Time record transaction file, 240
TOC, *see* Theory of constraints
Toshiba, 310, 316
Total quality environment (TQE), 290, 327–352
    and business process redesign, 340–342, 344–349
    business process redesign vs., 344
    controls in, 337
    cross-functional cooperation in, 330–331
    definition of, 327
    frame breaking in, 352
    functions within, 331
    implementation of, 332, 334–337
    and information technology, 342–344
    and nature of change, 328–329

and ongoing evolution of organization, 328
    and organizational learning, 349–352
    organizational system in, 329–330
    perception of work in, 350–351
    policies for, 336–337
    scope of, 327–328
    setting the stage for, 332–334
    tools used in, 337–340
Total quality management (TQM), 290
Toyota, 290, 311
TQE, *see* Total quality environment
TQM, *see* Total quality management
Training:
    of employees, 294
    using procedures manual for, 3
Transaction coding:
    in employee services management cycle, 239
    in expenditure cycle, 209–210
    in revenue cycle, 176–177
Transaction files, 178
Transaction processing, 133–134, 138–141
Transaction processing cycles, 132–133
Travel and entertainment expenses, 377

Uneven workloads, 367–368
Unintentional errors, 84
U.S. Customs Service, 374
Unit-level costs, 357
Upper-level executives, 75–76

Valuation, inventory, 255–258
Value, providing, 15
Value-added networks (VANs), 373
Value-adding elements (in illuminative approach to documentation), 35–36
Value chain, 99
Value exchange, 317
VANs (value-added networks), 373
Vendor master file, 210
Vendors, 76, 298
VF Corporation, 299–300
Violence, acts of, 85
Viruses, 395

Vision, shared, 293
Vitro, 316

Wal-Mart, 342
WANs, *see* Wide area networks
WebTrust, 400–402
White-collar crime, 95
Wide area networks (WANs), 371–372

Work, perception of, 350–351
Work-in-process, 266–267,
    271–272
Work location, 16
Xerox, 296, 305–307

Yamaha, 323
Yates, JoAnne, 1